RALLY YEARBOOK
World Rally Championship
2006

CHRONOSPORTS
ÉDITEUR

DPPI photographers:
François Baudin, Frédéric Le Floc'h, Claude Saulnier,
François Flamand, Thierry Bovy, Manrico Martella,
Alexandre Guillaumot and Eric Vargiolu.

ISBN 2-84707-114-8

For the french edition «L'Année Rallyes 2006»
ISBN 2-84707-113-X

© December 2006, Chronosports S.A.
Jordils Park, Rue des Jordils 40,
CH-1025 St-Sulpice, Suisse.
Tel. : (+41 21) 694 24 44.
Fax : (+41 21) 694 24 46.
e-mail: info@chronosports.com
Web: www.chronosports.com

Printed by Imprimerie Clerc, 18206 St-Amand-Montrond, France
Bound by Reliures Brun, 45331 Malesherbes, France.

All rights reserved. No part of this publication may be reproduced,
stored in a retrieval system, or transmitted in any form or by any
means, electronic, mechanical, photocopying, recording or
otherwise, without the prior written permission of the publishers.

Thanks Vicky! ;)

RALLY YEARBOOK
World Rally Championship

2006

Photos
DPPI

Words
Philippe Joubin
"L'Equipe"

Translated from french by
David Waldron

Artistic Director, coordination
Cyril Davillerd

Page Layout
Cyril Davillerd, Sidonie Perrin & Loraine Lequint

Results
Vicky Paradisgarten & Cyril Davillerd

CHRONOSPORTS
ÉDITEUR

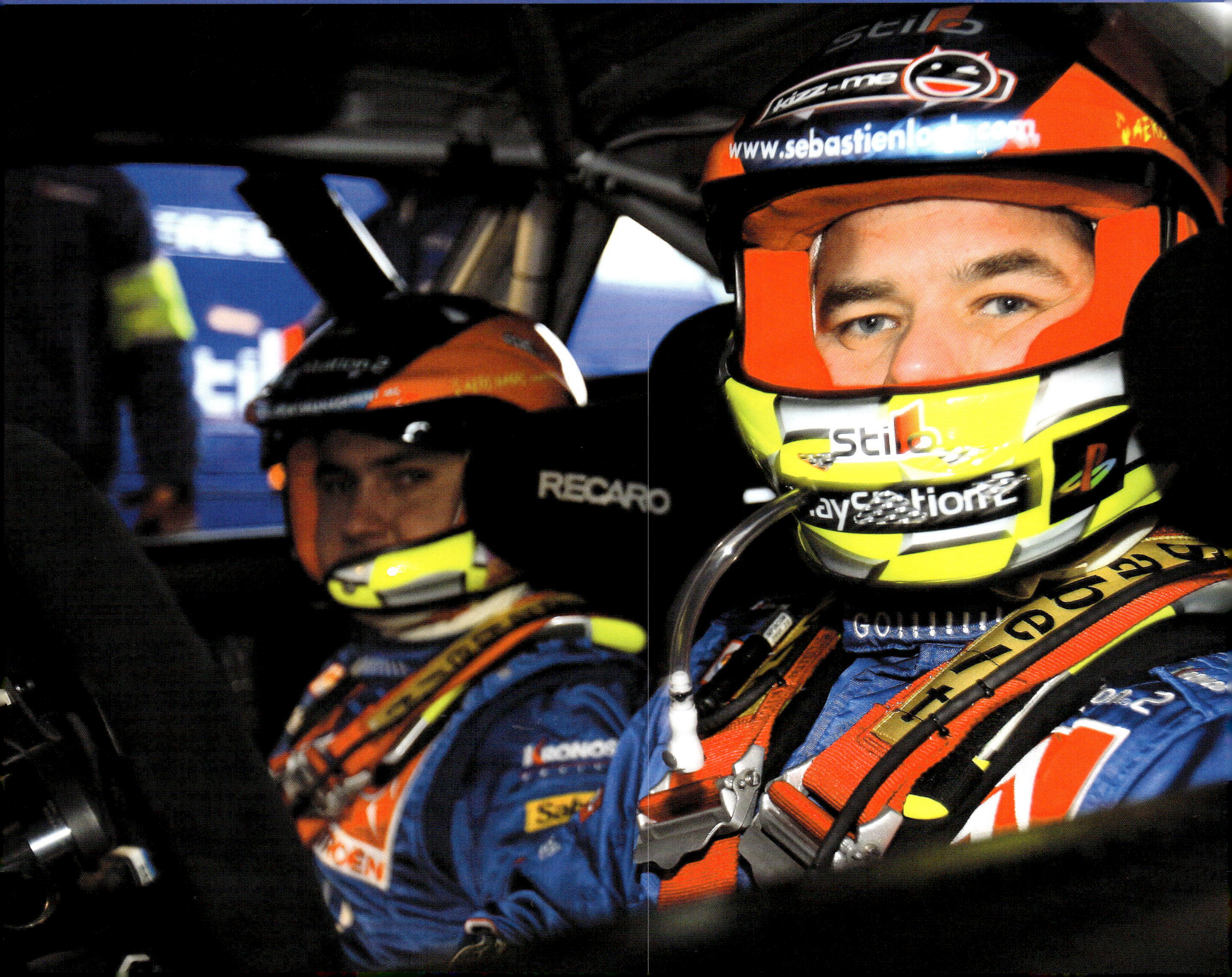
kizz-me
RECARO
Stilo

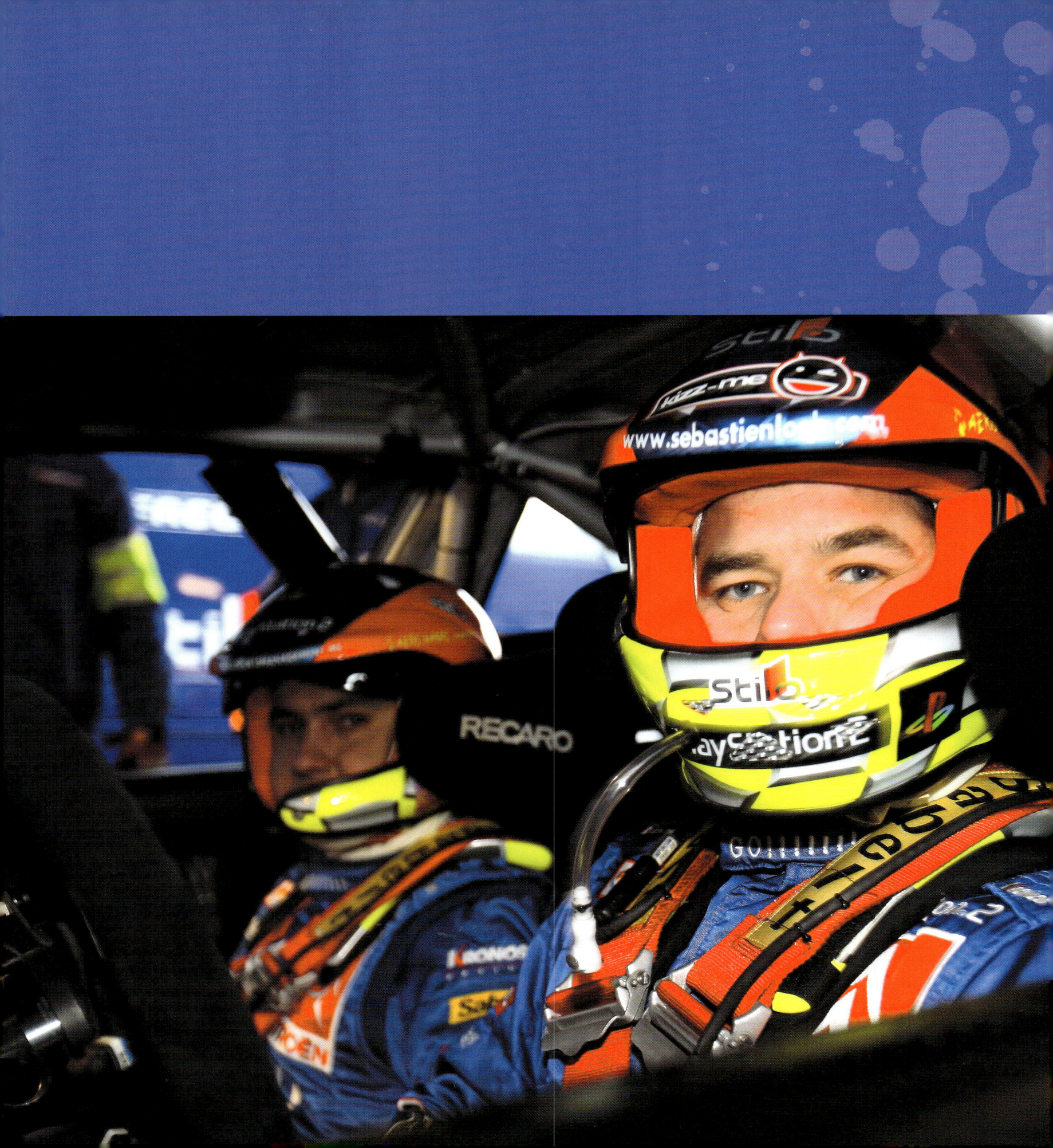

FOREWORD

Okay! It's a very hackneyed saying that good things come in threes! But that's how we like it. Next year at the start of the Monte Carlo Rally our helmets will have a third little star. And you can't imagine how proud of it we are. It has to be said that this title was obtained in unusual circumstances. The day we won it we were both in France while everything was unfolding 20,000 kilometres away in Australia. What has always been important for us is to win, not just to take part. And we came home first in eight out of the twelve rallies in which we raced.

Besides this third title, 2006 will be remembered as an exceptional year for us both for other reasons.

First of all, we beat the record number of victories for both drivers and co-drivers, which we really wanted to do. It is something people don't forget. And then there were the last rallies that we shared with the Xsara WRC.

It is an extraordinary car and we are going to miss it as it has brought us all our successes up till now.

And finally for the marvellous season we had with Kronos. Without the passion and devotion of all the members of the squad we could never have achieved such success. In 2007, we will be back in France but we are leaving our friends in the team with a heavy heart.

It is thanks to them that we are again writing the preface to the "Rally Yearbook", the unique reference work. It is the third time as it is always the pleasant duty of the reigning world champions to do the job. It is a wonderful tradition, and if we are back here again in 2007 it will mean that we have equalled the last record that has escaped us so far: four titles.

2007: Here we come. And next year: same place, same time!

Sébastien Loeb

Daniel Elena

SUBARU
Beta
TOTAL
PIRELLI
RECARO
CITROEN
TOTAL
CITROËN
GAULOISES
Red Bull
ultimate
.com

CONTENTS

- 4 Foreword by Sébastien Loeb and Daniel Elena
- 8 Analysis
- 16 Record: Loeb, 28 victories
- 18 Christian Loriaux: "A human history!"
- 22 Teams and Drivers
- 39 Production Championship
- 40 Junior Championship
- 41 Kronos, an up and down season
- 44 2006 FIA World Rally Championship
  - 46 01 Monte-Carlo
  - 54 02 Sweden
  - 62 03 Mexico
  - 70 04 Spain
  - 78 05 France
  - 86 06 Argentina
  - 94 07 Italy
  - 102 08 Greece
  - 110 09 Germany
  - 118 10 Finland
  - 126 11 Japan
  - 134 12 Cyprus
  - 142 13 Turkey
  - 150 14 Australia
  - 158 15 New Zealand
  - 166 16 Great Britain
- 174 The 2006 FIA World Rally Championships
- 176 Statistics

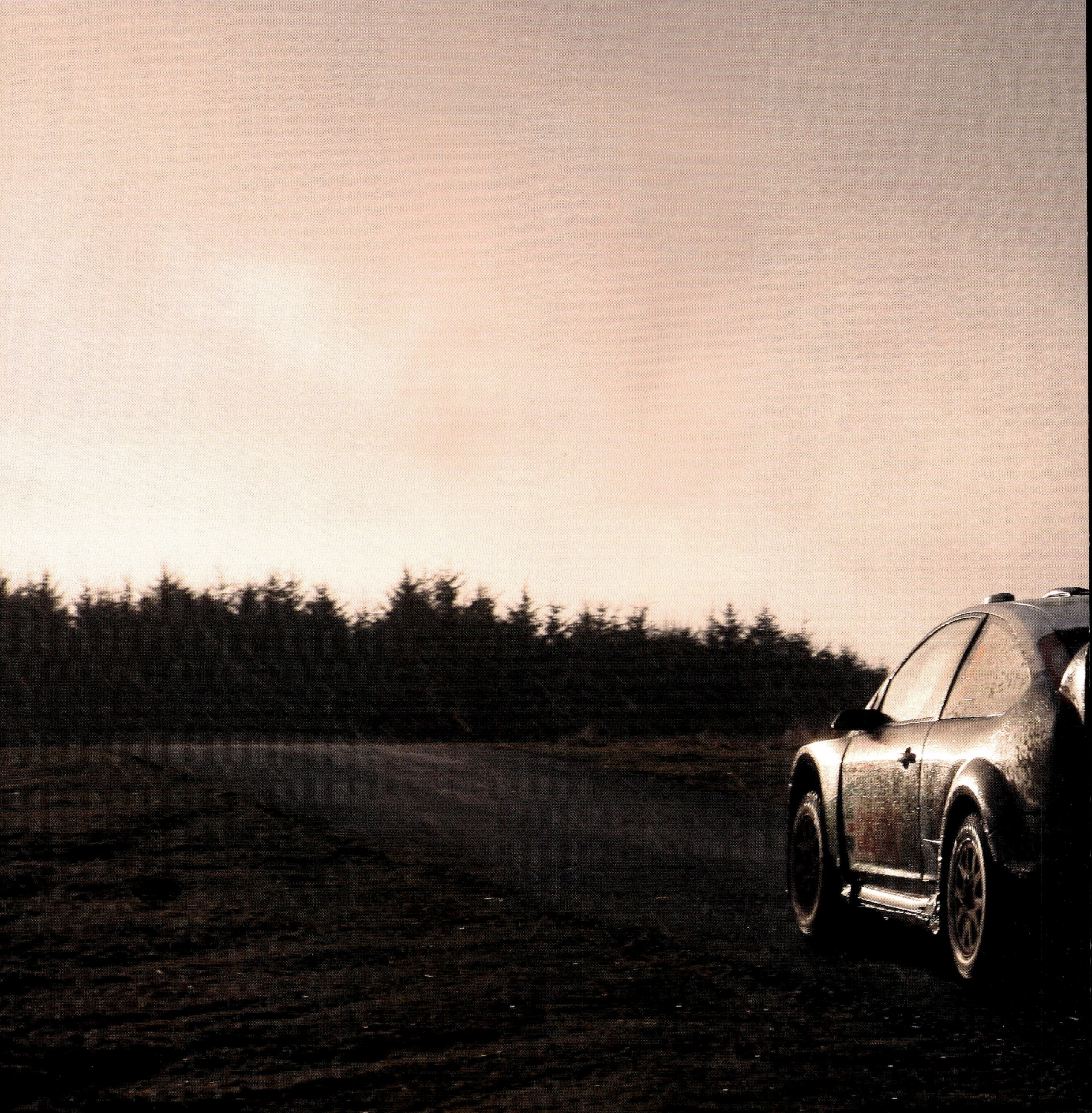

2006 FIA WRC

Analysis

It was an unusual season for Sébastien Loeb. He won the title for the third time but was not present on the day when it was awarded to him rather than his archrival Marcus Grönholm. Their duel, which ended prematurely when Loeb fell off his bicycle, was a breathtaking one and overshadowed the other drivers. After the last rally only 1 point separated them!

Analysis

Sébastien Loeb

Marcus Grönholm

The battle between Loeb and Grönholm began on 20th January 2006 in Monaco and it finally turned in the Frenchman's favour in the Eucalyptus forests of Perth in Australia when the big Finn's car made contact with a stone. It took 9 months for the 2006 championship to be decided and victory went to the same man as in the previous two years: Sébastien Loeb. The Alsatian's 2006 season was an extraordinary one. First of all he was driving for a semi-private team Kronos (read about the history of their collaboration elsewhere n this book). He did not win in Monte Carlo but then racked up a string of five victories (between Mexico and Italy) and broke his arm after another success (Cyprus), which effectively eliminated him from the last 4 events.

Sébastien Loeb and Daniel Elena joined the Kronos team for the 2006 season while awaiting the official return of Citroën in 2007 with the new C4. It took several months of prevarication before the responsibility of running the Xsaras in the world championship was finally entrusted to the Belgian outfit. In fact, it was only an illusion. Whether or not Sébastien Loeb's car ever saw the inside of the Namur

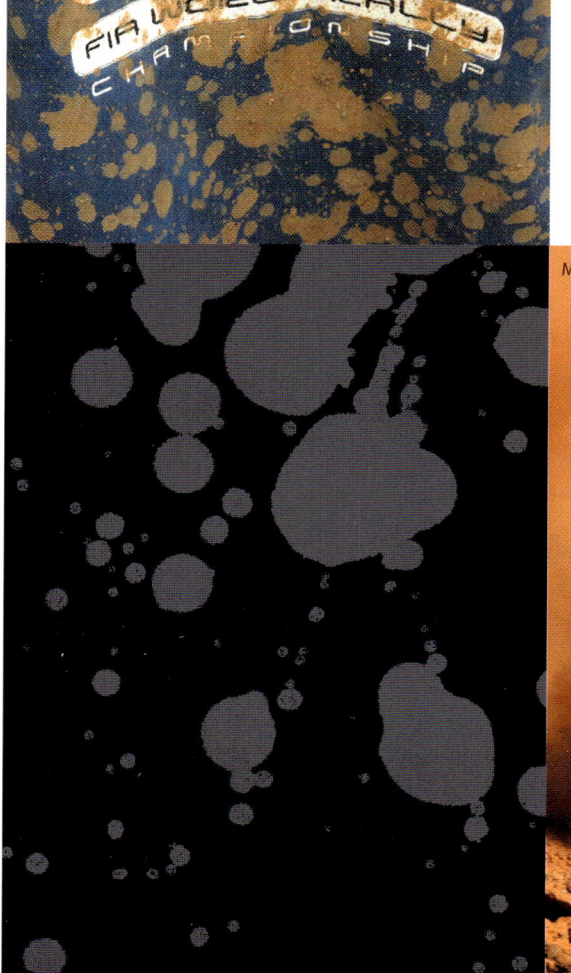

Marcus Grönholm

Gigi Galli

Chris Atkinson

workshops is a moot point. The car bearing no.1 was prepared and developed in the Satory workshops, and many of the company's engineers were on hand whenever it started a rally. Kronos is perhaps a private team but the no.1 Xsara was anything but a private entry in the strict sense of the term. It was allowed several homologation updates during the season, proof that it was constantly improved by Guy Fréquelin's men.

This "old" car was still as quick as ever- in the hands of Loeb in any case. The season got off to a poor start with the Frenchman's accident in the Monte Carlo Rally after which he was delayed and then dominated in Sweden. The Franco-Monegasque pair was back in the winning groove from Mexico onwards racking up five victories on the trot. It took an on-form Grönholm and a puncture in the Acropolis to prevent them from equalling their record of 6 consecutive successes, which they had racked up in 2005. Then in succession Daniel Elena followed by Loeb broke the records for the number of victories by a co-driver and driver in the World Rally Championship. Elena's moment came in Sardinia when he beat Luis Moya's record of 24 and in Cyprus the Frenchman broke the one held by his old tutor Carlos Sainz whose tally was 26. Loeb and Elena left this record standing at 28 in Cyprus.

Petter Solberg

Sébastien Loeb

Analysis

Daniel Sordo

So what was left for the others? During the season the real enthusiasts were enthralled by the incredible battles between Loeb and Grönholm, which reached their height in Finland and Japan writing some of the most exciting pages in the history of road events. The Finn's comeback at the end of the Japanese event, and the Frenchman's never-say-die courage near Jyväskylä were two sublime moments. Marcus never gave up but he also committed a number of faults under pressure from Loeb that played hell with his consistency, something he will regret for the rest of his days. In addition, the points system favours consistency over dash, so it was sometimes wiser to go for a place. Loeb, though, was never less than flat out in the 12 events in which he took part. But when he saw that victory was beyond his grasp he was content to settle for second as witnessed by his results because if he did not win that was where he always finished.

Consistency was what the fiery Grönholm lacked. It is difficult to say which of the two is the quicker but Loeb is certainly the more reliable. In addition, Marcus had to cope with the teething troubles on his new car.

Petter & Henning Solberg

Manfred Stohl
& Ilka Minor

Henning Solberg

All the other title contenders played walk-on roles. This included Petter Solberg, certainly one of the best, who ran into too many technical problems on his 2006 Impreza to hope to mix it with the two Titans. Whether or not the sharp edge of the Norwegian driver's talent has been blunted by his disastrous season remains to be seen. The best of the no. 2s was Mikko Hirvonen. The young Finn was able to cope with the pressure of driving for a major manufacturer. He said himself that he was unable to match the speed of Loeb and Grönholm. Nonetheless, he picked up seven second or third places making a large contribution to Ford's manufacturers' title. The cherry on the cake was his victory in Australia when his leader tripped up and Loeb was absent. He is a good driver who fully deserved his third place in the drivers' championship. However, he will have to be able to up his pace to show that he has what it takes to make it to the very top.

The duel between Grönholm and Loeb left a slightly bitter taste. At the end of the season when the Frenchman was absent after his bicycle accident, the Finn had no real

Toni Gardemeister

Analysis

Jari-Matti Latvala

opposition except himself. In Australia he destroyed his championship hopes in a stupid accident as he admitted afterwards. He racked up fastest times and victories and the only thing he had to fear was one of his own slip-ups.

In the opposite case it would have been the same. Without Grönholm the championship would be a cakewalk for Loeb. So where is the problem? There are obviously explanations. Solberg was out of it in 2006 because of his car. The next generation has not yet really confirmed its potential, and the lack of works cars does not help in this area. Obviously, the excellence of the two drivers is not in question. It seems that Marcus Grönholm is heading for retirement (his current contract expires at the end of 2007) so hopefully that other drivers will follow in his footsteps. Sébastien Loeb is such a sportsman that he would agree with this analysis, as winning without opposition is not part of his mentality.

Ford came out on top in the manufacturers' championship after 27 years. The last time was in 1979 thanks to Bjorn Waldegaard at the wheel of the bullet-proof Ford Escorts. In 1981, Ari Vatanen won the drivers' title but the American giant did not reckon such a long lapse of time between successes. From 1979 and 2006 the Rally World Championship was dominated by makes like Audi, Lancia, Peugeot and Subaru and drivers such as Auriol, Sainz, Mäkinen

Petter Solberg

Mikko Hirvonen

Mikko Hirvonen

and Kankkunen among others. Ford was always present even if at times the team was perturbed by internal and external threats as well as achieving some successes (Delacour in Monte Carlo, for example). It was only justice that Malcolm Wilson the man who epitomises the presence of the manufacturer at the highest level and his team M-Sport reaped the rewards. He was an excellent driver and is a great team chief as well as someone noted for his sporting fair play, so hopefully the Ford big cheeses will realise just how lucky they are to have his team representing them. They have trusted him since 1997 when the Boreham squad was floundering by giving him their road racing programme. In 2004, they told him that Ford was going to continue in top-level rallying for several years to come. Now the toughest part has to be faced: namely, defending the title in 2007 against the assaults of the red army! Citroën is sharpening its weapons and the C4 will make its first appearance in a rally on 19th January 2007 in Monaco. It will be out to recapture the Chevron-badged make's former glory, which will not be an easy task against Grönholm and the Ford Focus.

Alexandre Bengué

Xavier

LOEB RECORD 28

2004

2004

2004

2005

2005

2005

2006

2006

2006

2006

Christian Loriaux "A human victory!"

"A human victory!"
Christian Loriaux

Ford waited a long time. Twenty-seven years in fact to win the manufacturers' title again. Despite the tough opposition provided by Kronos-Citroën Malcolm Wilson's M-Sport team entrusted with the design, development and entry of the Ford Focuses in the world championship finally achieved its ultimate aim. One of the men behind this success is the chief engineer, Belgian Christian Loriaux, who was mainly responsible for Subaru's success. He then joined Ford and with his engineers came up with a car that brought the American giant victory in only its first season.

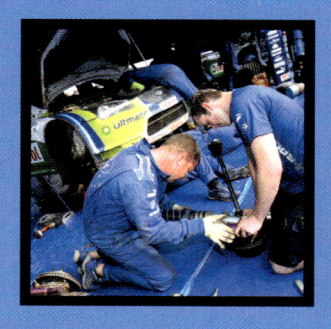

What was the Ford's strong point this season?

"The driving force of the team is its human potential. It took a huge amount of work to get the car up and running from the first sketches in the design studio where we began with a clean sheet to the first fastest time. That took a lot of work, and then the on-going development in all areas throughout the season was another enormous task. The title and the way we won are down to the human investment and the harmony between the personnel in M-Sport. The team is closely-knit and they work well together with tremendous enthusiasm. It was sheer passion that got us our result. Many things were done without any one person being directly responsible. It's rare in a company for people to take such responsibilities on themselves."

The car appeared at the end of 2005 and won first time out in 2006. It is now world champion at the end of its first season. Are you surprised, as the aim was to win in 2007?

We said that this would be a learning year. But the aim of my engineers and myself has always been to make cars that are very competitive out of the box even if it means taking technical risks. The first car that I was responsible for in terms of design, engineering and assembly was the 2000 Subaru and it triumphed in the first rally in which it raced. Then we made the 2001 Impreza and we won the championship with Richard Burns. After that came the 2003 Focus that was on the pace right away. I've got experience and so have my engineers and I'm lucky to be surrounded by a very good bunch of guys. Of course, when the car does its first special you're always a bit afraid. You ask yourself if you haven't got it wrong. What's really amazing is that between the car coming out of the workshop and its first rally we did only 6 days testing. We arrived in Australia with our drivers Kresta and Gardemeister neither of who had driven or even seen the Ford before. Tony set the second-quickest time in the first stage! It was fantastic all the more so as we were up against the works Peugeots and Citroëns. The car was quick out of the box and that reassured us though we were expecting to have more reliability problems."

Christian Loriaux *"A human victory!"*

But in 2006 you did have more problems than the Xsara...

"It's true. In Sweden we lost the water pump belt on Mikko's car a problem that we'd already had in Australia. We solved it by fitting housings on the pump to cover the belt. In Catalonia, Marcus was in the lead from Sébastien on asphalt, but we lost because the waste gates worked loose and fell off on both cars. There was a problem with the bolts and clips. We found that out to our cost. But apart from those two the others were minor. There was an electrical glitch in Argentina because the work had not been done properly; it could've happened on any car. And finally we broke a sump guard and an oil filter in Sardinia and retired. That was because of the car's newness but overall I'm very satisfied with the Focus's reliability. All the new technical systems that we factored in held. We also owe our title to the steadiness of our no.2 driver."

Speaking of drivers Grönholm was always ahead of Hirvonen but he's less consistent than Loeb...

"Well, let's look at the rallies one by one. Many people will say, 'Sébastien's quicker,' but Marcus was the only one who could match his pace and pressure him into making mistakes. In Sweden, he scored a dominant victory. In Mexico, he committed a big blunder. He got angry, wanted to win and pushed too hard when he was well in front of Loeb. In Spain there was a technical problem. And let's be honest in Corsica our rivals, both drivers and cars, were too strong. Sébastien drove a more technical rally on the island, and the Citroëns were better than we were. In Argentina, Marcus was again in the lead until he had a technical problem. In Sardinia, he drove a superb first loop; after three stages he had a 40-second lead! But the car broke the next day. We won the Acropolis. In Germany, we really screwed up and our settings were useless. The drivers lost confidence and gave up trying. Marcus won again in Finland but it was not easy as Sébastien was really superb.

In Japan and Cyprus they had fantastic battles. In the land of the rising sun the way Marcus pulled back 25 seconds on the last day shows just how quick he is. He failed to win because Loeb pressured him into making a mistake and he spun losing 30 seconds. It's difficult to say who is the better of the two. Sébastien is a great driver; he makes very few mistakes, keeps a cool head and he's calm and intelligent. He's won the world championship three times after such a short career in top-class rallying, so any body who says that he's not one of the greatest drivers in the history of the sport needs his head examined!"

Grönholm is more driven by his temperament...

"He is the most hot-blooded of the Finns. He has this thing that's really great; when he gets into his car he wants to be the quickest in the stage. It's good in one way but it would be better if he calculated a little more from time to time. In some rallies he didn't need to push like crazy. Mikko had a very good season. We

21

From left to right, up : Henning Solberg, Cato Menkerud, Gilles Panizzi, Hervé Panizzi, Xavier Pons, Carlos Del Barrio, Pieter Tsjoen, Eddy Chevalier, Chris Atkinson, Glenn MacNeall
Middle : Michael Orr, Stéphane Sarrazin, Stéphane Prévot, Klaus Wicha, Andreas Aigner, Mikko Hirvonen, Jarmo Lehtinen, Ilka Minor
Sitting : Matthew Wilson, Timo Rautiainen, Marcus Grönholm, Daniel Elena, Sébastien Loeb, Petter Solberg, Philip Mills, Manfred Stohl

Teams & Drivers

Kronos Total Citroën WRT — Teams & Drivers

CITROËN Manufacturer 1
Xsara WRC

It was a gamble that almost came off. Guy Fréquelin entrusted the semi-official entry of the Xsara WRCs to Kronos Racing, which was a big risk for the Citroën Sports boss. In the past the Belgian team had run the French cars with success in rallies, but placing a double world champion, Sébastien Loeb with it was a whole different ballgame as was its defence of the manufacturers' title. Marc Van Dalen and his merry men did a marvellous job adopting an approach that was as serious as it was successful (read about the Loeb-Kronos collaboration elsewhere). The Xsara, whose first chassis was built in 1999, was still as quick and reliable as ever when adapted to the 2006 regulations. The Citroën engineers were working on the development of the C4 that will make its debut in the 2007 Monte Carlo Rally; and they also continued to develop the 'old' Xsara by incorporating the modifications intended for its sister car.

It almost worked. Kronos led the manufacturers' championship for most of the season only being beaten by Ford towards the end. It is true that the loss of Loeb with four rallies still to go was a huge blow as the 2 Spaniards in the team failed to live up to expectations. Pons was nominated to score points in the manufacturers' championship at the start of the season. Then Dani Sordo proved the quicker of the two. In the second part of the year he was entrusted with this task after a superb drive in the German rally. He then made a lot of mistakes, and was unable to defend his corner in some very specific events. While Kronos gave Loeb what he needed to win, and his drivers' title owes a lot to the Belgian team, it lost out on the manufacturers' one. It would have been a marvellous feat if this private squad had managed to pull off the double from under the noses of works outfits like Ford and Subaru.

Next year Citroën will be back with the C4 entrusted to Loeb and Sordo. A question mark hangs over Kronos's future, but hopefully it will find a way of capitalising on its 2006 results: 8 victories, 2 doubles, the drivers' title and runner-up in the manufacturers' championship.

Sébastien Loeb, Jean-Pierre Mondron, Marc Van Dalen & Daniel Elena

Daniel Grataloup

Identity
Kronos S.A.
Rue Pieds d'Alouette, 37
5100 Namur (Naninne)
Belgium
- Tel.: +32 81 40 16 39
- Fax: +32 81 40 17 25
- Web: www.kronosracing.com

Team Members
- Director: Marc Van Dalen
- Administrator delegetade: Jean-Pierre Mondron
- Team Manager: Luc Manset
- Team Director: Michel Legros
- Team Coordinator: Daniel Grataloup
- Technical Managers:
  Jean-Pierre Debacker, Matthieu Bassou

Records
- Constructors Titles: 0
- Drivers Titles: 1 (2006)
- Victories: 8

- Team founded in: 1994
- Rally debut: 1994

Classification
- 2006 - 2°

Engine
- Type: XU7JP4
- Disposition: front transverse 30°
- Cylinders: 4 in line
- Valve: 4 per cyclinder
- Capacity: 1998 cc
- Camshaft: double overhead
- Bore x Stroke: 86 x 86 mm
- Power: 315 bhp @ 5500 rpm
- Torque max.: 580 Nm @ 2750 rpm
- Turbocharger: Garrett
- Engine Management: Magnetti-Marelli
- Lubrification: carbon wet sump
- Fuel / Lubrifiant: Total

Transmission
- Clutch: carbon triple-plate 140 mm
- Gearbox: X-tracs longitudinal 6-speed sequential
- Differentials: active centre differentials

Steerings
- Hydraulic power-assisted rack and pinion

Suspensions
- Front & rear: McPherson strut with helicoidal spring

Shock Absorbers
- Extremetech

Brakes
- Front: ventilated discs,
  376 mm ø (asphalt), 310 mm ø (gravel)
  6-pot calipers
- Rear: ventilated discs (318 mm ø),
  4-pot calipers

Tyres BFGoodrich
Wheels O.Z. magnesium 8 x 18"

Dimensions
- Wheelbase: 2555 mm
- Overall length: 4167 mm
- Overall width: 1770 mm
- Overall height: 1390 mm
- Car weight: 1230 kgs

Kronos Total Citroën WRT — Teams & Drivers

Sébastien LOEB #1

IDENTITY CARD
- Nationality: French
- Date of birth: February 26, 1974
- Place of birth: Haguenau (F)
- Resident: Bougy-Villars (CH)
- Marital status: Married to Séverine
- Co-driver: Daniel Elena (MC)
- Web: www.sebastienloeb.com

CAREER
- Rally debut: 1995
- Number of Rallies in WRC: 80
- Number of victories: 28

2001 - 15th in Championship; WORLD CHAMPION S1600
2002 - 10th in Championship
2003 - 2nd in Championship
2004 - WORLD CHAMPION
2005 - WORLD CHAMPION
2006 - WORLD CHAMPION

Daniel Elena

The problem with Sébastien Loeb is that one runs out of superlatives very quickly. The 2006 season will remain one of the most singular of his career. He set a new world record for rally victories with 28, which, for him and many observers was the most important thing, two more than Carlos Sainz and then racked up a third world championship title beating those who had scored two like Walter Röhrl, Carlos Sainz and Mikki Biaison plus Marcus Grönholm. His three on the trot has been bested by only one man in rally history Tommi Mäkinen who racked up four between 1996 and 1999. What, though, was different was the fact that he was crowned in absentia due to his mountain bike accident after the Cyprus rally. Up till then he had scored 112 points thanks to 8 victories and 4 second places so he was really out of reach of Marcus Grönholm, the only driver to pose a threat to him throughout the 2006 season. In addition, his third title was won in a car run by a private team, Kronos Racing. "I think that not many people reckoned that I could win driving for a non-works team," he explained when he had the title in his pocket. "Even if it was backed by Citroën Sport."

2005 was the season in which he earned his spurs and in 2006 he displayed a stunning amount of know-how. Drivers often say that they learn every day when they get into their cars, like Michael Schumacher, for example. Sébastien Loeb is not of that ilk. As a driver he reckons that he is at the top of his game using that extraordinary mixture of talent and hard work, which has brought him to a level probably never reached until now. Certain polls in motoring magazines prove that Loeb, a simple and appealing guy, is one the greatest drivers in the history of motor sport, all branches combined. It's not far from the truth but still needs a little further confirmation. His next challenge is to equal Tommi Mäkinen's record in 2007, and then to beat it the following year. Next season, though, will probably not be that easy. How will the new C4 WRC that has undergone an enormous amount of development behave? Will Marcus Grönholm, more motivated than ever in the last year of his career at the wheel of his Ford Focus that has proved to be very quick, be better than everyone? But the mark of a great driver is to overcome all these obstacles like Loeb did at the end of 2005. We shall see.

Xavier PONS #2 / #1

IDENTITY CARD
- Nationality: Spanish
- Date of birth: January 21, 1980
- Place of birth: Vic (E)
- Resident: Manlleu (E)
- Marital status: Single
- Co-driver: Carlos del Barrio (E)
- Web: www.xevipons.com

CAREER
- Rally debut: 2003
- Nbr of Rallies in WRC: 51
- Best result: 4th

2004 - 22nd in Championship
2005 - 16th in Championship
2006 - 7th in Championship

Pons was given the second seat in the Kronos-entered Citroën at the start of the year after a promising 2005 season in which he had taken part in some Production Championship rallies. He won in this category in New Zealand and put in a few good drives in a Xsara WRC. It was a big responsibility for the former enduro champion who, up till then, had never really achieved any major results in rallying. He made a modest start to the season and finished in the points on four out of eight events up to Greece with fourth as his best result. It was not what his employer had been expecting especially as he was up against an all-fired up Dani Sordo. He suffered mechanical problems and his driving became increasingly erratic until his accident in Corsica brought him down to earth with a bump. He was then stripped of his seat in the works car for the first four rallies of the second half of the season, but was called back after Colin McRea's disappointing performance in Australia where he came home fourth in one of the client version Kronos Xsaras. He was not really up to taking the fight to Ford, and Dani Sordo was chosen instead of him for the second works C4 seat in 2007.

Daniel SORDO #2

IDENTITY CARD
- Nationality: Spanish
- Date of birth: May 2, 1983
- Place of birth: Torrelavega (E)
- Resident: Puente San Miguel (E)
- Marital status: Single
- Co-driver: Marc Marti (E)
- Web: www.danielsordo.com

CAREER
- Rally debut: 2003
- Nbr of Rallies in WRC: 16
- Best result: 2nd

2005 – WORLD CHAMPION Jr.
2006 – 5th in Championship

Daniel Sordo has the unconditional backing of Carlos Sainz and has had a meteoric rise to fame in motor sport. In 2003 and 2004 he won the Spanish Junior Championship and the following year at the age of 22 he won the Junior World Championship. His skill behind the wheel, his combativeness gave him the drive in the third Kronos Xsara WRC (in 2005 spec) at the start of the season. He exploited this to the full by coming second in Catalonia, then third in Corsica and third in Sardinia. At the halfway mark he was in third place in the drivers' ratings. He was given the seat in the second works Xsara from Germany onwards, and immediately scored another second place behind Sébastien Loeb. Marc Van Dalen was obliged to tell him to cool it so as not to jeopardise the double that was on the cards. That was all Citroën Sport needed to take him on for 2007. But the latter part of the 2006 season was a bit of a disaster for the young Spaniard. He went off in both Finland and Cyprus, and was the victim of a stupid disqualification in Japan. He was overtaken by Hirvonen for third place in the drivers' championship. That he is quick there is no doubt but he will have to show more consistency at the wheel of the C4 if he wants Guy Fréquelin to keep him on.

Colin McRAE #1

IDENTITY CARD
- Nationality: Scotish
- Date of birth: August 5, 1968
- Place of birth: Lanark (GB)
- Resident: Monaco (MC), Lanark (GB)
- Marital status: Married to Alison, two children
- Co-driver: Nicky Grist (GB)
- Web: www.colinmcrae.com

CARREER
- Rally debut: 1986
- Nbr of Rallies in WRC: 152
- Number of victories: 25

1989 - 34th in Championship
1990 - 34th in Championship
1991 - Not classified
1992 - 8th in Championship
1993 - 5th in Championship
1994 - 4th in Championship
1995 - WORLD CHAMPION
1996 - 2nd in Championship
1997 - 2nd in Championship
1998 - 3rd in Championship
1999 - 6th in Championship
2000 - 4th in Championship
2001 - 2nd in Championship
2002 - 4th in Championship
2003 - 7th in Championship
2005 - 23rd in Championship
2006 - Not classified

In 2005, Citroën brought Carlos Sainz out of retirement after François Duval's poor showing. The Spaniard did a marvellous job scoring 11 points in the manufacturers' championship. When Loeb had his accident Kronos called in Colin McRae to replace him for the Turkish rally. The 38-year-old Scot, who never wanted to quit rallying in the first place, drove a marvellous race in Australia at the end of 2005 in a Skoda, and he was hoping to relaunch his career in the Citroën with his co-driver Nicky Grist. His first leg was okay (he finished 6th) but after that he fell back due to a wrong tyre choice; it has to be said he did not receive a lot of help for his team in this area. He retired with alternator problems near the end and that was that.

BP-Ford World Rally Team
Teams & Drivers

FORD Manufacturer 1
Focus RS WRC 06

In 1996, Ford took a big risk when it decided to entrust its entry in rallies to M-Sport. The team had already made a name for itself but did not seem to fit the bill for a worldwide campaign. It was founded in 1979 by Malcolm Wilson to enable him to fulfil his devouring passion: rallying. In the 80s the team grew in size along with the reputation of its owner/driver.

The arrival of the Ford Cosworth in the 90s gave it an additional boost as it entered cars in various championships winning titles in Italy, Portugal and the Middle East. Malcolm himself became British champion in 1994. Two years later Jarmo Kytolehto finished third in Finland in an Escort entered by M-Sport, and that result highlighted the qualities of the British team. At that moment Ford was enjoying little success with its Boreham-based squad, and was chasing after world titles in vain while suffering from a succession of internal crises. At the end of 1996, the manufacturer made up its mind and decided in favour of M-Sport. Its trust was soon rewarded as in 1997 the Escort WRC won two rallies: Greece and then Indonesia. For 1999, Ford entrusted M-Sport with the development of the first Focus WRC designed by Günther Steiner and destined for Colin McRae. The Scot was a big star and he made M-Sport pay a high price for his skills as he negotiated the biggest salary up to then in the history of rallying: over five million dollars! So it was victory or nothing. The Focus was quick out of the box, set fastest times on its first outing and then won the Safari showing itself at home on difficult terrain. There was, however, an obstacle on the path of M-Sport: Tommi Mäkinen and Mitsubishi. Ford and McRae fought some marvellous duels with the Finn but were unable to stop his run of victories. In 2002, the Scot and his team-mate since 2000 Carlos Sainz came close to winning the title. Unfortunately, they were let down by the poor quality of the Pirellis on asphalt.

McRae and then Sainz joined Citroën in 2003 and the following years were ones of transition with some good drivers like Markko Märtin, the best of the bunch, winning rallies while waiting for Ford to confirm its long-term engagement in the world championship. Which it did in 2004.

The Focus WRC RS 06 was designed by a technical team led by Belgian Christian Loriaux who had quit Subaru for Ford for the 2003 season. The car was a success and was quick on its debut in the 2005 Australian event. In 2006, its drivers won eight rounds of the championship between them, seven for Marcus Grönholm and one for Mikko Hirvonen. It had few teething troubles and scored points in 24 out of its 32 starts. The aim was to win the world title in 2007. The Focus achieved this a year in advance!

While there is no doubting the qualities of the Focus and its 2 drivers Sébastien Loeb's absence in the last four rallies certainly had an enormous bearing on the final outcome. The Frenchman was really the only driver capable of fighting Citroën's corner. The two Ford drivers, who allied consistency and speed especially towards the end of the 2006 season - even when Loeb was present like in Japan or Cyprus – reaped the rewards of their team's investment.

Malcolm Wilson made the right choice by hiring the two Finns. Once Peugeot had withdrawn Grönholm hesitated for a time between Citroën and Ford, and must have been delighted with his decision. The team quickly fell under his charm, straightforwardness, his talent and his fighting spirit.

Hirvonen was a Ford driver in 2003 and then went to Subaru in 2004 where he had a fairly poor season. In 2005, he did a limited programme and shone on each one of his outings so Malcolm Wilson gave him a second chance. It was the right decision as his steadiness allied to Grönholm's speed gave Ford the 2006 manufactures' title, the make's first since 1979, and only its second since the creation of the world championship in 1973.

Identity
Ford Motor Company, M-Sport Ltd
Dovenby Hall, Dovenby,
Cockermouth, Cumbria, CA13 OPN
Great Britain
- Tel.: +44 19 00 82 88 88
- Fax: +44 19 00 82 38 23
- Web: www.ford.co.uk

Team Members
- Director, Ford Team RS: Jost Capito
- Team Director: Malcolm Wilson
- Technical Director: Christian Loriaux

- Team founded in: 1986
- Rally debut: 1973

Records
- Constructors Titles: 2 (1979, 2006)
- Drivers Titles: 2 (1979, 1981)
- Victories: 56

Classifications
- 1973 - 3rd
- 1974 - 3rd
- 1975 - 6th
- 1976 - 3rd
- 1977 - 2nd
- 1978 - 2nd
- 1979 - 1st
- 1980 - 3rd
- 1980 - 8th
- 1981 - 3rd
- 1982 - 4th
- 1984 - 12th
- 1985 - 11th
- 1986 - 5th
- 1987 - 5th
- 1988 - 2nd
- 1989 - 13th
- 1990 - 8th
- 1991 - 4th
- 1992 - 3rd
- 1993 - 2nd
- 1994 - 3rd
- 1995 - 3rd
- 1996 - 3rd
- 1997 - 2nd
- 1998 - 4th
- 1999 - 4th
- 2000 - 2nd
- 2001 - 2nd
- 2002 - 2nd
- 2003 - 4th
- 2004 - 2nd
- 2005 - 3rd
- 2006 - 1st

Engine
- Type: Ford 2.0 liter Pipo I4 Duratec WRC
- Disposition: front transverse
- Number of cylinders: 4 in line
- Valve: 4 per cylinder
- Capacity: 1998 cc
- Camshaft: double overhead
- Bore x Stroke: 85 x 88 mm
- Power: 300 bhp @ 6500 rpm
- Torque: 550 Nm @ 4000 rpm
- Turbocharger: Garrett
- Engine Management: Pi electronic
- Lubrification: carbon wet sump
- Exchanger: air-air
- Fuel tank capacity: 94 litres

Transmission
- Clutch: M-Sport / Sachs multi disc carbon
- Gearbox: M-Sport / Ricardo sequential with electrico-hydraulically controlled shift.
- Differentials: Permanent four-wheel drive with M-Sport designed active, centre differential.

Steering Power-assisted rack and pinion

Suspensions
- Front and rear: MacPherson

Shock absorbers Reiger

Brakes Brembo
- Gravel (F & R): ventilated discs (300 mm ø), 4-piston monoblock calipers.
- Asphalt (F & R): ventilated discs (370 mm ø), 8-piston monoblock calipers.

Tyres BFGoodrich (650 mm)
Wheels Gravel: 7 x 15", asphalt: 8 x 18"

Dimensions
- Wheelbase: 2640 mm
- Overall lenght: 4362 mm
- Overall width: 1800 mm
- Overall height: 1420 mm
- Car weight: 1230 kgs

Marcus GRÖNHOLM #3

Timo Rautiainen

IDENTITY CARD
- Nationality: Finnish
- Date of birth: February 5, 1968
- Place of birth: Espoo (FIN)
- Resident: Inkoo (FIN)
- Marital status: Married, 3 children
- Co-driver: Timo Rautiainen (FIN)
- Web: www.mgr.fi

CAREER
- Rally debut: 1989
- Nbr of rallies in WRC: 133
- Number of victories: 25

- 1996 - 10th in Championship
- 1997 - 12th in Championship
- 1998 - 16th in Championship
- 1999 - 15th in Championship
- 2000 - WORLD CHAMPION
- 2001 - 4th in Championship
- 2002 - WORLD CHAMPION
- 2003 - 6th in Championship
- 2004 - 5th in Championship
- 2005 - 3rd in Championship
- 2006 - 2nd in Championship

Only 2 points separated him from his third world title at the end of the 2006 season. The big Finn will rue his mistake in Australia for the rest of his life. In the third stage his Ford hit a stone and went off into the scenery ending up on its roof. The accident and the time lost robbed him of his hopes of a third title.
Sébastien Loeb's accident in Switzerland had opened the door for his Finnish rival. After the Cyprus rally he was 35 points behind the Frenchman but there were still four to go and scoring 36* looked on the cards. He racked up 34 proving that he had no room for error.
The big Finn, as quick if not quicker than Loeb, despite his age and his long career lost his chances of the title in the rallies before Australian especially in Mexico and Japan. But overall, he had a great season with a total of 7 victories, a first in his career, scored in his favourite rallies like Sweden, Finland and Greece as well an in one of his last favourite Monte Carlo. He has now racked up a total of 25 victories, one behind Sainz, and is the only driver able to threaten the Frenchman's 28.
He starts the 2007 season as favourite in a team where he is as happy as a sand boy at the wheel of a car that he loves. His motivation will be all the stronger as he may retire at the end of the year, and would love to do so with a third title in his pocket.

*Had the 2 drivers finished the year with the same number of points Loeb would have won thanks to his greater number of victories.

Mikko HIRVONEN #4

Jarmo Lehtinen

IDENTITY CARD
- Nationality: Finnish
- Date of birth: July 31, 1980
- Place of birth: Kannonkoski (FIN)
- Resident: Jyväskylä (FIN)
- Marital status: Engaged to Karoliina
- Co-driver: Jarmo Lehtinen (FIN)
- Web: www.mikkohirvonen.com

CAREER
- Rally debut: 1998
- Nbr of rallies in WRC: 56
- Number of victory: 1

- 2003 - 15th in Championship
- 2004 - 7th in Championship
- 2005 - 10th in Championship
- 2006 - 3rd in Championship

In 2003, Mikko Hirvonen was a works Ford driver and he was back in that much sought-after position at the end of last year. His drives in private cars and at the wheel of M-Sport Focuses convinced Malcolm Wilson to give him a second chance. And he knew that there would not be a third so he seized it with both hands. His year got off to a cautious start as he ran into technical problems, but then things started to go his way with second place in Italy followed by third in Greece. These two results boosted his confidence and apart from Germany he was on the rostrum until the end of the season except in Great Britain. He came first in the Australian rally (his first WRC success) and was the only other winner in 2006 besides Loeb and Grönholm. His great end of season charge helped Ford to the manufacturers' title and with the raft of problems that hit Kronos he snatched third place in the drivers' championship from Dani Sordo.
26-year-old Hirvonen did exactly what was expected of him in the right place at the right time and will be part of the Ford squad for 2007. Now he has to up his pace if he wants to be more than just a good no.2.

Subaru World Rally Team
Teams & Drivers

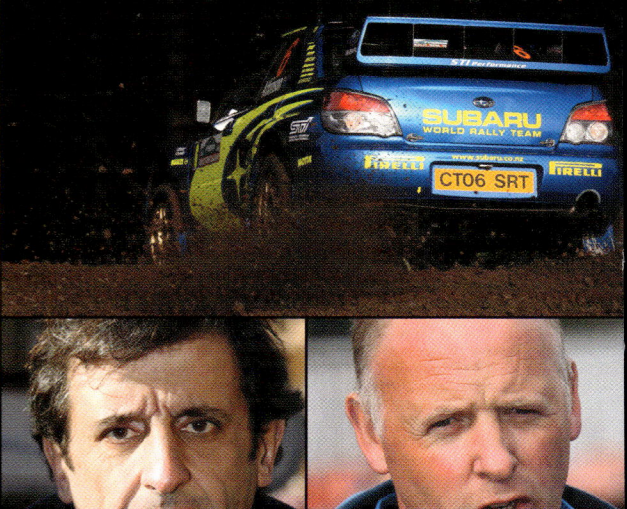

Luis Moya
Paul Howarth

SUBARU
Manufacturer 1
Impreza WRC 2006

It seems an age since Petter Solberg won the drivers' title. It was in 2003, and that seems a long time ago in comparison to the Japanese manufacturer's catastrophic 2006 season. The Impreza was a bad car right from the word go. It was unreliable and slow, and its drivers were never in a position to fight for victory. Given that Prodrive, the team that looks after and develops the Subaru, is very adept at concealing the truth, not many people expressed themselves openly concerning the car's faults. Petter Solberg occasionally spoke out of turn, but he is a professional and after each outburst Hollywood's broad smile was back on his face. The first to speak out was Toshio Araï, entered only for the Japanese rally, and as faithful to the make as they come. At the next rally in Cyprus the team management described the new evolution's faults. Its braking and road holding were erratic and in corners its behaviour was inconsistent. These were the car's main defects that were very difficult to correct due to the fact that the team had not really mastered its own technical choices.

There were a few bright spots like in Mexico and Australia where Solberg scored a couple of second places. But they were not followed up by the same kind of performance in the rally that followed on different terrain. 2006 was thus a winless season for Subaru, an infrequent occurrence for this make since its arrival in the world championship. This led to in-depth restructuring. During the season team manager David Lapworth was sent off to look after other projects: in particular Prodrive's F1 programme. Steve Farrell was made technical director and Belgian Christophe Chapelain was put in charge of design. Another Belgian Pierre-Yves Genon was asked to look after development, and ex-Peugeot engineer François-Xavier Demaison was given the job of race engineer. Subaru Japan also decided to become more involved. In 2007, the team will use BF Goodrich tyres replacing Pirelli, the team's long-term partner. It has put its trust in two of its three 2006 drivers, Solberg and Atkinson, for the coming season so Subaru has everything it takes to do well. Another faux pas is out of the question.

Identity
Subaru World Rally Team (Prodrive)
Banbury, Oxfordshire OX16 3ER
Great Britain
· Tel.: +44 12 95 27 33 35
· Fax: +44 12 95 27 11 88
· Web: www.swrt.com

Team members
· Managing Director SWRT: Richard Taylor
· Sporting Director: Luis Moya
· Rally Operations Director: Paul Howarth
· Director of Engineering: Steve Farrell
· Chief Engineer - Test & Development: Pierre Genon
· Senior Event Engineer: François-Xavier Demaison

Records
· Constructors Titles: 3 (1995, 1996, 1997)
· Drivers Titles: 3 (1995, 2001, 2003)
· Victories: 47

· Rally debut: 1982
· Team founded in: 1990

Classifications
· 1983 - 7th
· 1984 - 9th
· 1985 - 12th
· 1986 - 8th
· 1987 - 10th
· 1988 - 9th
· 1989 - 12th
· 1990 - 4th
· 1991 - 6th
· 1992 - 4th
· 1993 - 3rd
· 1994 - 2nd
· 1995 - 1st
· 1996 - 1st
· 1997 - 1st
· 1998 - 3rd
· 1999 - 2nd
· 2000 - 3rd
· 2001 - 3rd
· 2002 - 3rd
· 2003 - 3rd
· 2004 - 3rd
· 2005 - 4th
· 2006 - 3rd

Engine
· Type: flat 4-cylinder
· Valve: 4 per cylinder
· Capacity: 1994 cc
· Distribution: 2x double overhead
· Bore x Stroke: 92.0 x 75.0 mm
· Power: 300 bhp @ 5500 rpm
· Torque: 60 kg-m @ 4000 rpm
· Turbocharger: IHI
· Engine management: Subaru programmable electronic engine management system
· Spark plugs: Denso
· Fuel tank capacity: 80 litres

Transmission
· Gearbox: Prodrive longitudinal 6-speed electro-hydraulic, semi-automatic
· Differentials: Electro-hydraulic controlled

Steering
· Power-assisted rack and pinion

Suspensions
· Front: MacPherson strut
· Rear: MacPherson strut - longitudinal and transverse link

Shock absorbers Sachs

Brakes AP Racing
· Front and rear: ventilated discs (305 mm ø), 4-pot calipers
· Asphalt: front: ventilated discs (366 mm ø), 6-pot calipers

Tyres Pirelli

Wheels BBS

Dimensions
· Wheelbase: 2545 mm
· Overall lenght: 4425 mm
· Overall width: 1800 mm
· Overall height: 1390 mm
· Car weight: 1230 kgs

Petter SOLBERG #5

IDENTITY CARD
- Nationality: Norwegian
- Date of birth: November 18, 1974
- Place of birth: Askim (N)
- Resident: Monaco (MC)
- Marital status: Married, one son
- Co-driver: Phil Mills (GB)
- Web: www.pettersolberg.com

CAREER
- Rally debut: 1995
- Nbr of rallies in WRC: 108
- Number of victories: 13

1999 – 18th in Championship
2000 – 10th in Championship
2001 – 9th in Championship
2002 – 2nd in Championship
2003 – WORLD CHAMPION
2004 – 2nd in Championship
2006 – 6th in Championship

Petter Solberg's main wish this season was probably to have it over and done with as soon as possible. The Subaru Impreza version 2006 was a real dog that was incapable of matching the speed of the Xsara and the Ford Focus. The 2003 world champion was doomed to play a walk-on role. On the few occasions when the car actually performed properly like in Mexico he was able to up the pace and gave Loeb a run for his money. His was a frustrating season above all else and towards the end he voiced his dissatisfaction in public criticising both his car and his team. It was unusual behaviour for a guy who has always been very professional in his relationship with his employer. His car was too slow and his personal tally of victories remained stuck at 13, while he saw his two main rivals add further successes to their score. He ended the year in sixth place, which must have been hell for him, as since 2002 he had never finished lower than second. And in addition, it was his first season without a win since 2001. He used to be as quick as both Loeb and Grönholm and the question that now raises its head is: has he still got what it takes after the season from hell he has lived through? The two stars of the 2006 season have upped their game to such a level that it may be difficult for Solberg to match them.

Chris ATKINSON #6

IDENTITY CARD
- Nationality: Australian
- Date of birth: November 30, 1979
- Place of birth: Bega (AUS)
- Resident: Oxfordshire (GB)
- Marital status: Single
- Co-driver: Glenn Macneall (AUS)
- Web: chrisatkinson.com.au

CAREER
- Rally debut: 2000
- Nbr of rallies in WRC: 36
- Best result: 3rd

2004 – 16th in Championship
2005 – 12th in Championship
2006 – 10th in Championship

The Australian is a bit of an enigma. He was given the second Subaru seat while it was left up to Stéphane Sarrazin to score points in the asphalt rallies. It is difficult to judge whether or not he has made progress in relation to 2005 when he did a full season as a works driver with the exception of the Monte Carlo. Or was it a question of the technical problems with his car? Whatever the reason Atkinson was the driver who, together with Matthew Wilson, benefited from the most from the super rally system without which his appearances at the finish would have been very scarce indeed. His best result was fourth place in Japan, a rally that he likes very much. Chris was the worst of the no.2 drivers in terms of results and finished the championship behind Manfred Stohl and Henning Solberg. Subaru has decided to keep him on for 2007, a decision helped by the dollars of his personal sponsors. If the 2007 Impreza is competitive he will have to confirm the promise he showed on his brilliant debut in 2004.

Stéphane SARRAZIN #6

IDENTITY CARD
- Nationality: French
- Date of birth: November 2, 1975
- Place of birth: Alès (F)
- Resident: (CH)
- Marital status: Single
- Co-driver: Stéphane Prévot (B)
- Web: stephane-sarrazin.com

CAREER
- Rally debut: 2000
- Nbr of rallies in WRC: 15
- Best result: 4th

2004 – 11th in Championship
2005 – 17th in Championship
2006 – 18th in Championship

"Next season we'll invest all our efforts in two cars in all the championship rounds," explained Richard Taylor, the Subaru team manager on 3rd October 2006. "This means that there'll be no third car so no drive for Stéphane Sarrazin. We're very sorry to lose him."
What this meant was that Sarrazin was fired. The ex-F1 driver and French Rally Champion in 2004 on asphalt was probably the scapegoat for Subaru's miserable 2006 season. His programme was limited to 4 events: Monte Carlo, Catalonia, Corsica and Germany. He did not do too badly finishing fifth (highest-placed Subaru), 8th (just behind Solberg), 8th (only Subaru driver in the points) and in Germany he crashed out and retired. But his performances did not convince the team management. He was lucky enough to have a programme with Aston Martin in endurance. He scored a brilliant win at Laguna Seca in the American Le Mans Series, in which he was runner-up in the drivers' championship and first of the Aston regulars. The common point between the two is that Prodrive looks after both teams.

OMV - Peugeot Norway WRT
Teams & Drivers

Jacky Bozian & Henning Solberg

PEUGEOT Manufacturer 2
307 WRC

The French team Bozian began the year with a very ambitious programme. It had financial backing from OMV and entered 2005 spec 307 WRCs for the whole season for Manfred Stohl plus 12 rallies for Henning Solberg. The latter was also down to race in the Norwegian event a candidate for a place on the world championship calendar in 2007. In addition, it provided some 206s for certain clients and gave Gigi Galli a drive in a competitive car on a few occasions.

The OMV Peugeot Norway team was entered in the Manufacturers' 2 Championship. It had a good season. In Monte Carlo Manfred Stohl, its best driver, set the first two fastest times in 2006 and came home fourth. The Austrian set foot on the rostrum on four occasions and finished in fourth place in the championship in which the Bozian cars were always on the pace. Indeed, the team celebrated its 100th entry in the WRC in Turkey. OMV Peugeot Norway came home fourth in the manufacturers' title chase not far behind Subaru and first in the 2 category in addition to helping Henning Solberg to victory in the Norwegian rally. The French company withdrew officially from world rallying in 2005, but kept an eye on its cars and continued their development pleased to see them in such good hands.

Identity
Team Bozian racing
45 rue des Bruyères
69330 Pusignan
France
- Tel.: +33 (0)4 72 93 11 30
- Fax: +33 (0)4 72 93 11 31
- Web: www.bozian-racing.com
  www.owrt.com

Team members
- Directors:
  Arthur Bozian, Jacky Bozian
- Technical Director : Bruno Besset
- Technical Manager.
  Axel Verchere
- Cars Managers:
  Lionel Dupin, Alban Murugneux, Mickael Gardy, Nicolas Dupin, Frederic Stefunko, Arnaud Despont
- Engine Manager:
  Michel Pham

- Team founded in: 1969

Records
- Constructors Titles: 0
- Drivers Titles: 0

Classification
- 2006 - 4th

Engine
- Type: XU7JP4
- Disposition: front transverse
- Number of cylinders: 4 in line
- Valves: 4 per cylinder
- Capacity: 1997 cc
- Camshaft: double overhead
- Bore x Stroke: 85 x 88 mm
- Power: 300 bhp @ 5250 rpm
- Torque max.: 580 Nm @ 3500 rpm
- Turbocharger: Garrett Honeywell
- Engine Management: Magnetti-Marrelli Step 9
- Lubrification: carbon wet sump
- Supplying: electronical injection
- Exchanger: air-air
- Fuel tank capacity: 90 litres
- Fuel / Lubrifiant: F.I.A / Total

Transmission
- Clutch: Carbon, triple-plate
- Gearbox: Transverse Hewland, 5-speed
- Differentials: active front, centre and rear

Steering
Power-assisted rack and pinion

Suspensions
- Front and rear: pseudo McPherson

Shock absorbers
Peugeot

Brakes
- Front: ventilated discs (370 mm ø), 8-pot calipers
- Rear: ventilated discs (370 mm ø) 4-pot calipers

Tyres
BFGoodrich

Wheels
8 x 18"

Dimensions
- Wheelbase: 2610 mm
- Overall lenght: 4344 mm
- Overall width: 1770 mm
- Overall height: 1390 mm
- Car weight: 1230 kgs

Manfred STOHL #7

IDENTITY CARD
- Nationality: Austrian
- Date of birth: July 7, 1972
- Place of birth: Vienna (A)
- Resident: Vienna (A)
- Marital status: Single
- Co-driver: Ilka Minor (A)
- Web: www.stohl.at

CAREER
- Rally debut: 1991
- Nbr of rallies in WRC: 87
- Best result: 2nd

2003 - 20th in Championship
2004 - 18th in Championship
2005 - 9th in Championship
2006 - 4th in Championship

In 2005, the Austrian was at the wheel of a Xsara 2005 WRC and this year his mount was a 307 WRC entered by the Bozian squad. He made the best of it and scored four rostrum finishes (Mexico, Australia, New Zealand and Great Britain). He came fourth in the drivers' championship and first privateer. Stohl is a very reliable driver who does not seem to have attracted the eye of the works teams. He made a few blunders like in SS11 in Sweden (Sundjson 2) where his team-mate and himself went off in the same corner. He also had a big shunt during reconnaissance in Catalonia whose sequels he still felt in Corsica. Overall, he can be proud of his 2006 campaign, which ended on a high note with second place in the British rally.

Henning SOLBERG #8

IDENTITY CARD
- Nationality: Norwegian
- Date of birth: January 8, 1973
- Place of birth: Spydeberg (N)
- Resident: Spydeberg (N)
- Marital status: Married, two children
- Co-driver: Cato Menkerud (N)
- Web: henningsolberg.com

CAREER
- Rally debut: 1997
- Nbr of rallies in WRC: 40
- Best result: 3rd

2004 - 21st in Championship
2005 - 14th in Championship
2006 - 8th in Championship

In the same car compared with Stohl Solberg came off worse. Petter's elder brother did not take part in the whole championship missing 4 events (3 on asphalt which he doesn't like and Japan), but he was not as brilliant as the Austrian. Henning is a good driver, but not a no.1. Up to 2005, his best result in the championship was fourth and in 2006 he came home third in Turkey after his brother retired. A solid season but not much more.

Stobart VK M-Sport Ford Rally Team

FORD Manufacturer 2
Focus RS WRC 04 & 06

Malcolm Wilson wanted to help his 19-year-old son Matthew to break into rallying and set up a full programme with the help of the Stobart team, an M-Sport and Ford satellite. The young Englishman raced in all the 2006 events with more downs than ups, and he was a regular in the super rally at the wheel of a very quick Ford Focus WRC 05. He was not in the same ballpark as Marcus Grönholm or Mikko Hirvonen but he did shine from time to time.

Stobart was entered in the manufacturers' championship 2 and turned up with a second and even a third car when its drivers came up with the right amount of dosh. Thus, rich Argentinean Luis Perec-Companc raced 8 times for the team while Jari-Matti Latvala and Kosti Katajamäki had fewer drives and were often quicker than their team-mates. Pieter Tsjoen took part in the Monte Carlo without making much of a splash Overall, Stobart's results were disappointing mainly due to the poor quality of its drivers, and the British team was no match for OMV-Norway and its 307 WRCs.

Identity
Stobart Motorsport
Eddie Stobart Ltd,
Brunthill Road,
Kingstown Ind Est,
Carlisle, Cumbria, CA3 0EH
Great Britain
- Tel.: +44 1357 523188
- Fax: +44 1357 523188
- Web: www.stobartmotorsport.com

Team members
- Director: Andrew Tinkler
- Team Manager: Malcolm Wilson

- Team founded in: 1996

Crews
M. Wilson / M. Orr
P. Tsjoen / E. Chevalier
K. Katajamaki / T. Alanne
JM Latvala / M. Anttila
L. Perez Companc / J. Volta

Records
- Constructors Titles: 0
- Drivers Titles: 0

Classification
- 2006 - 5th

Engine
- Type: Ford 2.0 litre M-Sport Zetec WRC
- Disposition: Front transverse
- Number of cylinders: 4 in ine
- Valve: 4 per cylinder
- Capacity: 1998 cc
- Camshaft: double overhead
- Bore x Stroke: 85 x 88 mm
- Power: 300 bhp @ 6500 rpm
- Torque: 550 Nm @ 4000 rpm
- Turbocharger: Garrett
- Engine management: Pi electronic
- Lubrification: Carbon wet sump
- Supplying: electronical injection
- Exchanger: air-air
- Fuel tank capacity: 95 litres

Transmission
- Clutch: Carbon triple-plate
- Gearbox: M-Sport / XTrac 240 six-speed sequential gearbox with electro-hydraulically controlled shift.
- Differentials: M-Sport, active front, centre and rear

Steering Power-assisted rack and pinion

Suspensions
- Front and rear: MacPherson

Shock absorbers Reiger

Brakes Brembo
- Gravel (F & R): ventilated discs (300 mm ø), 4-piston monoblock calipers.
- Asphalt (F & R): ventilated discs (370 mm ø), 8-piston monoblock calipers.

Tyres BFGoodrich (650 mm)

Wheels Gravel: 7 x 15", asphalt: 8 x 18"

Dimensions
- Wheelbase: 2615 mm
- Overall lenght: 4270 mm
- Overall width: 1770 mm
- Overall height: 1420 mm
- Car weight: 1230 kgs

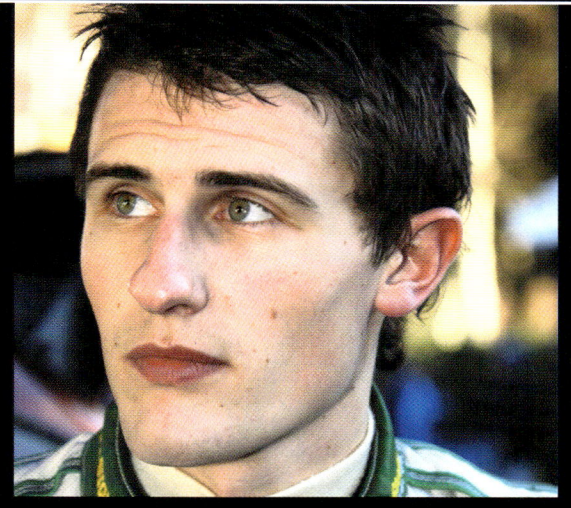

Teams & Drivers

Matthieu WILSON #9

IDENTITY CARD
- Nationality: British
- Date of birth: January 29, 1987
- Place of birth: Cockermouth (GB)
- Marital status: Single
- Co-driver: Michael Orr (GB)

CAREER
- Rally debut: 2004
- Nbr of rallies in WRC: 18
- Best result: 8th

2006 - 28th in Championship

Michael Orr

Kosti KATAJAMÄKI #10

IDENTITY CARD
- Nationality: Finnish
- Date of birth: February 26, 1977
- Marital status: Single
- Co-driver: Timo Alanne (FIN)

CAREER
- Rally debut: 2001
- Nbr of rallies in WRC: 17
- Best result: 5th

2004 - 54th in Championship
2005 - 41st in Championship
2006 - 14th in Championship

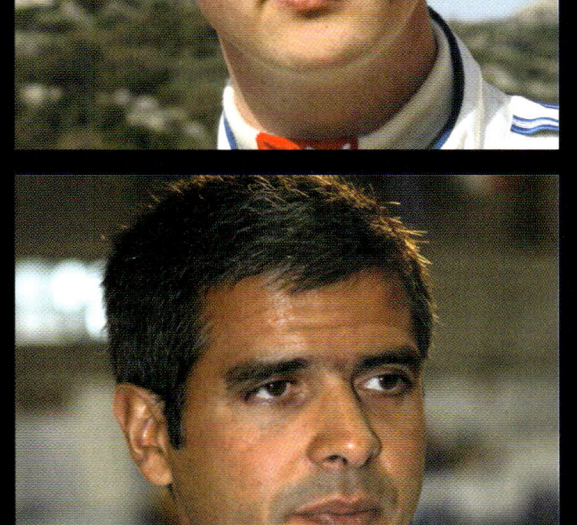

Luis PÉREZ COMPANC #10

IDENTITY CARD
- Nationality: Argentinean
- Date of birth: January 2, 1972
- Marital status: Single
- Co-driver: Jose Volta (RA)

CAREER
- Rally debut: 2001
- Nbr of rallies in WRC: 18
- Best result: 7th

2004 - 23rd in Championship
2005 - 54th in Championship
2006 - 26th in Championship

Jari-Matti LATVALA #10

IDENTITY CARD
- Nationality: Finnish
- Date of birth: April 3, 1985
- Marital status: Single
- Co-driver: Miikka Anttila (FIN)

CARREER
- Rally debut: 2001
- Nbr of rallies in WRC: 29
- Best result: 8th

2006 - 20th in Championship

Matthew Wilson is Malcolm's son, which may have helped him get a full world championship programme in a Ford entered by Stobart VK M-Sport. The 19-year-old had good and bad moments like a point and a fastest time in Argentina, becoming the youngest driver ever to win a stage in the world championship. On the down side he went off in Mexico and blundered in Japan. His turbo went and he parked his Focus on the side of the road to avoid hindering the cars coming after him. The Ford fell into a rut from which it was impossible to extract it! As Matthew's dad had decided to invest in him throughout the season it was globally positive. But he should be more careful on the liaison sections. He was always in a hurry and was caught speeding on ten occasions, which cost him a fine of 3800 euros and a minute's penalty before even the start of the British rally!

Marcus Grönholm's protégé, Kosti Katajamäki, did 5 rallies at the wheel of a Ford Focus entered by the same Stobart team. His best result was in Turkey where he finished fifth just behind Pons and Henning Solberg. But at 29 he can no longer be called a coming man.

Rich Argentinean Luis Perez Companc was more used to driving Group N cars than WRCs. He did 8 rallies as a pay-driver in the 06 Focus. He had a stupid accident in Mexico; then in Japan he drove well and crowned his year with an excellent seventh-place finish in New Zealand scoring 2 points for Stobart. Finally, the team called upon Finn Jari-Matti Latvala whose performances were steady rather than spectacular; he finished his season on a high note with fourth place in the British rally. Outside the WRC context he won 2 rounds of the Production championship.

Red Bull - Škoda Team
Teams & Drivers

SKODA Manufacturer 2
Fabia WRC

The team was managed by Raimund Baumschlager and Armin Schwartz who had given up driving. Finance came from the energy drinks producer Red Bull, present in all forms of motor sport including F1, NASCAR, Rally Raids, GP2 etc. The team used Skoda Fabias that were more or less factory entries even if the make officially withdrew from rallying in 2005. At the wheel of one of them was young Austrian, Andreas Aigner, the winner of a huge search for a star and an almost complete debutante in rallying. The Panizzi brothers were supposed to drive the other but they threw in the towel after only 2 events. Their replacement was the phlegmatic Harri Rovanperä who extended his long career a bit further.

Finally, Matthias Ekström did two events, Sweden and Germany, without showing that he had the makings of a rally driver. Throughout the season rumours about the team's precarious financial situation were doing the rounds. The only drivers to get some speed out of the Skodas were Jan Kopecky and François Duval. But both were driving cars entered by teams other than Red Bull, which was racing in the manufacturers' championship 2. At the end of 2006 a big question mark hung over a semi-works entry for the Czech make in 2007.

Identity
Baumschlager Rallye Racing GmbH. Schön 48
4563 Micheldorf
Austria
Tel: +43 7 5823 7508
Fax: +43 7 5823 7570
Web: www.brr.at

Red Bull GmbH
Am Brunnen 1
5330 Fuschl am See
Austria
Tel: +43 662 6582 0
Fax: +43 662 6582 7010
Web: www.redbullskoda.com

Team members
- Directors:
  Raimund Baumschlager,
  Rudolf Neuwirth
- Chief Engineer:
  Dietmar Metrich
- Team Manager: Armin Schwarz

Records
- Constructors Titles: 0
- Drivers Titles: 0
- Victories: 0
- Best result: 3rd

Classifications
- 1973 - 17th
- 1975 - 16th
- 1977 - 18th
- 1979 - 16th
- 1993* - 2nd
- 1994* - 1st
- 1995* - 3rd
- 1996* - 3rd
- 1997* - 2nd
- 1999 - 7th
- 2000 - 6th
- 2001 - 5th
- 2002 - 5th
- 2003 - 5th
- 2005 - 6th
- 2006 - 6th

(* = 2 litres)

Engine
- Type: DOHC - 4 cylinder
- Disposition: front transverse
- Valves: 5 per cylinder
- Capacity: 1997 cc
- Camshaft: double overhead
- Bore x Stroke: 82.5 x 93.5 mm
- Power: 320 bhp @ 5500 rpm
- Torque: 600 Nm @ 3500 rpm
- Turbocharger: Garrett
- Fuel tank capacity: 90 litres
- Lubrifiants/Fuel: Shell

Transmission
- Clutch: Carbon triple-plate
- Gearbox: transverse, sequential 5-speed semi-automatic gearshift
- Differentials: permanent drive with three active differentials, 2006 spec with mech. FR and RR differentials

Steering
Power-assisted rack and pinion

Suspensions
- Front and rear: MacPherson

Brakes
- Gravel (F & R): ventilated discs (304 mm ø), 4-pot calipers
- Asphalt: ventilated discs (F: 378 mm ø, R: 356 mm ø), 8-pot calipers

Tyres
BFGoodrich

Wheels
asphalt: 8 x 18",
gravel: 7 x 16",
snow: 5.5 x 16"

Dimensions
- Wheelbase: 2462 mm
- Overall lenght: 4002 mm
- Overall width: 1770 mm
- Overall height: 1390 mm
- Car weight: 1230 kgs

Gilles PANIZZI #11 Harri ROVANPERÄ #11

The Panizzi brothers were rarin' to go at the start of the Monte Carlo that Gilles considers as his home event. At the wheel of a Skoda Fabia he set the second-quickest time in SS 1 and then the third in SS 2. The end was less glorious as he went off depriving himself of seventh place. The pair then drove in Catalonia and came home in tenth place after many difficulties over 5 minutes behind the winner. When asked what pleased him most about his car, Gilles replied laconically, "the colour!" He was very disappointed and threw in the towel after this event missing the Tour of Corsica that was also part of his programme. The brothers have done a lot for rallying in France so hopefully Spain 2006 will not be their last world championship event. They were replaced by Harri Rovanperä who was celebrating his fortieth birthday this year. Enough said!

Mattias EKSTRÖM #11

IDENTITY CARD
- Nationality: Swedish
- Date of birth: July 14, 1978
- Place of birth: Falun (S)
- Resident: Krylbo (S), Salenstein (CH)
- Marital status: Engaged to Tina
- Co-driver: Jonas Andersson (FIN)
- Web: www.mattiasekstrom.se

CAREER
- Rally debut: 1999
- Nbr of rallies in WRC: 10
- Best result: 10th

2005 - 32nd in Championship
2006 - 38th in Championship

Like in 2005, the Swedish driver took advantage of the fact that his sponsor in the DTM also bankrolls Skoda in the World Rally Championship. In Sweden he was on his way to fifth place when he went off and in Germany he was nowhere on asphalt: a bit strange for a circuit racer!

Andreas AIGNER #11 #12

IDENTITY CARD
- Nationality: Austrian
- Date of birth: September 24, 1984
- Place of birth: Loeben (A)
- Resident: Weissenbach (A)
- Marital status: Single
- Co-drivers: Timo Gottschalk (D), Klaus Wicha (D)
- Web: www.andreasaigner.at

CAREER
- Rally debut: 2004
- Nbr of rallies in WRC: 10
- Best result: 6th

2006 - 23rd in Championship

Andreas Aigner has had a rapid rise to fame! The twenty-one-year-old who had practically no rally experience found himself with a 10-event programme at the wheel of a Skoda Fabia. He was the lucky winner of a spot-the-star campaign launched by Red Bull in Germany, Austria and Switzerland. After several events a jury composed of specialists like Armin Schwartz, Walter Röhrl and Klaus Wicha chose Aigner for the programme. In 2005, he cut his teeth at the wheel of a Group N Mitsubishi before plunging into the top category this season. He almost drowned! He made a disastrous start to the year in terms of performances but managed to stay on the road. Only in Germany did he show a glimmer of promise scoring his only points in 2006 thanks to a sixth place. He still has a long way to go.

Jan KOPECKY #17

IDENTITY CARD
- Nationality: Czech
- Date of birth: January 28, 1982
- Place of birth: Opocne (CZ)
- Resident: Svobodny (CZ)
- Marital status: Engaged to Orlici
- Co-driver: Filip Schovánek (CZ)
- Web: www.motorsport-kopecky.cz

CAREER
- Rally debut: 2002
- Nbr of rallies in WRC: 10
- Best result: 5th

2005 - 26th in Championship
2006 - 15th in Championship

The Czech Republic has always produced skilled rally drivers and of course Skoda's name has been associated with rallying. A number of them have taken part in the championship including Roman Kresta who drove a works Ford in 2005 but never confirmed his promise in the long term. The latest is Jan Kopecky and he was the best of the Skoda drivers throughout the season. He set fastest times and also scored points on 4 occasions.

François DUVAL #18

IDENTITY CARD
- Nationality: Belgian
- Date of birth: November 18, 1980
- Place of birth: Chimary (B)
- Resident: Cul-des-Sart (B)
- Marital status: Single
- Co-driver: Stéphane Prévot (B)
- Web: www.fduval.com

CAREER
- Rally debut: 1999
- Nbr of rallies in WRC: 73
- Number of victories: 1

2002 - 30th in Championship
2003 - 8th in Championship
2004 - 8th in Championship
2005 - 6th in Championship
2006 - 19th in Championship

Duval's Australian victory in 2005 should have opened a few doors for him. Unfortunately, his clashes at Citroën, allied to his unforthcoming personality before this success gave him a disastrous reputation. He had no works drive and only six outings in a Skoda entered by the First team. The Belgian was as quick as ever but his car did not allow him to shine and he scored a paltry 5 points.

Spectacular stand-ins!

Toni GARDEMEISTER #16 #14

IDENTITY CARD
- Nationality: Finnish
- Date of birth: March 31, 1975
- Place of birth: Kouvola (FIN)
- Resident: Monaco
- Marital status: Single
- Co-driver: Jakke Honkanen (FIN)
- Web: tonigardemeister.com

CAREER
- Rally debut: 1993
- Nbr of rallies in WRC: 87
- Best result: 2nd

1999 - 10th in Championship
2000 - 12th in Championship
2002 - 13th in Championship
2003 - 12th in Championship
2004 - 24th in Championship
2005 - 4th in Championship
2006 - 9th in Championship

Toni Gardemeister found himself at the wheel of a 307 followed a Xsara entered by Astra Racing and backed by the powerful Timo Joukhi. He had a programme limited to a few rallies on both asphalt and gravel to prove that he was not finished. The former works Skoda and Ford driver found a new lease of life and reminded the little world of rallying that he was still quick. He had good points finishes in events as different as Monte Carlo, the Acropolis, Germany and Cyprus.

Gianluigi GALLI #14 #25

IDENTITY CARD
- Nationality: Italian
- Date of birth: January 13, 1973
- Place of birth: Milan (I)
- Resident: Livigno (I)
- Marital status: Single
- Co-driver: Guido D'Amore (I)
- Web: gigigalli.com

CAREER
- Rally debut: 1994
- Nbr of rallies in WRC: 51
- Best result: 3rd

2004 - 15th in Championship
2005 - 11th in Championship
2006 - 11th in Championship

Galli found himself without a drive at the end of 2005 after Mitsubishi's withdrawal. It was a great shame for someone as talented and fiery as the Italian. This year he made a few promising appearances, two at the wheel of a Lancer (Monte Carlo and Sweden) and three in a 307 entered with the backing of Pirelli. He showed that he had lost none of his talent and finished on the rostrum in Argentina.

Jussi VÄLIMÄKI #26 #20 #18

IDENTITY CARD
- Nationality: Finnish
- Date of birth: September 10, 1974
- Place of birth: Tampere (FIN)
- Resident: Kangasala (FIN)
- Marital status: Single
- Co-driver: Jarkko Kalliolepo (FIN)
- Web: www.jussivalimaki.com

CAREER
- Rally debut: 1998
- Nbr of rallies in WRC: 35
- Best result: 5th

2004 - 28th in Championship
2006 - 17th in Championship

Välimäki only did three rallies in a Mitsubishi Lancer. The 2005 Asian/Pacific champion had his own private team, and finished fifth in Sardinia, ninth in Greece and seventh in Finland where he was up against tough opposition.

Alexandre BENGUÉ #19

IDENTITY CARD
- Nationality: French
- Date of birth: December 22, 1975
- Place of birth: Lourdes (F)
- Resident: Cauterets (F)
- Marital status: Single
- Co-driver: Caroline Escudero (F)
- Web: www.alexbengue.com

CAREER
- Rally debut: 1998
- Nbr of rallies in WRC: 13
- Best result: 4th

2005 - 21st in Championship
2006 - 12th in Championship

The 2003 French asphalt champion and former Skoda works driver had only 2 world championship events on his programme on asphalt. Where else? In both Catalonia and Corsica he proved that his talent was still intact at the wheel of a 307 WRC entered by BSA. In Spain he finished fourth and then fifth in the French round (highest-placed privateer on the two occasions) so he did not disgrace himself. In Great Britain, he drove in his third WRC round of the year in a Group N Mitsubishi.

FIA P-WRC

39

1. Nasser Al-Attiyah
2. Fumio Nutahara
3. Mirco Baldacci
4. Jari-Matti Latvala
5. Aki Teiskonen
6. Toshihiro Arai
7. Leszek Kuzaj
8. Stefano Marrini
10. Sergey Uspensky
11. Khalid Al-Qassimi
12. Dean Herridge
14. Nigel Heath
15. Takuma Kamada
17. Stepan Vojtech
18. Francisco Name

Production Championship
Mission accomplished !

In 2004, Nassar Al-Attiyah appeared on the WRC scene. He was no debutante but a skilled driver who was out to fulfil an ambitious 3-year mission. He was the reigning Asian-Pacific champion and his aim was to become the Production champion at the end of three years. In November 2006 after the New Zealand rally it was mission accomplished. "My Federation, my sponsors and myself set up this project," explained a very happy Qatari. He went into the championship lead in his Subaru after finishing second in the Mexican event, the second round on the calendar, following on from his third place in Monte Carlo, and was never headed for the rest of the year. He won the next 2 rounds (Argentina and Greece) and then controlled his lead. His only rival was Fumio Nutahara from Japan who won three times in his Mitsubishi (Monte Carlo, Japan and Cyprus). He was then the victim of a stupid exclusion in Japan, and under performed in both Australia and New Zealand so the title did not remain in the land of the rising sun. Toshihiro Araï, the 2005 champion, did not manage to beat Al-Attiyah and won only a single event (Sweden) after which he was victim of technical problems. The only other driver who looked capable of threatening the Qatari was Jari-Matti Latvala who won the last two rounds, but his poor start to the season compromised his chances.

Al-Attiyah was reliable and consistent and he gave his country its first-ever world title in motor sport. This all-round sportsman who is an excellent rally-raid driver was also getting ready for a very busy winter. It will start with his defence of his clay pigeon gold medal won in the 2002 Asian-Pacific Games as the 2006 Games were being held in his country. He will then race in the 2007 Dakar in an X-Raid team BMW after which he will be back to defend his world title.

Aged 36 Al-Attiyah is still a very ambitious man. He wants to race in WRC and should have a 6-race programme in 2007, and then win a gold medal in the 2008 Peking Olympics.

Nasser Al-Attiyah

FIA J-WRC

1. Patrick Sandell
2. Urmo Aava
3. Per-Gunnar Andersson
4. Guy Wilks
5. Conrad Rautenbach
6. Josef Beres
7. Kris Meeke
8. Julien Pressac
9. Martin Prokop
10. Jaan Mölder
11. Bernd Casier
12. Aaron Nicolai Burkart
13. Luca Betti
14. Brice Tirabassi
15. Pavel Valousek
16. Fatih Kara
17. Matti Rantanen
18. Barry Clark
19. Michal Kosciuszko
20. Kalle Pinomäki
22. Andrea Cortinovis
24. Yoann Bonato

Junior Championship
Sandell down to the wire

The winner of the Junior Championship was an outsider. Patrik Sandell clinched the title in Great Britain after a very exciting season. It was the Swede's debut year and he was not among the favourites at the start of the season as he was up against experienced drivers like Per-Gunnar Andersson, the 2004 champion, Urmo Aava from Estonia and Guy Wilks and Chris Meeke from Northern Ireland and England respectively. Sandell was very consistent throughout the year with a victory and three second places in a championship marked by the large number of different victors. Andersson (Sweden), Prokop (Catalonia), Tirabassi (Corsica), Sandell (Sardinia), Meeke (Germany), Aava (Turkey) and Mölder (Great Britain) all won a round. Wilks was the only one to score 2 victories (Argentina and Finland). They represented three different manufacturers. Suzuki won 5 rallies, Citroën 3 and Renault 1.

Before the final round of the year in Great Britain six drivers were still in with a change of the winning the title. Aava and Andersson in the first 2 places overall should have arrived in the British round in a stronger position but they had been victims of two disqualifications, the former in Finland for not wearing the fireproof underwear laid down by the FIA, and the latter for repairing his car in an unauthorised zone. All this was to Patrik Sandell's benefit. Although he did not win the event he was the only one of the contenders to avoid all the traps of a very demanding layout. He was third before the teams came to Wales, and his second-place finish was good enough to give him the title. The 23-year-old Swede arrived in the Junior Championship preceded by a flattering reputation. He is the leader of the Swedish Junior Team, and is closely followed by his Federation. He is very much at home on both snow and ice and looks to have a brilliant future.

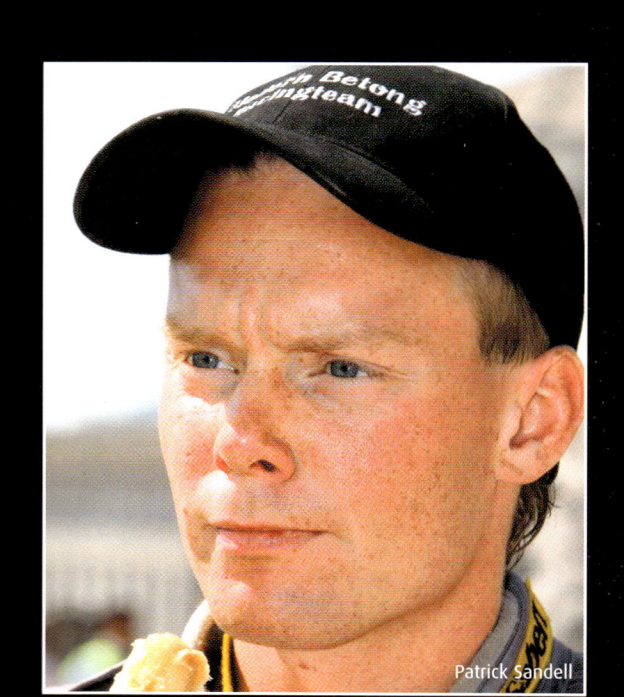

Patrick Sandell

Kronos, an up and down season

Sébastien Loeb with Guy Fréquelin.

Sébastien Loeb would certainly have liked his collaboration with the Kronos team to have got off to a better start. The triple Monte Carlo winner failed to add a fourth victory in the mythic rally to his tally, as he finally finished in second place in the blue colours of the Belgian team after a stunning comeback.

The Frenchman lost control of his Xsara in the final stage on the first day and the car fell ten metres into a ravine without sustaining much damage. The double world champion called Guy Fréquelin, the Citroën Sport competitions manager. It was the reflex of a driver who had not yet broken his links with the French make's headquarters. Loeb told Fréquelin that he had retired, but the "Grizzly" reminded him about the super rally regulations and that he still had a chance. He got back into the fray and after two days' pedal-to-metal driving fought his way back up to second place behind Grönholm.

He would have preferred starting his career with Kronos with a win. They, in turn, were amazed by his performance that weekend and saw that the Alsatian was worthy of his reputation, a man of his word and an exceptional driver. He had earned their trust. Two weeks later in Sweden it was the team that scored Brownie points with the Frenchman. Loeb was battling with Grönholm for the lead when he fell back after a mistake by Daniel Elena, his co-driver, who had forgotten to close the bonnet properly before the start of a special. The windscreen was cracked and the pair was given a 10-second penalty. Loeb was furious with his Monegasque friend.

Marc Van Dalen, the co-founder and general manager of Kronos took the two men aside and give them a firm but frank talking to boost the co-driver's morale. Frankness and humanity are two qualities that Van Dalen and Loeb share. The Frenchmen discovered this and came out of the meeting encouraged by the spirit that reigned in his new team. Their season then turned into a dream.

Kronos *an up and down season*

In Mexico, Loeb and Elena gave Kronos its first success in the World Rally Championship, which added a whole new dimension to this little Belgian team whose major results up till then consisted of a couple of victories in the Spa 24-Hour race. This Mexican win was confirmation of its know-how revealed in 2005 when it was the official tuner of the C2 Super 1600s that allowed Dani Sordo to win the Junior World Championship. Manfred Stohl also scored the best result of his career with a second place in the Cyprus rally at the wheel of a Xsara WRC rented from Kronos.

These two scintillating performances must have weighed in the balance when Guy Fréquelin had to choose between Kronos, ORECA and PH Sport to place Loeb for 2006 while awaiting Citroën's official return.

In Catalonia, Corsica, Argentina and Sardinia Loeb was back in the same winning groove at the wheel of his no.1 blue Xsara as in 2005 when he drove for Citroën Sport. He scored five victories on the trot while Grönholm and Ford kept tripping up. Before the halfway mark it looked like the championship was already sewn up, as after Sardinia Loeb was 31 points in front of the mighty Finn. It was a complete turnaround compared to the start of the season.

Many observers explained this domination by saying that Kronos was nothing more than a disguised works Citroën team. "It's a load of bullshit," exclaimed Petter Solberg when someone told him in Monte Carlo that Loeb would have problems in a private team.

Kronos is based near Namur and consists of some thirty people so on paper anyway it does not look like a factory outfit. At the rallies it was a different story. There were around sixty people present and from the chef to the engineers passing by the osteopath, car chief, weatherman, coordinator and press attaché they were all the same as in Citroën Sport. Loeb felt at home. The Kronos bosses wanted to provide the world champion with the best possible environment, and had recruited a number of people from the French outfit. Others were still employed by the manufacturer, and were on loan to the Belgian team as agreed in the contract signed between Guy Fréquelin and Marc Van Dalen.

It was not a very complicated one. As in 2005 when Kronos was running Manfred Stohl it rented Xsaras from Citroën. The 2006 price was higher as the cars were delivered "ready to race" with technical back-up. This meant that a chief engineer (Didier Clément, Cyrille Jourdain or Christophe Besse depending on the events) a car engineer and three or four mechanics from Citroën Sport looked after the no.1 Xsara. Loeb tested for Citroën Sport (which paid part of his salary) in a Xsara before each rally to give Kronos the basic settings for the event. After each one the Frenchman's car went back to Satory to be completely stripped down, revised and have evolutions added if necessary. In particular, this was the case after the Acropolis rally at the start of June which Grönholm dominated.

With a series of gravel rallies coming up, Citroën's management was worried that the Finn and his by-now-reliable and very quick Focus would get back in the title chase, and began a series of development tests with the Xsara. The aim was to supply its sub-contractor with the best possible car to develop its client competitions service, and give Loeb the opportunity to clinch the 2006 championship as quickly as possible so he could concentrate on the make's new weapon.

Citroën was developing the C4 in parallel and the manufacturer added all the compatible technical updates to the Xsara. Thus, the car was not the same from event to event thanks to the agreement that gave Kronos the status of a works-backed private team. Citroën looked after the development and maintenance while it was Kronos's job to run the car. However, the Belgian squad had to find the money to do this and pay all the expenses that it entailed. It managed to obtain the necessary funds from Total, Gauloises, BF Goodrich and some Spanish sponsors thanks to the presence of Sordo and Pons. All this helped it to snatch the contract from under the nose of ORECA when Guy Fréquelin was looking for a team for Loeb at the end of 2005.

In Greece, Loeb failed to win his sixth rally on the trot.

Van Dalen and Mondron, the outfit's co-founders, had the biggest budget ever in the history of Kronos but they kept their feet firmly on the ground and did not become swollen-headed even though a double world champion was joining their team. They had no helicopter, no fancy hostesses and no garish motorhomes in the service park. The only area in which they spent their money freely was on the car.

Otherwise the team lived within its budget, which was way below that of Ford and Subaru. They saved in other areas by renting fewer cars at rallies, providing more shuttles between hotels and the service parks for the mechanics, economy class flights and no rooms in the fanciest hotels in town (except for the drivers and management) no starters before meals etc.
Loeb appreciated this way of working and all the efforts made. He knew that Van Dalen and Mondron had been dropped by one of their major sponsors and had problems balancing the budget. So he put in the same effort as at Citroën and fought tooth and nail to help the team win. He did his best to fend off Ford's comeback, and tried to compensate for the mistakes of his two Spanish team-mates, Dani Sordo and Xevi Pons.

After the Cyprus rally, the twelfth round of the championship, Loeb had the title almost won. All he needed was fourth place in Turkey. Kronos's destiny took a hard hit on 25th September when the Alsatian broke his arm falling off his mountain bike. Things began to unravel. Colin McRae was called in as a replacement in Turkey but was completely off the pace. Kronos multiplied its mistakes in its tyre choices whereas when Loeb was there there had been no blunders since the start of the season. Van Dalen was resigned to letting the two Spaniards get on with it till the end of the championship. Ford scored two doubles on the trot and won the manufactures' championship in New Zealand while Kronos, whose season had turned into a nightmare since Loeb's accident, was losing money.
"It's been a paradoxical season. We've got the results and the ambience is fantastic. Everybody's happy but in the end the team's losing money. I'm losing sleep over it," said Van Dalen.

The aim of the Kronos directors when they recruited Sébastien Loeb was not to make a fortune out of the 2006 season. All the sponsors' money - and a lot more - was reinvested. What Van Dalen and Mondron were looking at were the long-term benefits of a successful year to attract sponsors or another manufacturer.

On the eve of the British rally as the curtain is rung down on the 2006 season, the 30 employees at Kronos still do not know what the future holds. Will they be present at the 2007 Monte Carlo Rally or will they be obliged to follow the exploits of Loeb in his Citroën no.1, that owes at lot to them, from a distance? Things could certainly have ended on a higher note for the Belgian outfit.

In Australia, a round of applause and a few sighs of relief after Loeb was finally crowned champion.

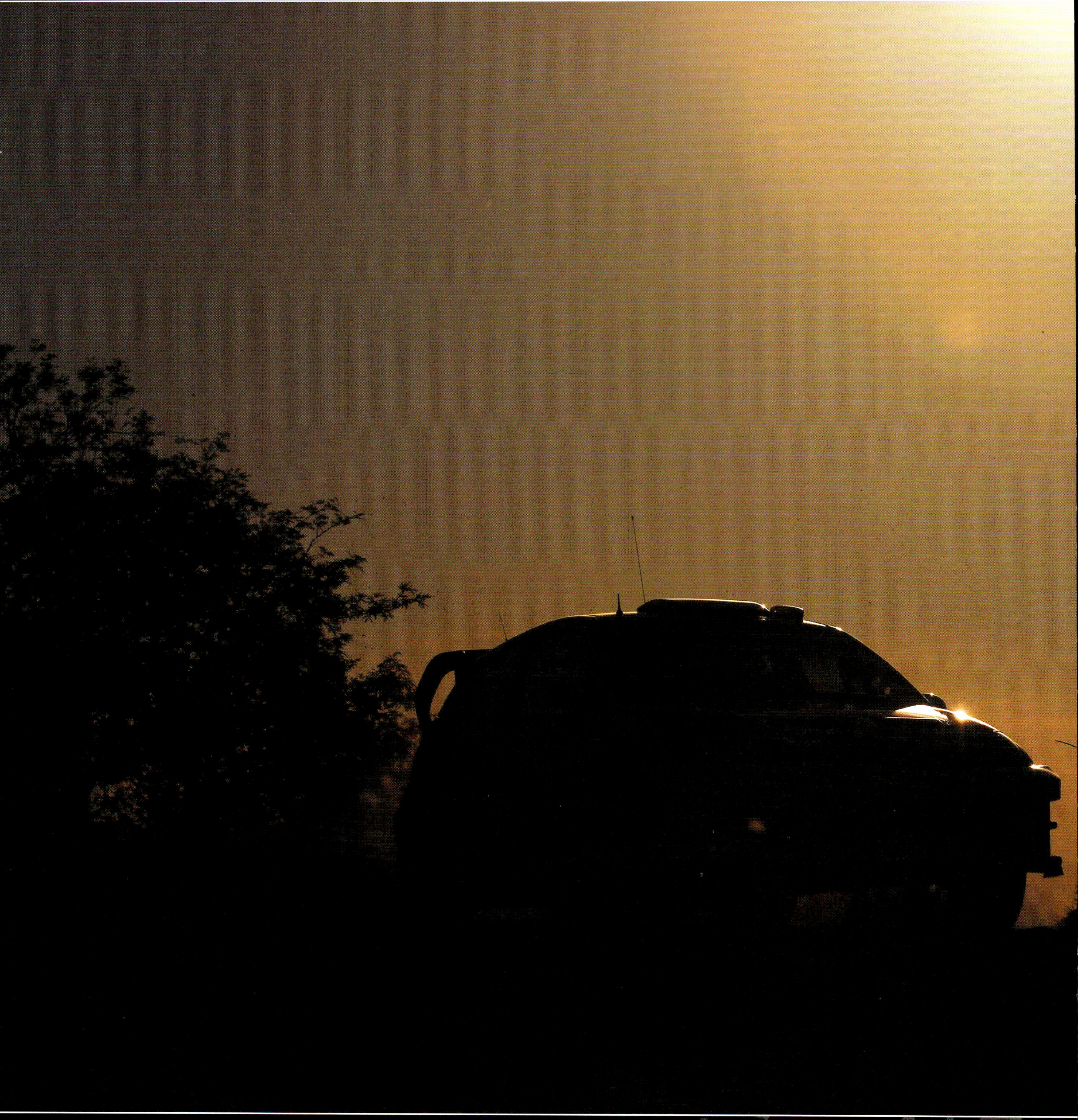

2006 FIA WRC

01	Monte-Carlo P-WRC	46
02	Sweden J-WRC	54
03	Mexico P-WRC	62
04	Spain J-WRC	70
05	France J-WRC	78
06	Argentina J-WRC + P-WRC	86
07	Italy J-WRC	94
08	Greece P-WRC	102
09	Germany J-WRC	110
10	Finland J-WRC	118
11	Japan P-WRC	126
12	Cyprus P-WRC	134
13	Turkey J-WRC	142
14	Australia P-WRC	150
15	New Zealand P-WRC	158
16	Great Britain J-WRC	166

Monte-Carlo

01

02
03
04
05
06
07
08
09
10
11
12
13
14
15
16

Grönholm stakes his claim.
The Finn won on his first time out in the new Ford Focus, which was only taking part in its second event. However, he owed his victory in large part to a rare Sébastien Loeb mistake, which resulted in the Frenchman snatching second place at the very end after a white-knuckle comeback.

01 Monte-Carlo

Chris Atkinson made a big impact on his Monte Carlo debut. He got as high as second and finished the event in sixth place.

François Duval was a late entrant in a First team Skoda.

Monte Carlo was Toni Gardemeister's first rally of the season. He did not have a full 2006 programme, and put on his usual impressive display in his 307 WRC with a third-place finish in one of his favourite events.

THE RALLY
Grönholm opens his score

The opening round of the world championship, the Monte, is always the moment to take stock of the situation. To see who is doing what, who is with which team, what cars and drivers have the most potential in terms of car/driver/tyre combination and so on. This assumed even more importance at the 2006 Monte Carlo as the little world of rallying had undergone some major changes since 2005. Mitsubishi and Peugeot had stopped their competition programmes and Marcus Grönholm, faithful to the

Marcus Grönholm is not addicted to the weed! It was winter in the Alps.

French make for so many years, had joined Ford whose previous no.1, Markko Märtin, had give up after the tragic accident that cost the life of his co-driver Michael Park. The big Finn's team-mate with the Blue Oval was his young fellow-countryman, Mikko Hirvonen. The latter had convinced Malcolm Wilson to give him another chance after his impressive performances as a privateer in 2005. Skoda was back in the form of an Austro-Czech-German team financed by Red Bull for the promising Austrian, Andreas Aigner, and Gilles Panizzi plus another entered by the First squad for veteran Frenchman, François Duval. As in the case of the Fabia WRCs there were more private 307s entered than the previous year thanks to private teams (Bozian, Astra and BSA) for Manfred Stohl, Henning Solberg, Toni Gardemeister and Olivier Burri. The only other works outfit besides Ford was Subaru with its usual three drivers: Petter Solberg, Stéphane Sarrazin and Chris Atkinson. Gigi Galli was also at the start in an old works WRC Lancer. While awaiting the arrival of the C4 WRC marking the return of Citroën as a works team the Xsaras were entrusted to the Belgian squad Kronos in which Guy Fréquelin had put his trust. Now painted blue the three cars entered were a couple of 2006 evolutions in C1 with mechanical differentials (see the 2006 rules) and a third, a 2005 model with an active differential for the promising Dani Sordo. BF Goodrich replaced Michelin but in fact it was only a marketing name change on the part of the Clermont-Ferrand manufacturer. The ex-Michelin rubber was used by the majority of the front-runners, Subaru being the odd man out with its Pirellis.

Overall the field consisted of twelve World Rally Cars in the world championship entered by six different teams plus a small number of squads in the Production Championship (six only). Overall there were fifty-three starters for the 74th Monte Carlo Rally that began on 20th January 2006, St Sébastien's day.

The world champion went off like a bat out of hell to celebrate his name day and also to rack up a fourth win on the trot in a rally that he had dominated since 2003. The first leg had all the right ingredients of a true Monte Carlo: frost, scattered snow, ice and a few streams of water plus dry asphalt. Right from the start Seb showed his rivals who was boss by winning the first stage: Saint-Sauveur-sur-Tinée – Beuil. He was helped by a wise tyre choice consisting of mini-studs perfectly suited to the morning frost and he pulled out a gap over his rivals (25.5s on Panizzi in second) while the unfortunate Grönholm (fourth 36.5s behind) had a spin. "It was in a right-hander three kilometres after the start," a bemused Finn explained. "In my notes, I put very slippery, but it was very, very slippery! Trying to get the car back facing in the right direction it stalled on several occasions. The tyre choice was difficult and I should've started on mini studs." Petter Solberg's decision was even worse. He set off on slicks that were worse than useless. He crawled through the stage and lost a couple of minutes.

Only eleven cars finished the special; all the others were blocked behind in a traffic jam at the start. The layout was such that only the first eleven cars could compete in the specials making up the first loop, and the third stage had to be cancelled after the field became split up.

The road conditions improved when the sun finally came out and Grönholm took advantage of this and his tyres to bang in the quickest time but only 2.5s in front of Loeb. Battle was joined between the two drivers and the others played walk-on roles. Second time through the Saint-Saveur-sur-Tinée-Beuil Loeb set his second scratch time of the day. In the following stage Duval created a bit of a surprise by coming out on top. Galli was already out. The Italian set good times right from the word go and was up in fourth place until his Lancer got away from him in the fourth stage. Result: one bent car and one very disappointed Italian. The face of the opening round of the championship changed between Pierlas and Ilonse. "I got caught out," said Loeb who doesn't usually make mistakes.

You had to judge the grip in each corner this afternoon even more than in the morning when the studs gave me a safety margin. I came into a fourth-gear left-hander and I thought that the tar was black in the braking zone because of dampness. In fact, it was very dirty. The car began to understeer and I tried to get it back on line with a quick tug on the handbrake. We spun immediately and slid backwards down a steep slope."

That was how the rally turned upside down and how Loeb honoured his patron saint! The Xsara slid into the ravine and luckily it was not too badly damaged. Loeb's chances of victory were almost non-existent, and all Grönholm had to do to win was to keep it between the hedges even if at that precise moment he was 1m 16.4s behind the Frenchman.

"I didn't like that leg very much," commented the mighty Finn at the end. "But I like being in the lead. I drove at a fairly conservative pace, too conservative at times, but the grip was dreadful and it was very difficult to find the right speed. What'll determine the outcome is the tyre choice."

The other major surprise came from Australian Chris Atkinson who was up in second place 1m 23.7s behind Grönholm and in front of Gardemeister in his 307. He made no driving mistakes, chose the right tyres and he was helped by his Impreza with its active differential.

In the night of Friday to Saturday the Kronos mechanics worked miracles. After the Xsara was brought back to Monaco they managed to put it back in running order as it was not too badly damaged in the accident. Thus, Sébastien was able to start the next day in the Super Rally thanks to this new rule that was first applied in 2004 and adopted in 2005. It allows drivers to rejoin the rally after

having retired in the previous leg (with a penalty of five minutes per stage missed). Loeb started the second leg in eighth place 3m 43.6s behind the leader.

The man from Alsace buckled down to the task in hand and did a pretty good job as he set the fastest times in all the day's specials whatever the tyres or the conditions, with the exception of no.11 which was cancelled because of more traffic jams. A spin between Saint Antonin and Toudon (SS8) did not slow him He picked off his rivals one by one and by the end of the day he and his co-driver Daniel Elena from Monaco were in fourth place behind Grönholm, Gardemeister and Stohl. Atkinson tried in vain to fend of the Xsara and lost thirty seconds with a couple of spins in SS9 falling behind Loeb as well as Manfred Stohl and his hard-charging team-mate Stéphane Sarrazin.

Gilles Panizzi was called in by Red Bull Skoda to do the asphalt rallies. He drove a good first stage, but then fell back handicapped by his car's unpredictable road holding.

Loeb was back in his favourite hunting ground. He was out to add another Monte Carlo victory to his tally, but it was not to be.

01 Monte-Carlo

Stéphane Sarrazin made the wrong tyre choice at the start and probably deprived himself of a rostrum finish.

>> Dani Sordo, the outgoing 2005 Junior Champion, had a full season ahead of him in the Xsara WRC.

Sébastien Loeb's second place was his worst Monte Carlo result since 2002!

Gardemeister's third place and Stohl's (seen here in action) fourth gave the Peugeot colours a good result, as not for a long time had the Lion been so well placed in the Monte Carlo.

Up front Marcus increased his lead over his immediate pursuer (2m 05.9s) but Loeb was now only 2m 41.6s behind the Ford and closing. The Finn was not all that relaxed as witnessed by his spin just after the Turini in SS12. "The conditions are horrible," he complained, as the Monte Carlo Rally is not one of his favourites. "They're the worst I've experienced here. Have I got a big enough lead over Loeb? I'm going to have a look at the times and see if I can find the right rhythm in the last leg. I just hope I won't make any blunders. It's all too easy on these kinds of roads."

Was he bluffing? Loeb reckoned that he had no chance of catching the leader. "The gap between me and Marcus is too big to close in normal conditions in under 117 kms, which is what we've still got left to cover. But we're only 35 seconds from second place."

This was his target and he went for it. The last leg consisted of six stages. He won three; two others went to Stohl who made the right tyre choice (slicks in the last two) and no.14 fell to Gardemeister.

"We knew that when Gardemeister was on slicks he could pip us," said an elated Elena after the finish. "We'd no information about Toni so the only solution was all-out attack. The Turini descent was mind-blowing. We were on snow tyres in the dry. I felt like I was going to be seasick, we were sliding about so much!" Neither of the two 307 drivers was able to fight off Loeb who finally snatched second place. For that he could thank the Super Rally rule that had not helped him up till then. "It was one hell of a chase. Just the kind of battle that I love. We found out that our Xsara has nothing to envy our rivals."

Grönholm was very pleased to have emerged victorious in a rally that he really does not like. "Frankly, I didn't think I could win it,' he said after the finish. "But I was handed a good lead and I wasn't involved in a real battle." Gardemeister was probably very happy to have finished third followed by Stohl and Sarrazin. "I'm delighted to have finished in the points with a brand-new car even if we lost too much time on Friday," smiled a happy Frenchman. The drivers who were most disappointed were Solberg and Panizzi. The Frenchman could probably have scored a points finish in his Skoda, but a slight off on a road that he knows like the back of his hand losing him three minutes when he was going through the Turini for the first time on Sunday morning. Petter had to retire with a blown engine at the end of the first leg, giving him a dreadful start to the 2006 season in which he was hoping to win the world title for the first time since 2003. He was out for revenge. Quickly! ∎

51

The Monte has never been one of Grönholm's favourite rallies. This year, though, he hassled Loeb and won the event.

Road events are very popular and pull in huge crowds as seen here with Mikko Hirvonen rounding a hairpin.

A worried-looking Petter Solberg. The Norwegian did not yet know that his retirement was only a foretaste of what was to be a disastrous season.

THE RULES
Muddying the waters!

World rallying is in a state of crisis. It has been obvious for several years and the absence of several major manufacturers at the start of the 2006 season only served to underline it. The rule makers decided to make some changes with two major objectives in mind: revive media interest and find a new challenge for the manufacturers at less expense. Before the start of the championship it was better to understand the greyer areas of the new regulations. Firstly, teams could enter in two categories. One was made up of direct works teams (Ford and Subaru). The other consisted of so-called private teams that were the direct representatives of a make (Citroën via Kronos). All those entered in this category had to take part in all the rounds and enter cars complying with the 2006 regs: mechanical front and rear differentials with the central one still driven by electronics (water injection forbidden). The no.1 driver of the entrants in Class 1 had to take part in all sixteen rounds: Grönholm, Loeb and Solberg. The second crew could change for each event.

Category 2 consisted of private teams (Bozian, Red Bull, First, Astyra BSA etc.). They had to take part in a minimum of ten events with cars complying with the 2005 regs (active differentials, water injection) and their drivers could be changed at will. Nonetheless, they should not have finished one of the five championships before the one in question in the first six in the drivers' classification. It was a fairly theoretical rule as for the Monte Carlo the FIA gave Gilles Panizzi a derogation. This division into two catagories was accompanied by several additional measures like extending the Super Rally to the third leg plus new restrictions regarding the mechanical parts such as gearboxes, suspension etc. to extend their life. ∎

01 Monte-Carlo results

74th RALLY OF MONTE-CARLO

Organiser Details
ACM
B.P. 464
23 Blvd Albert 1er
98012 MC Cedex, MC
Tel.: +377 9315 2600
Fax: +377 9315 8008

Rallye Automobile Monte-Carlo

1st leg of FIA 2006 World Rally Championship for constructors and drivers.
1st leg of FIA Production Car WRC Championship.

Date January 19 - 22, 2006

Route
1336.84 km divised in three legs.
18 special stages on tarmac roads
(366.39 km) and 16 raced (324.44 km)

Starting Procedure
Thursday, January 19 (18:30),
Place du Casino, Monaco

Leg 1
Friday, January 20 (08:33/16:11),
Monaco > Monaco, 508.40 km;
6 specials stages expected (118.10 km),
5 raced (94.88 km)

Leg 2
Saturday, January 21 (07:53/16:38),
Monaco > Monaco, 530.71 km;
6 special stages excpected (131.69 km),
5 raced (112.96 km)

Leg 3
Sunday, January 22 (07:55/12:45),
Monaco > Monaco, 297.73 km;
6 special stages (116.60 km)

Entry List (53) - 52 starters

N°	Driver (Nat.)	Co-driver (Nat.)	Team	Car	Group & FIA Priority
1.	S. LOEB (F)	D. ELENA (MC)	KRONOS TOTAL CITROEN WRT	Citroën Xsara WRC	A8 1
2.	X. PONS (E)	C. DEL BARRIO (E)	KRONOS TOTAL CITROEN WRT	Citroën Xsara WRC	A8 1
3.	M. GRÖNHOLM (FIN)	T. RAUTIAINEN (FIN)	BP FORD WORLD RALLY TEAM	Ford Focus RS WRC 06	A8 1
4.	M. HIRVONEN (FIN)	J. LEHTINEN (FIN)	BP FORD WORLD RALLY TEAM	Ford Focus RS WRC 06	A8 1
5.	P. SOLBERG (N)	P. MILLS (GB)	SUBARU WORLD RALLY TEAM	Subaru Impreza WRC 2006	A8 1
6.	S. SARRAZIN (F)	S. PREVOT (B)	SUBARU WORLD RALLY TEAM	Subaru Impreza WRC 2006	A8 1
7.	M. STOHL (A)	I. MINOR (A)	OMV - PEUGEOT NORWAY	Peugeot 307 WRC	A8 1
8.	H. SOLBERG (N)	C. MENKERUD (N)	OMV - PEUGEOT NORWAY	Peugeot 307 WRC	A8 1
9.	M. WILSON (GB)	M. ORR (GB)	STOBART - VK - M-SPORT FORD RALLY TEAM	Ford Focus RS WRC 04	A8 1
10.	P. TSJOEN (B)	E. CHEVAILLIER (B)	STOBART - VK - M-SPORT FORD RALLY TEAM	Ford Focus RS WRC 04	A8 1
11.	G. PANIZZI (F)	H. PANIZZI (F)	RED BULL - SKODA TEAM	Skoda Fabia WRC	A8 1
12.	A. AIGNER (A)	K. WICHA (D)	RED BULL - SKODA TEAM	Skoda Fabia WRC	A8 1
16.	T. GARDEMEISTER (FIN)	J. HONKANEN (FIN)	ASTRA RACING	Peugeot 307 WRC	A8 2
17.	F. DUVAL (B)	P. PIVATO (F)	FIRST MOTORSPORT	Skoda Fabia WRC	A8 2
18.	C. ATKINSON (AUS)	G. MACNEALL (AUS)	SUBARU RALLY TEAM AUSTRALIA	Subaru Impreza WRC 05	A8 2
25.	G. GALLI (I)	G. D'AMORE (I)	MITSUBISHI MOTORS MOTOR SPORTS	Mitsubishi Lancer	A8 1
26.	D. SORDO (E)	M. MARTI (E)	DANIEL SORDO	Citroën Xsara WRC	A8 2
33.	F. NUTAHARA (J)	D. BARRITT (GB)	ADVAN-PIAA RALLY TEAM	Mitsubishi Lancer Evo IX	N4 3
37.	J. LATVALA (FIN)	M. ANTTILA (FIN)	JARI-MATTI LATVALA	Subaru Impreza WRX Sti	N4 3
39.	N. AL-ATTIYAH (QAT)	C. PATTERSON (GB)	QMMF	Subaru Impreza	N4 3
40.	S. MARRINI (I)	T. SANDRONI (I)	ERRANI TEAM GROUP	Mitsubishi Lancer Evo VII	N4 3
43.	J. POPOV (BG)	D. POPOV (BG)	OMV CEE RALLY TEAM	Mitsubishi Lancer Evo VII	N4 3
44.	D. HIGGINS (GB)	R. BUTLER (GB)	DAVID HIGGINS	Mitsubishi Lancer Evo VII	N4 3
62.	F. KOPECKY (CZ)	F. SCHOVANEK (CZ)	JAN KOPECKY	Skoda Fabia WRC	A8 2
63.	O. BURRI (CH)	F. GORDON (F)	OLIVIER BURRI	Peugeot 307 WRC	A8 2
64.	G. MAC HALE (IRL)	P. MAGLE (IRL)	GARETH MAC HALE	Ford Focus WRC	A8 2
65.	P. ROUX (CH)	E. JORDAN (CH)	PHILIPPE ROUX	Peugeot 206 WRC	A8 2
66.	R. ERRANI (I)	S. CASADIO (I)	RICCARDO ERRANI	Skoda Octavia	A8
67.	A. MACHALE (IRL)	B. MURPHY (IRL)	AUSTIN MACHALE	Ford Focus WRC	A8 2
68.	E. BOLAND (IRL)	F. REGAN (IRL)	EAMONN BOLAND	Ford Focus WRC	A8 2
69.	S. TCHINE (MC)	P. DUPUY (F)	TCHINE	Mitsubishi Lancer	A8
71.	P. CATUDAL (F)	G. RAMOIN (F)	PHILIPPE CATUDAL	Peugeot 306 Maxi	A7
73.	M. DESSI (MC)	P. DESSI (MC)	LES CASINOS DE MONTE-CARLO	Renault Clio RS	A7
74.	P. BARBERO (F)	P. GULLINO (F)	PHILIPPE BARBERO	Renault Clio Ragnotti	A7
75.	M. AMOURETTE (F)	G. MARIE (F)	MARC AMOURETTE	Citroën C2	A6
76.	M. PROKOP (CZ)	J. TOMANEK (CZ)	MARTIN PROKOP	Citroën C2 S1600	A6
77.	M. GIOFFRE (I)	E. SGARRONI (F)	MICHEL GIOFFRE	Renault Clio kit car	A6
78.	M. SUHR (D)	I. MULLER (D)	MAIKE SUHR	Suzuki Ignis Sport	A6
79.	M. BOETTI (F)	E. NAS DE TOURRIS (F)	MICHEL BOETTI	Citroën Saxo	A6
80.	F. LO FIEGO (F)	C. RAYSSAC (F)	FABIANO LO FIEGO	Citroën C2	A6
81.	S. CORNU (F)	B. LEGRAS (F)	STÉPHANE CORNU	Citroën Saxo	A6
82.	A. BURKART (D)	K. ZEMANIK (D)	AARON BURKART	Citroën Saxo S1600	A6
83.	P. HEINTZ (CH)	R. SCHERRER (CH)	PATRICK HEINTZ	Subaru Impreza Sti	N4
84.	T. CSERHALMI (SK)	M. HULKA (CZ)	TIBOR CSERHALMI	Mitsubishi Lancer	N4
85.	M. BONFILS (F)	R. BELLEVILLE (F)	MICHEL BONFILS	Subaru Impreza WRX	N4
86.	M. CHVOJKA (CZ)	Z. CHVOJKOVA (CZ)	MILAN CHVOJKA	Mitsubishi Lancer Evo VIII	N4
87.	R. MARTINEZ SACO (E)	R. MARCHENA BAENA (E)	RAFAEL MARTINEZ SACO	Subaru Impreza Sti	N4
88.	R. FRAU (F)	S. LEGARS (F)	RICHARD FRAU	Mitsubishi Lancer Evo IX	N4
89.	A. JEREB (SLO)	M. KACIN (SLO)	ANDREJ JEREB	Subaru Impreza Sti	N4
90.	J. JALONEN (FIN)	T. SUOMINEN (FIN)	JUKKA JALONEN	Mitsubishi Lancer	N4
91.	J. SEBALJ (CR)	T. KLINC (HR)	JURAJ SEBALJ	Subaru Impreza WRX Sti	N4

Championship Classifications

FIA Drivers (1/16)

1. Grönholm 1🏆 10
2. Loeb 8
3. Gardemeister 6
4. Stohl 5
5. Sarrazin 4
6. Atkinson 3
7. Hirvönen 2
8. Sordo 1
9. Pons 0
10. Panizzi 0
11. Kopecky 0
12. Burri 0
13. Aigner 0
14. Tsjoen 0
15. Wilson 0
16. Mac Hale 0

FIA Constructors (1/16)

1. BP-Ford World Rally Team 1🏆 14
2. Kronos Total Citroën WRT 11
3. OMV-Peugeot Norway 6
4. Subaru World Rally Team 5
5. Red Bull-Skoda Team 3
6. Stobart VK M-Sport Ford WRT 0

FIA Production Car (1/8)

1. Nutahara 1🏆 10
2. Higgins 8
3. Al-Attiyah 6
4. Marrini 5
5. Latvala 4
6. Popov 0

Special Stages Times

www.acm.mc
www.wrc.com

SS1 St-Sauveur sur Tinée - Beuil 1 (22.23 km)
1.Loeb 15'14"0; 2.Panizzi +25"5;
3.Galli +26"0; 4.Grönholm +36"5;
5.Atkinson +45"8;
6.Gardemeister +58"5; 7.Stohl +1'05"1;
8.Sarrazin +1'18"8...
P-WRC > 11=Higgins/Latvala... 17'12"2

SS2 Guillaumes - Valberg 1 (13.60 km)
1.Grönholm 9'37"2; 2.Loeb +2"5;
3.Panizzi +7"9; 4.Galli +15"9;
5.Atkinson +29"4;
6.Gardemeister +47"6;
7.Sarrazin +50"7; 8.Stohl +56"8...
P-WRC > 9.Higgins 10'40"5

SS3 Pierlas - Ilonse 1 (23.22 Km)
Annulée

SS4 St-Sauveur sur Tinée - Beuil 2 (22.23 km)
1.Loeb 14'43"9; 2.Duval +20"8;
3.Grönholm +28"3; 4.Hirvönen +31"9;
5.P.Solberg +33"5;
6.Gardemeister +35"9; 7.Stohl +36"1;
8.Atkinson +38"0...
P-WRC > 21.Popov 16'49"4

SS5 Guillaumes - Valberg 2 (13.60 km)
1.Duval 9'43"3; 2.Sarrazin +5"7;
3.Loeb +5"9; 4.Stohl +8"1;
5.P.Solberg +8"4; 6.Gardemeister +9"2;
7.Hirvönen +14"9; 8.Grönholm +20"0...
P-WRC > 21.Popov 10'54"3

SS6 Pierlas - Ilonse 2 (23.22 Km)
1.Grönholm 18'47"6; 2.Stohl +17"8;
3.Gardemeister +20"7;
4.Atkinson +24"7; 5.Duval +31"0;
6.Pons +55"5; 7.Sordo +57"5;
8.Panizzi +1'06"3...
P-WRC > 15.Nutahara 21'15"4

Classification Leg 1
1.Grönholm 1h09'30"8;
2.Atkinson +1'23"7;
3.Gardemeister +1'27"1;
4.Panizzi +1'34"6; 5.Stohl +1'39"1;
6.Duval +2'05"5; 7.Sarrazin +2'46"8;
8.Loeb +3'43"6...
P-WRC > 17.Nutahara 1h17'25"8

SS7 Sigale - Bif. D10 / D110 (22.54 km)
1.Loeb 16'50"4; 2.Grönholm +15"7;
3.Stohl +15"8; 4.Sordo +17"2;
5.Gardemeister +19"0; 6.Duval +19"2;
7.Pons +19"4; 8.Hirvönen +19"8...
P-WRC > 19.Al-Attiyah 18'27"9

SS8 St Antonin - Toudon 1 (20.22 Km)
1.Loeb 14'41"2; 2.Sarrazin +2"3;
3.Grönholm +5"0; 4.Duval +5"2;
5.Hirvönen +9"0; 6.Gardemeister +9"1;
7.Stohl +16"9; 8.Pons +17"8...
P-WRC > 20.Al-Attiyah 16'09"9

SS9 La Tour sur Tinée - Utelle 1 (18.73 Km)
1.Loeb 15'41"5; 2.Grönholm +6"1;
3.Sarrazin +7"4; 4.Stohl +13"8;
5.Hirvönen +24"6; 6.Sordo +28"3;
7.Gardemeister +40"6; 8.Burri +47"9...
P-WRC > 14.Nutahara 16'46"4

SS10 St Antonin - Toudon 2 (20.22 Km)
1.Loeb 14'21"2; 2.Sordo +18"6;
3.Grönholm +19"5; 4.Hirvönen +20"2;
5.Pons +21"8; 6.Gardemeister +25"1;
7.Stohl +31"9; 8.Sarrazin +35"8...
P-WRC > 19.Nutahara 16'17"7

SS11 La Tour sur Tinée - Utelle 2 (18.73 Km)
Cancelled

SS12 La Bollene Vésubie - Sospel 1 (31.25 Km)
1.Loeb 24'03"1; 2.Gardemeister +7"0;
3.Sarrazin +7"3; 4.Stohl +13"3;
5.Grönholm +15"7; 6.Sordo +42"4;
7.Burri +1'02"0; 8.Hirvönen +1'16"9...
P-WRC > 17.Nutahara 27'19"0

Classification Leg 2
1.Grönholm 2h36'10"2;
2.Gardemeister +2'05"9;
3.Stohl +2'08"8; 4.Loeb +2'41"6;
5.Sarrazin +3'03"4; 6.Atkinson +4'42"8;
7.Sordo +5'01"6; 8.Panizzi +5'20"0...
P-WRC > 18.Nutahara 2h53'12"5

SS13 Col de Braus - La Cabanette 1 (12.60 Km)
1.Loeb 12'16"2; 2.Grönholm +3"5;
3.Gardemeister +16"9; 4.Stohl +17"0;
5.Hirvönen +18"7; 6.Panizzi +27"2;
7.Pons +34"5; 8.Atkinson +34"6...
P-WRC > 9.Latvala 12'53"9

SS14 Col St Roch - Lantosque 1 (14.45 Km)
1.Gardemeister 11'20"0; 2.Loeb +5"2;
3.Atkinson +8"6; 4.Sarrazin +9"9;
5.Grönholm +14"4; 6.Panizzi +16"9;
7.Stohl +17"2; 8.Hirvönen +23"6...
P-WRC > 15.Latvala 12'11"1

SS15 La Bollene Vésubie - Sospel 2 (31.25 Km)
1.Loeb 24'07"0; 2.Gardemeister +9"5;
3.Sarrazin +14"5; 4.Atkinson +16"5;
5.Grönholm +28"6; 6.Stohl +30"1;
7.Sordo +31"9; 8.Hirvönen +37"1...
P-WRC > 17.Latvala 25'54"8

SS16 Col de Braus - La Cabanette 2 (12.60 Km)
1.Loeb 11'38"5; 2.Gardemeister +2"3;
3.Grönholm +2"5; 4.Hirvönen +6"3;
5.Pons +7"3; 6.Atkinson +13"7;
7.Panizzi +18"3; 8.Sordo +27"2...
P-WRC > 9.Latvala 12'08"8

SS17 Col St Roch - Lantosque 2 (14.45 Km)
1.Stohl 10'56"4; 2.Sarrazin +0"9;
3.H.Solberg +7"1; 4.Loeb +9"1;
5.Gardemeister +15"1; 6.Sordo +19"6;
7.Grönholm +21"9; 8.Atkinson +22"6...
P-WRC > 15.Latvala 11'46"1

SS18 La Bollène Vesubie - Sospel 3 (31.25 Km)
1.Stohl 23'02"8; 2.Loeb +18"7;
3.Sarrazin +36"0; 4.Gardemeister +46"2;
5.Atkinson +56"4; 6.Grönholm +1'01"9;
7.Panizzi +1'09"5; 8.Hirvönen +1'11"0...
P-WRC > 15.Latvala 25'21"1

Results

	Driver - Co-driver	Car	Gr.	Time
1	Grönholm - Rautiainen	Ford Focus RS WRC 06	A8	4h11'43"9
2	Loeb - Elena	Citroën Xsara WRC	A8	+ 1'01"8
3	Gardemeister - Honkanen	Peugeot 307 WRC	A8	+ 1'23"1
4	Stohl - Minor	Peugeot 307 WRC	A8	+ 1'42"3
5	Sarrazin - Prévot	Subaru Impreza WRC 2006	A8	+ 3'20"2
6	Atkinson - Macneall	Subaru Impreza WRC 2005	A8	+ 5'02"4
7	Hirvönen - Lehtinen	Ford Focus RS WRC 06	A8	+ 6'19"5
8	Sordo - Marti	Citroën Xsara WRC	A8	+ 7'15"2
9	Pons - Del Barrio	Citroën Xsara WRC	A8	+ 7'42"9
10	Panizzi - Panizzi	Skoda Fabia WRC	A8	+ 9'29"8
17	**Nutahara - Barritt**	**Mitsubishi Lancer Evo IX**	**N4/P**	**+ 26'15"2**
21	Higgins - Butler	Mitsubishi Lancer Evo VII	N4/P	+ 32'47"0
29	Al-Attiyah - Patterson	Subaru Impreza	N4/P	+ 43'29"3

Leading Retirements (8)

TC18A	H. Solberg - Menkerud	Peugeot 307 WRC	Off
SF12	Popov - Popov	Mitsubishi Lancer Evo VIII	Off
SF9	Duval - Smeet	Skoda Fabia WRC	Off
TC9	Galli - Bernacchini	Mitsubishi Lancer WRC 05	Gearbox
TC6C	P. Solberg - Mills	Subaru Impreza WRC 2006	Engine

Marcus Grönholm

Performers

	1	2	3	4	5	6	C6	NbSS
Loeb	10	3	1	1	-	-	15	16
Grönholm	2	3	4	1	3	1	14	16
Stohl	2	-	2	4	-	1	9	16
Gardemeister	1	3	1	2	2	6	15	16
Duval	1	1	-	1	-	2	5	8
Sarrazin	-	3	4	1	-	-	8	16
Panizzi	-	1	1	-	-	2	4	16
Sordo	-	1	-	1	-	3	5	12
P. Solberg	-	1	-	-	2	-	3	5
Galli	-	-	1	1	-	-	2	3
Atkinson	-	-	1	1	4	1	7	16
H. Solberg	-	-	1	-	-	-	1	11
Hirvönen	-	-	-	3	3	-	6	16
Pons	-	-	-	-	2	-	2	12

Leaders

SS1 > SS5	Loeb
SS6 > SS18	Grönholm

Previous winners

1973	Andruet - "Biche" Alpine Renault A 110	1985	Vatanen - Harryman Peugeot 205 T16	1996	Bernardini - Andrié Ford Escort Cosworth
1975	Munari - Mannucci Lancia Stratos	1986	Toivonen - Cresto Lancia Delta S4	1997	Liatti - Pons Subaru Impreza WRC
1976	Munari - Maiga Lancia Stratos	1987	Biasion - Siviero Lancia Delta HF 4WD	1998	Sainz - Moya Toyota Corolla WRC
1977	Munari - Maiga Lancia Stratos	1988	Saby - Fauchille Lancia Delta HF 4WD	1999	Mäkinen-Mannisenmäki Mitsubishi Lancer Evo VI
1978	Nicolas - Laverne Porsche 911 SC	1989	Biasion - Siviero Lancia Delta Integrale	2000	Mäkinen-Mannisenmäki Mitsubishi Lancer Evo VI
1979	Darniche - Mahé Lancia Stratos	1990	Auriol - Occelli Lancia Delta Integrale	2001	Mäkinen-Mannisenmäki Mitsubishi Lancer Evo VI
1980	Rohrl - Geistdorfer Fiat 131 Abarth	1991	Sainz - Moya Toyota Celica GT-Four	2002	Mäkinen - Lindström Subaru Impreza WRC
1981	Ragnotti - Andrié Renault 5 Turbo	1992	Auriol - Occelli Lancia Delta HF Integrale	2003	Loeb - Elena Citroën Xsara WRC
1982	Rohrl - Geistdorfer Opel Ascona 400	1993	Auriol - Occelli Toyota Celica Turbo 4WD	2004	Loeb - Elena Citroën Xsara WRC
1983	Rohrl - Geistdorfer Lancia rally 037	1994	Delecour - Grataloup Ford Escort RS Cosworth	2005	Loeb - Elena Citroën Xsara WRC
1984	Rohrl - Geistdorfer Audi Quattro	1995	Sainz - Moya Subaru Impreza 555		

Sweden

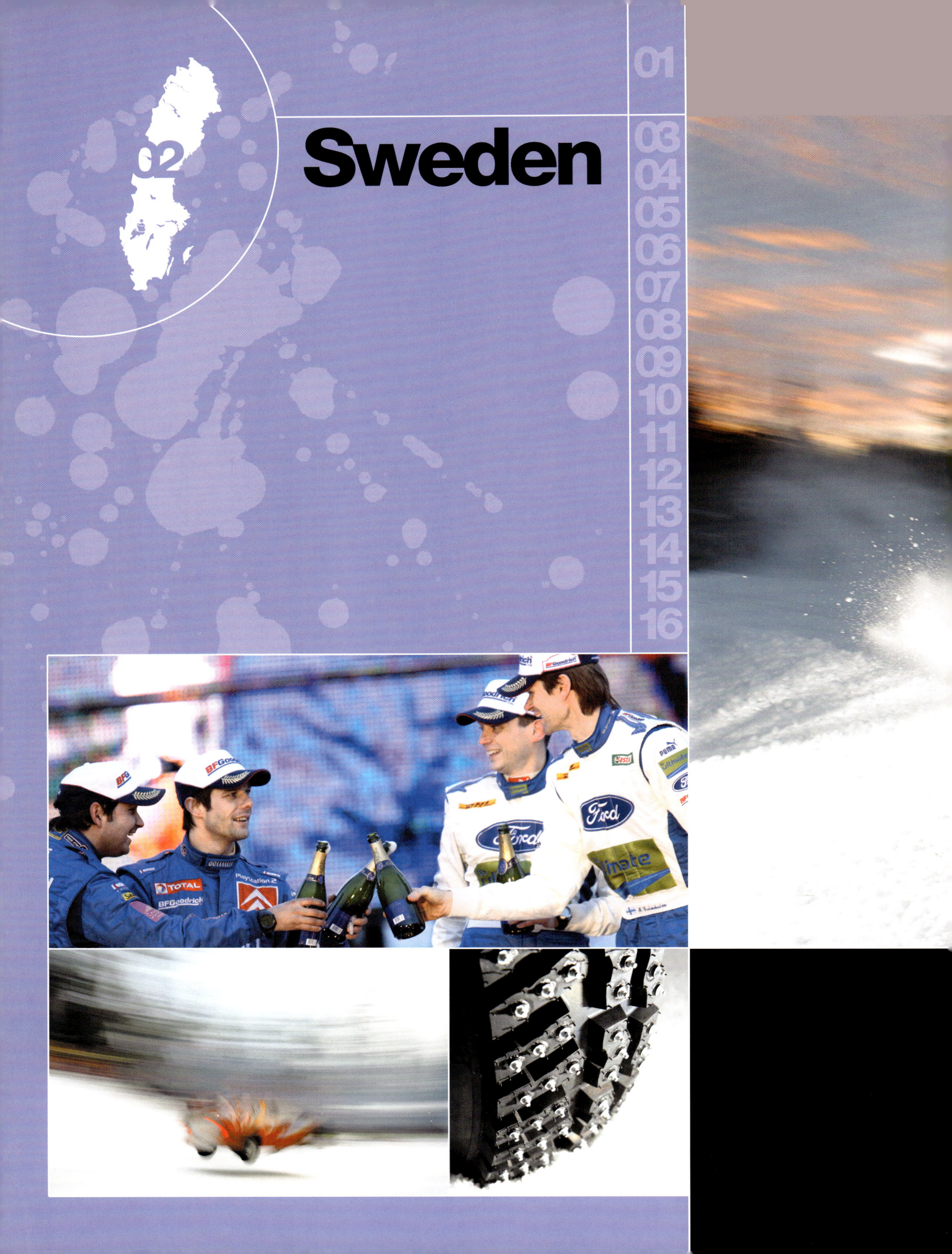

01
03
04
05
06
07
08
09
10
11
12
13
14
15
16

Ford doubles up !
Rally no. 2 and victory no.2 for Marcus Grönholm who dominated the Swedish event scoring his twentieth victory in the world championship. Once again Sébastien Loeb finished in the runner-up spot. Behind the two men there was a no-holds-barred battle between the two Mitsubishi drivers for third place on the rostrum.

02 Sweden

Petter Solberg, the 2005 winner, was one very disappointed Norwegian. He was unable to fight for victory and retired at the end of the rally when his engine refused to fire up.

Manfred Stohl made a good start to the event before going off.

THE RALLY
The mighty Finn scores no.2

Both Petter Solberg and his team were expecting a lot from the Swedish Rally. Too much perhaps. A year earlier they had scored an impressive victory in the Swedish snows but in 2006 they left with their tail between their legs after an immensely disappointing performance. Five miles into the first special the left-hand rear drive shaft broke on the Norwegian's Subaru Impreza. The former world champion lost a minute. In the second stage he lost another two. He stalled at the start of the third special and in the fourth his gearbox began to play up. Before the fifth his mechanics fitted a new box but it was not adapted to the specific characteristics of the Swedish terrain. So by the end of the day Petter was in eighth place 1m 48.4s behind the leader. It wasn't much better for his team-mate. In 2005, Chris Atkinson had not found it too difficult to come to grips with the Swedish roads. This year he made a big mistake in the Fredriksberg stage and went off. He hit a tree root, which bent his steering slowing him considerably. "It's not our day," sighed David Lapworth, the team manager at the end of the leg. "We were hoping for a good performance after a promising shakedown test which makes this result all the more disappointing. The most frustrating thing is that the technical problems we've run into have nothing to do with the new car but with tried and tested parts. Petter is really down in the dumps. He deserves more luck after what he's been through in the last two rallies." By Friday the Norwegian's rally was over like his team-mate's. They both continued over the next two days to do some

Sébastien Loeb was not destined to win the Swedish rally in 2006. He was defeated by a wrong stud choice and an on-form Grönholm.

Marcus Grönholm made the break in the first two legs, and then strolled home to a comfortable victory.

Dani Sordo, who had never raced on snow and ice before, receives some expert advice from Sébastien Loeb.

Gigi Galli had driven a fantastic rally in Sweden in 2005 followed by 4th place in 2006, which boosted Mitsubishi's hopes.

testing but without much hope of a result. In fact, things got even worse for Petter as at the start of the final stage his engine refused to fire up and he was eliminated from the event.

So the Subarus were out of contention early on, and like in the south of France two weeks earlier the battle for victory boiled down to a straight fight between two men, Marcus Grönholm and Sébastien Loeb. The Finn was full of confidence after his Monte Carlo success and set the two fastest times in the first two specials. This gave him a small lead over the Frenchman but not enough to relax. Marcus really went for it. "I made a few minor mistakes and ended up leaning on the snow walls but it was nothing serious," he laughed after the leg. "It looks like it's going to be one hell of a battle and I'll see if I can up the pace a bit more."

At the end of the first day he was in the lead but only 10.2s ahead of Loeb after an awesome duel as shown by the 0.8s between the two drivers at the end of the 20m 40s Vargasen stage (SS5, 39.9 kms). Sébastien set three scratch times during the first leg in his attempts to match the Finn's searing pace. But he was hit with a stupid 10-second penalty for turning up late for the start of SS2. The Xsara crew had lost time on the road stage trying to fasten the bonnet that had suddenly flown up, as Loeb and Elena had forgotten to put back the bonnet pins after removing the auxiliary spotlights. So it was pedal to metal time for the Frenchman. "We're not going to let that worry us throughout the rally,» he exclaimed. "Whatever the situation there was going to be a battle with Marcus. We're lucky enough to have perfect conditions and I'm really going for it. So's Marcus by the state of the walls after he's been through! We'll continue the hunt tomorrow!"

Behind the Frenchman and the Finn two other drivers were at it hammer and tongs, Gianluigi Galli and Daniel Carlsson in their Mitsubishi Lancers. The previous year the Italian had driven a good rally here and the Swede was getting to know the Lancer WRC05 on his home territory. The cars from the team's base in Rugby were works entries in all but name, and had made a lot of progress during the interseason as proved by the time sheets. Galli was quickest in SS3 and Carlsson was almost as fast; by the end of the first leg in Karlstadt they were in third and fourth places respectively separated by only 5.5s. It is a pity that the Mitsubishi participation this year is so limited.

The second leg was the theatre of three separate duels for the first six places. Loeb/Grönholm for the lead, Galli/Carlsson for third and fourth and Ekström/Tuohino in a Skoda and a Citroën respectively for fifth and sixth. Up front the two leaders set the fastest times with the advantage going to the Finn with six as against Loeb's two. In fact, it looked like Grönholm's tyre choice (long studs) was better than the Frenchman's who opted for the shorter ones on his BF Goodrichs. While there was only half-a-millimetre's difference between the two, it was enough to give the Ford driver that little edge that can make a big difference between two such skilled drivers. Little by little Marcus eked out an advantage: 4.9s in SS7, 2.8s in SS8, 3.3s in SS9. "I thought I'd made a mistake," Loeb admitted. "I didn't have the long studs when it mattered in the first loop and I put them on in the second when standard ones would've been better."

Thomas Radström, a former winner of the rally and ex-works Ford and Citroën driver among others, was at the start of the event that made his name. He came home 5th in a Subaru.

02 Sweden

Mattias Ekström, Swedish DTM driver, had another outing in rallying, a sport he likes very much.

Sweden gave Henning Solberg some valuable practice. He finished 8th in his 307 WRC and a few days later he won the Norwegian rally, an event that will be part of the 2007 calendar, in the same car.

The half-millimetre was an apt metaphor for the intensity of the battle between the two world champions. The Finn was trying to drive home his advantage while Sébastien was doing his utmost not to let his rival make the break. At the end of the second leg on Saturday they were separated by 25.1s. "It's not over yet," Loeb insisted. "I'm going to really go flat out at the start of tomorrow's leg to up the pressure." The battle for third turned in Carlsson's favour at the end of day 2, but by only 0.3s! "I've never driven like this," said the breathless Gigi. "You've just got to go flat out to pull back a second," declared the Swede.

The duel between Ekström and Tuohino was just as intense. Only 1/10s separated them at the end of the leg. The DTM driver loves his home rally and was able to take part in it this year thanks to the link-up between his sponsor in the DTM and Skoda, Red Bull. He was up against a Finn who was out to prove that he deserved his last-minute entry in a PH Sport Xsara in place of Harri Rovanperä.

The third leg looked like it was going to be just as exciting as the first two. And it was! Loeb went flat out from the start and won the first three stages. In only forty-five kilometres he closed the gap to Grönholm to 14.4s. The latter got his head down and drove without making any mistakes but ran into trouble in Malta (SS16) with an ill-handling car. The hydraulic filter on his Ford had burst and he had to use his spare gear lever. "We gave ourselves a big scare when the fluid began to spurt onto the windscreen in the middle of the stage." Luckily, a service halt was programmed after this special and the Ford mechanics got the car back into proper working order for the last three stages. The Finn was all-fired up and he set the three quickest times. Loeb was still trying to close the gap even further but once more the Frenchman got his tyre choices mixed up. Finally, the difference between first and second was 30.9s, and a very happy Marcus Grönholm and Timo Rautiainen scored their second win of the 2006 season on what Marcus considers his home territory.

The joy in the Ford camp would have been complete had not Mikko Hirvonen run into a problem with the alternator belt, which also drove the water pump, on his Ford. "We're continuing our good start to the season," smiled a delighted Malcolm Wilson. "I have to admit that I spent three pretty frantic days hoping that the problem we had on Mikko's car would not affect Marcus." This second win on the trot gave Ford the advantage in both championships ahead of Loeb and Kronos thanks to the latter's second places. Loeb's aim was to rack up his first victory in the 2006 campaign but he admitted after the finish,"Marcus was the strongest here. No regrets!"

Daniel Carlsson just scraped onto the third step of the rostrum and was in seventh heaven. "I've never had such a scrap with a team-mate. It's a dream. All the more so as I wasn't told that I'd be taking part in the event in the Mitsubishi until just before the start. I didn't even have time to test the car." The two drivers swapped third place ten times throughout the rally, and the outcome was decided in the last special when Galli

Kosti Katajamäki saw the flag in 6th place giving the Stobart VK-M team its first points of the season.

It as Xevi Pons's 4th time out in Sweden. His works responsibilities calmed his ardour a little and his seventh place brought his team 3 points.

Former Peugeot driver Daniel Carlsson was a happy man thanks to his rostrum finish in an old works Mitsubishi.

felt his engine tightening up and did the whole stage in fourth gear.
The battle between Ekström and Tuohino did not last until the end as the Swede went off in the first stage of the third leg. His rival thought that fifth was his for the taking until his engine seized 300 metres from the finish. He finally came home in tenth place thanks to the Super Rally. ■

THE JUNIORS
Good news for Andersson

The WRC Junior Championship began in Sweden for the first time in its short existence. Fourteen drivers mostly from the north (Swedes, Finns and Estonians) started the rally, which Per-Gunnar Andersson dominated from start to finish. He had won the championship in 2004 and crushed his rivals in Sweden at the wheel of his works Suzuki Swift. The only driver to threaten him was his fellow-countryman Patrick Sandell who snatched the lead briefly in his Clio in the fourth stage. Apart from this Andersson won as he pleased and came under no pressure from his stable-mate Guy Wilks who stuffed his Swift into a snow drift, which it took him twenty minutes to get out of.

"An ideal weekend," laughed the happy winner. "The rally was a bit of a doodle even if Patrick (who finished second) tried to put some pressure on me. But I always thought I had things under control especially as I feel really at home on this type of terrain." Aava from Estonia (Suzuki Swift) finished third. Another Swede, Peter Zachrisson, put on a stunning performance especially as he was a last-minute entry in a Swift (Ignis this time) by setting five quickest times. He finished seventh. ■

Chris Atkinson's fiery temperament did not mix with the ice in the 3rd stage. He went off and was obliged to do battle at the rear of the field.

02 Sweden results

55th SWEDISH RALLY

Organiser Details
International Swedish Rally
BOX 594
651 13 Karlstadt
Sweden
Tel.: +4654 102025
Fax: +4654 180530

Uddeholm Swedish Rally

2nd leg of FIA 2006 World Rally Championship for constructors and drivers.
1st leg of FIA WRC Junior Championship.

Date February 2 - 5, 2006

Route
1447.76 km divised in three legs.
19 special stages on snowy dirt roads (348.88 km)

Starting Procedure
Thursday, February 2 (19:00),
Grand Place, Karlstad
Leg 1
Friday, February 3 (08:01/17:07),
Hagfors > Hagfors, 549.68 km;
6 special stages (130.89 km)
Leg 2
Saturday, February 4 (08:00/16:57),
Hagfors > Hagfors, 518.50 km;
7 special stages (127.79 km)
Leg 3
Sunday, February 5 (07:58/12:52),
Hagfors > Karlstad, 379.43 km;
6 special stages (90.20 km)

Entry List (67) - 63 starters

N°	Driver (Nat.)	Co-driver (Nat.)	Team	Car	Group & FIA Priority
1.	S. LOEB (F)	D. ELENA (MC)	KRONOS TOTAL CITROEN WRT	Citroën Xsara WRC	A8 1
2.	X. PONS (E)	C. DEL BARRIO (E)	KRONOS TOTAL CITROEN WRT	Citroën Xsara WRC	A8 1
3.	M. GRÖNHOLM (FIN)	T. RAUTIAINEN (FIN)	BP FORD WORLD RALLY TEAM	Ford Focus RS WRC 06	A8 1
4.	M. HIRVONEN (FIN)	J. LEHTINEN (FIN)	BP FORD WORLD RALLY TEAM	Ford Focus RS WRC 06	A8 1
5.	P. SOLBERG (N)	P. MILLS (GB)	SUBARU WORLD RALLY TEAM	Subaru Impreza WRC 2006	A8 1
6.	C. ATKINSON (AUS)	G. MACNEALL (AUS)	SUBARU WORLD RALLY TEAM	Subaru Impreza WRC 2006	A8 1
7.	M. STOHL (A)	I. MINOR (A)	OMV - PEUGEOT NORWAY	Peugeot 307 WRC	A8 1
8.	H. SOLBERG (N)	C. MENKERUD (N)	OMV - PEUGEOT NORWAY	Peugeot 307 WRC	A8 1
9.	M. WILSON (GB)	M. ORR (GB)	STOBART - VK - M-SPORT FORD RALLY TEAM	Ford Focus RS WRC 04	A8 1
10.	K. KATAJAMÄKI (FIN)	T. ALANNE (FIN)	STOBART - VK - M-SPORT FORD RALLY TEAM	Ford Focus RS WRC 04	A8 1
11.	A. AIGNER (A)	T. GOTTSCHALK (D)	RED BULL - SKODA TEAM	Skoda Fabia WRC	A8 1
12.	M. EKSTRÖM (S)	S. BERGMAN (S)	RED BULL - SKODA TEAM	Skoda Fabia WRC	A8 1
14.	G. GALLI (I)	G. BERNACCHINI (I)	GIANLUIGI GALLI	Mitsubishi Lancer WR05	A8 2
15.	J. TUOHINO (FIN)	R. PIETILÄINEN (FIN)	HARRI ROVANPERÄ	Citroen Xsara WRC	A8 2
16.	T. RÅDSTRÖM (S)	J. SKALLMAN (S)	RALLYTEAM OLSBERGS	Subaru S10 WRC	A8 2
17.	J. KOPECKY (E)	F. SCHOVÁNEK (CZ)	CZECH RALLY TEAM SKODA- KOPECKY	Skoda Fabia WRC 5	A8 2
18.	K. SOHLBERG (FIN)	K. LINDSTROM (FIN)	TEAM RED DEVIL ATOLYE KAZAZ	Subaru Impreza WRC	A8 2
19.	J. JOGE (S)	M. ANDERSSON (S)	PEUGEOT SPORT SWEDEN	Peugeot 206 WRC	A8 2
20.	T. SCHIE (N)	G. BERGSTEN (S)	THOMAS SCHIE	Ford Focus WRC	A8 2
21.	D. SORDO (E)	M. MARTI (E)	DANIEL SORDO	Citroen Xsara WRC	A8 2
22.	L. PEREZ COMPANC (RA)	J. MARIA VOLTA (RA)	STOBART - VK - M-SPORT FORD RALLY TEAM	Ford Focus RS WRC 04	A8 2
33.	U. AAVA (EST)	K. SIKK (EST)	URMO AAVA	Suzuki Swift S1600	A6 3
35.	P. ANDERSSON (S)	J. ANDERSSON (S)	PG ANDERSSON	Suzuki Swift Super 1600	A6 3
37.	P. VALOUSEK (CZ)	P. SCALVINI (CZ)	PAVEL VALOUSEK	Suzuki Swift S1600	A6 3
40.	S. BLOMQVIST (S)	A. GONI (YV)	STIG BLOMQVIST	Subaru Impreza STi WRX	N4
41.	P. SANDELL (S)	E. AXELSSON (S)	PATRIK SANDELL	Renault Clio Super 1600	A6 3
43.	J. MÖLDER (EST)	K. BECKER (D)	JAAN MÖLDER	Ford Fiesta	A6 3
44.	M. KOSCIUSZKO (PL)	J. BARAN (PL)	MICHAL KOSCIUSZKO	Suzuki Ignis S1600	A6 3
45.	J. BÉRES (SK)	P. STARY (CZ)	JOZEF BÉRES	Suzuki Ignis	A6 3
46.	A. CORTINOVIS (I)	B. MASSIMILIANO (I)	ANDREA CORTINOVIS	Renault Clio	N3 3
47.	F. A BORDIGNON (I)	J. BARDINI (I)	FILIPPO BORDIGNON	Opel Astra OPC	N3 3
48.	G. WILKS (GB)	P. PUGH (GB)	GUY WILKS	Suzuki Swift Super 1600	A6 3
49.	M. PROKOP (CZ)	J. TOMÁNEK (CZ)	MARTIN PROKOP	Citroën C2 S1600	A6 3
50.	K. PINOMÄKI (FIN)	M. MARKKULA (FIN)	KALLE PINOMÄKI	Renault Clio Ragnotti	N3 3
59.	P. ZACHRISSON (S)	J. SVANSTRÖM (S)	PETER ZACHRISSON	Suzuki Ignis	A6 3
60.	J. KARLSSON (S)	M. GUSTAVSSON (S)	JOHAN KARLSSON	Peugeot 206 RC	N3 3
61.	M. ÖSTBERG (N)	R. ENGEN (N)	MADS ÖSTBERG	Subaru Impreza WRC	A8
62.	A. GRÖNDAL (NOR)	T. Inge ÖSTBYE (N)	ANDERS GRÖNDAL	Subaru Impreza WRC	A8
63.	D. CARLSSON (S)	B. HOLMSTRAND (S)	DANIEL CARLSSON	Mitsubishi Lancer WR05	A8 2
64.	P. FLODIN (S)	M. ANDERSSON (S)	PATRIK FLODIN	Subaru Impreza	N4
65.	J. KETOMÄKI (FIN)	K. RISBERG (FIN)	JUKKA KETOMÄKI	Subaru Impreza WRX STi	N4
66.	R. TAHKO (FIN)	O. LAHTINEN (FIN)	RIKU TAHKO	Mitsubishi Lancer Evo VII	N4
67.	O. SVEDLUND (S)	B. NILSSON (S)	OSCAR SVEDLUND	Subaru Impreza WRX STi	N4
69.	H. WENG (S)	A. FREDRIKSSON (S)	HANS-ERIK WENG	Mitsubishi Lancer Evo VIII	N4
70.	D. WICKSELL (S)	N. FRANSSON (S)	DICK WICKSELL	Subaru Impreza	N4
71.	M. SOLOWOW (PL)	M. BARAN (PL)	CERSANIT RALLY TEAM	Subaru Impreza GL WRC	A8
72.	G. MAC HALE (IRL)	P. NAGLE (IRL)	GARETH MACHALE	Ford Focus WRC	A8
73.	J. HÄNNINEN (FIN)	M. SALLINEN (FIN)	JUHO HÄNNINEN	Mitsubishi Lancer Evo IX	N4
74.	H. GUSTAVSSON (S)	N. EDVARDSSON (S)	HASSE GUSTAVSSON	Subaru Impreza WRX STi	N4
75.	E. STEFFENSEN (N)	J. Petter SIGVARTSEN (N)	EIVIND STEFFENSEN	Subaru Impreza	N4
76.	J. ROMAN (S)	J. CARLSSON (S)	JOAKIM ROMAN	Subaru Impreza WRX STi 6	N4
77.	A. ALÉN (FIN)	J. AARIAINEN (FIN)	Anton Alén	Mitsubishi Lancer Evo VII	N4
78.	P. BRYNILDSEN (N)	R. Espen OLSEN (N)	PER-ERIK BRYNILDSEN	Mitsubishi Lancer Evo VII	N4
79.	P. Mikael GUSTAFSSON (S)	L. Erik KRONBERG (S)	PER-MIKAEL GUSTAFSSON	Mitsubishi Lancer Evo VII	N4
80.	F. FRISIERO (I)	S. SCATTOLIN (I)	FABIO FRISIERO	Toyota Corolla	A8
81.	A. VILLANUEVA (E)	A. TRAMONT (F)	ALEXANDER VILLANUEVA	Mitsubishi Lancer	N4
82.	S. KARNABAL (PL)	B. BOBA (POL)	STEFAN KARNABAL	Mitsubishi Lancer	N4
83.	A. ARAUJO (P)	M. RAMALHO (P)	MITSUBISHI PORTUGAL	Mitsubishi Lancer Evo VIII	N4
84.	E. BRYNILDSEN (N)	A. RÖNNING (N)	EYVIND BRYNILDSEN	Mitsubishi Lancer Evo VII	N4
85.	L. HOELBLING (I)	T. SIENA (I)	LUCA HOELBLING	Subaru Impreza STi	N4
86.	R. SCANDOLA (I)	D. PASI (I)	RICCARDO SCANDOLA	Subaru Impreza STi	N4
87.	R. MARTINEZ SACO (ESP)	R. MARCHENA BAENO (E)	RAFAEL MARTINEZ SACO	Subaru Impreza STi Spec-C	N4
88.	A. MANCIN (PL)	R. CIUPKA (PL)	ANDRZEJ MANCIN	Mitsubishi Lancer Evo VII	N4
89.	P. STRAND (S)	P. ELLISON (S)	PER-ARNE STRAND	Citroen C2 Sport	A6
90.	L. STORM (S)	U. STORM (S)	LASSE STORM	Renault Clio Ragnotti	N3
91.	Z. PENZES (H)	A. THURZO (H)	ZSOLT PÉNZES	Renault Clio Ragnotti	N3
92.	E. GRANUM (N)	O. Johnny WINTHER (N)	ENDRE GRANUM	Nissan Almera GTI	N3

Championship Classifications

FIA Drivers (2/16)
1. Grönholm 2♕ 20
2. Loeb 16
3. Gardemeister 6
4. Carlsson 6
5. Stohl 5
6. Galli 5
7. Sarrazin 4
8. Rådström 4
9. Atkinson 3
10. Katajamäki 3
11. Pons 2
12. Hirvönen 2
13. Sordo 1
14. H. Solberg 1
15. Joge, Panizzi, Tuohino, Kopecky, Burri, Aigner, Wilson, Tsjoen, Hänninen, MacHale, Sandell 0

FIA Constructors (2/16)
1. BP-Ford World Rally Team 2♕ 26
2. Kronos Total Citroën WRT 24
3. OMV-Peugeot Norway 10
4. Subaru World Rally Team 8
5. Stobart VK M-Sport Ford WRT 7
6. Red Bull-Skoda Team 3

FIA Production Car (1/8)
1. Nutahara 1♕ 10
2. Higgins 8
3. Al-Attiyah 6
4. Marrini 5
5. Latvala 4
6. Popov 0

FIA Junior WRC (1/9)
1. Andersson 1♕ 10
2. Sandell 8
3. Aava 6
4. Valousek 5
5. Pinomäki 4
6. Béres 3
7. Zachrisson 2
8. Kosciuszko 1
9. Wilks 0
10. Molder 0
11. Prokop 0
12. Karlsson 0
13. Bordignon 0
14. Cortinovis 0

Special Stages Times

www.swedishrally.mc
www.wrc.com

SS1 Fredriksberg 1 (18.13 km)
1.Grönholm 10'25"7; 2.Loeb +2"8;
3.Hirvonen +7"8; 4.Stohl +11"2;
5.Ekström +11"6; 6.Atkinson +15"8;
7.Galli +16"8; 8.Rådström +17"6...
J-WRC > 32.Andersson 11'45"6

SS2 Lejen 1 (26.46 km)
1.Grönholm 14'20"9; 2.Loeb +6"2;
3.Hirvonen +18"8; 4.Galli +19"5;
5.Atkinson +20"1; 6.Carlsson +20"4;
7.Sohlberg +21"8; 8.Ekström +22"6...
J-WRC > 26.Andersson 15'49"5

SS3 Fredriksberg 2 (18.13 km)
1.Galli 10'29"1; 2.Ekström +1"2;
3.Tuohino +1"8; 4.Hirvonen +3"9;
5.Sohlberg +5"2; 6.Loeb +5"7;
7.Carlsson +5"9; 8.Rådström +11"7...
J-WRC > 28.Sandell 11'18"5

SS4 Lejen 2 (26.46 km)
1.Loeb 14'24"4; 2.Grönholm +0"8;
3.Carlsson +5"1; 4.Galli +5"5;
5.Hirvonen +5"8; 6.H.Solberg +12"2;
7.Tuohino +13"3; 8.Stohl +15"7...
J-WRC > 27.Andersson 15'35"7

SS5 Vargåsen 1 (39.95 km)
1.Loeb 20'40"5; 2.Grönholm +0"8;
3.Carlsson +23"2; 4.Galli +26"8;
5.Stohl +27"6; 6.P.Solberg +34"0;
7.H.Solberg +35"5; 8.Ekström +37"2...
J-WRC > 26.Andersson 22'49"5

SS6 Hagfors Sprint 1 (1.87 km)
1.Loeb 1'54"7; 2.Grönholm +0"6;
3.Galli +3"4; 4.Ekström +3"6;
5.Carlsson +4"5; 6.Sordo/Tuohino +4"8;
8.Stohl/Sohlberg +5"2...
J-WRC > 28.Zachrisson 2'09"4

Classification leg 1
1.Grönholm 1h12'29"8; 2.Loeb +10"2;
3.Galli +57"5; 4.Carlsson +1'03"0;
5.Ekström +1'22"4; 6.Stohl +1'28"7;
7.H.Solberg +1'40"3;
8.Sohlberg +1'48"4...
J-WRC > 24.Andersson 1h19'37"3

SS7 Hara 1 (11.31 km)
1.Grönholm 6'04"8; 2.Hirvonen +0"8;
3.P.Solberg +4"3; 4.Loeb +4"9;
5.Carlsson +6"9; 6.Stohl +7"5;
7.H.Solberg +7"6; 8.Atkinson +10"4...
J-WRC > 27.Andersson 6'49"4

SS8 Sundsjön 1 (20.78 Km)
1.Grönholm 11'07"4; 2.Loeb +2"8;
3.P.Solberg +11"0; 4.Hirvonen +13"1;
5.Sohlberg +13"8; 6.Tuohino +15"1;
7.H.Solberg +15"6; 8.Galli +15"7...
J-WRC > 27.Zachrisson 12'19"5

SS9 Likenäs (21.78 Km)
1.Grönholm 12'19"6; 2.Loeb +3"4;
3.P.Solberg +3"5; 4.Hirvonen +8"0;
5.Galli +9"8; 6.Tuohino +12"2;
7.Carlsson +15"6; 8.Stohl +16"3...
J-WRC > 31.Andersson 13'51"0

SS10 Hara 2 (11.31 Km)
1.Grönholm 6'02"4; 2.Loeb +0"3;
3.Hirvonen +1"3; 4.P.Solberg +3"6;
5.Carlsson +7"4; 6.Tuohino +7"7;
7.Stohl +9"1; 8.H.Solberg +11"9...
J-WRC > 27.Andersson 6'45"7

SS11 Sundsjön 2 (20.78 Km)
1.Grönholm 11'00"4; 2.Loeb +6"5;
3.Hirvonen +10"9; 4.Tuohino +14"7;
5.Sohlberg +17"4; 6.Ekström +19"6;
7.Rådström +20"6; 8.Carlsson +22"7...
J-WRC > 23.Andersson 12'08"0

SS12 Vargåsen 2 (39.95 Km)
1.Loeb 20'43"8; 2.Grönholm +2"3;
3.Galli +19"0; 4.Carlsson +19"9;
5.Ekström +21"4; 6.Hirvonen +26"1;
7.Atkinson +29"9; 8.Sohlberg +36"3...
J-WRC > 24.Andersson 22'56"7

SS13 Hagfors Sprint 2 (1.87 km)
1.Loeb 2'00"7;
2.Grönholm/Katajamäki +0"7;
4.Tuohino +1"4; 5.Joge +2"0;
6.Galli +2"2; 7.Sordo +2"8;
8.Carlsson +3"4...
J-WRC > 27.Andersson 2'12"7

Classification leg 2
1.Grönholm 2h21'51"9; 2.Loeb +25"1;
3.Carlsson +2'32"7; 4.Galli +2'33"0;
5.Ekström +3'28"1; 6.Tuohino +3'28"2;
7.Rådström +4'26"5;
8.H.Solberg +5'14"6...
J-WRC > 22.Anderson 2h36'53"3

SS14 Lesjöfors 1 (10.48 Km)
1.Loeb 5'56"3; 2.Grönholm +0"2;
3.Hirvonen +0"6; 4.Carlsson +3"5;
5.Galli +4"0; 6.H.Solberg +4"7;
7.Atkinson +4"9; 8.P.Solberg +6"2...
J-WRC > 24.Andersson 6'32"9

SS15 Rämmen 1 (23.35 Km)
1.Loeb 11'49"3; 2.Grönholm +1"5;
3.P.Solberg +3"4; 4.Hirvonen +6"3;
5.Galli +7"0; 6.Carlsson +9"5;
7.Atkinson +11"6; 8.Rådström +13"2...
J-WRC > 24.Zachrisson 13'10"8

SS16 Malta 1 (11.25 Km)
1.Loeb 5'47"7; 2.H.Solberg +2"9;
3.Carlsson +3"2; 4.Galli +5"6;
5.Hirvonen +6"4; 6.Rådström +6"7;
7.Atkinson +6"8; 8.P.Solberg +8"9...
J-WRC > 22.Zachrisson 6'32"5

SS17 Lesjöfors 2 (10.48 Km)
1.Grönholm 5'47"7; 2.Loeb +3"7;
3.Galli +5"9; 4.Carlsson +7"3;
5.H.Solberg +8"9; 6.P.Solberg +10"9;
7.Hirvonen +12"0; 8.Atkinson +12"9...
J-WRC > 22.Wilks 6'26"4

SS18 Rämmen 2 (23.35 Km)
1.Grönholm 11'50"3; 2.Loeb +3"2;
3.Hirvonen +10"2; 4.Carlsson +10"3;
5.Galli +11"2; 6.H.Solberg +12"8;
7.Atkinson +20"3; 8.Tuohino +20"4...
J-WRC > 21.Zachrisson 13'01"0

SS19 Malta 2 (11.25 Km)
1.Grönholm 5'48"0; 2.Carlsson +1"0;
3.Galli +7"8; 4.H.Solberg +8"1;
5.Atkinson +9"4; 6.Loeb +9"6;
7.Hirvonen +10"0; 8.Rådström +13"1...
J-WRC > 19.Wilks 6'24"3

Results 🇸🇪

	Driver - Co-driver	Car	Gr.	Time
1	Grönholm - Rautiainen	Ford Focus RS WRC 06	A8	3h09'01"9
2	Loeb - Elena	Citroën Xsara WRC	A8	+ 30"9
3	Carlsson - Holmstrand	Mitsubishi Lancer WRC05	A8	+ 2'56"8
4	Galli - Bernacchini	Mitsubishi Lancer WRC05	A8	+ 3'03"8
5	Rådström - Skallman	Subaru Impreza S10 WRC	A8	+ 5'53"3
6	Katajamäki - Alanne	Ford Focus RS WRC 04	A8	+ 7'34"8
7	Pons - Del Barrio	Citroën Xsara WRC	A8	+ 8'35"6
8	H. Solberg - Menkerud	Peugeot 307 WRC	A8	+ 9'01"5
9	Joge - Andersson	Peugeot 206 WRC	A8	+ 9'17"2
10	Tuohino - Pietiläinen	Citroën Xsara WRC	A8	+9'43"0
15	**Hänninen - Sallinen**	**Mitsubishi Lancer Evo IX**	**N4**	**+ 15'14"9**
19	**Andersson - Andersson**	**Suzuki Swift Super 1600**	**A6/J**	**+ 20'16"8**
20	Sandell - Axelsson	Renault Clio Super 1600	A6/J	+ 21'09"9
22	Aava - Sikk	Suzuki Swift Super 1600	A6/J	+ 23'11"9

Leading Retirements (12)

SS18	P. Solberg - Mills	Subaru Impreza WRC 2006	Off
TC16	Aigner - Gottschalk	Skoda Fabia WRC 05	Engine
TC15	Schie - Bergsten	Ford Focus WRC	Engine
SF15	Gröndal - Östbye	Subaru Impreza WRC	Off
SF14	Ekström - Bergman	Skoda Fabia WRC 05	Off
TC13A	Sohlberg - Lindstrom	Subaru Impreza WRC	Engine

Performers

	1	2	3	4	5	6	C6	NbSS
Grönholm	10	7	-	-	-	-	17	19
Loeb	8	8	-	1	-	2	19	19
Galli	1	-	4	4	4	1	14	19
Hirvonen	-	1	6	4	2	1	14	17
Carlsson	-	1	3	4	3	2	13	19
Ekström	-	1	-	1	2	1	5	13
H. Solberg	-	1	-	1	-	3	5	19
Katajamäki	-	1	-	-	-	-	1	19
P. Solberg	-	-	4	1	-	2	7	17
Tuohino	-	-	1	2	-	4	7	18
Stohl	-	-	-	1	1	1	3	16
Söhlberg	-	-	-	-	4	-	4	13
Atkinson	-	-	-	-	2	1	3	19
Joge	-	-	-	-	1	-	1	19
Rådström	-	-	-	-	-	1	1	19
Sordo	-	-	-	-	-	1	1	19

Leaders

SS1 > SS19   Grönholm

Previous Winners

1973	Blomqvist - Hertz Saab 96 V 4	1985	Vatanen - Harryman Peugeot 205 T16	1997	Eriksson - Parmander Subaru Impreza WRC
1975	Waldegaard - Thorszelius Lancia Stratos	1986	Kankkunen - Piironen Peugeot 205 T16	1998	Mäkinen - Mannisenmaki Mitsubishi Lancer Evo IV
1976	Eklund - Cederberg Saab 96 V 4	1987	Salonen - Harjanne Mazda 323 Turbo	1999	Mäkinen - Mannisenmaki Mitsubishi Lancer Evo VI
1977	Blomqvist - Sylvan Saab 99 ems	1988	Alen - Kivimaki Lancia Delta HF 4WD	2000	Grönholm - Rautiainen Peugeot 206 WRC
1978	Waldegaard - Thorszelius Ford Escort RS	1989	Carlsson - Carlsson Mazda 323 4WD	2001	Rovanperä - Pietilainen Peugeot 206 WRC
1979	Blomqvist - Cederberg Saab 99 Turbo	1991	Eriksson - Parmander Mitsubishii Galant VR-4	2002	Grönholm - Rautiainen Peugeot 206 WRC
1980	Kullang - Berglund Opel Ascona 400	1992	Jonsson - Backman Toyota Celica GT-Four	2003	Loeb - Elena Citroën Xsara WRC
1981	Mikkola - Hertz Audi Quattro	1993	Jonsson - Backman Toyota Celica Turbo 4WD	2004	Loeb - Elena Citroën Xsara WRC
1982	Blomqvist - Cederberg Audi Quattro	1994	Rådström - Backman Toyota Celica Turbo 4WD	2005	P. Solberg - Mills Subaru Impreza WRC 2004
1983	Mikkola - Hertz Audi Quattro	1995	Eriksson - Parmander Mitsubishi Lancer Evo II		
1984	Blomqvist - Cederberg Audi Quattro	1996	Mäkinen - Harjanne Mitsubishi Lancer Evo III		

Per-Gunnar Andersson

Mexico

03

01
02
04
05
06
07
08
09
10
11
12
13
14
15
16

Loeb back on top
Sébastien Loeb and Daniel Elena's first win of the 2006 season came after a mind-boggling duel with Petter Solberg-Phil Mills. Grönholm made a major error in the first leg and was never in a position to challenge the two leaders. Although the Xsara won out in the end the rally showed that at this juncture of the season Subaru was a force to be reckoned with.

Mexico

For once the 2006 Subaru spread its wings in Mexico enabling Petter Solberg to take the fight to Sébastien Loeb.

Hirvonen drove a good first leg and was second after the first day. Unfortunately, the young Finn made his only serious mistake of the season and crashed out the following morning.

Sébastien Loeb was dominated at the start of the rally but managed to up his pace at the end of the second leg, which he finished in third place.

THE RALLY
Back on gravel

Like the Monte Carlo the first gravel rally is an eagerly-awaited test for the different teams entered in the World Championship. As it is the surface on which the majority of events are run it always provides a lot of in-depth information about the strengths and weaknesses of the title contenders. There was a fair amount of tension as the cars lined up for the start of the third round of the 2006 Championship, an event celebrated with increasing intensity by the Leon region as the years roll by. Petter Solberg enjoyed a good starting position so he was spared the dust that was swept away by the first cars out on the routes, and he was able to go pedal to metal right away. For once it looked like the Subaru was capable of doing what he asked it to, and the Pirellis were much more at home on gravel than on asphalt. The Norwegian was ninth out while Loeb started from second place and Grönholm from first. Petter set his first three fastest times of the season. It was about time! In addition, there had been a bit of a reshuffle at Subaru, which had a new team manager since Sweden. Paul Howarth had replaced David Lapworth, David Richard's bosom buddy, after the disastrous start to the season by the blue cars. In the Japanese camp in Mexico was François-Xavier Demaison, Grönholm's engineer when he was at Peugeot. He was to look after Solberg's car. Lapworth, the former chief Subaru engineer was probably not really in the right place as team manager, and he was entrusted with managing the Prodrive F1 programme by Richards.

The fruit of these changes was that the Subarus were quick in Mexico. Solberg led the way and young Chris Atkinson also put on an excellent display despite an oversteering Impreza.

The main opposition to the Subarus came from Ford. Not from Grönholm but his team-mate Mikko Hirvonen who was also well placed in the starting order, sixth in fact. The young Finn went into second out of the starting blocks and stayed there all day. He had problems adapted to the handling of his car due to the altitude. "The engine is down on power," he said at midday. "That makes it very tricky to drive in the corners as you don't have the usual grunt to get it out of the bends. I'm also a bit surprised by the hardness of the terrain (it had not rained in the region for five months) and I hit quite a few stones. The brakes

Little-known Irishman Gareth McHale finished the rally in a brilliant sixth place in a Ford Focus WRC 03.

Manfred Stohl was on the rostrum for the first time in the 2006 season in his Bozian-entered 307, and went into third place in the drivers' Championship.

his bad old ways with an off in the fourth special. "I came into a left-handed curve too quickly," he groaned. "I slid into the ditch on the outside. The car ended up on its side and we had to give it a shove to get it back on its four wheels. My mistake! I was pushing too hard and I tried to brake as late as possible." The Ford Focus suffered from broken rear suspension and had to retire. The damage was not too serious and Grönholm was hoping to restart in the Super Rally to bag a few points for the Manufacturers' Championship.

Thus, an ecstatic Solberg was in the lead at the end of the first leg followed by Hirvonen. The Norwegian scented that a second victory was in the offing on the same surface on which he triumphed the previous year. "I'm really delighted to be in front. The car's been perfect so far. I made a good start thanks to my position and then it was a question of controlling my lead. Even if I'm dreaming of victory I'm making no forecast. I'm going to take the days as they come and we'll see what happens at the end."

Only 10 seconds separated Solberg, Hirvonen and Loeb while Stohl in fourth place was already 1m 45s behind and Sordo in fifth 2m 01s in arrears. Pons did not make to the end of the day and retired in the second stage when a broken piece of plug fell into a cylinder and that was that.

On Saturday morning Hirvonen set off like a scalded cat as he reckoned that he was in a position to score his first win in a World Championship event. His hopes lasted a full 2 kilometres! On landing after a bump he lost control of his Focus. "I wanted push even harder than yesterday," admitted the fiery

are working okay but they're on the limit temperaturewise. The thinner air means that they don't cool in the same way as elsewhere."

The two Championship leaders met with diverse fortunes. Loeb was one of the first out and he had to battle with low grip first time through the day's specials, but he was also a bit at sea with his differential adjustments. After three stages he was 33.1s behind Solberg with Grönholm only just over 4s in front of him.

Once Sébastien got the handling of the Xasra to his liking he was able to up the pace on the stages in the afternoon as they had been well swept. He set the fastest time in Gunajuato (SS5) and then again in El Cubilete (SS6) and pulled back a good chunk of his deficit. At the end of the third stage he was in third place only 9.5s behind Solberg. "It was a day of two very different halves," he declared on his return to Léon. "At midday it was difficult to calculate the sweep factor in the amount of ground lost. I'm very happy with the adjustments made between the two loops and the performance of the BF Goodrichs tyres on the hot, clean surface."

It was Henning Solberg's first time out on gravel in the 307. Petter's elder brother suffered brake problems and then a puncture that obliged him to change a wheel during a special stage.

Marcus Grönholm, who was back on the ex-Michelins after a year of hell with the Pirellis that were totally incompatible with the 307 WRC, should have been a happy bunny as well. Unfortunately, the Ford team leader had fallen back into

Mexico

Dani Sordo's marvellous performance on his first time out on gravel made everybody sit up and take notice. In Mexico, the 2005 Junior Champion came home fourth in his WRC.

Marcus is never one to make excuses. "I came into a left-handed curve too quickly. The car ended up on its side in the ditch and we had to push it to get it back on four wheels. My mistake!" It probably cost him the rally.

Finn. "I arrived on a little hill and the car slid a bit. On landing a rear wheel hit the ground first and the impact sent us cartwheeling off the road onto the side." After Grönholm's misadventure it was all over for Ford as Matthew Wilson had also gone off in the same special as Hirvonen.

So the rally saw the two old sparring partners Solberg and Loeb going at it hammer and tongs. The Citroën driver was quickest in El Zauco (SS8) and took the lead. The Norwegian fought back in the next one and then Loeb was fastest again in Derramedero (SS10). Halfway though the leg they were separated by just two seconds with Solberg in front while Stohl in third was 2m 44s back. "We're on the ragged edge," gasped the Frenchman at the break.

There was no lull in the battle. Loeb set the two quickest times and scraped back in front. Then a strange incident happened in El Zauco second time round. During reconnaissance they had crossed a bridge which they had included in their pace notes. When the Franco-Monegasque pair arrived they saw a barrier in place to prevent it from being crossed. "I grabbed the handbrake and then I went down onto the river bed," explained Sébastien. "I came up the other side and got back on the road." According to the Subaru's readout there was no sign of it slowing down when it crossed the ford! Nonetheless, the battle continued. When the cars set off on Derramadero (SS13) the split times showed that Solberg was pulling away helped by the fact that his rival had to hit the handbrake once again to avoid a herd of cattle blocking the road;

they were standing around the dead body of an animal that Stohl had knocked over. The Norwegian was blasting along until he hit a stone three kilometres after the start breaking his power steering. "It really was a pity having that setback," he moaned. "We were so close to Sébastien." It was a costly error losing him 23.7s. Things got worse in the super special rounding off the day. The Subaru driver made a mistake on this little 4.4 km special, spun and stalled. At the end of the leg he was 37.7s behind Loeb in the lead. "It was a good fight anyway," he grinned. "The most important thing is that we're back on the pace. The car keeps getting better and better. The last leg's going to be exciting. I'm here to win. Even if the eight points for second place are important, I'll do my damnedest to come first."

There were three specials and 60.42 kms left to decide the outcome. Not a lot. Solberg knew it and he drove his heart out. But in the first stage on Sunday, the longest in the rally (37.9 kms) his Subaru's brakes began to overheat and the Norwegian backed off. The Citroën driver was kept informed of the gap along the special and slowed down too. It was all over bar the shouting. Solberg was not too disappointed when he received the flag in second place 48.9s behind the winner. "I'm very very happy with this result. Of course I'd like to have won but that wasn't possible. It shows that we're on our way back to the top. And it's good to have scored some points. Now I want some more. There's still a long way to go."

Loeb was very happy after opening his score in 2006. "It's a good first victory with Kronos," he said gleefully after the finish. "I've collected it in a rally in which I've not had much luck up till now (it was the 14th different World Championship rally that he had won with Elena). And I emerged victorious after a tough battle and that makes it all the more rewarding."

The Kronos team was over the moon. Not only had they won their first World Championship rally, but also Sordo came home in fourth place after a good scrap with Stohl who finished third in his Peugeot 307.

Chris Atkinson was in his usual wheel-twirling mode and pushed the envelope a bit too far, once again. Thanks to the super rally he finished in seventh place.

Daniel Elena and Sébastien Loeb were happy bunnies at the end of the rally. They scored their first win of the season and also went into the lead in the drivers' Championship.

Mexico gave the Belgian team's hopes a big boost in the Championship. The win put Citroën in the lead in the manufacturers' title chase and Loeb was now in front in the drivers' one. Ford and Grönholm's total (he finally finished eighth) were not enough to stem the Franco-Belgian tide. Subaru was back; Loeb and Citroën-Kronos were in front. Grönholm was down but far from out and Sébastien was back on top. There did not seem much to choose between drivers and teams on gravel so the 2006 Championship looked like being a hotly-contested one if what had happened in Central America was anything to go by. ■

PRODUCTION
Araï, makes his comeback

The Production Championship had got off to a slow start in Monte Carlo where Japanese Fumio Nutahara in his Mitsubishi was the class of a very sparse field. It really took off in Mexico as there were twelve crews entered including regulars Araï, Al-Attiyah, Baldacci, Ligato, Pozzo in either Lancers or Imprezas. Jari-Matti Latvala, the former Ford driver and Junior Championship contender, shot off into the lead setting the fastest times in the first two specials. Araï, the reigning champion, who had given Monte Carlo* a miss, was quickly back in the groove and took first place second time through the stages.

Latvala was then delayed by broken transmission and after that Araï was never threatened by his rivals even if Al-Attiyah set four fastest times. The Japanese driver strolled on to another win followed by the man from Qatar 48.9s behind (the same gap that separated Loeb and Solberg) with Baldacci almost 6m back in third! Into the lead in the Championship went Al-Attiyah after his third place in Monaco. It was not Nutahara's lucky day as he was disqualified. The Mitsubishi driver was delayed by a puncture in SS2 and then ran into turbo trouble. He used the tools that Araï had lent him to carry out emergency repairs on the side of the road, which did not go down well with the Stewards and out he went. ■

* It consists of eight rounds and each team must take part in six.

Petter Solberg was well pleased with the 2006 version of the Impreza WRC, which he drove to second place. It boded well for the rest of the season. Which, unfortunately, turned into a nightmare for the Japanese team.

Mexico results

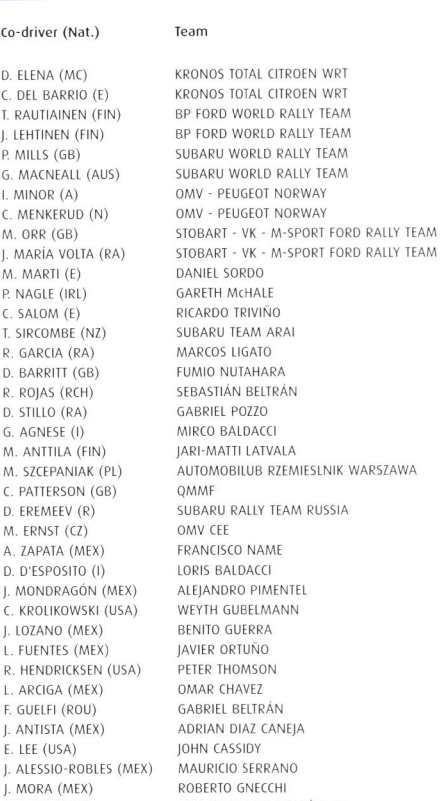

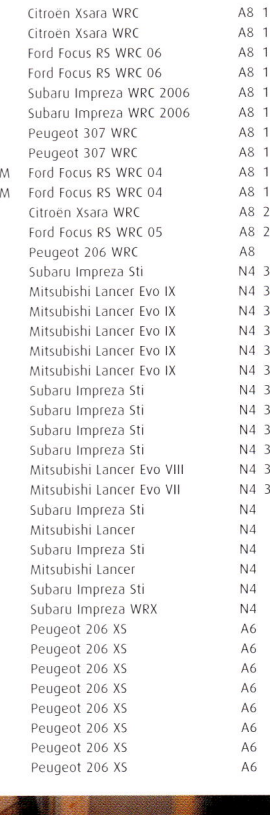

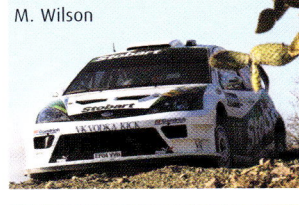

20th RALLY OF MEXICO

Organiser Details
Reforma 2608,
Piso 15,
Lomas Altas,
Mexico DF 11950
Tel.: +44 1483 459555
Fax: +44 7887 508890

Corona Rally Mexico

3rd leg of the 2006 World Rally Championship for constructors and drivers.
2nd leg of FIA Production Car WRC Championship.

Date March 3-5, 2006

Route
1002.47 km divised in 3 legs.
17 special stages on dirt roads (359.54 km)

Starting Procedure
Thursday March 2 (21:00), Guanajuato
Leg 1
Friday Mach 3 (09:37/19:17),
León > León, 452.70 km;
7 special stages (150.20 km)
Leg 2
Saturday March 4 (10:08/19:49),
León > León, 397.70 km;
7 special stages (148.92 km)
Leg 3
Sunday March 5 (08:28/11:26),
León > León, 152.07 km;
3 special stages (60.42 km)

Entry List (42) - 39 starters

N°	Driver (Nat.)	Co-driver (Nat.)	Team	Car	Group & FIA Priority
1.	S. LOEB (F)	D. ELENA (MC)	KRONOS TOTAL CITROEN WRT	Citroën Xsara WRC	A8 1
2.	X. PONS (E)	C. DEL BARRIO (E)	KRONOS TOTAL CITROEN WRT	Citroën Xsara WRC	A8 1
3.	M. GRÖNHOLM (FIN)	T. RAUTIAINEN (FIN)	BP FORD WORLD RALLY TEAM	Ford Focus RS WRC 06	A8 1
4.	M. HIRVONEN (FIN)	J. LEHTINEN (FIN)	BP FORD WORLD RALLY TEAM	Ford Focus RS WRC 06	A8 1
5.	P. SOLBERG (N)	P. MILLS (GB)	SUBARU WORLD RALLY TEAM	Subaru Impreza WRC 2006	A8 1
6.	C. ATKINSON (AUS)	G. MACNEALL (AUS)	SUBARU WORLD RALLY TEAM	Subaru Impreza WRC 2006	A8 1
7.	M. STOHL (A)	I. MINOR (A)	OMV - PEUGEOT NORWAY	Peugeot 307 WRC	A8 1
8.	H. SOLBERG (N)	C. MENKERUD (N)	OMV - PEUGEOT NORWAY	Peugeot 307 WRC	A8 1
9.	M. WILSON (GB)	M. ORR (GB)	STOBART - VK - M-SPORT FORD RALLY TEAM	Ford Focus RS WRC 04	A8 1
10.	L. PEREZ COMPANC (RA)	J. MARÍA VOLTA (RA)	STOBART - VK - M-SPORT FORD RALLY TEAM	Ford Focus RS WRC 04	A8 1
14.	D. SORDO (E)	M. MARTI (E)	DANIEL SORDO	Citroën Xsara WRC	A8 2
15.	G. McHALE (IRL)	P. NAGLE (IRL)	GARETH McHALE	Ford Focus RS WRC 05	A8 2
16.	R. TRIVINO (MEX)	C. SALOM (E)	RICARDO TRIVIÑO	Peugeot 206 WRC	A8
31.	T. ARAI (J)	T. SIRCOMBE (NZ)	SUBARU TEAM ARAI	Subaru Impreza Sti	N4 3
32.	M. LIGATO (RA)	R. GARCIA (RA)	MARCOS LIGATO	Mitsubishi Lancer Evo IX	N4 3
33.	F. NUTAHARA (J)	D. BARRITT (GB)	FUMIO NUTAHARA	Mitsubishi Lancer Evo IX	N4 3
34.	S. BELTRÁN (RA)	R. ROJAS (RCH)	SEBASTIÁN BELTRÁN	Mitsubishi Lancer Evo IX	N4 3
35.	G. POZZO (RA)	D. STILLO (RA)	GABRIEL POZZO	Mitsubishi Lancer Evo IX	N4 3
36.	M. BALDACCI (RSM)	G. AGNESE (I)	MIRCO BALDACCI	Mitsubishi Lancer Evo IX	N4 3
37.	J. LATVALA (FIN)	M. ANTTILA (FIN)	JARI-MATTI LATVALA	Subaru Impreza Sti	N4 3
38.	L. KUZAJ (PL)	M. SZCEPANIAK (PL)	AUTOMOBILUB RZEMIESLNIK WARSZAWA	Subaru Impreza Sti	N4 3
39.	N. AL-ATTIYAH (QAT)	C. PATTERSON (GB)	QMMF	Subaru Impreza Sti	N4 3
42.	S. USPENSKIY (RUS)	D. EREMEEV (R)	SUBARU RALLY TEAM RUSSIA	Subaru Impreza Sti	N4 3
43.	S. VOJTECH (CZ)	M. ERNST (CZ)	OMV CEE	Mitsubishi Lancer Evo VIII	N4 3
60.	F. NAME (MEX)	A. ZAPATA (MEX)	FRANCISCO NAME	Mitsubishi Lancer Evo VII	N4 3
61.	L. BALDACCI (RSM)	D. D'ESPOSITO (I)	LORIS BALDACCI	Subaru Impreza Sti	N4
62.	A. PIMENTEL (MEX)	J. MONDRAGÓN (MEX)	ALEJANDRO PIMENTEL	Mitsubishi Lancer	N4
63.	W. GUBELMANN (USA)	C. KROLIKOWSKI (USA)	WEYTH GUBELMANN	Subaru Impreza Sti	N4
65.	B. GUERRA (MEX)	J. LOZANO (MEX)	BENITO GUERRA	Mitsubishi Lancer	N4
66.	J. ORTUÑO (MEX)	L. FUENTES (MEX)	JAVIER ORTUÑO	Subaru Impreza Sti	N4
67.	P. THOMSON (CAN)	R. HENDRICKSEN (USA)	PETER THOMSON	Subaru Impreza WRX	N4
68.	O. CHAVEZ (MEX)	L. ARCIGA (MEX)	OMAR CHAVEZ	Peugeot 206 XS	A6
69.	G. BELTRÁN (ROU)	F. GUELFI (ROU)	GABRIEL BELTRÁN	Peugeot 206 XS	A6
70.	A. DIAZ CANEJA (MEX)	J. ANTISTA (MEX)	ADRIAN DIAZ CANEJA	Peugeot 206 XS	A6
71.	J. CASSIDY (USA)	E. LEE (USA)	JOHN CASSIDY	Peugeot 206 XS	A6
72.	M. SERRANO (MEX)	J. ALESSIO-ROBLES (MEX)	MAURICIO SERRANO	Peugeot 206 XS	A6
73.	R. GNECCHI (MEX)	J. MORA (MEX)	ROBERTO GNECCHI	Peugeot 206 XS	A6
74.	L. A. RODRÍGUEZ (MEX)	F. ISLAS (MEX)	LUIS ARMANDO RODRÍGUEZ	Peugeot 206 XS	A6
75.	O. URIBE F (MEX)	O. URIBE B (MEX)	OSCAR URIBE	Peugeot 206 XS	A6

Championships

FIA Drivers (3/16)
1. Loeb   1🏆   26
2. Grönholm   2🏆   21
3. Stohl   11
4. P. Solberg   8
5. Gardemeister   6
6. Carlsson   6
7. Sordo   6
8. Galli   5
9. H. Solberg   5
10. Atkinson   5
11. Sarrazin   4
12. Rådström   4
13. Mac Hale   3
14. Katajamäki   3
15. Pons   2
16. Hirvönen   2
17. Joge, Arai, Panizzi, Tuohino, Al-Attiyah Kopecky, Baldacci, Burri, Perez Companc, Aigner, Kuzaj, Wilson, Tsjoen, Hänninen, Uspenskiy, Sandell   0

FIA Constructors (3/16)
1. Kronos Total Citroën WRT   1🏆   34
2. BP-Ford World Rally Team   2🏆   30
3. OMV-Peugeot Norway   21
4. Subaru World Rally Team   20
5. Stobart VK M-Sport Ford WRT   9
6. Red Bull-Skoda Team   3

FIA Production Car WRC (2/8)
1. Al-Attiyah   14
2. Nutahara   1🏆   10
3. Arai   1🏆   10
4. Higgins   8
5. Baldacci   6
6. Marrini   5
7. Kuzaj   5
8. Latvala   4
9. Uspenskiy   4
10. Ligato   3
11. Vojtech   2
12. Name   1
13. Popov   0
14. Pozzo   0

FIA Junior WRC (1/9)
1. Andersson   1🏆   10
2. Sandell   8
3. Aava   6
4. Valousek   5
5. Pinomäki   4
6. Béres   3
7. Zachrisson   2
8. Kosciuszko   1
9. Wilks   0
10. Molder   0
11. Prokop   0
12. Karlsson   0
13. Bordignon   0
14. Cortinovis   0

Special Stages Times

www.rallymexico.com
www.wrc.com

SS1 Ibarrilla 1 (22.40 km)
1.P.Solberg 13'17"3; 2.Hirvonen +6"1;
3.Loeb +12"1; 4.Grönholm +12"3;
5.Atkinson +17"6; 6.Sordo +19"0;
7.Pons +22"1; 8.Stohl +27"0...
P-WRC > 13.Latvala 14'33"5

SS2 Guanajuato 1 (28.87 km)
1.P.Solberg 16'56"4; 2.Hirvonen +2"0;
3.Grönholm +13"0; 4.Loeb +14"4;
5.Atkinson +16"6; 6.Stohl +27"8;
7.Wilson +34"1; 8.Sordo +56"8...
P-WRC > 11.Latvala 18'17"7

SS3 El Cubilete 1 (21.61 km)
1.P.Solberg 12'06"8; 2.Hirvonen +2"3;
3.Grönholm +4"1; 4.H.Solberg +6"2;
5.Loeb +6"6; 6.Stohl +10"7;
7.Atkinson +12"9; 8.Sordo +17"2...
P-WRC > 13.Arai 12'56"2

SS4 Ibarrilla 2 (22.40 km)
1.P.Solberg 13'17"0; 2.Hirvonen +1"1;
3.Loeb +1"2; 4.H.Solberg +5"3;
5.Sordo +10"3; 6.Atkinson +13"0;
7.Stohl +16"5; 8.Wilson +34"8...
P-WRC > 11.Arai 14'33"5

SS5 Guanajuato 2 (28.87 km)
1.Loeb 16'33"9; 2.Hirvonen +8"9;
3.P.Solberg +9"7; 4.Sordo +22"6;
5.Stohl +39"8; 6.Wilson +49"4;
7.McHale +1'24"8; P-WRC >
8.Arai +1'39"5 (18'13"4)

SS6 El Cubilete 2 (21.61 km)
1.Loeb 11'45"4; 2.Hirvonen +5"8;
3.Stohl +10"5; 4.P.Solberg +12"9;
5.Sordo +13"2; 6.H.Solberg +14"2;
7.Wilson +29"1; 8.McHale +38"9...
P-WRC > 10.Arai 12'52"5

SS7 Nextel Superspecial 1 (4.42 km)
1.Stohl 3'21"6; 2.H.Solberg +1"2;
3.Loeb +1"6; 4.Wilson +2"9;
5.P.Solberg +3"8; 6.Hirvonen +5"0;
7.Sordo +8"6; P-WRC > 8.Al-
Attiyah +10"8 (3'32"44)

Classification Leg 1
1.P.Solberg 1h27'44"8;
2.Hirvonen +4"8, 3.Loeb +9"5;
4.Stohl +1'45"9; 5.Sordo +2'01"3;
6.Wilson +2'56"2;
7.McHale/H.Solberg +5'37"3...
P-WRC > 9.Arai 1h35'07"6

SS8 El Zauco 1 (25.22 Km)
1.Loeb 16'30"4; 2.P.Solberg +10"2;
3.Grönholm +20"5; 4.Sordo +29"1;
5.Stohl +31"1; 6.Atkinson +40"7;
7.H.Solberg +41"0;
8.Perez Companc +1'12"4...
P-WRC > 11.Arai 18'18"1

SS9 Duarte 1 (23.75 Km)
1.P.Solberg 18'07"4; 2.Loeb +4"2;
3.Grönholm +14"4; 4.Stohl +17"0;
5.Atkinson +27"0; 6.Sordo +34"6;
7.H.Solberg +59"9; 8.McHale +1'10"3...
P-WRC > 10.Arai 19'36"1

SS10 Derramadero 1 (23.27 Km)
1.Loeb 14'03"6; 2.P.Solberg +1"5;
3.Stohl +18"3; 4.Atkinson +21"3;
5.Sordo +22"5; 6.Grönholm +31"1;
7.H.Solberg +50"2;
8.Perez Companc +1'07"9...
P-WRC > 10.Arai 15'24"9

SS11 El Zauco 2 (25.22 Km)
1.Loeb 16'21"4; 2.P.Solberg +0"3;
3.Grönholm +12"6; 4.Sordo +22"4;
5.Atkinson +23"1; 6.Stohl +23"2;
7.H. Solberg +27"9;
8.Perez Companc +1'22"3...
P-WRC > 10.Arai 18'07"7

SS12 Duarte 2 (23.75 Km)
1.Loeb 17'44"0; 2.P.Solberg +6"5;
3.Atkinson +17"0; 4.Grönholm +17"6;
5.Sordo +20"7; 6.Stohl +12"2;
7.H.Solberg +58"9; 8.McHale +1'12"6...
P-WRC > 10.Al-Attiyah 19'40"8

SS13 Derramadero 2 (23.27 Km)
1.Loeb 13'50"1; 2.Grönholm +10"9;
3.Stohl +18"9; 4.Atkinson +19"0;
5.Sordo +22"9; 6.P.Solberg +23"7;
7.H.Solberg +54"6; 8.McHale +1'00"0...
P-WRC > 10.Arai 15'15"9

SS14 Nextel Superspecial 2 (4.42 km)
1.Loeb 3'21"7; 2.Grönholm +1"9;
3.Stohl +2"2; 4.H.Solberg +4"7;
5.Sordo +6"3; 6.Atkinson/Perez
Companc +7"8; 8.P.Solberg +9"2...
P-WRC > 10.Al-Attiyah 3'34"4

Classification Leg 2
1.Loeb 3h07'57"1; 2.P.Solberg +37"7;
3.Stohl +3'49"7; 4.Sordo +4'21"9;
5.H.Solberg +10'20"8;
6.McHale +13'12"7;
P-WRC > 7.Arai +18'52"1 (3h26'49"2);
8.Trivino +19'28"0...

SS15 León (37.99 Km)
1.Loeb 25'32"1; 2.Grönholm +5"3;
3.P.Solberg +12"6; 4.Stohl +32"2;
5.Atkinson +38"9; 6.Sordo +59"6;
7.Hirvonen +1'00"1; 8.Wilson +1'15"3...
P-WRC > 12.Arai 28'02"5

SS16 Silao (18.10 Km)
1.P.Solberg 10'20"8; 2.Grönholm +0"3;
3.Loeb +1"3; 4.Sordo +6"3;
5.Hirvonen +15"8, 6.Atkinson +18"5;
7.Stohl +19"0; 8.H.Solberg +23"8...
P-WRC > 13.Arai 11'19"6

ES17 Nextel Superspecial 3 (4.42 Km)
1.Stohl 3'17"0; 2.P.Solberg +0"4;
3.Loeb/H.Solberg +0"5; 5.Sordo +1"7;
6.Grönholm +2"1;
7.Perez Companc +3"3;
8.Hirvonen +4"9...
P-WRC > 13.Al-Attiyah 3'29"9

Results 🇲🇽

	Driver - Co-driver	Car	Gr.	Time
1	**Loeb - Elena**	**Citroën Xsara WRC**	A8	**3h47'08"8**
2	P. Solberg - Mills	Subaru Impreza WRC 2006	A8	+ 48"9
3	Stohl - Minor	Peugeot 307 WRC	A8	+ 4'39"1
4	Sordo - Marti	Citroën Xsara WRC	A8	+ 5'27"7
5	H. Solberg - Menkerud	Peugeot 307 WRC	A8	+ 12'35"4
6	McHale - Nagle	Ford Focus RS WRC 05	A8	+ 16'02"3
7	Atkinson - Macneall	Subaru Impreza WRC 2006	A8	+ 20'39"5
8	Grönholm - Rautiainen	Ford Focus RS WRC 06	A8	+ 21'44"2
9	**Arai - Sircombe**	**Subaru Impreza Sti**	N4/P	**+ 22'34"6**
10	Al-Attiyah - Patterson	Subaru Impreza Sti	N4/P	+ 23'23"5
11	Baldacci - Agnese	Mitsubishi Lancer Evo IX	N4/P	+ 28'23"8
27	**Diaz Caneja - Antista**	**Peugeot 206 XS**	A6	**+ 1h22'59"8**

Leading Retirements (6)
TC17D	Trivino - Salom	Peugeot 206 WRC	Excluded
SF8	Pozzo - Stillo	Mitsubishi Lancer Evo IX	Engine
TC7D	Pons - Del Barrio	Citroën Xsara WRC	Engine
TC7D	Beltrán - Rojas	Mitsubishi Lancer Evo IX	Off
SF6	Nutahara - Barritt	Mitsubishi Lancer Evo IX	Excluded

Performers

	1	2	3	4	5	6	C6	N°SS
Loeb	9	1	5	1	1	-	17	17
P. Solberg	6	5	2	1	1	1	17	17
Stohl	2	-	3	2	3	4	14	17
Hirvonen	-	6	-	-	1	1	8	10
Grönholm	-	4	5	2	-	2	13	13
H. Solberg	-	1	1	3	-	1	6	17
Sordo	-	-	1	4	6	3	14	17
Atkinson	-	-	1	2	5	4	12	14
Wilson	-	-	-	1	-	1	2	10
Perez-Companc	-	-	-	-	-	1	1	15

Leaders

SS1 > SS7	P. Solberg
SS8	Loeb
SS9 > SS11	P. Solberg
SS12 > SS17	Loeb

Previous winners

2004	Märtin - Park	2005	P. Solberg - Mills
	Ford Focus RS WRC 03		Subaru Impreza WRC 2005

Spain

Loeb triumphs again

Sébastien Loeb and Daniel Elena won again on asphalt. Unfortunately, a shadow was cast over the rally by the accidental death of Jörg Bastuck, the co-driver of a Citroën C2, who was hit by another car when he was changing a wheel. Loeb's success was his twenty-second and he increased his lead in the drivers' World Championship over Grönholm who finished third in Spain.

Spain

THE RALLY
Another blow to Ford's hopes...

Marcus Grönholm likes asphalt. The mighty Finn should already have won many rallies on this surface, with the exception of Monte Carlo, which is an atypical event in itself. But his one major stumbling block is called Sébastien Loeb. In addition, he has often been unlucky and his occasional fits of red mist have not helped things either leading to his retirement on numerous occasions. In Spain, Grönholm was in a brand-new Focus which was very much at home on this kind of surface and his BF Goodrich tyres were just what the doctor ordered. He went for it right from the start and on the long sweeping stages in the Spanish rally he set the fastest times in the first three stages dominating his rivals with almost insolent ease. His performance was overshadowed by Bastuck's fatal accident (see below).

Dani Sordo was obviously inspired by his home crowd. The young Spaniard drove a mind-boggling rally and finished second behind Loeb giving Kronos its first double of the season.

The reigning world champion was unbeatable on the Catalonian asphalt despite a few brake and set-up problems in the first leg.

At the end of the third special (Querol 2) he was 11.1s ahead of Sébastien Loeb who seemed a bit perplexed by this. The Citroën driver had a brake problem on the first stage; he had not chosen the same tyres as Grönholm but what really worried him was his car's set-up. The Ford seemed glued to the road helped by its very efficient aerodynamics.

In the fourth special Loeb fought back and managed to reduce the Finn's lead by 1.8s but he did not really know how to up his pace even more.

Lady Luck was to come to his help. A third of the way through the next stage (SS5, Colldejou) the Focus suddenly slowed with a broken turbo so the

Marcus Grönholm was determined to win his first 100% asphalt rally. A belt problem on the water pump put a premature end to his hopes.

4-cylinder engine was unable to give its full power. A few minutes later Hirvonen in the second Ford was the victim of the same problem in almost exactly the same spot when he was in fourth place overall. The rally had been turned on its head in the space of just a few minutes. Grönholm had no time for repairs between the fifth and sixth specials and he tackled no.6 (Riudecanyes) in a very sick motorcar. Overall he lost 2m 42s. "It's very difficult to race without a turbo," he complained. "All the more so as it went from bad to worse and there was nothing I could do about it. The turbo is placed just behind the engine and it was all so hot that I couldn't repair it between the two stages. It's all the more disappointing, as we didn't meet this kind of problem in testing before the rally. It was all going so well. For the first time I was actually dominating Sébastien on asphalt!"

Hirvonen was more severely hit losing a total of 4m 30s. This meant that the two Ford drivers were now too far behind to

Mikko Hirvonen was not yet on the same level on asphalt as his team leader. Nonetheless, the Ford no.2 put on a good performance before technical problems led to his retirement.

Alexandre Bengué was the pick of the 307 WRC drivers and had a good Catalonian rally. He held third for a long time until Grönholm snatched it from him in the closing stages.

hope to fight back to the front in the remaining two legs. At the end of the first Grönholm was in tenth place 2m 33.6s behind Loeb while Hirvonen was down in fourteenth over 5 minutes in arrears. Three Citroëns were in the first three places led by the Frenchman followed by Sordo and Pons 27.3s and 1m 01.5 s behind respectively. In fourth was Petter Solberg a bit surprised at being so well placed.
The new Pirelli asphalt rubber were more at home on this surface than usual but they were still not good enough to allow the Norwegian and his team-mates Stéphane Sarrazin and Chris Atkinson to take the fight to the leaders on BF Goodrich tyres. "It's been a good day," said Solberg in his usual optimistic manner. "I'm pretty happy with the car which is much quicker than last year's on asphalt. We've still got a lot of work to do but we're on the right track. We're going to have to drive like crazy to hold on to our places."
All Loeb had to do in the second leg was to control his lead over Dani Sordo. The reigning WRC Junior Champion really showed his talent in this event, only his fourth World Championship rally, and in his private Xsara matched the pace of the Frenchman. In the tenth special (Duesaigües) he set his first-ever fastest time in the World Championship, and kept up the pressure on Loeb who was obliged to keep pushing to fend off the young Spaniard. His fellow-countryman Xavier Pons did not exactly distinguish himself in the same stage. Loeb's Kronos team-mate went off in a slow left-hander when his car suddenly lost all grip. The Citroën slipped down a slope into a small ravine in an incident that recalled his team-mate's in the 2006 Monte Carlo Rally. His retirement let Alexandre Bengué into third place in his 307 WRC entered by the Beuzelin team. It was a good performance by the former French asphalt champion (2003) who was in Catalonia to prepare for the Tour of Corsica. However, he had a fire-breathing Marcus Grönholm on his tail as the Finn had put in another of his amazing comeback drives. He set three fastest times out of a possible six and ended the day only 4.1s behind Bengué.
When the third leg began he quickly swallowed up the Frenchman and came first in all four specials held that day. But there were no worries up front for an unruffled Loeb who won the Spanish Rally from Daniel Sordo.
"After my problems on Friday, the car went like a dream," smiled Marcus. "Honestly, when I found myself in tenth place I really didn't think I'd finish on

François Duval was back in the WRC at the wheel of a Skoda. He scored his first 3 points in the 2006 Championship after setting one fastest time.

Spain

Petter Solberg already had to cope with a difficult start to the 2006 season. Things did not get much better on asphalt on which the Impreza and its Pirellis were not at home despite fourth place at the end of the first leg.

Reigning Junior Champion Dani Sordo made a big impression in Catalonia in what was only his fourth event at the wheel of a WRC.

Skoda expected a lot from François Duval. In fact, it was Kopecky who shone for the Cezch make finishing in fourth place.

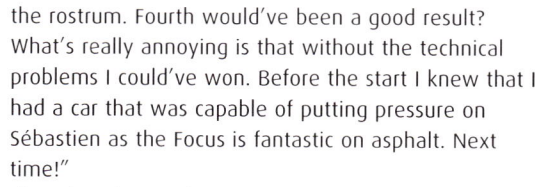

the rostrum. Fourth would've been a good result? What's really annoying is that without the technical problems I could've won. Before the start I knew that I had a car that was capable of putting pressure on Sébastien as the Focus is fantastic on asphalt. Next time!"

The other driver who left his mark on this event was Dani Sordo, Carlos Sainz's protégé. The young Spaniard at the wheel of his 2005 competition-client Xsara gave Kronos its first World Championship double and confirmed his position as one of the rally stars of the future.

In addition to Sordo another couple of drivers proved that they have what it takes to make it to the top in the World Championship: Alexandre Bengué and Jan Kopecky. The Frenchman finished fourth and Kopecky in a Skoda Fabia came home in fifth place in front of some of the more fancied runners in the Championship. The rally provided a lot of information about the speed of certain drivers and opened up fresh horizons for Sébastien Loeb.

It was his second victory after Mexico and he increased his lead over Grönholm and Sordo. Next up was the Tour of Corsica before which he was down to do some testing at the wheel of the Pescarolo in view of the 2006 Le Mans 24 Hours. Sébastien left Spain still ruminating over Grönholm's fantastic comeback in the event. ■

THE JUNIORS
Tragedy and a first

The Catalonian rally was the scene of the second round of the 2006 Junior Championship, which saw a first with the victory of the Czech pairing of Prokop-Tomanek in a Citroën C2. Not only had no Czech driver ever won a rally at this level, but it was also the best result by an inhabitant of this country in the World Championship.

Unfortunately, a tragic accident overshadowed their performance. During the second special (El Montmell 1) German Jörg Bestuck, Aaron Burkhart's co-driver, was killed when he was hit by another car. The two guys were in the process of repairing their Citroën after an off. Bestuck was just finishing putting on a wheel when an out-of-control Group N Ford Fiesta driven by Brits Barry Clark-Scott Martin knocked him over. He was immediately helicoptered to the nearest hospital where he succumbed to his injuries. Thirty-six-year-old Bestuck, a passionate rally enthusiast and a former co-driver for names like Roman Kresta, was helping out his young fellow-countryman who was making his Junior World Championship debut. It was an avoidable accident that cast a pall over the whole event.

The rally continued, however. Kris Meeke (Citroën C2) opening up a gap over his rivals right from the start until El Montmell second time round. It was the fourth special and he hit Latvala's Ford Focus WRC that had

A few cheesy grins from the Subaru team. Once again the rally was a disappointment for both drivers and team members.

Sébastien Loeb's second win on the trot increased his lead in the drivers' Championship. His performance was saluted by the Spanish crowd, which knows a thing or two about rallying.

Prokop from Czechoslovakia (Citroën) scored his first victory in the Junior Championship. The event was marred by German Jörg Bastuck's death. He was Aaron Burkart's co-driver and succumbed to his injuries after being hit by another car.

broken down and was stopped on the side of the road. The impact sliced a tyre that came off soon afterwards. He finished the stage on three wheels and lost 2m 32s allowing Prokop to take the lead. Meeke went pedal to metal afterwards and set fourteen fastest times out of the sixteen possible (the other two going to the Czech) but he was unable to make up lost ground and finished third behind Bernd Casier from Belgium in his Renault Clio and Prokop. Bernd had come under severe pressure from Frenchman Julien Pressac until the engine on the Citroën Challenge Champion's C2 went bang! Despite the accident Prokop was very happy with his win: "I was hoping for a good result before the rally, but not victory. The team did a lot of hard work and the car was the best I've ever driven on asphalt. New car, new co-driver; it's really great." He was all the more delighted as his victory propelled him into the joint lead in the Championship with Swede Andersson, winner of the first round held in Sweden, who had decided to give the Spanish event a miss. ∎

Spain results

42nd RALLYE OF CATALUNYA

Organiser Details
RACC - Area Esportiva,
Av Diagonal 687,
08028 Barcelona,
Spain
Tél.: +3493 4955029
Fax: +3493 4482490

Rally RACC Catalunya – Costa Daurada

4th leg of FIA 2006 World Rally Championship for constructors and drivers.
2nd leg of FIA WRC Junior Championship.

Date March 24 - 26, 2006

Route
1376.14 km divised in 3 legs.
16 special stages on tarmac (346.43 km)

Starting Procedure
Thursday, March 23 (20:00),
Podium Salou
Leg 1
Friday, March 24 (08:05/17:24),
Port Aventura > Port Aventura, 532.57 km;
6 special stages (137.25 km)
Leg 2
Saturday, March 25 (07:50/15:18),
Port Aventura > Port Aventura, 477.62 km;
6 special stages (111.36 km)
Leg 3
Sunday, March 26 (07:53/13:08),
Port Aventura > Salou, 365.95 km;
4 special stages (97.82 km)

Entry List (71) - 66 starters

N°	Driver (Nat.)	Co-driver (Nat.)	Team	Car	Group & FIA Priority
1.	S. LOEB (F)	D. ELENA (MC)	KRONOS TOTAL CITROEN WRT	Citroën Xsara WRC	A8 1
2.	X. PONS (E)	C. DEL BARRIO (E)	KRONOS TOTAL CITROEN WRT	Citroën Xsara WRC	A8 1
3.	M. GRÖNHOLM (FIN)	T. RAUTIAINEN (FIN)	BP FORD WORLD RALLY TEAM	Ford Focus RS WRC 06	A8 1
4.	M. HIRVONEN (FIN)	J. LEHTINEN (FIN)	BP FORD WORLD RALLY TEAM	Ford Focus RS WRC 06	A8 1
5.	P. SOLBERG (N)	P. MILLS (GB)	SUBARU WORLD RALLY TEAM	Subaru Impreza WRC 2006	A8 1
6.	S. SARRAZIN (F)	S. PREVOT (B)	SUBARU WORLD RALLY TEAM	Subaru Impreza WRC 2006	A8 1
7.	M. STOHL (A)	I. MINOR (A)	OMV - PEUGEOT NORWAY	Peugeot 307 WRC	A8 2
9.	M. WILSON (GB)	M. ORR (GB)	STOBART - VK - M-SPORT FORD RALLY TEAM	Ford Focus RS WRC 04	A8 1
10.	J. LATVALA (FIN)	M. ANTTILA (FIN)	STOBART - VK - M-SPORT FORD RALLY TEAM	Ford Focus RS WRC 04	A8 1
11.	G. PANIZZI (F)	H. PANIZZI (F)	RED BULL - SKODA TEAM	Skoda Fabia WRC	A8 1
12.	A. AIGNER (A)	T. GOTTSCHALK (D)	RED BULL - SKODA TEAM	Skoda Fabia WRC	A8 1
15.	D. SORDO (E)	M. MARTI (E)	DANIEL SORDO	Citroën Xsara WRC	A8 2
16.	C. ATKINSON (AUS)	G. MACNEALL (AUS)	SUBARU AUSTRALIA	Subaru Impreza WRC 2005	A8 2
17.	G. MAC HALE (IRL)	P. NAGLE (IRL)	GARETH MAC HALE	Ford Focus RS WRC 04	A8 2
18.	F. DUVAL (B)	P. PIVATO (F)	FIRST MOTORSPORT	Skoda Fabia WRC	A8 2
19.	A. BENGUÉ (F)	C. ESCUDERO (F)	ALEXANDRE BENGUÉ	Peugeot 307 WRC	A8 2
21.	J. KOPECKY (CZ)	F. SCHOVÁNEK (CZ)	CZECH RALLY TEAM SKODA- KOPECKY	Skoda Fabia WRC	A8 2
22.	S. VOJTECH (CZ)	M. ERNST (CZ)	OMV RALLY TEAM	Peugeot 206 WRC	A8 2
23.	S. PEREZ (GB)	S. HARRIS (GB)	STEVE PEREZ	Ford Focus 2005 WRC	A8 2
32.	K. MEEKE (GB)	G. PATTERSON (GB)	KRIS MEEKE	Citroën C2	A6 3
36.	L. BETTI (E)	P. CAPOLONGO (I)	LUCA BETTI	Renault Clio Super 1600	A6 3
39.	C. RAUTENBACH (ZW)	D. SENIOR (GB)	CONRAD RAUTENBACH	Renault Clio	A6 3
42.	J. PRESSAC (F)	G. DE TURCKHEIM (F)	JULIEN PRESSAC	Citroën C2	A6 3
44.	M. KOSCIUSZKO (PL)	J. BARAN (PL)	MICHAL KOSCIUSZKO	Suzuki Ignis S1600	A6 3
45.	J. BERES (SK)	P. STAR? (CZ)	JOZEF BERES	Suzuki Ignis	A6 3
47.	F. A. BORDIGNON (I)	J. BARDINI (I)	FILIPPO BORDIGNON	Opel Astra OPC	N3 3
49.	M. PROKOP (CZ)	J. TOMÁNEK (CZ)	JIPOCAR CZECH NATIONAL TEAM	Citroën C2	A6 3
50.	K. PINOMÄKI (FIN)	M. MARKKULA (FIN)	KALLE PINOMÄKI	Renault Clio RS Ragnotti	N3 3
51.	F. KARA (TR)	C. BAKANCOCUKLARI (TR)	FATIH KARA	Renault Clio S1600	A6 3
52.	B. CASIER (B)	F. MICLOTTE (B)	BERND CASIER	Renault Clio S1600	A6 3
53.	B. CLARK (GB)	S. MARTIN (GB)	STOBART, VK	Ford Fiesta	N3 3
54.	A. Nicolai BURKART (D)	J. BASTUCK (D)	BURKART AARON NICOLAI	Citroën C2 GT	A6 3
55.	B. TIRABASSI (F)	J. RENUCCI (F)	PH-SPORT	Citroën C2	A6 3
61.	M. BARRETT (IRL)	B. GOODMAN (IRL)	BARRY GOODMAN	Subaru Impreza WRC	A8
62.	J. ZURITA (E)	M. MUÑOZ (E)	BAPORO MOTORSPORT	Seat Cordoba WRC	A8
66.	M. CANELLA (I)	S. GRIA (I)	CANELLA MASSIMO	Renault Clio	A6
67.	A. PIATTO (I)	F. VACCA (I)	4 AS SPORT-FN SPECIALCARS	Renault Clio S1600	A6
68.	S. PINTARELLI (I)	M. MARCHIORI (I)	SILVANO PINTARELLI	Renault Clio S1600	A6
69.	P. FONT (E)	B. FLUXÀ (E)	ESC. CIUTAT DE MANACOR DA-LIGAS	Peugeot 206 Super 1600	A6
70.	A. ORRIOLS (E)	J. RIBA (E)	ESCUDERIA VOLTEGRÀ	Subaru Impreza STI	N4
71.	O. SVEDLUND (S)	B. NILSSON (S)	OSCAR SVEDLUND	Subaru STI N12	N4
72.	T. KUHLMANN (D)	D. RUF (D)	THORSTEN KUHLMANN	Mitsubishi Carisma Evo IV	N4
73.	F. FRISIERO (I)	J. BARRABÉS (E)	FABIO FRISIERO	Mitsubishi Lancer Evo VIII	N4
74.	A. LLOVERA (AND)	L. S. CRUZ (E)	ALBERT LLOVERA	Mitsubishi Lancer Evo VIII	N4
75.	T. CSERHALMI (SK)	M. HULKA (CZ)	TIBOR CSERHALMI	Mitsubishi Lancer	N4
76.	S. JONES (GB)	C. PARRY (GB)	STUART JONES	Mitsubishi Evo IX	N4
77.	H. WENG (SWE)	A. FREDRIKSSON (S)	HANS-ERIK WENG	Mitsubishi Lancer Evo VIII	N4
78.	S. CANALS (E)	J. PUCHOL (E)	ESCUDERIA PENEDÈS	Mitsubishi Lancer Evo VIII	N4
79.	M. BIASION (F)	C. BÉYNET (F)	MATHIEU BIASION	Ford Fiesta ST	N3
80.	A. BETTEGA (I)	S. SCATOLLIN (I)	TRT Srl	Ford Fiesta ST	N3
81.	K. KESKINEN (FIN)	J. KOLJONEN (FIN)	KALLE KESKINEN	Ford Fiesta ST	N3
82.	G. SCHAMMEL (LUX)	R. JAMOUL (B)	JPS JUNIOR TEAM LUXEMBOURG	Ford Fiesta ST	N3
83.	S. HUGHES (GB)	C. MOLE (GB)	SIMON HUGHES	Ford Fiesta ST	N3
84.	L. ATHANASSOULAS (GR)	N. MOUZAKIS (GR)	TEAM GREECE	Ford Fiesta ST	N3
85.	T. CURTIS (GB)	A. BARGERY (GB)	TOM CURTIS	Ford Fiesta ST	N3
86.	Y. PHILIPPEDES (GR)	M. CLARKE (GB)	YORGO PHILIPPEDES	Ford Fiesta ST	N3
87.	S. PEREZ (E)	P. MARCOS (E)	SERGIO PEREZ DONOSTI	Peugeot 206 RC	N3
88.	E. MIR (E)	S. ORIHUELA (E)	MCS. MOTOR CLUB SABADELL	Renault Clio Sport	N3
89.	R. MONTLLEO (E)	R. SUBIRANAS (E)	MCS. MOTOR CLUB SABADELL	Renault Clio Sport	N3
90.	A. GIBERT (E)	E. CODINA (E)	ESCUDERIA OSONA	Renault Clio RS	N3
91.	J. FORNELL (E)	O. SANCHEZ (E)	GAMACE MC COMPETICIÓ	Renault Clio RS S	N3
92.	C. PUIG (E)	J. ANTICH (E)	ESCUDERIA COSTA DAURADA	Renault Clio RS 2000	N3
93.	F. LEYMARIE (F)	P. VIEUX-ROCHAT (F)	FRANCIS LEYMARIE	Peugeot 306 16S	N3
94.	J. Mª LOPEZ (E)	A. DOMINGUEZ (E)	ESCUDERIA LALIN-DEZA	Peugeot 206 RC	N3
95.	C. SCHMIDT (D)	M. SCHENDY (D)	CHRISTIAN SCHMIDT	Suzuki Ignis Sport	N2
96.	J. Antonio MARTÍNEZ DEL RIO (E)	D. BERNARDEZ (E)	ESCUDERIA RIAS BAJAS	Fiat Seicento Sporting	A5

Championship Classifications

FIA Drivers (4/16)

1. Loeb — 2🏆 36
2. Grönholm — 2🏆 27
3. Sordo — 14
4. Stohl — 11
5. P. Solberg — 10
6. Gardemeister — 6
7. Carlsson — 6
8. Galli — 5
9. Bengué — 5
10. Sarrazin — 5
11. H. Solberg — 5
12. Atkinson — 5
13. Rådström — 4
14. Kopecky — 4
15. Mac Hale — 3
16. Katajamäki — 3
17. Duval — 3
18. Hirvönen — 2
19. Pons — 2
20. Joge, Arai, Panizzi... — 0

FIA Constructors (4/16)

1. Kronos Total Citroën WRT — 2🏆 44
2. BP-Ford World Rally Team — 2🏆 42
3. Subaru World Rally Team — 31
4. OMV-Peugeot Norway — 21
5. Stobart VK M-Sport Ford WRT — 10
6. Red Bull-Skoda Team — 8

FIA Production Car (2/8)

1. Al-Attiyah — 14
2. Nutahara — 1🏆 10
3. Arai — 1🏆 10
4. Higgins — 8
5. Baldacci — 6
6. Marrini — 5
7. Kuzaj — 5
8. Latvala — 4
9. Uspenskiy — 4
10. Ligato — 3
11. Vojtech — 2
12. Name — 1
13. Popov — 0
14. Pozzo — 0

FIA Junior WRC (2/9)

1. Prokop — 1🏆 10
2. Andersson — 1🏆 10
3. Sandell — 8
4. Casier — 8
5. Béres — 8
6. Aava — 6
7. Meeke — 6
8. Valousek — 5
9. Kosciuszko — 5
10. Pinomäki — 4
11. Rautenbach — 3
12. Zachrisson — 2
13. Kara — 2
14. Tirabassi — 1
15. Bordignon — 0
16. Wilks — 0
17. Molder — 0
18. Karlsson — 0
19. Cortinovis — 0

Special Stages Times

www.rallycatalunya.com
www.wrc.com

SS1 Querol 1 (25.43 km)
1.Grönholm 13'36"7; 2.Loeb +6"1;
3.Hirvonen +9"2; 4.Sordo +15"9;
5.Pons +17"3; 6.Kopecky +21"2;
7.P.Solberg +21"8; 8.Atkinson +26"0...
J-WRC > 18.Meeke 15'18"0

SS2 El Montmell 1 (24.14 km)
1.Grönholm 12'35"6; 2.Loeb +1"2;
3.Sordo +3"0; 4.Hirvonen +8"5;
5.P.Solberg +11"2; 6.Bengué +13"1;
7.Pons +14"3; 8.Kopecky +16"4...
J-WRC > 18.Meeke 13'50"3

SS3 Querol 2 (25.43 km)
1.Grönholm 13'44"4; 2.Loeb +3"8;
3.Sordo +5"5; 4.Hirvonen +6"4;
5.Pons +7"6; 6.Kopecky +16"4;
7.Sarrazin +17"6; 8.Duval +18"0...
J-WRC > 18.Meeke 15'18"9

SS4 El Montmell 2 (24.14 km)
1.Loeb 12'31"8; 2.Grönholm +1"8;
3.Sordo +2"6; 4.Hirvonen +5"2;
5.Pons +5"3; 6.P.Solberg +10"7;
7.Bengué +14"7; 8.Kopecky +15"5...
J-WRC > 17.Prokop 14'09"7

SS5 Colldejou 1 (26.51 km)
1.Loeb 15'42"1; 2.Sordo +7"3;
3.Pons +13"0; 4.Bengué +14"1;
5.P.Solberg +20"0; 6.Sarrazin +20"3;
7.Kopecky +21"0; 8.Atkinson +31"1...
J-WRC > 16.Meeke 17'09"1

SS6 Riudecanyes 1 (11.60 km)
1.Loeb 7'45"3; 2.Sordo +4"1;
3.Bengué +13"4; 4.P.Solberg +14"4;
5.Pons +15"1; 6.Stohl +16"4;
7.Kopecky +16"6; 8.Sarrazin +18"0...
J-WRC > 15.Prokop 8'44"3

Classification Leg 1
1.Loeb 1h16'07"0; 2.Sordo +27"3;
3.Pons +1'01"5; 4.P.Solberg +1'25"6;
5.Bengué +1'32"6; 6.Kopecky +1'36"0;
7.Sarrazin +1'50"4;
8.Atkinson +2'25"5...
J-WRC > 17.Prokop 1h25'32"5

SS7 Duesaigües 1 (11.50 km)
1.Hirvonen/Grönholm/Duval 7'47"8;
4.Pons +4"7; 5.Bengué +5"1;
6.Loeb +6"3; 7.Stohl +8"0;
8.Panizzi +8"7...
J-WRC > 17.Meeke 8'37"6

SS8 Vilaplana 1 (28.33 Km)
1.Grönholm 16'36"4; 2.Hirvonen +0"9;
3.Sordo +6"4; 4.Panizzi +12"3;
5.Pons +12"4; 6.Loeb +13"0;
7.Bengué +15"4; 8.Kopecky +20"2...
J-WRC > 18.Meeke 18'23"2

SS9 Margalef - la Palma d'Ebre 1 (15.85 Km)
1.Loeb 9'35"2; 2.Grönholm +0"9;
3.Bengué +9"0; 4.Hirvonen +9"8;
5.Duval +11"4; 6.Sordo +13"1;
7.Pons/Latvala +14"0...
J-WRC > 18.Meeke 10'33"7

SS10 Duesaigües 2 (11.50 Km)
1.Sordo 8'04"7; 2.Grönholm +1"0;
3.Kopecky +1"3; 4.Bengué +2"3;
5.Loeb +3"6; 6.Panizzi +4"9;
7.Hirvonen +5"9; 8.Latvala +6"2...
J-WRC > 17.Meeke 8'43"9

SS11 Vilaplana 2 (28.33 Km)
1.Grönholm 16'44"7; 2.Sordo +1"0;
3.Hirvonen +2"5; 4.Loeb +6"0;
5.Bengué/Panizzi +15"8;
7.Kopecky +17"9; 8.Duval +24"9...
J-WRC > 15.Meeke 18'14"5

SS12 Margalef - la Palma d'Ebre 2 (15.85 Km)
1.Loeb 9'33"2; 2.Grönholm +2"9;
3.Sordo +4"8; 4.Hirvonen +5"0;
5.Latvala +10"8; 6.Duval +13"1;
7.Kopecky +13"5; 8.Atkinson +13"7...
J-WRC > 16.Meeke 10'35"5

Classification Leg 2
1.Loeb 2h24'57"9; 2.Sordo +34"4;
3.Bengué +2'05"4;
4.Grönholm +2'09"5;
5.Kopecky +2'23"9; 6.Duval +3'30"2;
7.P.Solberg +3'42"0;
8.Sarrazin +3'56"5...
J-WRC > 17.Prokop 2h42'20"4

SS13 El Lloar - La Figuera 1 (22.43 Km)
1.Grönholm 12'41"5; 2.Panizzi +2"3;
3.Bengué +2"5; 4.Duval +2"8;
5.Loeb +3"8; 6.Hirvonen +4"2;
7.Latvala +6"3; 8.P.Solberg +6"8...
J-WRC > 17.Meeke 13'41"3

SS14 Pratdip 1 (26.48 Km)
1.Grönholm 15'36"5; 2.Bengué +8"2;
3.Loeb +8"6; 4.Hirvonen +9"3;
5.P.Solberg +12"0; 6.Duval +13"2;
7.Sordo +14"8; 8.Latvala +15"6...
J-WRC > 17.Meeke 17'01"6

SS15 El Lloar - La Figuera 2 (22.43 Km)
1.Grönholm 12'41"5; 2.Hirvonen +2"9;
3.Sordo +3"0; 4.P.Solberg +4"6;
5.Kopecky +4"7; 6.Bengué +5"6;
7.Duval +5"7; 8.Latvala +8"4...
J-WRC > 16.Meeke 13'43"8

SS16 Pratdip 2 (26.48 Km)
1.Grönholm 15'40"6; 2.Loeb +2"0;
3.Bengué +3"9; 4.Hirvonen +5"2;
5.P.Solberg +6"5; 6.Latvala +9"3;
7.Duval +9"6; 8.Atkinson +10"4...
J-WRC > 15.Meeke 17'00"9

Results

	Driver - Co-driver	Car	Gr.	Time
1	**Loeb - Elena**	**Citroën Xsara WRC**	A8	**3h22'01"7**
2	Sordo - Marti	Citroën Xsara WRC	A8	+ 48"2
3	Grönholm - Rautiainen	Ford Focus RS WRC 06	A8	+ 1'45"8
4	Bengué - Escudero	Peugeot 307 WRC	A8	+ 2'01"9
5	Kopecky - Schovanek	Skoda Fabia WRC 05	A8	+ 2'57"2
6	Duval - Privato	Skoda Fabia WRC 05	A8	+ 3'37"8
7	P. Solberg - Mills	Subaru Impreza WRC 2006	A8	+ 3'48"2
8	Sarrazin - Prévot	Subaru Impreza WRC 2006	A8	+ 4'36"4
9	Hirvonen - Lehtinen	Ford Focus RS WRC 06	A8	+ 5'01"6
10	Panizzi - Panizzi	Skoda Fabia WRC 05	A8	+ 5'04"4
17	**Prokop - Tomanek**	**Citroën C2**	A6/J	+ 24'02"3
18	Casier - Miclotte	Renault Clio S1600	A6/J	+ 24'44"6
19	Meeke - Patterson	Citroën C2	A6/J	+ 25'07"7
22	**Svedlund - Nilsson**	**Subaru Sti N12**	N4	+ 27'58"6

Leading Retirements (10)

TC12D	Pons - Del Barrio	Citroën Xsara WRC	Off
TC12D	Betti - Capolongo	Renault Clio Super 1600	Off
TC12D	Pressac - De Turckheim	Citroën C2	Engine
SF2	Burkart - Bastuck	Citroën C2 GT	Accident
SF1	Mac Hale - Nagle	Ford Focus RS WRC 04	Off

Performers

	1	2	3	4	5	6	C6	NbSS
Grönholm	10	4	-	-	-	-	14	16
Loeb	5	4	1	2	1	2	15	16
Sordo	1	3	6	1	-	1	12	16
Hirvonen	1	2	2	7	-	1	13	16
Duval	1	-	-	1	1	2	5	16
Bengué	-	1	4	2	1	3	11	16
Panizzi	-	1	-	1	1	1	4	16
Pons	-	-	1	1	5	-	7	9
Kopecky	-	-	1	-	1	2	4	16
P. Solberg	-	-	-	2	4	1	7	16
Latvala	-	-	-	-	1	1	2	13
Sarrazin	-	-	-	-	-	1	1	16
Stohl	-	-	-	-	1	1	16	

Leaders

SS1 > SS4	Grönholm
SS5 > SS16	Loeb

Previous winners

1991	Schwarz - Hertz	1996	McRae - Ringer	2001	Auriol - Giraudet
	Toyota Celica GT-Four		Subaru Impreza		Peugeot 206 WRC
1992	Sainz - Moya	1997	Mäkinen - Harjanne	2002	Panizzi - Panizzi
	Toyota Celica Turbo 4WD		Mitsubishi Lancer Evo IV		Peugeot 206 WRC
1993	Delecour - Grataloup	1998	Auriol - Giraudet	2003	Panizzi - Panizzi
	Ford Escort RS Cosworth		Toyota Corolla WRC		Peugeot 206 WRC
1994	Bertone - Chiapponi	1999	Bugalski - Chiaroni	2004	Märtin - Park
	Toyota Celica Turbo 4WD		Citroën Xsara Kit Car		Ford Focus RS WRC 04
1995	Sainz - Moya	2000	C. McRae - Grist	2005	Loeb - Elena
	Subaru Impreza		Ford Focus WRC		Citroën Xsara WRC

Martin Prokop

France

05

01 02 03 04 05 06 07 08 09 10 11 12 13 14 15 16

Loeb wins in a canter on home turf.
Sébastien Loeb came out on top again in another asphalt rally. He won in a canter from Marcus Grönholm, who was less of a threat than in Spain, tightening his stranglehold on the drivers' World Championship classification. Daniel Soro showed that his performance in Catalonia was no flash in the pan by taking third on the French island, and also third overall in the Championship ratings.

France

Sébastien Loeb and Daniel Elena scored another dominant victory in Corsica less than 6 months after their previous record-breaking success in the same event.

Mikko Hirvonen was not really at home in the Corsican heat. He looked good for third for a long time but the Ford no.2 was passed by Dani Sordo and came home fourth.

Nicolas Vouilloz wanted to get in some practice in a 307 WRC for the French Championship. He ended the first leg in eighth place and on Saturday morning hit a wall at the entry to a bridge.

THE RALLY
A doddle for Loeb

Sébastien Loeb talked up the threat posed by Marcus Grönholm in his new Ford Focus on BF Goodrich tyres after the Finn's performance in Catalonia. The Frenchman reckoned that Marcus was in with a good chance of stealing victory in this rally in which he (Loeb) had achieved the unique exploit of winning all the stages in 2005. Five months after the previous Tour of Corsica, the protagonists in the World Championship arrived on the French island in the spring for the fiftieth running of the event to tackle a layout that was the spitting image of the one on which Loeb had achieved his feat. Everybody was expected a daggers-drawn duel between Loeb/Elena and Grönholm/Rautiainen as each pair had won two rallies so far in 2006. The action began straight away. Loeb put on an awesome performance in the first stage (Ampaza-col Saint Eustache) with a time of 20m 45.5s the quickest ever on the 32,8 km special shattering his own record by 17 seconds! Grönholm hit back immediately and snatched fastest time in the next stage between Aullène and Arbellara 3.4s ahead of the Frenchman who still had a small lead (4.9s). "I wonder if I didn't back off a little after opening up a lead of over 8 seconds in the first stage. I didn't push as hard as I could have in the second." He made up for this with the two fastest times in the following stages: Ampazza-col Saint Eustache 2: 20m 48.8s and Aullène-Arbellara 2: 15m 51.4s. At the end of the first leg that consisted of only 4 stages Loeb was in the lead with 19.9s in hand over Grönholm. It was in keeping with the early-season pattern.

" I lost time on Sébastien at the end of this first leg," grumbled the Finn, "and I don't really know why. Maybe it was the driver as there was nothing wrong with the car. I used hard tyres in the rally for the first time and I wasn't really used to them. Overall, I wasn't very happy with my driving. So it's going to be very difficult tomorrow in the second leg."

If Grönholm was unhappy, Loeb was delighted. "In Catalonia when I got the car really set up to my liking; Marcus had a problem. So I was curious to see what would happen here. It's like we expected; it's very close and the Xsara is really flying. I had to push very hard. It's tense but not too scary. We'll have to try and continue like that."

Behind the two leaders Alexandre Bengué put on another good performance in his 307 WRC, and took over third place overall behind Grönholm and Loeb in front of Hirvonen and Sordo in fourth and fifth both of whom had better cars. The Subarus were having a very disappointing event so far. They were completely outpaced and in addition were victims of either technical or driving errors. In SS1 Solberg went off and lost 1m 30s and in the following one he ran into gearbox problems. In the middle of SS3 Atkinson spun and destroyed his exhausts after which his gearbox also began to act up.

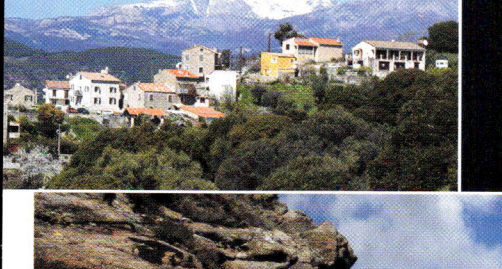

François Duval was not able to take part in the shakedown tests due to brake problems. He tried to do his best in the rally itself but went off at the end of the second leg when his brakes failed.

performance. He had set a fastest time in Spain and repeated this exploit in Corsica during the second leg, which he finished in third place. In contrast, Bengué's day was a rather disappointing one. He had to struggle with ill-chosen settings on his 307 in relation to the previous afternoon and lost second after second; he was overtaken by Sordo and Hirvonen separated by under 6 seconds both of whom had designs on third place overall in the rally.

In the second leg Loeb set two quickest times while the other two fell to Hirvonen (SS6, Uciani-Bastelica) and Sordo (SS8, Uciani-Bastelica 2). Grönholm was completely out of it. "Sébastien was very quick and I was not happy with my pace. I felt that the car was not 100% in the morning so I didn't push too hard, as the roads were very tricky. They were covered with gravel and very twisty. Not my cup of tea, really! Driving was like being on the razor's edge. I used more classic damper settings, as they were the only things that had changed since the day before. I don't know if I'm going to push tomorrow. Second is not too bad and I'm not in a position to tempt fate to try for a victory that's out of my reach." Grönholm's reasoning was perfectly logical. He was 39.7s behind the Frenchman who was in control of the situation. "I went for it in the first stage and then I based my rhythm on Marcus's," said the cunning Alsatian. "It seems like he's backed off a little. I'm happier as always when I have a bit of a lead. And the Xsara is really fantastic in the narrow, twisty sections." This was not the case for the Ford that was very much at home on the wide Catalonian roads but ill at ease on the island hairpins. The Citroën camp was very impressed not only with Loeb's stranglehold on the event, but even more so by Dani Sordo's

The only interest of the third leg was the battle between the Spaniard and the second Ford driver. Sordo set another fastest time in SS10 (Pont de Calzola-Agosta) and managed to fend off his Scandinavian rival so the overall classification was the same for the first eight as the previous day.

Ford was hoping to put one over on Citroën in Corsica, but despite Grönholm's Homeric efforts there was no catching Loeb.

Stéphane Sarrazin was the Subaru star on asphalt. Despite a hard-charging drive the Frenchman was unable to compensate for the team's overall lack of competitiveness.

France

Grönholm set two fastest times but it was not enough to close the gap to Loeb. At the finish 29s separated them. It was another very successful rally for Kronos with two cars on the rostrum after its Catalonian success. Indeed, its three cars finished in the first six places as Xavier Pons came home sixth. "Both Marcus and I had a fairly untroubled event" said Loeb afterwards. "The Xsara and the BF Goodrich tyres were very quick, the team made no mistakes and we won this round which is very important for us. It's in Corsica and it's an event that I like. What's more, it's the French rally in front of my home crowd. It's a very precious victory as I now have a 10-point lead in the drivers' Championship. It gives me a little breathing space because it's going to be a whole lot tougher in the next rallies that are on gravel. Looking a bit further ahead it brings me closer to Carlos Sainz's record that I'd really like to beat!"

Grönholm was in two minds about the rally in which he would have liked to have carried the fight to Loeb so he left it to his team boss Malcolm Wilson, to sum things up. "This second place comforted by Mikko's fourth proves that we're on the pace before we tackle rallies that are more suitable for our car. What's more apart from Citroën we're the only team to have won specials in this event, which is a real boost for me." A little bit of self-congratulation in the face of the Xsara's domination was not a bad thing for the Blue Oval's morale.

Alexandre Bengué finished in the points behind the two Fords and the two Xsaras outclassing Pons and Stohl (also in a 307 WRC), and Stéphane Sarrazin the only Subaru driver to survive what was another disastrous rally for the Japanese make. ∎

Xavier Pons had a hard time on the "Island of Beauty" as the French call Corsica! He was Loeb's team-mate in a car that was identical to the one driven by the new star in the rally firmament, Dani Sordo, and put on a pretty dismal performance.

Alexandre Bengué was back in the World Championship after his drive in Catalonia again at the wheel of a BSA 307 WRC. He was in third place at the end of the first leg after a fault-free drive.

Petter Solberg's poor performance was not due to a slight off on Friday. The reason was his 2006 Subaru Impreza that was totally off the pace.

THE JUNIORS
Tirabassi's comeback

Kris Meeke Kris Meeke knows what it's like to go quickly but learned to his cost that a rally lasts three days. Two weeks earlier in Spain the Ulsterman had gone straight into the lead. He did the same thing in Corsica in his C2 but at the end of the first special he was in second spot. He then racked up the fastest times in four stages on the trot and pulled out a big lead over second-placed man Urmo Aava (Suzuki) and almost 2m 30s on Tirabassi. Such was Meeke's domination that he looked well on the way to victory at this early stage.

Manfred Stohl was still suffering from the after-effects of his accident in Spain and was unable to get the best out of his Bozian-entered Peugeot 307 WRC.

This is a very heavy right foot when it comes to pressing an accelerator!

But like Julien Pressac in Catalonia Meeke's car's engine went bang at the twenty-seventh kilometre in the seventh special, and it was all over for the driver from Northern Ireland. Aava took up the running but not for long as he was badly delayed by electrical gremlins in his little Japanese car towards the end of the rally. "I hit problems in the middle of the eleventh stage," complained the Estonian. "We lost ignition on one of the 4 cylinders. In the following one we lost it on anther cylinder but we battled onto the finish. That's racing but it's a pity as the car was really good. And I'm also pretty happy about the speed we've shown on asphalt."

Brice Tirabassi emerged a surprise winner. "What a remarkable finish," laughed the Frenchman. "When we caught Aava after eight kilometres in the last special, my co-driver reckoned that we could beat him. So in the final sprint I really really pushed. It's a great result and I can't wait to be in Sardinia." Tirabassi won with only 8.2s in hand over the unfortunate Aava with the Zimbabwean Rautenbach almost 3mn behind in third place. It was not all gloom and doom for Aava as he went into the Junior Championship lead after the Corsican rally thanks to his second place on the island and third in Sweden. He was 2 points ahead of Czech Beres, fifth in the French Rally, who was the only driver to have scored points in all three rounds held so far. ∎

Loeb's third win of the 2006 season put him in the running for another World Championship title. But it was to be more difficult than he had imagined!

Dani Sordo drove an awesome rally in Corsica although hit by a few minor electrical problems.

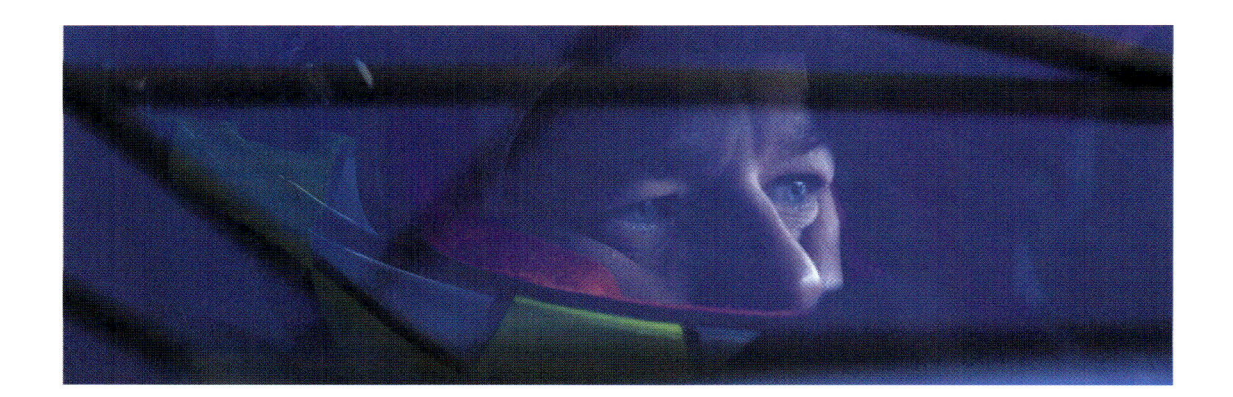

France results

50th RALLY OF FRANCE

Organiser Details
FFSA,
17 - 21 Avenue du General Mangin,
75781 Paris Cedex 16,
France
Tel.: +33 (0)4 95 23 61 43
Fax: +33 (0)4 95 23 61 55

Tour de Corse - Rally of France -

5th leg of FIA 2006 World Rally Championship for constructors and drivers.
3rd leg of FIA WRC Junior Championship.

Date April 7-9, 2006

Route
1045.68 km divised in 3 legs.
12 special stages on tarmac (354.18 km)

Starting Procedure
Thursday, April 6 (20:00),
Ajaccio, Place d'Austerlitz
Leg 1
Friday, April 7 (09:38/15:27),
Ajaccio > Ajaccio, 395,68 km;
4 special stages (121.34 km)
Leg 2
Saturday, April 8 (09:53/16:32),
Ajaccio > Ajaccio, 406.07 km;
4 special stages (120.74 km)
Leg 3
Sunday, April 9 (08:08/12:17),
Ajaccio > Ajaccio, 243.93 km;
4 special stages (112.10 km)

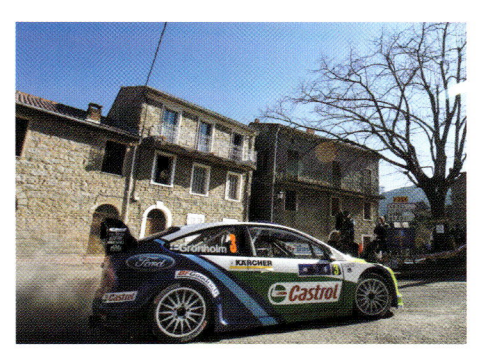

Entry List (79) - 75 starters

N°	Driver (Nat.)	Co-driver (Nat.)	Team	Car	Group & FIA Priority
1.	S. LOEB (F)	D. ELENA (MC)	KRONOS TOTAL CITROEN WRT	Citroën Xsara WRC	A8 1
2.	X. PONS (E)	C. DEL BARRIO (E)	KRONOS TOTAL CITROEN WRT	Citroën Xsara WRC	A8 1
3.	M. GRÖNHOLM (FIN)	T. RAUTIAINEN (FIN)	BP FORD WORLD RALLY TEAM	Ford Focus RS WRC 06	A8 1
4.	M. HIRVONEN (FIN)	J. LEHTINEN (FIN)	BP FORD WORLD RALLY TEAM	Ford Focus RS WRC 06	A8 1
5.	P. SOLBERG (N)	P. MILLS (GB)	SUBARU WORLD RALLY TEAM	Subaru Impreza WRC 2006	A8 1
6.	S. SARRAZIN (F)	S. PREVOT (B)	SUBARU WORLD RALLY TEAM	Subaru Impreza WRC 2006	A8 1
7.	M. STOHL (A)	I. MINOR (A)	OMV - PEUGEOT NORWAY	Peugeot 307 WRC	A8 2
9.	M. WILSON (GB)	M. ORR (GB)	STOBART - VK - M-SPORT FORD RALLY TEAM	Ford Focus RS WRC 04	A8 1
10.	J. LATVALA (FIN)	M. ANTTILA (FIN)	STOBART - VK - M-SPORT FORD RALLY TEAM	Ford Focus RS WRC 04	A8 1
11.	H. ROVANPERÄ (FIN)	R. PIETILÄINEN (FIN)	RED BULL - SKODA TEAM	Skoda Fabia WRC	A8 1
12.	A. AIGNER (A)	T. GOTTSCHALK (D)	RED BULL - SKODA TEAM	Skoda Fabia WRC	A8 1
15.	D. SORDO (E)	M. MARTI (E)	DANIEL SORDO	Citroën Xsara WRC	A8 2
16.	C. ATKINSON (AUS)	G. MACNEALL (AUS)	SUBARU AUSTRALIA	Subaru Impreza WRC 2005	A8 2
17.	J. KOPECKY (CZ)	F. SCHOVANEK (CZ)	CZECH RALLY TEAM SKODA- KOPECKY	Skoda Fabia WRC	A8 2
18.	F. DUVAL (B)	P. PIVATO (F)	FIRST MOTORSPORT	Skoda Fabia WRC	A8 2
19.	A. BENGUE (F)	C. ESCUDERO (F)	ALEXANDRE BENGUE	Peugeot 307 WRC	A8 2
20.	N. VOUILLOZ (F)	J. BOYERE (F)	EQUIPE DE FRANCE FFSA	Peugeot 307 WRC	A8 2
21.	P. ROUX (CH)	E. JORDAN (CH)	OMV - PEUGEOT NORWAY	Peugeot 206 WRC	A8 2
25.	G. GALLI (I)	G. BERNACCHINI (I)	GIANLUIGI GALLI	Peugeot 307 WRC	A8 2
32.	K. MEEKE (GB)	G. PATTERSON (GB)	KRIS MEEKE	Citroën C2	A6 3
33.	U. AAVA (EE)	K. SIKK (EE)	URMO AAVA	Suzuki Swift S1600	A6 3
36.	L. BETTI (E)	P. CAPOLONGO (I)	LUCA BETTI	Renault Clio S1600	A6 3
37.	P. VALOUSEK (CZ)	P. SCALVINI (CZ)	PAVEL VALOUSEK	Suzuki Swift S1600	A6 3
39.	C. RAUTENBACH (ZW)	D. SENIOR (GB)	CONRAD RAUTENBACH	Renault Clio S1600	A6 3
42.	J. PRESSAC (F)	G. DE TURCKHEIM (F)	JULIEN PRESSAC	Citroën C2	A6 3
45.	J. BERES (SK)	P. STARY (CZ)	JOZSEF BERES	Suzuki Ignis S1600	A6 3
46.	A. CORTINOVIS (I)	M. BOSSI (I)	ANDREA CORTINOVIS	Renault Clio	N3 3
50.	J. PINOMÄKI (FIN)	M. SALLINEN (FIN)	KALLE PINOMÄKI	Renault Clio RS Ragnotti	N3 3
51.	F. KARA (TR)	C. BAKANCOCUKLARI (TR)	FATIH KARA	Renault Clio S1600	A6 3
52.	B. CASIER (B)	F. MICLOTTE (B)	BERND CASIER	Renault Clio S1600	A6 3
53.	B. CLARK (GB)	S. MARTIN (GB)	STOBART - VK - M-SPORT FORD RALLY TEAM	Ford Fiesta ST	N3 3
54.	A. Nicolai BURKART (D)	T. GEILHAUSEN (D)	AARON NICOLAI BURKART	Citroën C2 GT	A6 3
55.	B. TIRABASSI (F)	J. JULIEN RENUCCI (F)	PH-SPORT	Citroën C2	A6 3
59.	Y. BONATO (F)	B. BOULLOUD (F)	EQUIPE DE FRANCE FFSA	Renault Clio S1600	A6 3
61.	F. LEANDRI (F)	G. LUIGI (F)	FRANÇOIS LEANDRI	Subaru Impreza	A8
62.	J. MICHELI (F)	M. MACCIONI (F)	JOSÉ MICHELI	Peugeot 206 WRC	A8
63.	S. CRNOJEVIC (CR)	M. MARETIC (CR)	SINISA CRNOJEVIC	Skoda Fabia RS TDi	A8
64.	M. VALLICCIONI (F)	M. Josée POYO CHANZA (F)	MARC VALLICCIONI	Mitsubishi Lancer Evo VII	N4
65.	G. FIORI (F)	C. BLANC RAFFINI (F)	GUY FIORI	Mitsubishi Lancer Evo VIII	N4
66.	M. BRANCA (F)	G. FORNS (F)	MICHEL BRANCA	Mitsubishi Lancer Evo VII	N4
67.	G. TANEV (BUL)	P. SIVOV (BG)	GEORGES TANEV	Subaru Impreza	N4
68.	D. ILIEV (BG)	Y. YANAKIEV (BG)	DIMITAR ILIEV	Mitsubishi Lancer Evo IX	N4
69.	J. MATTEI (F)	U. GREGORJ (F)	JEAN-DOMINIQUE MATTEI	Mitsubishi Lancer Evo IX	N4
70.	M. LEANDRI (F)	E. BURESI (F)	MARC LEANDRI	Mitsubishi Lancer	N4
71.	L. OTTO (CZ)	M. FANTA (CZ)	LUDVIK OTTO	Subaru Impreza	N4
72.	P. HEINTZ (CH)	R. SCHERRER (CH)	PATRICK HEINTZ	Subaru STI	N4
73.	H. GUIGNARD (F)	D. MEFFRE (F)	HERVE GUIGNARD	Mitsubishi Lancer Evo VIII MR	N4
74.	S. VOUILLON (F)	J. IMBERT (F)	STEPHANE VOUILLON	Subaru STI	N4
75.	T. CSERHALMI (SK)	M. HULKA (CZ)	TIBOR CSERHALMI	Mitsubishi Lancer	N4
76.	J. BARBOLOSI (F)	P. POLI (I)	JULIEN BARBOLOSI	Peugeot 306 Maxi	A7
77.	J. POISSON (F)	O. LESIGNE (F)	JEAN-MARC POISSON	Honda Integra	A7
78.	J. Michel RAOUX (F)	S. POGUT (F)	JEAN MICHEL RAOUX	Citroën C2 Challenge	A6
79.	J. SUCCI (F)	M. ANZIANI (F)	JEAN-FRANCOIS SUCCI	Citroën Saxo Kit Car	A6
80.	J. MUSELLI (F)	F. BUFFA (F)	JEAN-PHILIPPE MUSELLI	Citroën Saxo VTS	A6
82.	M. PROKOP (CZ)	J. TOMANEK (CZ)	MARTIN PROKOP	Citroën C2	A6
83.	C. BENSIMON (F)	J. Paul MARCHINI (F)	CLAUDE BENSIMON	Citroën Saxo VTS	A6
84.	P. COLLEIE (F)	F. POISSON (F)	PATRICK COLLEIE	Citroën Saxo 16S	A6
85.	F. ANDREUCCI (F)	J. Michel PERRIN (F)	FRÉDÉRIC ANDREUCCI	Renault Clio Cup	A6
86.	B. MURACCIOLI (F)	D. FOLACCI (F)	BASTIEN MURACCIOLI	Peugeot 206 XS	A6
87.	J. CASABIANCA (F)	L. VITALI (F)	JACQUES CASABIANCA	Peugeot 306 S16	N3
88.	P. QUILICI (F)	B. GRANGIE BIANCAMARIA (F)	PIERRE QUILICI	Renault Clio	N3
89.	S. ROVINA (F)	T. BARICHELLA (F)	STÉPHANE ROVINA	Renault Clio Ragnotti	N3
90.	P. Antoine GUGLIELMI (F)	G. CLER (F)	PIERRE ANTOINE GUGLIELMI	Renault Clio RS	N3
91.	P. GIOVANNI (F)	J. CASAMATTA (F)	PHILIPPE GIOVANNI	Peugeot 206 RC	N3
92.	J. Jean PAPINI (F)	E. FOURMY (F)	JACQUES JEAN PAPINI	Peugeot 206 RC	N3
93.	S. PEREZ DONOSTI (E)	P. MARCOS SELADES (E)	SERGIO PEREZ DONOSTI	Peugeot 206 RC	N3
94.	J. FABREGAT (F)	T. PIGEYRE (F)	JACQUES FABREGAT	Renault Clio Ragnotti	N3
95.	D. CASANOVA (F)	K. RENUCCI (F)	DENIS CASANOVA	Peugeot 206 RC	N3
96.	A. BETTEGA (I)	S. SCATOLIN (I)	TRT S.R.L	Ford Fiesta ST	N3
97.	M. BIASION (F)	C. BEYNET (F)	MATHIEU BIASION	Ford Fiesta ST	N3
98.	S. HUGHES (GB)	C. MOLE (GB)	SIMON HUGHES	Ford Fiesta ST	N3
99.	G. SCHAMMEL (LUX)	R. JAMOUL (B)	JPS JUNIOR TEAM LUXEMBOURG	Ford Fiesta ST	N3
100.	K. KESKENEN (FIN)	J. KOLJONEN (FIN)	PROGRESS MOTORSPORT	Ford Fiesta ST	N3
102.	L. ATHANASSOULAS (GR)	N. MOUZAKIS (GR)	TEAM GREECE	Ford Fiesta ST	N3
103.	E. VERTUNOV (RUS)	G. TROSHKIN (RUS)	EVGENY VERTUNOV	Ford Fiesta ST	N3

C. Rautenbach
G. Galli 
B. Tirabassi 
H. Rovanperä 
Y. Bonato 

Championship Classifications

FIA Drivers (5/16)
1. Loeb — 3🏆 46
2. Grönholm — 2🏆 35
3. Sordo — 20
4. Stohl — 13
5. P. Solberg — 10
6. Bengué — 9
7. Hirvonen — 7
8. Gardemeister — 6
9. Carlsson — 6
10. Sarrazin — 6
11. Galli — 5
12. H. Solberg — 5
13. Atkinson — 5
14. Pons — 5
15. Rådström — 4
16. Kopecky — 4
17. Mac Hale — 3
18. Katajamäki — 3
19. Duval — 3
20. Joge, Arai, Panizzi... — 0

FIA Constructors (5/16)
1. Kronos Total Citroën WRT — 3🏆 59
2. BP-Ford World Rally Team — 2🏆 56
3. Subaru World Rally Team — 38
4. OMV-Peugeot Norway — 21
5. Red Bull-Skoda Team — 11
6. Stobart VK M-Sport Ford WRT — 10

FIA Production Car (2/8)
1. Al-Attiyah — 14
2. Nutahara — 1🏆 10
3. Arai — 1🏆 10
4. Higgins — 8
5. Baldacci — 6
6. Marrini — 5
7. Kuzaj — 5
8. Latvala — 4
9. Uspenskiy — 4
10. Ligato — 3
11. Vojtech — 2
12. Name — 1
13. Popov — 0
14. Pozzo — 0

FIA Junior WRC (3/9)
1. Aava — 14
2. Béres — 12
3. Tirabassi — 1🏆 11
4. Prokop — 1🏆 10
5. Andersson — 1🏆 10
6. Rautenbach — 9
7. Sandell — 8
8. Casier — 8
9. Meeke — 6
10. Valousek — 5
11. Pressac — 5
12. Kosciuszko — 5
13. Kara — 5
14. Pinomäki — 4
15. Zachrisson — 2
16. Burkart — 2
17. Bonato — 1
18. Bordignon — 0
19. Wilks — 0
20. Clark — 0
21. Molder — 0
22. Cortinovis — 0
23. Karlsson — 0

Special Stages Times

www.rallyedefrance.com
www.wrc.com

SS1 Ampaza - Col St Eustache 1 (32.89 km)
1.Loeb 20'45"5; 2.Grönholm +8"3;
3.Pons +31"3; 4.Bengué +32"2;
5.Hirvonen +32"7; 6.Duval +36"5;
7.Stohl +40"3; 8.Vouilloz +40"8...
J-WRC > 19.Tirabassi 22'51"1

SS2 Aullène - Arbellara 1 (27,78 km)
1.Grönholm 15'49"8; 2.Loeb +3"4;
3.Bengué +15"1; 4.Sordo +17"5;
5.Hirvonen +20"6; 6.Pons +24"2;
7.Latvala +24"4; 8.Vouilloz +25"7...
J-WRC > 19.Meeke 17'14"0

SS3 Ampaza - Col St Eustache 2 (32.89 km)
1.Loeb 20'48"8; 2.Grönholm +10"6;
3.Sordo +18"0; 4.Hirvonen +18"5;
5.Bengué +25"1; 6.Pons +28"0;
7.Latvala +28"9; 8.Stohl +29"6...
J-WRC > 18.Meeke 22'51"8

SS4 Aullène - Arbellara 2 (27.78 km)
1.Loeb 15'51"4; 2.Grönholm +4"4;
3.Bengué +6"6; 4.Sordo +8"8;
5.Hirvonen +15"0; 6.Sarrazin +17"9;
7.Latvala +23"5; 8.Galli +24"3...
J-WRC > 19.Meeke 17'18"4

Classification Leg 1
1.Loeb 1h13'18"9; 2.Grönholm +19"9;
3.Bengué +1'15"6; 4.Hirvonen +1'23"4;
5.Sordo +1'36"6; 6.Pons +1'44"6;
7.Latvala +1'54"4; 8.Vouilloz +2'04"5...
J-WRC > 18.Meeke 1h20'15"4

SS5 Vico - Col de Sarzoggiu 1 (34.17 km)
1.Loeb 24'05"6; 2.Sordo +6"7;
3.Grönholm +7"8; 4.Pons +10"7;
5.Hirvonen +12"7; 6.Latvala +16"5;
7.Bengué +24"0; 8.Stohl +26"2...
J-WRC > 15.Meeke 26'15"9

SS6 Ucciani - Bastelica 1 (26.20 km)
1.Hirvonen 16'56"9; 2.Sordo +1"6;
3.Loeb +4"9; 4.Grönholm +6"2;
5.Bengué +9"7; 6.Pons +15"6;
7.Galli +18"5; 8.Stohl +19"9...
J-WRC > 14.Aava 18'35"6

SS7 Vico - Col de Sarzoggiu 2 (34,17 km)
1.Loeb 24'03"6; 2.Sordo +3"1;
3.Grönholm +3"7; 4.Hirvonen +9"7;
5.Bengué +14"1; 6.Pons +16"7;
7.Sarrazin +24"0; 8.Stohl +29"2...
J-WRC > 15.Aava 26'19"9

SS8 Ucciani - Bastelica 2 (26.20 km)
1.Sordo 16'56"8; 2.Loeb +4"7;
3.Hirvonen +7"9; 4.Grönholm +11"7;
5.Galli +15"6; 6.Pons +18"4;
7.Sarrazin/Stohl +24"5...
J-WRC > 15.Aava 18'46"7

Classification Leg 2
1.Loeb 2h35'31"4; 2.Grönholm +39"7;
3.Sordo +1'38"4; 4.Hirvonen +1'44"1;
5.Bengué +2'28"4; 6.Pons +2'36"4;
7.Stohl +3'40"6; 8.Sarrazin +4'16"2...
J-WRC > 14.Aava 2h51'00"0

SS9 Penitencier Coti Chiavari - Pietra Rossa 1 (24.24 Km)
1.Loeb 14'43"0; 2.Grönholm +0"5;
3.Hirvonen +3"1; 4.Sordo +8"4;
5.Bengué/Pons +9"6;
7.P.Solberg +13"4; 8.Sarrazin +17"9...
J-WRC > 16.Bonato 16'19"6

SS10 Pont de Calzola - Agosta 1 (31.81 Km)
1.Sordo 18'57"7; 2.Grönholm +0"4;
3.Loeb +0"5; 4.Bengué +4"6;
5.Hirvonen +7"3; 6.Pons +12"6;
7.Sarrazin +16"6; 8.Stohl +17"9...
J-WRC > 16.Bonato 20'47"9

SS11 Penitencier Coti Chiavari - Pietra Rossa 2 (24.24 Km)
1.Grönholm 14'44"7; 2.Hirvonen +0"6;
3.Sordo +3"1; 4.Loeb +6"8;
5.Pons +7"6; 6.Bengué +9"8;
7.Sarrazin +15"2; 8.Galli +15"9...
J-WRC > 16.Bonato 16'19"5

SS12 Pont de Calzola - Agosta 2 (31.81 Km)
1.Grönholm 18'57"0; 2.Loeb +4"3;
3.Bengué +6"9; 4.Sordo +10"4;
5.Pons +15"6; 6.Hirvonen +15"7;
7.Galli +22"2; 8.Kopecky +25"3...
J-WRC > 16.Bonato 20'45"5

Results

	Driver - Co-driver	Car	Gr.	Time
1	Loeb - Elena	Citroën Xsara WRC	A8	3h43'05"4
2	Grönholm - Rautiainen	Ford Focus RS WRC 06	A8	+ 29'0
3	Sordo - Marti	Citroën Xsara WRC	A8	+ 1'48"7
4	Hirvonen - Lehtinen	Ford Focus RS WRC 06	A8	+ 1'59"2
5	Bengué - Escudero	Peugeot 307 WRC	A8	+ 2'47"7
6	Pons - Del Barrio	Citroën Xsara WRC	A8	+ 3'10"2
7	Stohl - Minor	Peugeot 307 WRC	A8	+ 5'01"3
8	Sarrazin - Prévot	Subaru Impreza WRC 2006	A8	+ 5'21"9
9	Galli - Bernacchini	Peugeot 307 WRC	A8	+ 5'42"5
10	Kopecky - Schovanek	Skoda Fabia WRC 05	A8	+ 6'11"4
14	**Tirabassi - Renucci**	**Citroën C2**	A6/J	+ 26'15"8
17	Aava - Sikk	Suzuki Swift S1600	A6/J	+ 28'08"2
18	Rautenbach - Senior	Renault Clio S1600	A6/J	+ 29'09"2
21	**Valliccioni - Poyo Chanza**	**Mitsubshi Lancer Evo VII**	N4	+ 33'15"7

Leading Retirements (15)

TC12A	Prokop - Tomanek	Citroën C2	Off
SF8	Duval - Privato	Skoda Fabia WRC 05	Off
SF7	Meeke - Patterson	Citroën C2	Engine
SF6	Latvala - Anttila	Ford Focus RS WRC 04	Off
TC6	Vouilloz - Boyère	Peugeot 307 WRC	Off
TC6	Betti - Capolongo	Renault Clio S1600	Off

Performers

	1	2	3	4	5	6	C6	Nb SS
Loeb	6	3	2	1	-	-	12	12
Grönholm	3	5	2	2	-	-	12	12
Sordo	2	3	2	4	-	-	11	12
Hirvonen	1	1	2	2	5	1	12	12
Bengué	-	-	3	2	4	1	10	12
Pons	-	-	1	1	3	6	11	12
Galli	-	-	-	-	1	-	1	12
Sarrazin	-	-	-	-	-	1	1	12
Latvala	-	-	-	-	-	1	1	5

Leader

SS1 > SS12	Loeb

Brice Tirabassi

Previous winners

1973	Nicolas - Vial / Alpine Renault A 110
1974	Andruet - "Biche" / Lancia Stratos
1975	Darniche - Mahé / Lancia Stratos
1976	Munari - Maiga / Lancia Stratos
1977	Darniche - Mahé / Fiat 131 Abarth
1978	Darniche Mahé / Fiat 131 Abarth
1979	Darniche - Mahé / Lancia Stratos
1980	Thérier - Vial / Porsche 911SC
1981	Darniche - Mahé / Lancia Stratos
1982	Ragnotti - Andrié / Renault 5 Turbo
1983	Alen - Kivimaki / Lancia Rally 037
1984	Alen - Kivimaki / Lancia Rally 037
1985	Ragnotti - Andrié / Renault 5 Turbo
1986	Saby - Fauchille / Peugeot 205 T16
1987	Béguin - Lenne / BMW M3
1988	Auriol - Occelli / Ford Sierra RS Cosworth
1989	Auriol - Occelli / Lancia Delta Integrale
1990	Auriol - Occelli / Lancia Delta Integrale
1991	Sainz - Moya / Toyota Celica GT-Four
1992	Auriol - Occelli / Lancia Delta HF Integrale
1993	Delecour - Grataloup / Ford Escort RS Cosworth
1994	Auriol - Occelli / Toyota Celica Turbo 4WD
1995	Auriol - Giraudet / Toyota Celica GT-Four
1996	Bugalski - Chiaroni / Renault Maxi Megane
1997	McRae - Grist / Subaru Impreza WRC
1998	McRae - Grist / Subaru Impreza WRC
1999	Bugalski - Chiaroni / Citroën Xsara Kit Car
2000	Bugalski - Chiaroni / Peugeot 206 WRC
2001	Puras - Marti / Citroën Xsara WRC
2002	Panizzi - Panizzi / Peugeot 206 WRC
2003	Solberg - Mills / Subaru Impreza WRC 2003
2004	Märtin - Park / Ford Focus RS WRC 04
2005	Loeb - Elena / Citroën Xsara WRC

Argentina

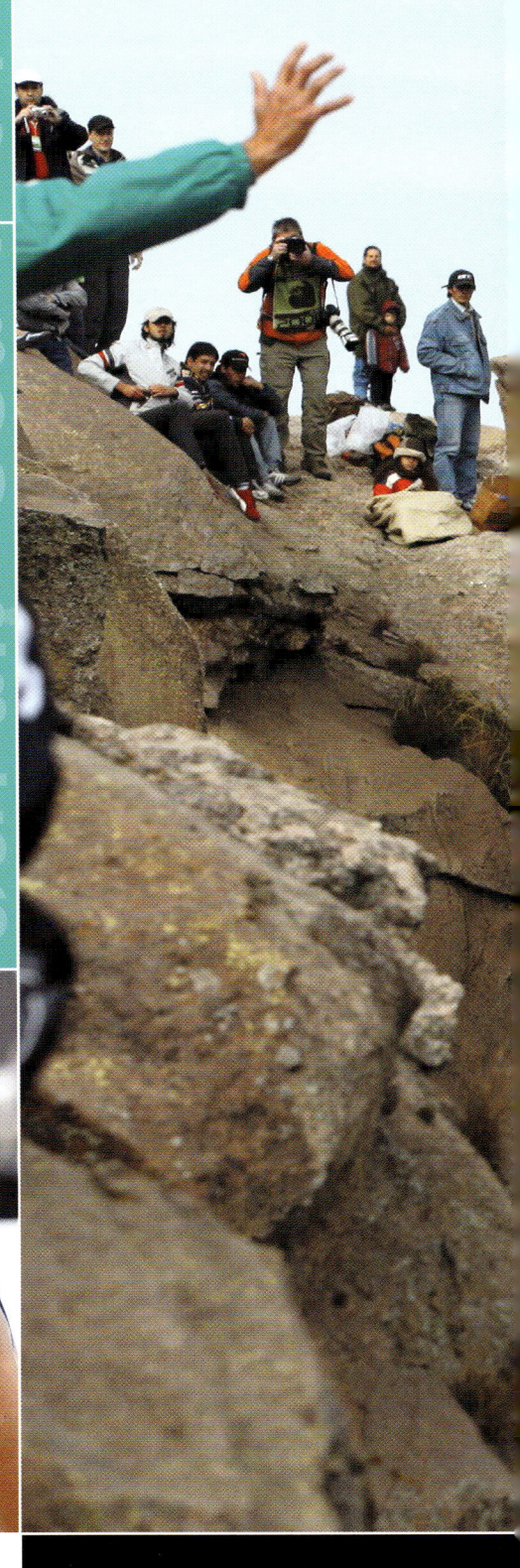

06

01 02 03 04 05
07 08 09 10 11 12 13 14 15 16

No stopping Loeb
Grönholm was slowed by technical problems. Solberg fought his way back to the front but was never in a position to challenge for victory. Loeb and Elena won the sixth round of the 2006 World championship, their twenty-fourth as well as their fourth on the trot. After an exciting start the event was a bit of an anti-climax. The first leg saw Loeb having to fight off the attacks of his challengers, after which he was able to pace himself and cope with the difficulties of this atypical rally.

Argentina

THE RALLY
A fantastic drive

For several years now a Subaru had always hit the front in the first specials of the Argentinean Rally whose stages are the most beautiful on the calendar, and seem to suit the blue cars and their Pirelli rubber down to the ground. The opening special in the grassy pampas in the Cordoba province was no exception to the rule. It was, though, difficult to believe that it would last, as the Japanese team had been a pale shadow of itself since Monte Carlo. The flat-four engine seemed to like the Argentinean air and Solberg won the first super special in the Château Carreras stadium in front of 45 000 spectators with Grönholm taking the honours in no.2. The serious business started the next day and Solberg again emerged in front at the end of SS3 (Ascochinga-La Cumbre). Battle was well and truly joined between the top three and Loeb, who had spun in SS3, hit back with a couple of fastest times in the next two stages. Solberg smacked a gatepost and broke the window on his co-driver's right in SS4 while Grönholm hovered just behind awaiting developments. The big Finn took the lead after SS5 after the Norwegian punctured his right-hand rear tyre and crawled to the end of the stage, which he finished in third place overall.

Marcus was on top and aimed to stay there as he showed by setting the fastest time in SS6. Loeb hit back immediately. It was a great scrap between the Ford and Citroën drivers with Solberg hanging on in there followed by Hirvonen. Something had to give and it did. In this case Grönholm's Ford's engine. "Eight kilometres into the special," muttered a downcast Finn, "I came into a corner and the engine stalled. I restarted but I couldn't find a gear. I blocked the differentials and managed to cover around 300 metres but in the tight corner that followed the car ground to a halt. I don't know what the problem is but I'm bitterly disappointed at having to retire just when everything was going so well. I was in the lead but not by much (8s over Loeb until his retirement) and I pushed hard this morning without taking huge risks." Grönholm's retirement was just the start of Ford's woes. At the end of the same Capilla del Monte-San Marcos special (SS8) Hirvonen up into third following his team leader's retirement also ran into engine trouble.

"On the liaison stage after the halt it suddenly went onto three cylinders. We stopped and changed the plugs but to no avail. We went on a bit farther and stopped again to change the black box. No use. As there were still two stages to go before we reached the service crew, we decided to throw in the towel because we didn't want to damage the engine any more hoping that we could restart in the morrow's Super Rally."

Malcolm Wilson, the M-Sport boss who looks after the works Fords in the World Championship was really down in the dumps: "Another race in which we were in the lead and again we ran into mechanical problems. It's a pity as both cars and drivers proved that they were able to win it. The engine failures we've had on both Focuses seem different, and we've never run into them before in testing."

Ford's double retirement left the way open for a two-horse race between Loeb and Solberg. The Norwegian was hit with a 10-second penalty for having arrived late after a long stop to change tyres on a liaison stage, and fought back by setting the fastest time between San Marcos and Cuchi Corral. The final stage of the day was won by Stohl taking part in his 100th rally from an all-fired up Galli.

The Cordoba stadium hosted the super special. Each duel between the front-runners like Loeb against Solberg had the crowd in ecstasy.

Manfred Stohl raced in his 100th rally in Argentina and was rewarded with fourth place in his Bozian-entered 307 WRC.

Henning Solberg had a very different rally from his Subaru-mounted younger brother. His 307 WRC was bedevilled with tyre and differential problems that lost him a lot of time.

Norwegian Petter Solberg really believed that his moment had come. He made a flying start to the rally setting the first four fastest times in the first leg. It was not good enough, though, to allow him to challenge Sébastien Loeb so he must have felt rather frustrated.

At end of the first leg, which had been as exciting as anything so far this season, Loeb returned to Cordoba with a lead of 19.8s over Solberg. Galli in third was already 59.4s further back. The Norwegian was one happy bunny to be back at the front: "It's been a very exciting day. A lot of things happened and it was really great to be able to battle for the lead and win a few stages."

The second leg was run in a very different landscape and the drivers set off to tackle the La Calamuchita valley with its long, bumpy stages. In addition, it was raining and the four specials in the Punilla valley were soaking wet with fog in some places. Loeb drove an intelligent race on soft tyres that were perfectly adapted to the terrain, and increased his lead in the mud and the mist. At the halfway mark he was 57.1s in front of Solberg who was totally unable to match the Frenchman's pace as he had chosen the wrong tyres. He was not helped by he paddle shift breaking in the opening special forcing him to use the spare lever. In the afternoon the Norwegian fought back setting two fastest times (dead-heating in one with his brother Henning) and he managed to reduce Loeb's lead by 14 seconds by the end of the leg. Grönholm was back in the Super Rally and showed just how quick the Ford was by setting four scratch times. This performance put him in tenth place some 14 minutes behind the leader. The battle for third place raged between three Peugeot-mounted drivers, Galli, Henning Solberg and Stohl separated by 1m 5s.

"It wasn't all that easy," commented Loeb once he was back in Cordoba. "It was very bumpy and I had to cross a lot of little streams at high speed. I've managed to open up a small gap and I'll try and maintain it in the third leg in which there are a couple of narrow, car-breaking stages where you can't afford to make any mistakes."

Solberg, on the other hand, was all fired up at the prospect of the challenges to come, in particular the Giulio and El Condor stages, two of the best in the World Championship. He announced to everybody within earshot, "the rally's not over yet. We've got to get through those stages and come out unscathed."

But it was no use counting on Sébastien at his very best with victory in his sights to make a mistake. He took things cautiously maintaining just the pace he needed to stay in front allowing Stohl and then Solberg to set the fastest times in the above-mentioned specials. There were no changes the first three positions from the previous day in the third leg, which finished in Château-Carreras with a couple of Mickey Mouse specials. Gigi Galli stepped up onto the rostrum for the first time in an event counting for the World Championship, a reward that was all the more well-deserved as it was only his second outing in a Peugeot 307 WRC. Stohl managed to move up a place and finished fourth from Dani Sordo, Chris Atkinson and Henning Solberg. The latter was the day's big loser as his clutch went in the last super special held in the Cordoba stadium.

Grönholm was one very disappointed Finn. He was in the lead at the end of the first leg, but was forced to retire with transmission problems generated by a defective electrical system.

Dani Sordo was having his first outing on the tricky Argentinean terrain and also his first on gravel in a WRC. He came home in a promising sixth place.

Argentina

This is the Argentinean rally at its most grandiose as Gigi Galli in his 307 WRC splashes across a river.

Loeb and Elena were over the moon with their twenty-fourth victory together. The Frenchman equalled the mythic Tommi Mäkinen's score and the Monegasque did the same for Luis Moya's. "It's fantastic," laughed Daniel. "But I'll really let it all hang out if I beat him!" Sébastien told everybody just how happy he was to have won this legendary rally for the second time: "It's a really thrilling event what with the decor, the bumps that throw the car into impossible positions, crossing the streams at high speed and above all the warm welcome of the most enthusiastic fans in the world. My Citroën was as quick, reliable and driveable as usual. It had to be because the rally was very difficult this year especially with the weather. I had a good scrap with Marcus on the first day and then with Petter for the rest of the event. For these reasons I'm really delighted to have won. In addition, Daniel and I have increased our lead in the drivers' Championship and Kronos has done the same in the manufacturers' one. It looks good in view of the tough battles still to come." Knowing that the Finn had not added any points to his tally was also a source of satisfaction for the Frenchman.

Another who was particularly elated was Petter Solberg as he was happy to be back at the sharp end of the field. "I wanted to win but coming second is a good result. We can't really complain as things turned out more or less as we'd imagined. I drove my heart out and the outcome is very positive. The car's getting better and better and I can really push without too many constraints. Roll on the next rally!" ■

Loeb and Elena have a particular affection for the Argentinean event. They had to buckle down to fend off the attacks of Grönholm and Solberg before being able to control their lead.

PRODUCTION
Let the storm pass...

Local honour was at stake and the Argentineans entered in the production category were pawing the ground with impatience before the start! Beltran, Pozzo and Ligato set off like it was a sprint race rather than a long-distance rally and tackled the first stages flat out. Inevitably, mayhem followed. But it was Mirco Baldacci who set the first two fastest times until Pozzo got the bit between his teeth and came first in the next three (SS3-SS5) putting him in the lead from his fellow-countrymen Beltran and Ligato: three Argentineans in the first three places all in Mitsubishis! The crowd went wild and so did the drivers. In the next couple of stages the face of the

Gigi Galli sprays the bubbly with Sébastien Loeb after his surprise appearance on the rostrum.

The South American event is one of the musts on the calendar year after year. The spectators are of an enthusiasm rarely found elsewhere. They line the roads often spending the whole night on the long stages just to catch a glimpse of the cars flashing past.

Suzuki driver Guy Wilks caught in a reflective mood. Helped by the absence of his main rivals, he won the Argentinean round of the Junior Championship adding 10 points to his tally.

category underwent a brutal change. Ligato destroyed a push rod in SS6 and Pozzo stove in his radiator after crossing a stream at far too high a speed in SS7. This put Beltran in front ahead of Al-Attiyah and Baldacci. The man from Qatar who won here in 2005, saw his hopes dashed when he was handed a 2-minute penalty for checking in too early by mistake. But what he wasn't counting on was Beltran's accident in the fourteenth special when he hit a rock destroying his Mitsubishi's suspension. Thus, Al-Attiyah found himself in a totally unexpected lead in his Subaru which he held to the chequered flag followed home by the Polish driver Kuzaj in another Subaru. Despite several penalties Baldacci finished third more than fourteen minutes behind the winner. "We had a good game plan," said a happy Al-Attiyah after the rally. "We had to stick to it - which we did - as it's a very difficult rally."

This victory increased his lead in the Championship from the two drivers who followed him home in Argentina: Kuzaj and Baldacci. ∎

Chris Atkinson confirmed that the Subarus were back in the ballpark. After many problems he came home in sixth place.

Argentina results

26th ARGENTINEAN RALLY

Organiser Driver
Automovil Club Argentino,
Avda del Libertador 1850,
1425 Buenos Aires,
Argentina
Tel.: +5435 14265252
Fax: +5435 14265000

Rally Argentina

6th leg of FIA 2006 World Rally Championship for constructors and drivers.
3rd leg of FIA Production Car Championship.
4th leg of FIA WRC Junior Championship.

Date April 28 - 30, 2006

Route
1474.82 km divised in 3 legs.
22 special stages on dirt roads (351.44 km).

Starting Procedure
Thursday, April 27 (19:05),
Estadio Córdoba
2 special stages (4.40 km)

Leg 1
Friday, April 28 (08:33/16:59),
Córdoba > La Cumbre > Córdoba, 546.63 km;
8 special stages (155.33 km)

Leg 2
Saturday, April 29 (08:07/17:26),
Córdoba > Santa Rosa de la Calamuchita > Córdoba, 640.09 km;
8 special stages (150.41 km)

Leg 3
Sunday, April 30 (09:43/13:08),
Córdoba > Mina Clavero > Córdoba, 288.10 km;
4 special stages (41.30 km)

Entry List (77) - 68 starters

N°	Driver (Nat.)	Co-driver (Nat.)	Team	Car	Group & FIA Priority
1.	S. LOEB (F)	D. ELENA (MC)	KRONOS TOTAL CITROEN WRT	Citroën Xsara WRC	A8 1
2.	X. PONS (E)	C. DEL BARRIO (E)	KRONOS TOTAL CITROEN WRT	Citroën Xsara WRC	A8 1
3.	M. GRÖNHOLM (FIN)	T. RAUTIAINEN (FIN)	BP FORD WORLD RALLY TEAM	Ford Focus RS WRC 06	A8 1
4.	M. HIRVONEN (FIN)	J. LEHTINEN (FIN)	BP FORD WORLD RALLY TEAM	Ford Focus RS WRC 06	A8 1
5.	P. SOLBERG (N)	P. MILLS (GB)	SUBARU WORLD RALLY TEAM	Subaru Impreza WRC 2006	A8 1
6.	C. ATKINSON (AUS)	G. MACNEALL (AUS)	SUBARU WORLD RALLY TEAM	Subaru Impreza WRC 2006	A8 1
7.	M. STOHL (A)	I. MINOR (A)	OMV - PEUGEOT NORWAY	Peugeot 307 WRC	A8 1
8.	H. SOLBERG (N)	C. MENKERUD (N)	OMV - PEUGEOT NORWAY	Peugeot 307 WRC	A8 1
9.	M. WILSON (GB)	M. ORR (GB)	STOBART - VK - M-SPORT FORD RALLY TEAM	Ford Focus RS WRC 04	A8 1
10.	L. PEREZ COMPANC (RA)	J. MARIA VOLTA (RA)	STOBART - VK - M-SPORT FORD RALLY TEAM	Ford Focus RS WRC 04	A8 1
11.	D. SORDO (E)	M. MARTI (E)	DANIEL SORDO	Citroën Xsara WRC	A8 2
12.	G. MAC HALE (IRL)	P. NAGLE (IRL)	GARETH MACHALE	Ford Focus RS WRC 04	A8 2
25.	G. GALLI (I)	B. GIOVANNI (I)	GIANLUIGI GALLI	Peugeot 307 WRC	A8 2
31.	T. ARAI (J)	T. SIRCOMBE (NZ)	SUBARU TEAM ARAI	Subaru Impreza STi	N4 3
32.	M. LIGATO (RA)	R. GARCIA (RA)	MARCOS LIGATO	Mitsubishi Lancer Evo IX	N4 3
34.	S. BELTRÁN (RA)	R. ROJAS (RCH)	SEBASTIAN BELTRAN	Mitsubishi Lancer Evo IX	N4 3
35.	G. POZZO (RA)	D. STILLO (RA)	GABRIEL POZZO	Mitsubishi Lancer Evo IX	N4 3
36.	M. BALDACCI (RSM)	A. GIOVANNI (I)	MIRCO BALDACCI	Mitsubishi Lancer Evo IX	N4 3
38.	L. KUZAJ (PL)	M. SZCZEPANIAK (PL)	AUTOMOBILKUB RZEMIESLNIK WARSZAWA	Subaru Impreza STi	N4 3
39.	N. AL-ATTIYAH (QAT)	C. PATTERSON (GB)	QMMF	Subaru Impreza Spec C	N4 3
40.	S. MARRINI (I)	T. SANDRONI (I)	ERRANI TEAM GROUP	Mitsubishi Lancer Evo VIII	N4 3
41.	T. KAMADA (J)	H. ICHINO (J)	SUBARU TEAM QUASYS	Subaru Impreza	N4 3
42.	S. USPENSKIY (RUS)	D. EREMEEV (R)	SUBARU RALLY TEAM RUSSIA	Subaru Impreza Spec C	N4 3
45.	A. TEISKONEN (FIN)	M. TEISKONEN (FIN)	SYMS RALLY TEAM	Subaru Impreza	N4 3
46.	N. HEATH (GB)	S. LANCASTER (GB)	HEATH NIGEL	Subaru Impreza Spec C	N4 3
61.	F. VILLAGRA (RA)	D. CURLETTO (RA)	VRS RALLY TEAM	Mitsubishi Lancer Evo VIII	N4
62.	E. OMAR (RA)	S. GARCIA (RA)	BARATTERO YOMA	Subaru Impreza STi WRX Spec	N4
63.	N. MADERO (RA)	G. PIAZZANO (RA)	VRS RALLY TEAM	Mitsubishi Lancer Evo VIII	N4
64.	C. MENZI (RA)	M. VERA (RA)	BARATTERO SUBARU	Subaru Impreza	N4
66.	S. VOJTECH (CZ)	M. ERNST (CZ)	OMV RALLY TEAM	Mitsubishi Lancer Evo	N4
67.	M. Oriol GÓMEZ (E)	J. Pascual ORIOL (E)	GAMACE COMPETICIÓN	Subaru Impreza WRX STi Spec	N4
68.	D. Arias QUIÑONES (PY)	H. NUNES (PY)	GORDEN COMPETICIÓN	Subaru Impreza WRX	N4
69.	D. Dominguez STROSSNER (PY)	C. Fabrizi CHIRIANI (PY)	DOMINGUEZ STROESSNER	Mitsubishi Lancer Evo VI	N4
70.	M. SAS (RA)	R. KEMBER (RA)	VRS RALLY TEAM	Mitsubishi Lancer Evo VIII	N4
71.	D. Elio MARROCCHI (RA)	T. Tba (Tba)	PRO RALLY	Mitsubishi Lancer Evo VI	N4
72.	L. BALDACCI (RSM)	D. D'ESPOSITO (I)	LORIS BALDACCI	Subaru Impreza STI	N4
73.	J. MARCHETO (RA)	T. Tba (Tba)	JORGE MARCHETO	Mitsubishi Lancer Evo VIII MR	N4
74.	G. KLUS (RA)	C. RAVAZA (RA)	GERARDO KLUS	Mitsubishi Lancer Evo VIII	N4
75.	L. Alexandre BURGOS MONTEIRO (RA)	D. Anibal CAGNOTTI (RA)	BURGOS MONTEIRO	Mitsubishi Lancer Evo VIII	N4
77.	M. KAHLFUSS (D)	R. BAUER (D)	MIKA TEAM	Mitsubishi Lancer Evo VI	N4
78.	L. Fernando BARBERY PAZ (BOL)	D. Filippi MARCELO (RA)	HAEDO COMPETICIÓN	Mitsubishi Lancer Evo VIII	N4
79.	J. CARLOS ALONSO (RA)	M. MERCADAL (RA)	EZD COMPETITION	Subaru Impreza Spec	N4
80.	J. RITTA (RA)	E. CAPREITO (RA)	HORACIO CIRES	Mitsubishi Lancer Evo VI	N4
82.	P. NOBRE (BR)	E. PAULA (BR)	PALMEIRINHA RALLY	Mitsubishi Lancer Evo VII	N4
84.	M. GALLUSER (RA)	J. CARLOS UBERTI (RA)	LOS QUIRQUINCHOS RALLY	Mitsubishi Lancer Evo VIII	N4
85.	N. Arturo ABELLA (RA)	R. BULACIO (RA)	ABELLA NAZAR RALLY TEAM	Mitsubishi Lancer Evo VI	N4
86.	R. ALENAZ (RA)	L. GRIGERA (RA)	KONICA MINOLTA RALLY	Mitsubishi Lancer Evo VIII	N4
87.	J. Luis GONZALEZ (RA)	H. Roberto OROPEL (RA)	PRO RALLY	Mitsubishi Lancer Evo VI	N4
88.	M. ANDRES (CR)	G. EDSARDO (RA)	ANC MOTOR SPORT	Subaru Impreza WRX	N4
90.	P. MARANZANA (RA)	L. SUAYA (RA)	TANGO RALLY TEAM	Renault Clio Sport	N3
91.	M. MACHINEA (RA)	E. MARONGIU (RA)	VILLA MARIA RALLY TEAM	Seat Ibiza	N3
92.	S. Massimo MECCHIA (RA)	A. GONZÁLEZ (RA)	SERGIO MECCHIA	Peugeot 206 XS	N3
93.	J. ERNESTO ANGELONI (RA)	P. Rodolfo ORELLANA (RA)	ANGELONI RALLY COMPETICIÓN	Seat Ibiza	N3
95.	E. AGUIRRE (RCH)	C. PEÑA WISHNIEWSKY (RCH)	AGUIRRE RALLY TEAM	Peugeot 206 RC	A7
96.	J. Alberto NICOLÁS (RA)	S. Dante PERUGINI (RA)	JOSÉ ALBERTO NICOLÁS	Renault Clio Dynamique	A6
97.	B. ALVAREZ (RA)	L. OYOLA (RA)	VILLA MARIA RALLY TEAM	Seat Ibiza	N3
98.	E. BUSTOS (RA)	A. SUAREZ (CR)	EMILIO BUSTOS	Fiat Palio	A6
100.	N. RAIES (RA)	J. DÍAZ (RA)	RAIES COMPETICIÓN	Renault Clio Sport	N3
101.	L. Maria VEGA (RA)	M. Javier ARMANDO (RA)	VEGA RALLY TEAM	Fiat Palio	N2
103.	J. DÍAZ (RA)	E. NOVELLI (RA)	ARIES AUTOMOTORES	Fiat Palio	N2
104.	G. BOTTAZZINI (RA)	D. DE LUCA (RA)	GUILLERMO BOTTAZZINI	Honda Civic VTi	N2
105.	L. PEREZ LOBO (RA)	G. CARCIOTTO (RA)	ZUNINO RACING	Renault Clio Sport	N2
106.	R. JAUREGUI (RA)	L. JAÑEZ (RA)	TITO JAUREGUI RALLY TEAM	Opel Corsa	N2
107.	H. CASTRO CARLOS (RA)	R. Pablo BAGLIANI (RA)	FAB - CAR	Opel Corsa	N2
135.	P. ANDERSSON (S)	J. ANDERSSON (S)	PG ANDERSSON	Suzuki Swift Super 1600	A6 3
141.	P. SANDELL (SWE)	E. AXELSSON (SWE)	PATRIK SANDELL	Renault Clio Super 1600	A6 3
143.	J. MÖLDER (EE)	K. BECKER (D)	JAAN MÖLDER	Ford Fiesta Super 1600	A6 3
148.	G. WILKS (GB)	P. PUGH (GB)	SUZUKI SPORT EUROPE UK	Suzuki Swift Super 1600	A6 3

Championship Classifications

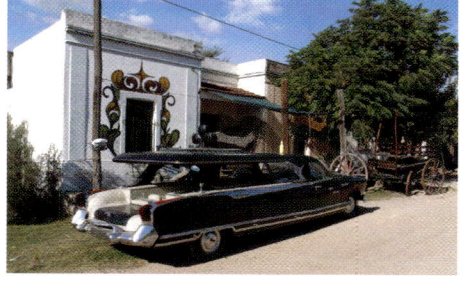

FIA Drivers (6/16)
1. Loeb — 4🏆 56
2. Grönholm — 2🏆 35
3. Sordo — 24
4. P. Solberg — 18
5. Stohl — 18
6. Galli — 11
7. Bengué — 9
8. Atkinson — 8
9. Hirvonen — 7
10. H. Solberg — 7
11. Gardemeister — 6
12. Carlsson — 6
13. Sarrazin — 6
14. Pons — 5
15. Kopecky — 4
16. Rådström — 4
17. Mac Hale — 3
18. Duval — 3
19. Katajamäki — 3
20. Wilson — 1
21. Perez Companc, Arai... — 0

FIA Constructors (6/16)
1. Kronos Total Citroën WRT — 4🏆 69
2. BP-Ford World Rally Team — 2🏆 57
3. Subaru World Rally Team — 51
4. OMV-Peugeot Norway — 31
5. Stobart VK M-Sport Ford WRT — 15
6. Red Bull-Skoda Team — 11

FIA Production Car (3/8)
1. Al-Attiyah — 1🏆 24
2. Kuzaj — 13
3. Baldacci — 12
4. Arai — 1🏆 11
5. Nutahara — 1🏆 10
6. Higgins — 8
7. Marrini — 7
8. Ligato — 6
9. Heath — 5
10. Latvala — 4
11. Uspenskiy — 4
12. Beltrán — 4
13. Vojtech — 2
14. Name — 1
15. Pozzo — 0
16. Teiskonen — 0
17. Kamada — 0
18. Popov — 0

FIA Junior WRC (4/9)
1. Andersson — 1🏆 16
2. Sandell — 16
3. Aava — 14
4. Béres — 12
5. Tirabassi — 1🏆 11
6. Wilks — 1🏆 10
7. Prokop — 1🏆 10
8. Rautenbach — 9
9. Casier — 8
10. Meeke — 6
11. Valousek — 5
12. Pressac — 5
13. Molder — 5
14. Kosciuszko — 5
15. Kara — 5
16. Pinomäki — 4
17. Zachrisson — 2
18. Burkart — 2
19. Bonato — 1
20. Bordignon — 0
21. Clark — 0
22. Cortinovis — 0
23. Karlsson — 0

…

Special Stages Times

www.rallyargentina.com
www.wrc.com

SS1 Super Especial 1 (2.20 km)
1.P.Solberg 2'26"4; 2.Loeb +0"3;
3.Grönholm +0"5; 4.Galli +1"2;
5.Pons +1"5; 6.Stohl +1"6;
7.Hirvonen +2"4; 8.Wilson +2"8...
P-WRC > 15.Baldacci 2'34"8
J-WRC > 28.Wilks 2'41"1

SS2 Super Especial 2 (2.20 km)
1.Grönholm 2'25"9; 2.Hirvonen +0"5;
3.Atkinson +1"8; 4.P.Solberg +2"3;
5.Loeb +2"6; 6.Galli +3"0;
7.H.Solberg +3"2; 8.Sordo +3"6...
P-WRC > 14.Baldacci 2'34"7
J-WRC > 31.Andersson/Wilks 2'42"9

SS3 Ascochinga - La Cumbre 1 (23.28 km)
1.P.Solberg 14'49"8; 2.Stohl +8"2;
3.Atkinson +9"3; 4.Grönholm +9"8;
5.Pons +12"6; 6.Hirvonen +13"2;
7.Loeb +22"7; 8.Galli +22"8...
P-WRC > 13.Pozzo 15'46"9
J-WRC > 24.Wilks 16'38"3

SS4 Capilla del Monte - San Marcos 1 (22.95 km)
1.Loeb 17'27"0; 2.Grönholm +1"4;
3.P.Solberg +6"3; 4.Stohl +11"0;
5.Hirvonen +13"5;
6.Atkinson/H.Solberg +17"0;
8.Galli +19"4...
P-WRC > 12.Pozzo 18'08"2
J-WRC > 25.Sandell 19'18"0

SS5 San Marcos - Cuchi Corral 1 (19.24 km)
1.Loeb 11'39"7; 2.Grönholm +4"1;
3.Galli +8"3; 4.Hirvonen +8"4;
5.H.Solberg +11"0; 6.Stohl +11"6;
7.P.Solberg +16"4; 8.Pons +20"7...
P-WRC > 12.Pozzo 12'23"2
J-WRC > 22.Wilks 13'05"4

SS6 Cabalango - Carlos Paz 1 (14.53 km)
1.Grönholm 9'51"9; 2.Loeb +2"9;
3.P.Solberg +5"4; 4.H.Solberg +7"3;
5.Galli +9"6; 6.Hirvonen +9"7;
7.Atkinson +16"9; 8.Sordo +20"6...
P-WRC > 14.Beltrán 10'43"2
J-WRC > 22.Wilks 11'06"0

SS7 La Falda - Villa Giardino 1 (11.77 km)
1.Loeb 7'34"9; 2.Grönholm +4"7;
3.H.Solberg +8"0; 4.P.Solberg +9"4;
5.Hirvonen +10"7; 6.Galli +11"8;
7.Stohl +12"1; 8.Sordo +13"7...
P-WRC > 15.Beltrán 8'29"6
J-WRC > 26.Wilks 9'00"9

SS8 Capilla del Monte - San Marcos 2 (22.95 km)
1.Loeb 17'10"8; 2.P.Solberg +0"3;
3.Stohl +3"7; 4.Galli +4"9;
5.Hirvonen +5"4; 6.H.Solberg +12"2;
7.Sordo +12"5; 8.Atkinson +21"0...
P-WRC > 13.Al-Attiyah 18'32"5
J-WRC > 21.Sandell 19'14"4

SS9 San Marcos - Cuchi Corral 2 (19.24 km)
1.P.Solberg 11'30"0; 2.Loeb +0"9;
3.Galli +12"1; 4.Stohl +12"5;
5.Sordo +14"4; 6.H.Solberg +14"9;
7.Atkinson +24"9; 8.Wilson +44"1...
P-WRC > 12.Al-Attiyah 12'43"6
J-WRC > 17.Wilks 13'17"2

SS10 La Cumbre - Agua de Oro 1 (21.37 Km)
1.Stohl 18'26"3; 2.Galli +2"3;
3.P.Solberg +5"7; 4.Loeb +6"6;
5.Sordo +16"0; 6.H.Solberg +16"5;
7.Wilson +19"7; 8.Atkinson +30"1...
P-WRC > 12.Beltrán 19'23"7
J-WRC > 20.Wilks 20'20"0

Classification Leg 1
1.Loeb 1h53'58"7; 2.P.Solberg +19"8;
3.Galli +59"4; 4.Stohl +1'12"1;
5.H.Solberg +1'31"8; 6.Sordo +2'15"1;
7.Atkinson +2'25"4; 8.Wilson +4'08"7...
P-WRC > 11.Beltrán 2h02'37"3
J-WRC > 20.Wilks 2h07'29"8

SS11 La Falda - Villa Giardino 2 (11.77 km)
1.Grönholm 7'45"6; 2.Loeb +5"3;
3.P.Solberg +8"3; 4.Stohl +10"0;
5.H.Solberg +13"6; 6.Pons +14"7;
7.Sordo +16"0; 8.Atkinson +18"2...
P-WRC > 14.Ligato 8'41"0
J-WRC > 26.Andersson 9'14"4

SS12 La Cumbre - Agua de Oro 2 (21.37 Km)
1.Grönholm 18'19"0; 2.Pons +6"3;
3.Loeb +6"5; 4.Galli +30"1;
5.P.Solberg +31"0; 6.Atkinson +39"1;
7.H.Solberg +44"5; 8.Sordo +45"8...
P-WRC > 13.Arai 19'54"0
J-WRC > 23.Andersson 21'14"9

SS13 Ascochinga - La Cumbre 2 (23.28 km)
1.Pons 15'06"1; 2.Grönholm +1"2;
3.Loeb +6"1; 4.P.Solberg +14"8;
5.Atkinson +28"1; 6.Galli +28"4;
7.Sordo +37"0; 8.H.Solberg +50"2...
P-WRC > 13.Arai 16'36"8
J-WRC > 24.Andersson 18'08"3

SS14 Cabalango - Carlos Paz 2 (14.53 km)
1.Loeb 9'46"7; 2.Grönholm +1"0;
3.P.Solberg +1"5; 4.Galli +2"0;
5.H.Solberg +8"5; 6.Stohl +12"0;
7.Sordo +12"2; 8.Atkinson +13"2...
P-WRC > 13.Ligato 10'39"8
J-WRC > 23.Wilks 11'12"1

SS15 Santa Rosa - San Augustín 1 (21.41 Km)
1.Grönholm 13'08"5; 2.P.Solberg +2"8;
3.Loeb +4"0; 4.Stohl +12"6;
5.Galli +15"1; 6.H.Solberg +15"2;
7.Atkinson +16"1; 8.Pons +33"0...
P-WRC > 17.Al-Attiyah 14'39"8
J-WRC > 21.Wilks 15'00"2

SS16 Las Bajadas - Villa del Dique (16.35 Km)
1.P.Solberg/H.Solberg 8'50"5;
3.Grönholm +3"7; 4.Loeb +3"8;
5.Stohl +7"2; 6.Galli +10"5;
7.Atkinson +11"5; 8.Pons +16"6...
P-WRC > 15.Kuzaj 9'53"1
J-WRC > 21.Andersson 10'14"3

SS17 Amboy - Santa Mónica (20.29 Km)
1.P.Solberg 10'30"1; 2.Loeb +5"8;
3.Grönholm +6"3; 4.Stohl +11"4;
5.Atkinson +12"6; 6.H.Solberg +14"4;
7.Galli +15"8; 8.Sordo +25"3...
P-WRC > 15.Al-Attiyah 11'51"2
J-WRC > 19.Andersson 12'09"1

SS18 Santa Rosa - San Augustín 2 (21.41 Km)
1.Grönholm 13'02"5; 2.P.Solberg +0"8;
3.Loeb +4"4; 4.Stohl +10"0;
5.Galli +12"8; 6.Sordo +13"5;
7.Atkinson +14"4; 8.H.Solberg +14"5...
P-WRC > 17.Al-Attiyah 14'39"6
J-WRC > 20.Andersson 14'51"1

Classification Leg 2
1.Loeb 3h31'03"6; 2.P.Solberg +43"1;
3.Galli +2'36"4; 4.H.Solberg +3'36"8;
5.Stohl +3'41"1; 6.Sordo +5'04"0;
7.Atkinson +5'22"7;
8.Perez Companc +9'26"6...
P-WRC > 14.Al-Attiyah 3h53'40"0
J-WRC > 19.Wilks 4h03'51"2

SS19 Mina Clavero - Giulio Cesare (20.08 Km)
1.Stohl 17'03"2; 2.P.Solberg +4"2;
3.Grönholm +4"7; 4.Loeb +7"5;
5.Atkinson +14"1; 6.Sordo +22"8;
7.Pons +23"8; 8.H.Solberg +26"9...
P-WRC > 13.Arai 18'12"6
J-WRC > 23.Andersson 19'14"7

SS20 El Condor - Copina (16.82 Km)
1.P.Solberg 13'40"2; 2.Grönholm +0"8;
3.Loeb +6"9; 4.Stohl +8"8;
5.Atkinson +10"9; 6.Sordo +19"8;
7.Galli +21"0; 8.Pons +23"8...
P-WRC > 13.Arai 14'37"8
J-WRC > 25.Wilks 15'29"1

SS21 Super Especial 3 (2.20 km)
1.Grönholm 2'22"5; 2.Pons +1"3;
3.P.Solberg +2"4; 4.Loeb +2"9;
5.Wilson +3"9; 6.Galli +4"0;
7.Mac Hale +4"4; 8.Stohl +5"7...
P-WRC > 9.Ligato 2'28"5
J-WRC > 28=.Sandell 2'36"8

SS22 Super Especial 4 (2.20 km)
1.Wilson 2'23"7; 2.Grönholm +0"5;
3.Loeb +0"8; 4.Pons +1"5; 5.Stohl +2"5;
6.Mac Hale +2"7; 7.P.Solberg +3"0;
8.Galli +4"6...
P-WRC > 10.Beltrán 2'29"7
J-WRC > 23.Sandell 2'35"4

Results

	Driver - Co-driver	Car	Gr.	Time
1	Loeb - Elena	Citroën Xsara WRC	A8	4h06'51"3
2	P. Solberg - Mills	Subaru Impreza WRC 2006	A8	+ 44"6
3	Galli - Bernacchini	Peugeot 307 WRC	A8	+ 3'24"3
4	Stohl - Minor	Peugeot 307 WRC	A8	+ 3'40"0
5	Sordo - Marti	Citroën Xsara WRC	A8	+ 5'40"2
6	Atkinson - Macneall	Subaru Impreza WRC 2006	A8	+ 5'43"8
7	H. Solberg - Menkerud	Peugeot 307 WRC	A8	+ 9'28"7
8	Wilson - Orr	Ford Focus RS WRC 04	A8	+ 10'34"6
9	Perez Companc - Volta	Ford Focus RS WRC 04	A8	+ 10'52"3
10	Grönholm - Rautiainen	Ford Focus RS WRC 06	A8	+ 14'08"7
12	Villagra - Curletto	Mitsubishi Lancer Evo VIII	N4	+ 22'49"8
15	Al-Attiyah - Patterson	Subaru Impreza Spec C	N4/P	+ 25'52"7
16	Kuzaj - Szczepaniak	Subaru Impreza STi	N4/P	+ 27'23"1
19	Wilks - Pugh	Suzuki Swift S1600	A6/J	+ 37'55"6
21	Baldacci - Agnese	Mitsubishi Lancer Evo IX	N4/P	+ 40'00"9
22	Sandell - Axelsson	Renault Clio S1600	A6/J	+ 47'15"1
34	Andersson - Andersson	Suzuki Swift S1600	A6/J	+ 1h06'56"6

Leading Retirements (11)
TC10C Hirvonen - Lehtinen — Ford Focus RS WRC 06 — Engine
TC6A Pozzo - Stillo — Mitsubishi Lancer Evo IX — Engine

Performers

	1	2	3	4	5	6	C6	NbSS
Grönholm	7	7	4	1	-	-	19	22
P. Solberg	6	4	6	3	1	-	20	22
Loeb	5	5	6	4	1	-	21	22
Stohl	2	1	1	7	2	3	16	22
Pons	1	2	-	1	2	1	7	15
H. Solberg	1	-	1	1	3	6	12	22
Wilson	1	-	-	-	1	-	2	22
Galli	-	1	2	4	3	5	15	22
Hirvonen	-	1	-	1	3	2	7	8
Atkinson	-	-	2	-	4	2	8	22
Sordo	-	-	-	-	2	3	5	22
Mac Hale	-	-	-	-	-	1	1	22

Leaders

SS1	P. Solberg
SS2	Grönholm
SS3 > SS4	P. Solberg
SS5 > SS7	Grönholm
SS8 > SS22	Loeb

Previous winners

1980	Röhrl - Geistdorfer / Fiat 131 Abarth	1990	Biasion - Siviero / Lancia Delta Integrale 16v	1999	Kankkunen - Repo / Subaru Impreza WRC
1981	Fréquelin - Todt / Talbot Sunbeam Lotus	1991	Sainz - Moya / Toyota Celica GT4	2000	Burns - Reid / Subaru Impreza WRC 2000
1983	Mikkola - Hertz / Audi Quattro	1992	Auriol - Occelli / Lancia Delta HF Integrale	2001	C. McRae - Grist / Ford Focus RS WRC 01
1984	Blomqvist - Cederberg / Audi Quattro	1993	Kankkunen - Grist / Toyota Celica Turbo 4WD	2002	Sainz - Moya / Ford Focus RS WRC 02
1985	Salonen - Harjanne / Peugeot 205 T16	1994	Auriol - Occelli / Toyota Celica Turbo 4WD	2003	Grönholm - Rautiainen / Peugeot 206 WRC
1986	Biasion - Siviero / Lancia Delta S4	1995	Recalde - Christie / Lancia Delta HF Integrale	2004	Sainz - Marti / Citroën Xsara WRC
1987	Biasion - Siviero / Lancia Delta HF Turbo	1996	Mäkinen - Harjanne / Mitsubishi Lancer Evo III	2005	Loeb - Elena / Citroën Xsara WRC
1988	Recalde - Del Buono / Lancia Delta Integrale	1997	Mäkinen - Harjanne / Mitsubishi Lancer Evo IV		
1989	Ericsson - Billstam / Lancia Delta Integrale	1998	Mäkinen - Mannisenmäki / Mitsubishi Lancer Evo V		

Italy

07

01
02
03
04
05
06
08
09
10
11
12
13
14
15
16

Sebastien's big five
Sébastien Loeb won his fifth rally on the trot although Marcus Grönholm was quicker than him in terms of sheer speed. Unfortunately for the Finn his rally ended at the start of the second leg. This success gave the Frenchman a big lead in the drivers' championship, while his co-driver Daniel Elena scored his twenty-fifth World championship victory beating the record held by Luis Moya.

Italy

The Ford Focus in the hands of Marcus Grönholm dominated the first leg. At the end of it he was 35 seconds in front of Sébastien Loeb.

Petter Solberg's Subaru kicks up the dust as he tries to make the car go faster - to no avail.

THE RALLY
Loeb: who else?

The Ford Focus RS WRC 06 is a good car and is in expert hand since it has been entrusted to Marcus Grönholm. It is able to match the pace of the leading rally car, the Xsara, and on occasions beat it, especially when development testing increases its speed. At the end of the first leg of the Sardinian rally, the Italian round of the World championship, the Finn made no bones about expressing his satisfaction. "I was very surprised at the lead I pulled out this morning. The car's great and I'm completely at home behind the steering wheel. We really sweated blood and tears in the last tests to improve the way the dampers, the differentials and the engine work. That pays off. So I feel really comfortable in the driving seat. In addition, I managed to avoid any punctures in the afternoon even though the roads were very rough in the second loop. That proves the quality of the BF Goodrichs and the work done by the tyre men."

The Finn was a very happy man on the warm Friday evening as the temperature had dropped but little in relation to the daytime. He was in the overall lead with 35.5s in hand over the Xsara, and had set four fastest times out of the six specials run with only two going to Loeb. The Frenchman had the difficult task of opening the road on the first loop but he was barely

Marcus Grönholm has very right to be disappointed. He hit a stone in the second leg which, in his own words, led to " one of the most frustrating retirements of my career."

quicker in the afternoon when they had been swept by the morning runs. "It was slippery," he moaned, "but it was the same thing for Marcus as he set off just after me. I don't really know why but I couldn't get into the right rhythm and I could do nothing; the gap just got bigger and bigger."

It was a strange first leg in which nobody could do anything about Grönholm who was at his very best in a car that was obviously faster than the others. This was proved by the third place of his team-mate Mikko Hirvonen ahead of a tightly-packed squabbling group consisting of Henning Solberg, Dani Sordo and Gigi Galli. Chris Atkinson in seventh place was the highest-placed of the Subaru drivers who were overall very disappointing. Peter Solberg was hit with a succession of punctures (two in three stages) and threw in the towel in the last special. One of his tyres exploded and as he was racing with two filled with foam due to punctures, and he had no spare he preferred to stop rather than finishing on the rim. This meant that he could restart in the super rally but without having much hope of a good placing in the overall classification.

97

The Sardinian rally is one of the most scenic in the championship whether one likes it or not.

Dani Sordo sprouted wings in 2006. The Spaniard confirmed his great start to the season by finishing third.

Gigi Galli was the pick of the Italian drivers and missing his national rally was unthinkable. He was at the wheel of a 307 WRC thanks to the backing of Pirelli.

"It's a real pain," grumbled Luis Moya the team's technical director. "After our progress in Argentina, we were hoping to be able to battle for the lead here." It was yet another setback for Subaru in the 2006 Championship.
Sébastien Loeb's aim right from the start of the second leg was to push really hard to see if he could match the leader's pace. If the answer was yes then he would do everything in his power to go after him: if not, he would wait and drive a patient rally either waiting for Grönholm to make a mistake or failing that to collect a further eight points in the Championship thanks to second place. Loelle (SS7) just about killed the Frenchman's hopes. Without really pushing the Ford driver was again the quickest.

Then came the next special, Monte-Lerno. Once again Grönholm set a blistering pace: on the split times he was fastest and he knew it calculating his efforts and the demands made on his car on the speed of his direct rival. Suddenly it all went south. "It was going great," growled the Finn. "We came into a left-hander, which was just before a right-handed hairpin. I braked much earlier than I had to as I was under no pressure. I was not pushing and I was pacing myself on Séb's split

Chris Atkinson drove a hard-charging rally. The feisty Australian saved Subaru's bacon as the Japanese team was once again completely at sea.

times. I felt really confident. There was a big stone on the right on my line and I hit it under braking. I was very surprised, as I just did not see it. There was a huge bang as the stone hit the sump. Immediately, the oil pressure warning light came on and Timo and me thought that it was a problem with a sensor. I drove on for another 800 metres but there was no more oil and we stopped. I just hit a stone in the wrong place. A couple of centimetres to the left or the right and it would've been okay." The big Finn was completely devastated: "It's one of the most heartbreaking retirements of my career," he sighed.

Into the lead went Loeb even if he too had a big scare with the same rock in the same place. "At the twenty-fourth kilometre," Loeb revealed later, "Daniel said there was a big impact in a left-hander against a stone that raised the whole front of the car. Similar incidents

Italy

that had stopped me in Mexico and in Catalonia in 2004 immediately sprang to mind. But I also knew that in relation to them I'd hit on the right side of the car; under the gearbox and not under the engine. The car's behaviour didn't suffer and I continued pushing." Once he reached the halt, his team told him what had happened to Grönholm. "I gave the Xsara a thorough examination," he went on. "There was no real damage. A Citroën's a solid piece of motor car!"
The outcome of this special was that Loeb went from being second 36.7s behind the Ford to first 1m 14.7s in front of Mikko Hirvonen. Barring any unforeseen incidents he had the rally won. Seb realised this immediately. "I had to control the situation by pushing just enough to master the car. This rhythm's the safest."

This is exactly what he did and combining steadiness with a fault-free drive went on to his twenty-fifth World championship victory, and his fifth in 2006 giving him an enormous 31-point lead in the drivers' title chase over the unfortunate Grönholm.

The battle for the lead had come to a premature end and Hirvonen was solidly installed in second place, which he held till the finish – his best result in the World championship - so the interest in the rally swung to the scrap for third. Dani Sordo was mighty impressive in what was only his third rally on gravel in a WRC. After the second passage through the specials on Saturday afternoon he succeeded in overcoming a very tenacious Galli, even if the latter was unable to reach the service park after breaking down on the final stage due to a water leak. This incident promoted

Sébastien Loeb and Daniel Elena were a cut above the rest in the world championship with five victories out of the seven rallies held so far.

Mitsubishi was back near the front again thanks to Välimäki who finished in fifth place.

After Grönholm's retirement Ford's no.2 Mikko Hirvonen did what was expected of him by finishing in second place.

Xavier Pons to fourth putting three Citroëns in the first four places. There were no changes in the final leg as everybody held position. Loeb won, Sordo and Pons came home third and fourth helping Kronos to tighten its grip on the manufacturers' championship as it now had 20 points in hand over Ford. So there was a fair amount of celebrating in the Kronos camp that evening.

Junior Championship: Sandell's first

Another very happy man at the end of the Sardinian Rally was Swede Patrick Sandell who, with his co-driver Emil Alexsson, scored his first victory in the Junior Championship. Renault too was delighted as Zimbabwean Conrad Rautenbach's second place gave the French make's Clio S 1600s a double.
The two men emerged victorious from what turned into an elimination race among whose victims were the favourites: the Suzukis.

Like Välimäki, Kristian Solberg from Finland put on an eye-catching performance in the rally, and saw the flag in sixth place in his Red Devil team's Subaru.

François Duval had another drive in a Skoda and came home eighth overall.

The front-runners set off like bats out of hell in the opening stages and paid the price for their impetuosity in a rally that is very hard on cars. The first victim was Aava who had four punctures in two specials (SS5 and 6) letting Guy Wilks into the lead. The Ulsterman ran into an oil pressure problem that slowed him enormously in the fifteenth special, and he was passed by Sandell and Rautenbach. Aava finally managed to scrape onto the rostrum in third place. Other favourites suffered in this rally like Andersson who set ten fastest times –the best performance of the event – but he too fell victim ot a succession of punctures that dropped him back to fourth where he finished. Brice Tirabassi ran into a lot of problems with his tyres and suspension and was never among the front-runners.
Sandell's unexpected victory was proof of just how open the 2006 Junior Championship was. He was the fifth different winner in five events. His success backed up by his two second places in Sweden and Argentina propelled him into the Championship lead from Andersson and Aava. ■

Xavier Pons's fourth place made it three Citroëns in the first four helped by Loeb (first) and Sordo (third).

THE RECORD
Record for Elena !

"And twenty-five for Daniel!" Sébastien Loeb praised his co-driver to the skies after the Sardinian Rally and dedicated his victory to him. At the finish draped in a jersey in Monegasque colours bearing the number 25 the usually jovial Elena suddenly became a bit serious. "It's because the feeling is indescribable. It's a great joy and I'd like to dedicate it to my family, my daughter Dorin and to "Beef" Park, my friend." It was an incredible performance to beat the record held by Luis Moya after only 77 World Championship rallies, a watershed in the life of a sportsmen. Moya was Carlos Sainz's right-hand man and is now Subaru team manager. It was a fitting consecration for a guy who is as pleasant as he is funny, as professional in his work as in his comradeship with his team, and above all Sébastien Loeb's faithful and indispensable friend. "It's always pleasant to savour the moment of victory, " commented Loeb. "But this one has a particular flavour; it's a red-letter day for Daniel. Knowing to what point I want to beat Carlos's record of twenty-six World Championship victories, I can well imagine what he must feel by becoming the first co-driver to score twenty-five wins." ■

Italy results

3rd RALLY ITALIA SARDINIA

Organiser Details
ACI - CSAI
Porto Industriale Cocciani
(Località Cala Saccaia)
Settore 1 – Edificio B
07026 Olbia (OT)
Italy
Tél.: +39 079 5551234
Fax: +39 079 5551244

Rally Italia Sardinia

7th leg of FIA 2006 World Rally Championship for constructors and drivers.
5th leg of FIA WRC Junior Championship.

Date May 19 - 21, 2006

Route
1140.18 km divised in 3 legs.
18 special stages on dirt roads (344.94 km).

Starting Procedure
Thursday, May 18 (20:00),
Porto Cervo
Leg 1
Friday, May 19 (08:46/17:00),
Olbia > Olbia, 459.52 km;
6 special stages (129.64 km)
Leg 2
Saturday, May 20 (09:30/16:23),
Olbia > Olbia, 400.98 km;
6 special stages (137.36 km)
Leg 3
Sunday, May 21 (07:49/12:32),
Olbia > Porto Cervo, 279.68 km;
6 special stages (77.94 km)

Entry List (82) - 79 starters

N°	Driver (Nat.)	Co-driver (Nat.)	Team	Car	Group & FIA Priority
1.	S. LOEB (F)	D. ELENA (MC)	KRONOS TOTAL CITROEN WRT	Citroën Xsara WRC	A8 1
2.	X. PONS (E)	C. DEL BARRIO (E)	KRONOS TOTAL CITROEN WRT	Citroën Xsara WRC	A8 1
3.	M. GRÖNHOLM (FIN)	T. RAUTIAINEN (FIN)	BP FORD WORLD RALLY TEAM	Ford Focus RS WRC 06	A8 1
4.	M. HIRVONEN (FIN)	J. LEHTINEN (FIN)	BP FORD WORLD RALLY TEAM	Ford Focus RS WRC 06	A8 1
5.	P. SOLBERG (N)	P. MILLS (GB)	SUBARU WORLD RALLY TEAM	Subaru Impreza WRC 2006	A8 1
6.	C. ATKINSON (AUS)	G. MACNEALL (AUS)	SUBARU WORLD RALLY TEAM	Subaru Impreza WRC 2006	A8 1
7.	M. STOHL (A)	I. MINOR (A)	OMV - PEUGEOT NORWAY	Peugeot 307 WRC	A8 1
8.	H. SOLBERG (N)	C. MENKERUD (N)	OMV - PEUGEOT NORWAY	Peugeot 307 WRC	A8 1
9.	M. WILSON (GB)	M. ORR (GB)	STOBART - VK - M-SPORT FORD RALLY TEAM	Ford Focus RS WRC 04	A8 1
10.	K. KATAJAMAKI (FIN)	T. ALANNE (FIN)	STOBART - VK - M-SPORT FORD RALLY TEAM	Ford Focus RS WRC 04	A8 1
11.	H. ROVANPERA (FIN)	R. PIETILAINEN (FIN)	RED BULL - SKODA TEAM	Skoda Fabia WRC	A8 1
12.	A. AIGNER (A)	T. GOTTSCHALK (D)	RED BULL - SKODA TEAM	Skoda Fabia WRC	A8 1
21.	D. SORDO (E)	M. MARTI (E)	DANIEL SORDO	Citroën Xsara WRC	A8 2
22.	F. DUVAL (B)	P. PIVATO (F)	FIRST MOTORSPORT	Skoda Fabia WRC	A8 2
23.	L. PEREZ COMPANC (RA)	J. MARIA VOLTA (RA)	STOBART - VK - M-SPORT FORD RALLY TEAM	Ford Focus RS WRC 04	A8 2
24.	G. MACHALE (IRL)	P. NAGLE (IRL)	GARETH MACHALE	Ford Focus RS WRC 04	A8 2
25.	G. GALLI (I)	G. BERNACCHINI (I)	GIANLUIGI GALLI	Peugeot 307 WRC	A8 2
26.	J. VALIMAKI (FIN)	J. KALLIOLEPO (FIN)	JUSSI VALIMAKI	Mitsubishi Lancer WRC	A8 2
27.	K. SOHLBERG (FIN)	T. TUOMINEN (FIN)	TEAM RED DEVIL ATOLYE KAZAZ	Subaru Impreza WRC	A8 2
28.	J. KOPECKY (CZ)	F. SCHOVANEK (CZ)	CZECH RALLY TEAM SKODA- KOPECKY	Skoda Fabia WRC	A8 2
33.	U. AAVA (EE)	K. SIKK (EE)	URMO AAVA	Suzuki Swift Super 1600	A6 3
35.	P. ANDERSSON (S)	J. ANDERSSON (S)	PER-GUNNAR ANDERSSON	Suzuki Swift Super 1600	A6 3
36.	L. BETTI (E)	P. CAPOLONGO (I)	LUCA BETTI	Renault Clio Super 1600	A6 3
37.	P. VALOUSEK (CZ)	P. SCALVINI (CZ)	PAVEL VALOUSEK	Suzuki Swift Super 1600	A6 3
39.	C. RAUTENBACH (ZW)	D. SENIOR (GB)	CONRAD RAUTENBACH	Renault Clio Super 1600	A6 3
41.	P. SANDELL (SWE)	E. AXELSSON (SWE)	PATRIK SANDELL	Renault Clio Super 1600	A6 3
42.	J. PRESSAC (F)	G. DE TURCKHEIM (F)	JULIEN PRESSAC	Citroën C2 Super 1600	A6 3
43.	J. MOLDER (EE)	K. BECKER (D)	JAAN MOLDER	Suzuki Ignis Super 1600	A6 3
44.	M. KOSCIUSZKO (PL)	J. BARAN (PL)	MICHAL KOSCIUSZKO	Suzuki Ignis Super 1600	A6 3
46.	A. CORTINOVIS (I)	M. BOSSI (I)	ANDREA CORTINOVIS	Renault Clio	N3 3
47.	F. Alessan BORDIGNON (I)	J. BARDINI (I)	FILIPPO ALESSANDRO BORDIGNON	Opel Astra OPC	N3 3
48.	G. WILKS (GB)	J. PUGH (GB)	SUZUKI SPORT EUROPE UK	Suzuki Swift Super 1600	A6 3
49.	M. PROKOP (CZ)	J. TOMANEK (CZ)	JIPOCAR CZECH NATIONAL TEAM	Citroën C2 Super 1600	A6 3
51.	F. KARA (TR)	T. BAKANCOCUKLARI (TR)	FATIH KARA	Renault Clio Super 1600	A6 3
52.	B. CASIER (B)	F. MICLOTTE (B)	BERND CASIER	Renault Clio Super 1600	A6 3
53.	B. CLARK (GB)	S. MARTIN (GB)	STOBART, VK	Ford Fiesta	N3 3
54.	A. Nicolai BURKART (D)	T. GEILHAUSEN (D)	AARON NICOLAI BURKART	Citroën C2 Super 1600	A6 3
55.	B. TIRABASSI (F)	J. JULIEN RENUCCI (F)	PH-Sport	Citroën C2 Super 1600	A6 3
71.	R. ERRANI (I)	S. CASADIO (I)	RICCARDO ERRANI	Skoda Octavia WRC	A8
72.	I. SOKOLOV (RUS)	V. MIRKOTAN (RUS)	SYRUS RALLY TEAM	Mitsubishi Lancer WRC	A8
73.	M. CASALLONI (I)	C. PICCINNU (I)	MARCO CASALLONI	Peugeot 306	A7
74.	A. PERICO (I)	F. CARRARA (I)	ALESSANDRO PERICO	Subaru Impreza	N4
75.	J. HÄNNINEN (FIN)	M. SALLINEN (FIN)	JUHO HANNINEN	Mitsubishi Lancer Evo IX	N4
76.	F. FRISIERO (I)	F. COZZULA (I)	FABIO FRISIERO	Mitsubishi Lancer Evo VIII	N4
77.	P. ZANCHI (I)	D. D'ESPOSITO (I)	PIERLORENZO ZANCHI	Subaru Impreza	N4
78.	S. CAMPEDELLI (I)	D. FAPPANI (I)	SIMONE CAMPEDELLI	Mitsubishi Lancer Evo VIII	N4
79.	M. VINCIGUERRA (I)	G. VOLPATO (I)	MARIO VINCIGUERRA	Subaru Impreza Sti	N4
81.	A. SCORCIONI (I)	C. CERLINI (I)	ALAN SCORCIONI	Subaru Impreza	N4
82.	W. EUGENI (I)	M. BUSINARO (I)	WALTER EUGENI	Subaru Impreza	N4
83.	B. BENTIVOGLI (I)	A. CECCHI (I)	BRUNO BENTIVOGLI	Subaru Impreza	N4
84.	D. CECCOLI (RSM)	A. MICHELET (I)	DANIELE CECCOLI	Subaru Impreza	N4
85.	P. BIOLGHINI (I)	S. GIRELLI (I)	PABLO BIOLGHINI	Subaru Impreza	N4
86.	F. PISTIS (I)	M. PALITTA (I)	FABIO PISTIS	Subaru Impreza	N4
87.	G. TOGNOZZI (I)	M. PELLEGRINI (I)	GABRIELE TOGNOZZI	Subaru Impreza	N4
88.	A. ALÉN (FIN)	J. AARIAINEN (FIN)	ANTON ALÉN	Subaru Impreza	N4
89.	D. CATANIA (I)	F. VESCARELLI (I)	DAVIDE CATANIA	Subaru Impreza	N4
90.	S. BENONI (I)	E. CANTONI (I)	STEFANO BENONI	Subaru Impreza	N4
91.	W. LAMONATO (I)	O. TOBALDO (I)	WALTER LAMONATO	Subaru Impreza	N4
92.	L. PETROCCO (I)	A. SAVINI (I)	LUCIO PETROCCO	Subaru Impreza	N4
94.	F. SCHIRRU (I)	S. MURTAS (I)	FABRIZIO SCHIRRU	Subaru Impreza	N4
95.	C. MURA (I)	G. PITTURRU (I)	COSTANTINO MURA	Mitsubishi Lancer Evo VIII	N4
96.	T. PILERI (I)	M. PILI (I)	TOMASO PILERI	Mitsubishi Lancer Evo VIII	N4
97.	G. DETTORI (I)	M. CORDA (I)	GIUSEPPE DETTORI	Mitsubishi Lancer Evo VIII	N4
98.	B. Anto CARAGLIU (I)	M. ATZEI (I)	BERNARDINO ANTONIO CARAGLIU	Mitsubishi Lancer Evo VI	N4
99.	G. CELLINO (I)	C. PISANO (I)	GIORGIO CELLINO	Subaru Impreza Sti	N4
100.	F. MARRONE (I)	M. PIGA (I)	FRANCESCO MARRONE	Mitsubishi Lancer Evo VI	N4
101.	M. BIASION (F)	C. BEYNET (F)	MATHIEU BIASION	Ford Fiesta ST	N3
102.	A. BETTEGA (I)	S. SCATTOLIN (I)	ALESSANDRO BETTEGA	Ford Fiesta ST	N3
103.	L. ATHNASSOULAS (GR)	N. MOUZAKIS (GR)	TEAM GREECE	Ford Fiesta ST	N3
104.	K. KESKINEN (FIN)	J. KOLJONEN (FIN)	KALLE KESKINEN	Ford Fiesta ST	N3
105.	G. SCHAMMEL (LUX)	R. JAMOUL (B)	JPS JUNIOR TEAM LUX	Ford Fiesta ST	N3
106.	E. VERTUNOV (RUS)	G. TROSHKIN (RUS)	EVGENY VERTUNOV	Ford Fiesta ST	N3
107.	T. CURTIS (GB)	A. BARGERY (GB)	TOM CURTIS	Ford Fiesta ST	N3
108.	N. TALI (I)	M. MIRABELLA (I)	NICOLA TALI	Opel Astra OPC	N3
110.	C. BERTOLIN (I)	M. ZANOTTO (I)	CORRADO BERTOLIN	Opel Astra Gsi	N3
111.	A. FRESI (I)	A. Martcel ORECCHIONI (I)	ANTONIO PIETRO FRESI	Seat Ibiza	N3
112.	G. PRANZONI (I)	P. PRANZONI (I)	GERRI PRANZONI	Renault Clio RS	N3
113.	S. FILIGHEDDU (I)	G. DE LUCA (I)	SALVATORE FILIGHEDDU	Peugeot 106	N2
114.	F. BUSCARINI (I)	M. GIOVANNINI (I)	FERDINANDO BUSCARINI	Rover MG ZR	N1

Championship Classifications

FIA Drivers (7/16)
1. Loeb — 5🏆 66
2. Grönholm — 2🏆 35
3. Sordo — 30
4. Stohl — 20
5. P. Solberg — 18
6. Hirvonen — 15
7. Galli — 11
8. Pons — 10
9. Bengué — 9
10. Atkinson — 8
11. H. Solberg — 7
12. Gardemeister — 6
13. Carlsson — 6
14. Sarrazin — 6
15. Kopecky — 4
16. Välimäki — 4
17. Rådström — 4
18. Duval — 4
19. Mac Hale — 3
20. Katajamäki — 3
21. Sohlberg — 3
22. Wilson — 1
23. Perez Companc, Arai... — 0

FIA Constructors (7/16)
1. Kronos Total Citroën WRT — 5🏆 85
2. BP-Ford World Rally Team — 2🏆 65
3. Subaru World Rally Team — 58
4. OMV-Peugeot Norway — 36
5. Stobart VK M-Sport Ford WRT — 15
6. Red Bull-Skoda Team — 14

FIA Production Car (3/8)
1. Al-Attiyah — 1🏆 24
2. Kuzaj — 13
3. Baldacci — 12
4. Arai — 1🏆 11
5. Nutahara — 1🏆 10
6. Higgins — 8
7. Marrini — 7
8. Ligato — 6
9. Heath — 5
10. Latvala — 4
11. Uspenskiy — 4
12. Beltrán — 4
13. Vojtech — 2
14. Name — 1
15. Pozzo — 0
16. Teiskonen — 0
17. Kamada — 0
18. Popov — 0

FIA Junior WRC (5/9)
1. Sandell — 1🏆 26
2. Andersson — 1🏆 21
3. Aava — 20
4. Rautenbach — 17
5. Béres — 12
6. Wilks — 1🏆 11
7. Tirabassi — 1🏆 11
8. Prokop — 1🏆 10
9. Casier — 8
10. Pressac — 7
11. Meeke — 6
12. Burkart — 6
13. Molder — 5
14. Valousek — 5
15. Kosciuszko — 5
16. Kara — 5
17. Pinomäki — 4
18. Betti — 3
19. Zachrisson — 2
20. Bonato — 1
21. Bordignon, Clark, Cortinovis, Karlsson — 0

Special Stages Times

www.rallyitaliasardegna.com
www.wrc.com

SS1 Terranova 1 (24.10 km)
1.Grönholm 17'06"9; 2.Atkinson +12"1;
3.Hirvonen +14"1; 4.P.Solberg +17"8;
5.Loeb +18"0; 6.Sordo +24"8;
7.Pons +29"2; 8.Välimäki +31"6...
J-WRC > 19.Aava 19'04"9

SS2 Onanì 1 (18.47 km)
1.Grönholm 12'46"0; 2.Hirvonen +6"4;
3.Galli +8"7; 4.H.Solberg +10"4;
5.Loeb +11"5; 6.Pons +12"1;
7.P.Solberg +13"1; 8.Atkinson +16"9...
J-WRC > 18.Aava 13'56"0

SS3 Siniscola 1 (22.25 km)
1.Grönholm 17'29"3;
2.H.Solberg +10"6; 3.Loeb +10"9;
4.P.Solberg +18"0; 5.Hirvonen +19"6;
6.Välimäki +23"0; 7.Atkinson +25"6;
8.Galli +26"8...
J-WRC > 20.Aava 19'28"0

SS4 Terranova 2 (24.10 km)
1.Loeb 16'32"4; 2.Grönholm +1"2;
3.Hirvonen +5"7; 4.H.Solberg +8"3;
5.P.Solberg +8"7; 6.Galli +17"5;
7.Sordo +18"6; 8.Pons +19"0...
J-WRC > 19.Wilks 18'38"9

SS5 Onanì 2 (18.47 km)
1.Loeb 12'27"4; 2.Grönholm +3"9;
3.Hirvonen +7"1; 4.Galli +11"0;
5.Stohl +12"3; 6.Sordo +13"0;
7.H.Solberg +17"3;
8.Atkinson/Pons +21"0...
J-WRC > 18.Wilks 14'08"5

SS6 Siniscola 2 (22.25 km)
1.Grönholm 17'12"8; 2.Loeb +0"1;
3.Hirvonen +16"4; 4.Sordo +18"6;
5.Galli +25"8; 6.H.Solberg +30"1;
7.Pons +30"3; 8.Atkinson +37"7...
J-WRC > 17.Wilks 19'33"8

Classification Leg 1
1.Grönholm 1h33'39"9; 2.Loeb +35"4;
3.Hirvonen +1'04"2;
4.H.Solberg +1'44"5; 5.Sordo +2'04"3;
6.Galli +2'06"8; 7.Atkinson +2'14"1;
8.Pons +2'29"6...
J-WRC > 18.Wilks 1h45'06"6

SS7 Loelle 1 (25.20 km)
1.Grönholm 15'30"8; 2.Loeb +1"1;
3.P.Solberg +9"0; 4.Hirvonen +20"2;
5.Galli +20"5; 6.H.Solberg +25"0;
7.Sordo +28"1; 8.Atkinson +28"6...
J-WRC > 22.Aava 17'38"8

SS8 Monte Lerno 1 (31.20 km)
1.Loeb 20'32"8; 2.P.Solberg +16"7;
3.Hirvonen +26"8; 4.Sordo +32"4;
5.Galli +38"3; 6.Atkinson +39"0;
7.Pons +42"6; 8.H.Solberg +51"8...
J-WRC > 20.Aava 23'11"6

SS9 Su Filigosu 1 (12.28 km)
1.Loeb 8'17"8; 2.Galli +2"3;
3.P.Solberg +4"6; 4.Sordo +9"4;
5.Pons +12"0; 6.Atkinson +13"5;
7.Välimäki +18"1; 8.Stohl +22"3...
J-WRC > 20.Andersson 9'07"0

SS10 Loelle 2 (25.20 Km)
1.P.Solberg 15'22"3; 2.Galli +6"6;
3.Sordo +6"9; 4.Loeb +7"1;
5.Hirvonen +10"4; 6.Atkinson +14"9;
7.Pons +23"3; 8.Stohl +25"5...
J-WRC > 19.Andersson 17'14"6

SS11 Monte Lerno 2 (31.20 km)
1.Loeb 20'12"7; 2.Sordo +14"4;
3.Hirvonen +14"9; 4.Galli +20"1;
5.Atkinson +20"4; 6.P.Solberg +24"7;
7.Pons +36"9; 8.Stohl +49"2...
J-WRC > 19.Andersson 22'47"8

SS12 Su Filigosu 2 (12.28 km)
1.Loeb 8'06"1; 2.Hirvonen +3"5;
3.Sordo +4"1; 4.P.Solberg +5"7;
5.Atkinson +9"8; 6.Pons +14"7;
7.Välimäki +15"4; 8.Sohlberg +15"9...
J-WRC > 18.Andersson 8'51"6

Classification Leg 2
1.Loeb 3h02'26"0; 2.Hirvonen +2'17"0;
3.Sordo +2'56"0; 4.Pons +4'27"1;
5.Atkinson +5'56"7;
6.Välimäki +6'01"6;
7.Sohlberg +6'29"1;
8.P.Solberg +6'57"8...
J-WRC > 18.Wilks 3h24'58"6

SS13 S. Giacomo 1 (13.46 km)
1.P.Solberg 10'09"3; 2.Loeb +0"9;
3.Hirvonen +6"3; 4.Atkinson +9"8;
5.Sordo +10"2; 6.Stohl +18"4;
7.Pons +18"6; 8.Välimäki +19"2...
J-WRC > 18.Andersson 11'13"5

SS14 La Prugnola 1 (9.59 km)
1.Atkinson 4'56"0; 2.Loeb +4"3;
3.Hirvonen +5"8; 4.P.Solberg +7"6;
5.Sordo +8"0; 6.Pons +9"3;
7.Sohlberg +9"8; 8.Välimäki +10"0...
J-WRC > 19.Andersson 5'27"2

SS15 Campovaglio 1 (15.92 Km)
1.Loeb 10'53"4; 2.Atkinson +6"7;
3.P.Solberg +7"5; 4.Sordo +16"0;
5.Hirvonen +16"1; 6.Kopecky +16"6;
7.Välimäki +17"7; 8.Duval +18"3...
J-WRC > 18.Andersson 12'02"9

SS16 La Prugnola 2 (9.59 Km)
1.P.Solberg 4'50"5; 2.Hirvonen +0"3;
3.Atkinson +0"5; 4.Loeb +1"1;
5.Duval +2"6; 6.Sordo +5"6;
7.Pons +7"1; 8.Välimäki +7"2...
J-WRC > 17.Andersson 5'18"5

SS17 Campovaglio 2 (15.92 Km)
1.Loeb 10'40"1; 2.P.Solberg +1"1;
3.Sordo/Atkinson +4"4;
5.Kopecky +5"2; 6.Välimäki +7"6;
7.Hirvonen +10"1; 8.Stohl +11"0...
J-WRC > 17.Andersson 11'40"0

SS18 S. Giacomo 2 (13.46 Km)
1.Kopecky 10'09"2; 2.Hirvonen +0"2;
3.Sordo +1"9; 4.Sohlberg +4"5;
5.Duval +6"0; 6.Pons +7"4;
7.Stohl +7"6; 8.Loeb +8"1...
J-WRC > 15.Aava/Andersson 11'11"9

Results

	Driver - Co-driver	Car	Gr.	Time
1	Loeb - Elena	Citroën Xsara WRC	A8	3h54'18"9
2	Hirvonen - Lehtinen	Ford Focus RS WRC 06	A8	+ 2'41"4
3	Sordo - Marti	Citroën Xsara WRC	A8	+ 3'27"7
4	Pons - Del Barrio	Citroën Xsara WRC	A8	+ 5'28"3
5	Välimäki - Kalliolepo	Mitsubishi Lancer WRC 05	A8	+ 7'08"8
6	Sohlberg - Tuominen	Subaru Impreza WRC	A8	+ 7'36"9
7	Stohl - Minor	Peugeot 307 WRC	A8	+ 8'18"4
8	Duval - Privato	Skoda Fabia WRC	A8	+ 9'45"8
9	P. Solberg - Mills	Subaru Impreza WRC 2006	A8	+ 10'19"9
10	Atkinson - Macneall	Subaru Impreza WRC 2006	A8	+ 11'03"9
14	Hänninen - Sallinen	Mitsubishi Lancer Evo IX	N4	+ 28'04"1
15	Sandell - Axelsson	Renault Clio S1600	A6/J	+ 32'06"3
16	Rautenbach - Senior	Renault Clio S1600	A6/J	+ 37'14"7
18	Aava - Sikk	Suzuki Swift S1600	A6/J	+ 37'43"1

Leading Retirements (19)

TC12D	Grönholm - Rautiainen	Ford Focus RS WRC 06	Oil pressure
TC12D	H. Solberg - Menkerud	Peugeot 307 WRC	Off
TC12D	Katajamaki - Alanne	Ford Focus RS WRC 04	Off
TC12D	Galli - Bernacchini	Peugeot 307 WRC	Radiator
TC12D	Casier - Miclotte	Renault Clio S1600	Engine

Performers

	1	2	3	4	5	6	C6	Nb SS
Loeb	8	4	1	2	2	-	17	18
Grönholm	5	2	-	-	-	-	7	7
P. Solberg	3	2	3	4	1	1	14	18
Atkinson	1	2	2	1	1	4	11	17
Kopecky	1	-	-	-	1	1	3	12
Hirvonen	-	4	8	1	3	-	16	18
Galli	-	2	1	2	4	1	10	12
Sordo	-	1	4	4	2	3	14	18
H. Solberg	-	1	-	2	-	2	5	8
Duval	-	-	-	2	-	-	2	18
Sohlberg	-	-	-	1	-	-	1	18
Pons	-	-	-	-	1	3	4	18
Stohl	-	-	-	-	1	1	2	18
Välimäki	-	-	-	-	2	2	18	

Leaders

SS1 > SS7	Grönholm
SS8 > SS18	Loeb

Previous winners

2004	Solberg - Mills	2005	Loeb - Elena
	Subaru Impreza WRC 2004		Citroën Xsara WRC

Greece

01
02
03
04
05
06
07

09
10
11
12
13
14
15
16

Gronholm back in the winner's circle
Sébastien Loeb and Daniel Elena's run of victories came to an end on Greek soil. They did not manage to rack up number 6 on the trot but finished second after being slowed by the damage to their car caused by a puncture. Marcus Grönholm scored his third win of the season and the Ford Focus's fifth in Greece. Despite this success he was still a long way behind Loeb in the title chase.

Greece

Manfred Stohl was heavily delayed by a fire at the start of the event and went pedal to metal to make up lost ground. He crashed out in the final leg destroying his 307 WRC.

Sébastien Loeb is not worried despite appearances. His second place in Greece helped him maintain his comfortable lead in the championship.

THE RALLY
Ford wins on familiar territory

What would have happened if the rally had not been suddenly turned on its head? Would Marcus Grönholm have managed to stay in front of Sébastien Loeb for whom second place is equivalent to a defeat? Would the Citroën driver have been able to up his game to match the pace of his Ford-mounted rival, who had been particularly quick since the start of the rally taking the lead at the end of the second stage? All these questions must remain unanswered, as the winner of the Greek rally was decided at the end of the second leg.

Toni Gardemeister drove a stonking rally on his first time in a Xsara. It was his first rally since Monte Carlo and he came home in fourth place.

When Marcus Grönholm does not make any driving mistakes he is unbeatable as proved by his display in the Acropolis rally.

3rd June 2006: Special stage 13: Psatha 2, length 7.4 kms, final timed section on the second day. Grönholm and Timo Rautiainen were in front with a lead of 25.1s over Sébastien Loeb and 1m 16.6s in hand over Petter Solberg. The others were way behind as Mikko Hirvonen in fourth was already over 3 minutes in arrears. Solberg in his Subaru was not too unhappy with the first part of the rally. The car was quicker but he was obliged to let his two main rivals past after going off in Psatha first time round. He was looking good for third place on the rostrum, but it all went wrong on the liaison section leading to SS13 on which he almost had a head-on collision with a car coming in the opposite direction. He just managed to avoid it and hit a big rock instead breaking a steering arm. "It was bloody amazing," he said afterwards. "I was coming into a right-hander when I was obliged to swerve to avoid a car coming in the wrong direction!"

The midnight blue Impreza never made it to the start of the stage. So only Loeb looked like he could pose a threat to Grönholm. It was a vain hope. "After the start of this loop and particularly in Kineta (SS12), the car and the above all tyres were subjected to hell. A kilometre-and-a-half after the start of Psatha we had a puncture on the right-hand rear. Filling it with foam was no help. We decided to continue and lost less time than if we had stopped to change the wheel."

The loss of time, though, was horrendous. Grönholm was again fastest in 11m 23.6s while Loeb finished the stage in twelfth place with a time that was 1m 22.1s slower than the Finn's.

When he arrived at the halt he saw the extent of the damage: "It was impossible to fix the wheel again," he continued. "The suspension had suffered too much. We continued like this, and then stopped to replace the

Bozian put a new 307 at the disposal of Henning Solberg after his other one was destroyed in Sardinia. He drove it to fifth place in the Greek classic.

And rightly so as their work allowed the Franco-Monegasque pairing to hang on to second place. After the second leg they were 1m 47.2s behind their Finnish rivals but the eight points for second place were well within their grasp.

It was a pity that the puncture had brought the battle with Grönholm to a premature halt. As they had shown in the first leg and then in nine-tenths of the second, they had the speed if not to pass the Finn at least to put pressure on him and maybe force him into making a mistake. The proof was that on the first day when they were first out the roads they fought like lions not to concede too much time. Which they did pretty well as in the evening they were 35.5s behind Marcus and 9.2s down on Solberg. The Ford driver was in scintillating form, and set all the fastest times with the exception of the super special programmed in the Olympic stadium that was packed to the gills. While Nikos Aliagas, a Franc-Greek rock star warmed up the crowd, Loeb beat his rival by exactly 2 seconds.

After that, on a day when the specials were run in suffocating heat the only notable incidents among the front-runners hit Atkinson (broken rear differential) and Gardemeister (minor off). There was also a succession of punctures whose effects were attenuated by the foam in the BF Goodrich and Pirelli tyres.

On Saturday morning Loeb went for it until he was slowed by the incident mentioned above. He was quickest in Kineta 1 (the longest special of the event, 37.3 kms), which enabled him to slip past Solberg into second place. He was again fastest in Kineta second time through while all the other stages fell to Grönholm.

Solberg and Loeb were not the only victims of the second leg. Kopecky and Duval in their private Skodas also came to grief: wheel torn off for the former and rear cradle twisted for the latter in Kineta second time through. Henning Solberg was suffering from defective suspension and Atkinson twisted a

right-hand rear wheel with the spare that was already filled with foam and which held as best it could. Finally, we clocked in on time on two wheels and a rim!"

Luckily, the Greek police were understanding and allowed the truncated Xasra to cover around 50 kilometres including a section on the motorway! In the past their British counterparts were less accommodating with Tommi Mäkinen in the 1999 RAC Rally when he was battling for the title, or the New Zealand cops with Colin McRae. Lucky Loeb! When such misadventures befall him they do so in countries where the local arm of the law is more sympathetic like in Turkey last year when he finished on 3 wheels. Daniel Elena had calculated the right average to enable them to clock into the service park on time without having to ask too much of the car. Immediately it arrived the Kronos mechanics swarmed round it and in 45 minutes it was as good as new! It was not an easy job, however. All the underbody protection had to be replaced, as had the inside of the wings, the gearbox, the rear axle, all the transmission and the exhausts. They did it in 43 minutes! Just as Loeb and Elena were getting back into their cars they applauded their mechanics which triggered a spontaneous ovation from the spectators. Marc Van Dalen, the man in charge of the Belgian team, was very

moved. "I was all goose flesh. Moments like that are unforgettable in the life of a rally lover. It's in difficult circumstances that you can judge the value of a team. I'm proud of them."

Although the route was considerably modified for the 2006 event the Acropolis is still a magnificent event even if Loeb and Elena haven't got much time to admire the scenery.

Greece

Mikko Hirvonen followed up his second place in Italy with a third in Greece after Petter Solberg went off at the end of the rally.

It was the stupidest retirement of the year. Petter Solberg was eliminated when he swerved to avoid a car coming in the opposite direction on the liaison section breaking his suspension and steering.

wishbone. And of course, there were the usual punctures.

So what was to be expected from the third leg? Not a lot in fact. A battle between Sordo and Henning Solberg for fourth place? Petter Solberg getting back into the points in the Super Rally? A scrap between Stohl-Pons for seventh? There was a bit of all that but the classification was decided more by retirements and technical problems on this car-breaking terrain than by pure speed. Stohl cartwheeled out of the rally in the first stage. Sordo's engine was firing on 3 cylinders (plug), which slowed him a lot. Pons finished the sixteenth special on the rim. Petter Solberg took advantage of Marcus's cautious approach, as victory was all that counted for the mighty Finn, and set all the scratch times in the final leg. In fact, the Ford driver gave himself a bit of a scare when he broke a damper in the seventeenth special. The final timed stage was in the Athens' stadium – almost empty this time due to the high price of the tickets – and it went to Grönholm giving him a total of eleven fastest times out of a possible eighteen. "It's very satisfactory to win such a difficult rally," acknowledged the big Finn. "The Ford was very solid and quick throughout the event. The terrain was terrible and I could never really drive with complete freedom, because I realised just how easy it would be to damage the car on a rock. The BF Goodrich tyres also proved very tough on such demanding roads and each time we had a puncture the foam worked perfectly. The Focus has real potential and I'm sure we'll be up there fighting for victory in the rallies to come."

Xavier Pons's display was not very impressive. The Spaniard finished eighth after a battle with Manfred Stohl.

Dani Sordo again showed his talent by scoring points for the seventh time (3 for sixth place) since the start of the season.

It was devoutly to be hoped. After the eighth round of the championship before the summer break he was 29 points behind Loeb; in other words he had pulled back only 2 in Greece. Thanks to Hirvonen's rather fortunate third place as his gearbox was acting up and he had to cover the final super special in second, Ford scored more points than Citroën-Kronos in the manufacturers' championship. The Blue Oval manufacturer was now only 15 points behind the Franco-Belgian team. The Acropolis Rally has always been a happy hunting ground for Ford, which won the event for the fifth time in 7 years. ■

PRODUCTION
Down to the wire

If in the WRC there was no suspense after the end of the second leg it went down to the wire in the Production category. There was a terrific battle for victory between the front-runners. Right from the start Baldacci (Mitsubishi), Al-Attiyah (Subaru) and Teiskonen from Finland (Subaru) went at it hammer and tongs for victory. Gabriel Pozzo soon put everybody in their place and took up the running after stage 5. He stayed in the lead in his Mitsubishi until almost the end of the second leg. Unfortunately in SS12 he damaged his car's radiator leading to overheating so he had to lift off. He fell back to fourth letting Al-Attiyah into first place. But the Qatari was under intense pressure from Teiskonen and the two drivers swapped the lead like a hot potato! The Finn was given a big help by the

Petter Solberg's Impreza kicks up the dust in his 100th WRC event that ended in a seventh place finish thanks to the super rally. It was a far cry from what he expected.

Marcus Grönholm's hard-charging drive in his Ford Focus was a delight for the spectators in Greece.

Loeb reached the service park at the end of the second leg on three then two wheels, the result of a puncture. He still managed to hang on to his second place.

5-minute penalty inflicted on his rival on Saturday evening for not following the road book. But Al-Attiyah finally scored a narrow win and returned triumphant to the big Olympic Stadium, which he particularly likes. Two years ago he paraded therein as an athlete representing his country in clay pigeon shooting in which he came fourth. He finished with just 23 seconds in hand over Pozzo who had fought his way back to the front. The latter had to push his car to the finishing line in the final stage as the engine gave up the ghost! Into third came a lucky Teiskonen. On Sunday morning when he reckoned that he would win after Al-Attiyah's penalty he was delayed by broken suspension. He fell back to fourth spot but inherited third after Baldacci (who finished third on the road) was disqualified because his Mitsubishi's bumpers were not in place.

Thanks to his second victory (after Argentina) Al-Attiyah left Greece with a comfortable lead of 17 points in the championship from Baldacci. The Qatari had scored points in all 4 rounds held up till then and was the man to beat in the first half of the season. ■

Marcus Grönholm and Timo Rautiainen express their delight at scoring their third victory of the season after a scintillating display.

Greece results

53rd ACROPOLIS RALLY

Organiser Details
Automobile & Touring Club of Greece - ELPA,
395 Messogion Ave,
153 43 Agia Paraskevi,
Athens, Greece
Tel.: +3021 09792572
Fax: +3021 06068983

BP Ultimate Acropolis Rally

8th leg of FIA 2006 World Rally Championship
for constructors and drivers.
4th leg of FIA Production Car World Championship.

Date June 1st - 4, 2006

Route
1279.29 km divised in 3 legs.
18 special stages on dirt roads (355.62 km).

Starting Procedure - Super Special
Thursday, June 1st (18:00),
Olympic Stadium Athens
1 special stage (2.80 km)

Leg 1
Friday, June 2nd (08:38/16:56),
Lamia > Lamia, 505.45 km;
6 special stages (120.80 km)

Leg 2
Saturday, June 3rd (08:57/16:24),
Lamia > Lamia, 450.92 km;
7 special stages (134.68 km)

Leg 3
Sunday, June 4 (07:47/14:15),
Lamia > Lamia, 322.92 km;
5 special stages (100.14 km)

Entry List (91) - 84 starters

N°	Driver (Nat.)	Co-driver (Nat.)	Team	Car	Group & FIA Priority
1.	S. LOEB (F)	D. ELENA (MC)	KRONOS TOTAL CITROEN WRT	Citroën Xsara WRC	A8 1
2.	X. PONS (E)	C. DEL BARRIO (E)	KRONOS TOTAL CITROEN WRT	Citroën Xsara WRC	A8 1
3.	M. GRÖNHOLM (FIN)	T. RAUTIAINEN (FIN)	BP FORD WORLD RALLY TEAM	Ford Focus RS WRC 06	A8 1
4.	M. HIRVONEN (FIN)	J. LEHTINEN (FIN)	BP FORD WORLD RALLY TEAM	Ford Focus RS WRC 06	A8 1
5.	P. SOLBERG (N)	P. MILLS (GB)	SUBARU WORLD RALLY TEAM	Subaru Impreza WRC 2006	A8 1
6.	C. ATKINSON (AUS)	G. MACNEALL (AUS)	SUBARU WORLD RALLY TEAM	Subaru Impreza WRC 2006	A8 1
7.	M. STOHL (A)	I. MINOR (A)	OMV - PEUGEOT NORWAY	Peugeot 307 WRC	A8 1
8.	H. SOLBERG (N)	C. MENKERUD (N)	OMV - PEUGEOT NORWAY	Peugeot 307 WRC	A8 1
9.	M. WILSON (GB)	M. ORR (GB)	STOBART - VK - M-SPORT FORD RALLY TEAM	Ford Focus RS WRC 04	A8 1
10.	K. KATAJAMAKI (FIN)	T. ALANNE (FIN)	STOBART - VK - M-SPORT FORD RALLY TEAM	Ford Focus RS WRC 04	A8 1
11.	H. ROVANPERÄ (FIN)	R. PIETILÄINEN (FIN)	RED BULL - SKODA TEAM	Skoda Fabia WRC	A8 1
12.	A. AIGNER (A)	K. WICHA (D)	RED BULL - SKODA TEAM	Skoda Fabia WRC	A8 1
14.	D. SORDO (E)	M. MARTI (E)	DANIEL SORDO	Citroën Xsara WRC	A8 2
16.	T. GARDEMEISTER (FIN)	J. HONKANEN (FIN)	ASTRA RACING	Citroën Xsara WRC	A8 2
17.	J. KOPECKY (CZ)	F. SCHOVANEK (CZ)	CZECH RALLY TEAM SKODA- KOPECKY	Skoda Fabia WRC	A8 2
18.	F. DUVAL (B)	P. PIVATO (F)	FIRST MOTORSPORT	Skoda Fabia WRC	A8 2
19.	A. VOVOS (GR)	". EL - EM " (GR)	EGNATIA ASFALISTIKI SA	Subaru Impreza S11 WRC	A8 2
20.	J. VÄLIMÄKI (FIN)	J. KALLIOLEPO (FIN)	JUSSI VÄLIMÄKI	Mitsubishi Lancer WRC	A8 2
31.	T. ARAI (J)	T. SIRCOMBE (NZ)	SUBARU TEAM ARAI	Subaru Impreza	N4 3
32.	M. LIGATO (RA)	R. GARCIA (RA)	MARCOS LIGATO	Mitsubishi Lancer Evo 9	N4 3
34.	S. BELTRÁN (RA)	R. ROJAS (RCH)	SEBASTIÁN BELTRÁN	Mitsubishi Lancer Evo 9	N4 3
35.	G. POZZO (RA)	D. STILLO (RA)	GABRIEL POZZO	Mitsubishi Lancer Evo 9	N4 3
36.	M. BALDACCI (RSM)	G. AGNESE (I)	MIRCO BALDACCI	Mitsubishi Lancer Evo 9	N4 3
37.	J. LATVALA (FIN)	M. ANTTILA (FIN)	JARI-MATTI LATVALA	Subaru Impreza WRX Sti Spec	N4 3
38.	L. KUZAJ (PL)	M. SZCZEPANIAK (PL)	AUTOMOBILKUB RZEMIESLNIK WARSZAWA	Subaru Impreza	N4 3
39.	N. AL-ATTIYAH (QAT)	C. PATTERSON (GB)	QMMF	Subaru Impreza Spec C 06	N4 3
40.	S. MARRINI (I)	T. SANDRONI (I)	ERRANI TEAM GROUP	Mitsubishi Lancer Evo 9	N4 3
41.	T. KAMADA (J)	H. ICHINO (J)	SUBARU TEAM QUASYS	Subaru Impreza	N4 3
42.	S. USPENSKIY (RUS)	D. EREMEEV (RUS)	SUBARU RALLY TEAM RUSSIA	Subaru Impreza WRX Sti Spec	N4 3
43.	A. JEREB (SLO)	M. KACIN (SLO)	OMV CEE RALLY TEAM	Mitsubishi Lancer Evo 9	N4 3
45.	A. TEISKONEN (FIN)	M. TEISKONEN (FIN)	SYMS RALLY TEAM	Subaru Impreza WRX Sti Spec	N4 3
46.	N. HEATH (GB)	S. LANCASTER (GB)	NIGEL HEATH	Subaru Impreza N12 Spec C	N4 3
60.	D. NASSOULAS (GR)	M. PATRIKOUSSIS (GR)	DIMITRIS NASSOULAS	Mitsubishi Lancer Evo 7	N4
61.	G. NIORAS (GR)	A. GOUSSETIS (GR)	HELLENIC POLICE	Mitsubishi Lancer Evo 7	N4
62.	E. HALKIAS (GR)	L. MAHAERAS (GR)	EFTHIMIOS HALKIAS	Mitsubishi Lancer Evo 8	N4
63.	D. PSYLOS (GR)	K. KONDOS (GR)	PSYLOS DIMITRIS - ALAMAP TEAM	Mitsubishi Lancer Evo 8	N4
65.	K. AL QASSIMI (UAE)	N. BEECH (GB)	KHALID AL-QASSIMI	Subaru WRX Sti	N4
66.	K. APOSTOLOU (GR)	M. KRIADIS (GR)	APOSTOLOU KONSTANTINOS	Mitsubishi Lancer Evo 6	A8
67.	E. STEFANIS (GR)	K. STEFANIS (GR)	EMMANUEL STEFANIS	Ford Focus WRC	A8
68.	K. PARADISSIS (GR)	M. TAKOU (GR)	LION HELLAS SA	Peugeot 206 Super 1600	A6
69.	M. KOSCIUSZKO (PL)	J. BARAN (PL)	MICHAL KOSCIUSZKO	Suzuki Ignis Super 1600	A6
70.	". LEONIDAS " (GR)	G. KOTSALIS (GR)	"LEONIDAS"	Renault Clio Super 1600	A6
73.	K. PITSOS (GR)	S. Jason KARAPAPAZIS (GR)	KONSTANTINOS PITSOS	Mitsubishi Lancer Evo 8	N4
74.	C. PLATIS (GR)	G. MELISSOURGOS (GR)	CHRISTOS PLATIS	Subaru Impreza WRX	N4
76.	". TAZ " (GR)	K. SOUKOULIS (GR)	"TAZ"	Mitsubishi Lancer Evo 8	N4
77.	". TROFONIOS " (GR)	A. PALEOLOGOS (GR)	"TROFONIOS"	Mitsubishi Lancer Evo 8	N4
78.	". KIRKOS " (GR)	I. SENGOS (GR)	"JUNIOR KIRKOS"	Mitsubishi Lancer Evo 7	A8
79.	G. KANTZAVELOS (GR)	M. STAVROPOULOU (GR)	GEORGE KANTZAVELOS	Mitsubishi Lancer Evo 7	A8
80.	P. MOSHOUTIS (GR)	G. KAIRIS (GR)	PAVLOS MOSHOUTIS	Mitsubishi Lancer Evo 7	N4
81.	C. RAUTENBACH (ZW)	D. SENIOR (GB)	CONRAD RAUTENBACH	Subaru Impreza	N4
82.	H. KALTSOUNIS (GR)	K. EXARHOS (GR)	HARIS KALTSOUNIS	Opel Corsa Super 1600	A6
83.	I. PLAGOS (GR)	K. KAKALIS (GR)	HELLENIC POLICE	Nissan Micra K11 Kit Car	A5
84.	D. HATZIRIGAS (GR)	M. MIHAELAKIS (GR)	GEORGE HATZIRIGAS	MG ZR 105	A5
85.	H. GAZETAS (GR)	G. FASKIOTIS (GR)	GAZETAS H. - ALAMAP TEAM	Toyota Yaris	A5
86.	S. STRATELIS (GR)	T. GAGAKAS (GR)	STERGIOS STRATELIS	Subaru Impreza Spec C	N4
87.	L. BALDACCI (RSM)	D. D'ESPOSITO (I)	LORIS BALDACCI	Subaru Impreza Spec C	N4
88.	A. KRATTIGER (CH)	E. CARNELOS (I)	ANDREAS KRATTIGER	Mitsubishi Lancer Evo 8	N4
89.	F. TREVISIN (I)	A. BORDIN (I)	FRANCESCO TREVISIN	Subaru Impreza Sti	N4
90.	D. SPANOS (GR)	S. GOTOVOS (GR)	DIONYSSIS SPANOS	Subaru Impreza Sti	N4
91.	M. FURIBONDI (I)	M. DI EGIDIO (I)	MARCELLO FURIBONDI	Subaru Impreza Sti	N4
92.	A. TSILIS (GR)	". KAS " (GR)	ATHANASSIOS TSILIS	Mitsubishi Lancer Evo 6	N4
93.	S. STAVRIANOUDAKIS (GR)	P. KONDYLIS (GR)	STELIOS STAVRIANOUDAKIS	Subaru Impreza 555	N4
94.	". PANOS " (GR)	". VAS " (GR)	PANOS - ALAMAP TEAM	Mitsubishi Lancer Evo 8	N4
95.	G. KLOUVATOS (GR)	A. VLAHOGENIS (GR)	GEORGE KLOUVATOS	Mitsubishi Lancer Evo 8	N4
96.	D. GAZETAS (GR)	A. PAPAGEORGIOU (GR)	DIONISSIS GAZETAS	Mitsubishi Lancer Evo 7	A8
97.	I. MARGARONIS (GR)	K. MIKES (GR)	IOANNIS MARGARONIS	Hyundai Accent	A6
98.	G. LADOGIANNIS (GR)	N. LADOGIANNIS (GR)	GRIGORIS LADOGIANNIS	Fiat Seicento	A5
99.	C. EKONOMOU (GR)	T. HATZITHEODORIDIS (GR)	CHRISTOS EKONOMOU	Citroën C2 R2 Kit Car	A6
100.	D. MAVRODIS (GR)	D. KEHAGIAS (GR)	DIONISSIS MAVRODIS	Nissan Micra K11	A5
101.	D. ARVANITIS (GR)	M. TSAOUSGLOU (GR)	DIMITRIS ARVANITIS	Honda Civic	A6
102.	". CASTOR " (GR)	E. KAFAOGLOU (GR)	"CASTOR"	Peugeot 206 Kit Car	A6
103.	M. HONDA (CZ)	L. VICIKOVA (CZ)	MICHAEL HONDA	Citroën Saxo Kit Car	A6
104.	K. LABOURAS (GR)	A. KOTZIAS (GR)	KONSTANTINOS LABOURAS	Toyota Corolla AE 111	A6
105.	C. STATHAKI (GR)	J. SABANIKOU (GR)	CHRISTINA MYRTO STATHAKI	Peugeot 206 Kit Car	A6
106.	D. VASSILIS (GR)	". IKAROS " (GR)	DIMITRIS VASSILIS	Peugeot 206 XS	A6
107.	N. PARAPERAS (GR)	P. Kritikos KYRATZIS (GR)	NIKOS PARAPERAS	MG ZR 160	A7
108.	I. ZOUNIS (GR)	S. DEMETZIS (GR)	SOMA PIROSVESTIKO	MG ZR-105	A5
109.	D. KAPNIAS (GR)	E. SEVASTOPOULOS (GR)	KAPNIAS D - ALAL TEAM	Toyota Yaris	A5
110.	K. PAPADIMITROPOULOS (GR)	S. SEIMENIS (GR)	KONSTANTINOS PAPADIMITROPOULOS	Toyota Yaris	A5
111.	D. ANGELETOS (GR)	E. VELENTZAS (GR)	DIMITRIS ANGELETOS	Nissan Micra	A5
112.	T. KATSABEKIS (GR)	C. FLAKOS (GR)	THEMISTOKLIS KATSABEKIS	VW Polo	A5
113.	". IRAKLIS " (GR)	G. PAPAGEORGIOU (GR)	"IRAKLIS"	Nissan Almera	A7
114.	A. NICOLAOU (CY)	I. IORDANOU (CY)	ANDREAS NICOLAOU	Suzuki Ignis Sport	N2
115.	P. HATZITSOPANIS (GR)	N. PETROPOULOS (GR)	PANAYIOTIS HATZITSOPANIS	Mitsubishi Lancer Evo 8	N4

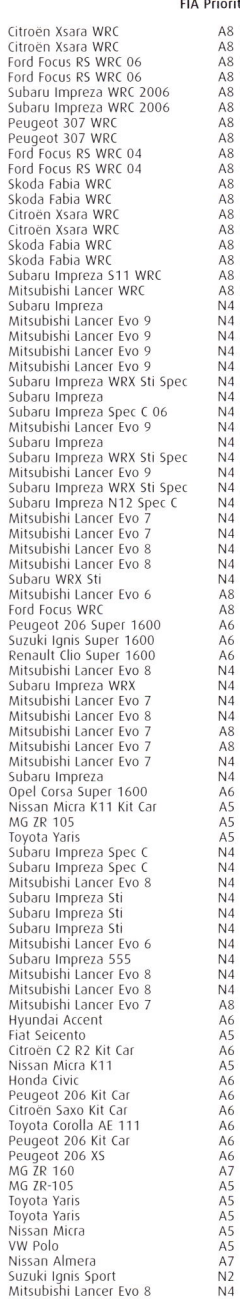

Championship Classifications

FIA Drivers (8/16)
1. Loeb 5🏆 74
2. Grönholm 3🏆 45
3. Sordo 33
3. Hirvonen 21
5. P. Solberg 20
6. Stohl 20
7. Galli 11
8. Gardemeister 11
9. Pons 11
10. H. Solberg 11
11. Bengué 9
12. Atkinson 8
13. Carlsson 6
14. Sarrazin 6
15. Välimäki 4
16. Kopecky 4
17. Rådström 4
18. Duval 4
19. MacHale 3
20. Katajamäki 3
21. Sohlberg 3
22. Wilson 1
23. Perez Companc, Arai... 0

FIA Constructors (8/16)
1. Kronos Total Citroën WRT 5🏆 96
2. BP-Ford World Rally Team 3🏆 81
3. Subaru World Rally Team 63
4. OMV-Peugeot Norway 41
5. Stobart VK M-Sport Ford WRT 17
6. Red Bull-Skoda Team 14

FIA Production Car (4/8)
1. Al-Attiyah 2🏆 34
2. Baldacci 17
3. Arai 1🏆 15
4. Kuzaj 13
5. Nutahara 1🏆 10
6. Higgins 8
7. Pozzo 8
8. Marrini 8
9. Ligato 8
10. Latvala 7
11. Teiskonen 6
12. Heath 5
13. Uspenskiy 4
14. Beltrán 4
15. Vojtech 2
16. Name 1
17. Kamada 0
18. Popov 0
Higgins Excluded 8

FIA Junior WRC (5/9)
1. Sandell 1🏆 26
2. Andersson 1🏆 21
3. Aava 20
4. Rautenbach 17
5. Béres 12
6. Wilks 1🏆 11
7. Tirabassi 1🏆 11
8. Prokop 1🏆 10
9. Casier 8
10. Pressac 7
11. Meeke 6
12. Burkart 6
13. Molder 5
14. Valousek 5
15. Kosciuszko 5
16. Kara 5
17. Pinomäki 4
18. Betti 3
19. Zachrisson 2
20. Bonato 1
21. Bordignon, Clark... 0

A. Aigner
J. Välimäki
M. Baldacci
N. Heath
G. Pozzo
A. Teiskonen

Special Stages Times

www.acropolisrally.gr
www.wrc.com

SS1 Oaka 1 (2.80 km)
1.Loeb 2'21"4; 2.Grönholm +2"0;
3.Hirvonen +2"8; 4.Duval +3"4;
5.Sordo +4"0; 6.Atkinson +4"8;
7.H.Solberg/Kopecky +5"0...
P-WRC > 20.Baldacci 2'33"0

SS2 Imittos 1 (11.44 km)
1.Grönholm 7'03"9; 2.P.Solberg +0"8;
3.Loeb +6"4; 4.Hirvonen +8"8;
5.Atkinson +9"3; 6.Duval +9"9;
7.Gardemeister +11"1; 8.Pons +11"3...
P-WRC > 19.Al-Attiyah 7'56"4

SS3 Skourta 1 (23.80 km)
1.Grönholm 14'40"1; 2.P.Solberg +6"1;
3.Loeb +8"0; 4.PHirvonen +19"7;
5.Duval +22"1; 6.Gardemeister +23"2;
7.Sordo +27"3; 8.Stohl +29"0...
P-WRC > 19.Pozzo 16'20"6

SS4 Thiva 1 (23.76 km)
1.Grönholm 17'16"9; 2.P.Solberg +1"8;
3.Duval +8"8; 4.Loeb +9"4
5.Välimäki +9"8; 6.H.Solberg +10"8;
7.Hirvonen +11"1; 8.Pons +13"8...
P-WRC > 18.Teiskonen 18'28"6

SS5 Imittos 2 (11.44 km)
1.Grönholm 6'58"3; 2.P.Solberg +1"5;
3.Loeb +2"1; 4.Hirvonen +4"5;
5.Sordo +6"1; 6.Stohl +7"0;
7.H.Solberg +7"9; 8.Pons +9"4...
P-WRC > 19.Pozzo 7'52"7

SS6 Skourta 2 (23.80 km)
1.Grönholm 14'29"6; 2.P.Solberg +2"1;
3.Loeb +6"7; 4.Stohl +12"4;
5.H.Solberg +14"2;
6.Gardemeister +15"9; 7.Sordo +16"0;
8.Hirvonen +19"0...
P-WRC > 18.Pozzo 16'23"6

SS7 Thiva 2 (23.76 km)
1.Grönholm 16'54"1; 2.Loeb +4"9;
3.P.Solberg +8"8; 4.Atkinson +11"6;
5.Hirvonen +12"0; 6.Stohl +13"2;
7.Välimäki +14"0; 8.Duval +14"5...
P-WRC > 18.Baldacci 18'22"1

Classification Leg 1
1.Grönholm 1h19'45"7;
2.P.Solberg +26"3; 3.Loeb +35"5;
4.Hirvonen +1'15"9; 5.Duval +1'29"4;
6.Stohl +1'38"1; 7.H.Solberg +1'39"8;
8.Gardemeister +1'42"1...
P-WRC > 18.Pozzo 1h28'33"6

SS8 Mandra 1 (12.60 km)
1.Grönholm 8'50"7; 2.Loeb +2"4;
3.P.Solberg +4"3; 4.Atkinson +6"5;
5.H.Solberg +14"3; 6.Hirvonen +15"1;
7.Duval +15"6; 8.Gardemeister +16"6...
P-WRC > 18.Arai/Pozzo/Ligato 9'53"7

SS9 Kineta 1 (37.33 km)
1.Loeb 25'39"1; 2.Grönholm +9"7;
3.P.Solberg +16"9; 4.Atkinson +29"5;
5.Hirvonen +32"7; 6.Stohl +42"1;
7.Gardemeister +48"7; 8.Sordo +50"6...
P-WRC > 19.Arai 28'25"8

SS10 Psatha 1 (17.41 Km)
1.Grönholm 11'21"3; 2.Loeb +1"0;
3.Atkinson +8"8; 4.H.Solberg +14"6;
5.P.Solberg +19"4; 6.Sordo +21"6;
7.Hirvonen +22"1; 8.Stohl +34"7...
P-WRC > 18.Arai 12'42"9

SS11 Mandra 2 (12.60 km)
1.Grönholm 8'43"1; 2.Loeb +0"8;
3.P.Solberg +3"1; 4.Sordo +7"2;
5.Hirvonen +9"7;
6.Gardemeister +10"4;
7.H.Solberg +10"8; 8.Stohl +16"0...
P-WRC > 19.Pozzo 9'45"9

SS12 Kineta 2 (37.33 km)
1.Loeb 25'20"2; 2.Grönholm +4"9;
3.P.Solberg +21"5;
4.Sordo/Hirvonen +31"9;
6.Stohl +35"2; 7.Gardemeister +37"8;
8.H.Solberg +40"8...
P-WRC > 17.Pozzo 28'28"3

SS13 Psatha 2 (17.41 km)
1.Grönholm 11'23"6; 2.H.Solberg +2"6;
3.Hirvonen +6"4; 4.Sordo +11"2;
5.Stohl +11"4; 6.Gardemeister +16"2;
7.Vovos +20"1; 8.Välimäki +25"3...
P-WRC > 13.Arai 12'54"5

Classification Leg 2
1.Grönholm 2h51'18"3;
2.Loeb +1'47"2; 3.Hirvonen +2'59"2;
4.Sordo +3'57"5; 5.H.Solberg +4'03"4;
6.Gardemeister +4'15"2;
7.Stohl +5'30"4; 8.Pons +5'50"3...
P-WRC > 19.Teiskonen 3h12'53"1

SS14 Avlonas 1 (23.90 km)
1.P.Solberg 14'07"2; 2.Grönholm +3"6;
3.Gardemeister +4"5; 4.Loeb +12"8;
5.H.Solberg +17"3; 6.Duval +18"2;
7.Hirvonen +20"2; 8.Pons +30"9...
P-WRC > 16.Al-Attiyah 15'43"2

SS15 Agia Sotira 1 (24.77 km)
1.P.Solberg 17'02"0; 2.Grönholm +9"0;
3.Duval +11"4; 4.Gardemeister +13"9;
5.Sordo +16"4; 6.Loeb +18"4;
7.Hirvonen +19"3; 8.H.Solberg +28"4...
P-WRC > 17.Al-Attiyah 18'51"1

SS16 Avlonas 2 (23.90 Km)
1.P.Solberg 14'00"6; 2.Duval +6"5;
3.Gardemeister +7"5;
4.Grönholm +12"1; 5.Sordo +13"6;
6.Hirvonen +15"1; 7.H.Solberg +17"4;
8.Atkinson/Loeb +23"7...
P-WRC > 17.Ligato 15'40"3

SS17 Agia Sotira 2 (24.77 Km)
1.P.Solberg 16'49"6; 2.Sordo +6"5;
3.Grönholm +22"7;
4.Gardemeister +23"6;
5.Hirvonen +27"8; 6.Loeb +29"6;
7.H.Solberg +31"4; 8.Atkinson +49"6...
P-WRC > 13.Pozzo 18'50"7

SS18 Oaka 2 (2.80 Km)
1.Grönholm 2'21"7; 2.Sordo +2"0;
3.Loeb +2"5; 4.Pons +2"9;
5.Gardemeister +3"5; 6.Atkinson +4"7;
7.P.Solberg +4"9; 8.H.Solberg +5"1...
P-WRC > 13.Baldacci/Hirvonen 2'31"3

Results

	Driver - Co-driver	Car	Gr.	Time
1	Grönholm - Rautiainen	Ford Focus RS WRC 06	A8	3h56'26"8
2	Loeb - Elena	Citroën Xsara WRC	A8	+ 2'26"8
3	Hirvonen - Lehtinen	Ford Focus RS WRC 06	A8	+ 3'43"8
4	Gardemeister - Honkanen	Citroën Xsara WRC	A8	+ 4'20"8
5	H. Solberg - Menkerud	Peugeot 307 WRC	A8	+ 4'55"6
6	Sordo - Marti	Citroën Xsara WRC	A8	+ 4'56"4
7	P. Solberg - Mills	Subaru Impreza WRC 2006	A8	+ 5'34"4
8	Pons - Del Barrio	Citroën Xsara WRC	A8	+ 8'19"0
9	Välimäki - Kalliolepo	Mitsubishi Lancer WRC 05	A8	+ 11'28"7
10	Wilson - Orr	Ford Focus RS WRC 04	A8	+ 13'30"8
17	Al-Attiyah - Patterson	Subaru Impreza Spec C 06	N4/P	+ 32'16"5
18	Pozzo - Stillo	Mitsubishi Lancer Evo IX	N4/P	+ 32'28"5
19	Teiskonen - Teiskonen	Subaru Impreza WRX Sti Spec C	N4/P	+ 32'46"9

Leading Retirements (15)
| SF18 | Stohl - Minor | Peugeot 307 WRC | Off |
| SF4 | Kuzaj - Szczepaniak | Subaru Impreza | Off |

Performers

	1	2	3	4	5	6	C6	Nb SS
Grönholm	11	5	1	1	-	-	18	18
P. Solberg	4	5	4	-	1	-	14	17
Loeb	3	4	5	2	-	2	16	18
Sordo	-	2	-	3	4	1	10	18
Duval	-	1	2	1	1	2	7	16
H. Solberg	-	1	-	1	3	1	6	18
Gardemeister	-	-	2	2	1	4	9	18
Hirvonen	-	-	2	3	5	2	12	18
Atkinson	-	-	1	3	1	2	7	18
Stohl	-	-	-	1	1	4	6	18
Pons	-	-	-	1	-	-	1	18
Välimäki	-	-	-	-	1	-	1	18

Leaders

| SS1 | Loeb |
| SS2 > SS18 | Grönholm |

Previous winners

1973	Thérier - Delferrier Alpine Renault A110	1985	Salonen - Harjanne Peugeot 205 T16	1996	McRae - Ringer Subaru Impreza
1975	Rohrl - Berger Opel Ascona	1986	Kankkunen - Piironen Peugeot 205 T16	1997	Sainz - Moya Ford Escort WRC
1976	Kallstrom - Andersson Datsun 160J	1987	Alen - Kivimaki Lancia Delta HF Turbo	1998	McRae - Grist Subaru Impreza WRC
1977	Waldegaard - Thorszelius Ford Escort RS	1988	Biasion - Siviero Lancia Delta Integrale	1999	Burns - Reid Subaru Impreza WRC
1978	Rohrl - Geistdorfer Fiat 131 Abarth	1989	Biasion - Siviero Lancia Delta Integrale	2000	C. McRae - Grist Ford Focus WRC
1979	Waldegaard - Thorszelius Ford escort RS	1990	Sainz - Moya Toyota Celica GT4	2001	C. McRae - Grist Ford Focus RS WRC 01
1980	Vatanen - Richards Ford Escort RS	1991	Kankkunen - Piironen Lancia Delta Integrale 16v	2002	C. McRae - Grist Ford Focus RS WRC 02
1981	Vatanen - Richards Ford Escort RS	1992	Auriol - Occelli Lancia Delta Integrale	2003	Märtin - Park Ford Focus RS WRC 03
1982	Mouton - Pons Audi Quattro	1993	Biasion - Siviero Ford Escort RS Cosworth	2004	P. Solberg - Mills Subaru Impreza WRC 2004
1983	Rohrl - Geistdorfer Lancia Rally 037	1994	Sainz - Moya Subaru Impreza	2005	Loeb - Elena Citroën Xsara WRC
1984	Blomqvist - Cederberg Audi Quattro	1995	Vovos - Stefanis Lancia Delta Integrale		

Nasser Al-Attiyah

Germany

09

01
02
03
04
05
06
07
08

10
11
12
13
14
15
16

Loeb bags another record
After a long break the World Championship resumed in Germany where Loeb and Elena had held sway over the past four years. 2006 wasn't any different and they won the rally for the fifth time from another Xsara in the hands of Sordo-Marti. Marcus Grönholm was all-fired up before the start but could do nothing against the French cars and in addition, he was delayed by a poor tyre choice.

09 Germany

For Subaru it was going from worse to worst! Petter Solberg destroyed his Impreza during the shakedown tests. Luckily, the mechanics were able to rebuild the car in time for the start.

Dani Sordo was in unstoppable mode in Germany. He finished second and was the only driver capable of hassling Loeb.

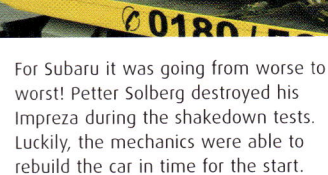

THE RALLY
Sordo struts his stuff

Marcus Grönholm was out to prove a point. He was going to take the World champion apart on his favourite terrain. The big Finn was after his first victory on asphalt, which had escaped him on so many occasions (Monte Carlo excepted because of its very special character). When the Ford team arrived in Trèves, an air of confidence reigned in the Anglo-American camp as the victory in the Greek rally was still fresh in their minds.

But the weather was to play a nasty trick on Malcolm Wilson and his merry men. In the shade the temperature was 11° (not bad for 11th August!) and the start was given under cloudy skies on roads soaked by the previous night's torrential rain. They were, however, beginning to dry and there were only a few scattered showers. The conditions were very tricky and Marcus Grönholm's motivation took a hit at the start of the first stage, Ruwertal-Fell. Once again tyre choice was to play a crucial role in this rally that the drivers call the summer Monte Carlo. It was a real head-scratcher.

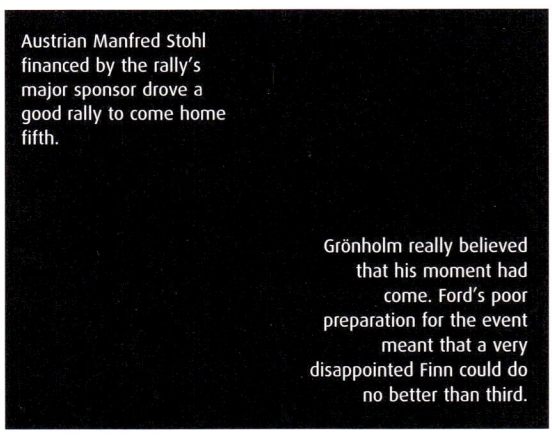

Austrian Manfred Stohl financed by the rally's major sponsor drove a good rally to come home fifth.

Grönholm really believed that his moment had come. Ford's poor preparation for the event meant that a very disappointed Finn could do no better than third.

All the front-runners opted for intermediates –except Aigner who put slicks on his Skoda – and had the tread re-cut as more rain was expected. Despite this Grönholm went off almost straight away-not once but four times in the 20,05 kms of the first special. The result was that he lost 20s to Loeb who set the fastest time. "My set-up was too soft," he explained, "and there was too much oversteer and understeer. I went off so many times that I couldn't believe it was happening to me!" At least he was lucky enough not to have been knocked out of the rally. Mikko Hirvonen, the Finn's team-mate, did not do much better either. He had a couple of off-course excursions, fortunately for him without damage.

In the second stage run in the dry things went from bad to worse for the Blue Oval boys. Dani Sordo set the quickest time with Loeb and Gardemeister on his heels making it a Xsara one, two, three. Back in fourth was Petter Solberg.
The Fords were way off the pace in the following special as their soft tyres were incapable of coping with the asphalt. The result was that the big Finn found himself almost 40s behind the leader with Hirvonen a further minute in arrears.

More difficulties were in store for the Focuses. On Friday afternoon the weather forecasts (from two different sources) received by Malcolm Wilson's team announced that there would be no rain. This time hard tyres were fitted to the Fords. The team couldn't have got it more wrong if they'd tried. Heavy showers began to fall from the fifth stage (Ruwertal-Fell 2) onwards. The Focuses were completely at sea. Grönholm lost seconds by the bagful: 14.1s in SS5, 31.6s in SS6 and 43.6s in SS7. The punishment was completely out of proportion to the crime! "The rain was unbelievable," groaned the Finnish driver after the end of the first leg that effectively put paid to his

He finished the first leg in fourth place 2m 11.4s behind Loeb, and his team-mate Hirvonen was in seventh place a further 2m 48.6s back. It was the end of the team's hopes of a victory in Germany. "When you've got the right tyres, it's easier," smiled the World champion. "We had the right information and we made the right choice. Great team work."

The Franco-Belgian team's astute evaluation of the conditions was shown by Dani Sordo's second place after he set 3 fastest times. He was only 42.7s behind his team leader. In third was another Xsara driven by Gardemeister not Pons as might have been expected. It

Solberg's big shunt during the shakedown tests. The blue cars set some good times early in the day including a second-fastest but then fell back. The Norwegian made the wrong tyre choice before his engine gave up the ghost in the first special on Saturday. Atkinson was like a fish out of water on the asphalt and Sarrazin was way off his best. The Japanese cars never posed a threat to the leaders.

So the only driver who looked as if he was capable of taking the fight to Loeb was the young promising Spaniard, Dani Sordo, Carls Sainz's protégé, driving in a well-structured WRC team for the first time.

Loeb's annual walk in the park in Germany...

Ford's wrong tyre choice meant that neither Hirvonen (9th) nor Grönholm could really show their talent.

And about time too! Young Austrian Andreas Aigner, sponsored by Red Bull and managed by Armin Schwartz, at last scored some points in the World Championship by finishing sixth.

chances. "The weather forecast was dry for the afternoon so we put on hard tyres. All I could do was to try and stay on the road. I did my best to remain calm in the rain as there was nothing else I could do." To crown it all the Focus had never done any rain testing so the set-up was completely ill adapted to the conditions. "We've never run on wet asphalt as we didn't have any rain in winter testing," was how a very disgruntled Grönholm summed it up.

was entered by PH Sport for the Finn's third rally of the year. As for Pons he should have been in third but slid off in the fourth stage. "It broke our rhythm," admitted the Spaniard. "It has to be said that going off into the vines in a WRC is probably not the best way to boost confidence on treacherous roads.
Citroën was in a dominant position at the end of the first leg. Besides Ford's problems Subaru was in deep trouble once again. What had not helped matters was

From the start of the second leg Sordo went for it and pulled back fifteen seconds on his leader who had lifted off a little as he wanted to assure what looked like a sure victory. However, the young Spaniard's pedal-to-metal approach was not exactly what the Kronos team manager had in mind. Marc Van Dalen got his two drivers together and told them that a Citroën-Kronos double was much too important to be jeopardised by a personal desire to achieve a headline-

Germany

Grönholm set only 2 scratch times. His team will have to have a rethink for the 2007 German rally.

the semi-automatic gear linkage plus hydraulics) after which he retired. Stohl met with clutch failure, and then Sarrazin made a poor start in the closing super special after which he set a time that would have been fastest were it not for his poor getaway.
The final leg did not see any major changes. Toni Gardemeister was the only one to provide a little excitement by going pedal to metal to oust Grönholm from third. He did his best but did not manage to knock his fellow-countryman off the third step of the rostrum despite setting three fastest times. It all went south for Stéphane Sarrazin whose future at Subaru did not look very rosy after his disappointing performance. The Frenchman (8th overall) went off and retired after

Citroën-Kronos preferred Sordo rather than Pons to score points in the manufacturers' Championship so the latter was at the wheel of a 2005 Xsara.

grabbing exploit. So it was necessary to read between the lines of the official declarations made by the drivers. Sordo: "The second part of the day was easier than the first so we took it quietly. I really want this second place!" Meaning: I respect my employer's orders. Loeb: "Dani was very quick this morning in difficult conditions. This afternoon we were thinking more about the Championships." Meaning: I did not react to his attacks; he was briefed and he understood what he had to do. In the tricky conditions reigning in the German Rally with half dry/half wet surfaces that were also greasy in parts, the leaders held position leaving the way open for a few individual exploits like Jan Kopecky's two scratch times in his Skoda. Grönholm was finally back on the pace and managed to snatch third place from Toni Gardemeister after SS12 in which he set his first scratch time of the day. Ford's speed in the dry was underlined by Hirvonen's fifth place. Others were not so lucky. Pons was hit with all kinds of mechanical problems (suspension,

Chris Atkinson does not really like asphalt and drove a very anonymous rally in Germany.

It was Toni Gardemeister's third 2006 outing and third points-scoring finish after Monte Carlo and Greece thanks to his fourth-place in Germany.

the first special. Mikko Hirvonen suffered a broken alternator on the road section after the last timed stage, but appeared in the classification thanks to the Super Rally.
The ninth round of the Championship was completely dominated by Citroën and enabled Loeb to increase his lead even more (33 points). In addition, the Frenchman was now on level pegging with Carlos Sainz in terms of victories in World Championship events, and also became the first driver to win the same rally on five consecutive occasions, a record. Kronos scored its

second double thanks mainly to Sordo's pace, as he was the only one capable of matching or even exceeding Loeb's speed, and extended its lead over Ford in the manufacturers' Championship. ■

THE JUNIORS
Meeke's exploit

Some people say that the Junior Championship does not serve a useful purpose. It is worth remembering that the first title winner was Sébastien Loeb and that in 2004 it revealed Dani Sordo's talent. The reigning champion really made his mark on the WRC scene in the German Rally. "When I see Dani's performances this year it gives me a lot of hope," said Chris Meeke at the finish after scoring a comfortable victory in Germany. Without wishing to denigrate the quality of his achievement it should be pointed out that the Championship leaders Sandell, Andersson and Aava had decided to give this asphalt rally a miss, as none of them is very much at home on this type of surface. Out of the 9 events on the Junior calendar each team has to take part in six.
The Northern Irishman at the wheel of his Citroën C2 went into the lead from the green light. He had a big scare in SS4 as he found himself without brakes and lost the lead as well as 2m 30s. "It was the most terrifying stage of my life. All I had to slow the car was the handbrake," he said. Belgian Bernd Casnier in his Clio took advantage of Meeke's mishap to take up the running. Chris, though, was all-fired up and drove flat out to claw his way back in front. He won stage after stage and by SS15 he was back in the lead by 6/10s. Finally, he won by 38.6s from Casnier and 1m 28.7s from the Czech Valousek (Suzuki) who had managed to snatch third place from the French driver Pressac in his Citroën. Tirabassi also Citroën-mounted looked on the way to a rostrum finish until he had an accident in the seventh special in which he damaged his vertebrae, luckily not seriously. After Germany, Meeke still has all the remaining rallies to do, but his win put him right back in the title chase even if he was still 10 points behind Sandell. ■

The German rally is an atypical one. But not for Loeb and Elena who won it for a record fifth time on the trot.

Young Czech Jan Kopecky showed his skills by setting two fastest times in his Skoda Fabia WRC.

Kris Meeke in his Citroën C2 dominated the German round of the Junior Championship and got back in the title hunt.

Germany results

25th RALLY OF GERMANY

Organiser Details
ADAC Motorsport Ltd,
Garmisher Strasse 19 - 21,
81377 Munchen,
Germany
Tel.: +4922 195 74 34 34
Fax: +4922 195 74 34 44

ADAC Rallye Deutschland

9th leg of FIA 2006 World Rally Championship for constructors and drivers.
6th leg of FIA WRC Junior Championship.

Date August 11 - 13, 2006

Route
1300.48 km divised in 3 legs.
19 special stages on tarmac (351.55 km)

Starting Procedure
Thursday, August 10 (20:00),
Trier, Porta Nigra

Leg 1
Friday, August 11 (09:23/16:52),
Trier > Bostalsee > Trier, 508.95 km;
8 special stages (134.72 km)

Leg 2
Saturday, August 12 (08:36/17:19),
Trier > Bostalsee > Trier, 531.20 km;
7 special stages (148.64 km)

Leg 3
Sunday, August 13 (08:38/10:44),
Trier > Bostalsee > Trier, 260.33 km;
4 special stages (68.19 km)

Entry List (77) - 73 starters

N°	Driver (Nat.)	Co-driver (Nat.)	Team	Car	Group & FIA Priority
1.	S. LOEB (F)	D. ELENA (MC)	KRONOS TOTAL CITROEN WRT	Citroën Xsara WRC	A8 1
2.	D. SORDO (E)	M. MARTI (E)	KRONOS TOTAL CITROEN WRT	Citroën Xsara WRC	A8 1
3.	M. GRÖNHOLM (FIN)	T. RAUTIAINEN (FIN)	BP FORD WORLD RALLY TEAM	Ford Focus RS WRC	A8 1
4.	M. HIRVONEN (FIN)	J. LEHTINEN (FIN)	BP FORD WORLD RALLY TEAM	Ford Focus RS WRC	A8 1
5.	P. SOLBERG (N)	P. MILLS (GB)	SUBARU WORLD RALLY TEAM	Subaru Impreza WRC 2006	A8 1
6.	S. SARRAZIN (F)	S. PREVOT (B)	SUBARU WORLD RALLY TEAM	Subaru Impreza WRC 2006	A8 1
7.	M. STOHL (A)	I. MINOR (A)	OMV - PEUGEOT NORWAY	Peugeot 307 WRC	A8 2
9.	M. WILSON (GB)	M. ORR (GB)	STOBART - VK - M-SPORT FORD RALLY TEAM	Ford Focus RS WRC 04	A8 1
10.	J. LATVALA (FIN)	M. ANTTILA (FIN)	STOBART - VK - M-SPORT FORD RALLY TEAM	Ford Focus RS WRC 04	A8 1
11.	M. EKSTRÖM (S)	J. ANDERSSON (S)	RED BULL - SKODA TEAM	Skoda Fabia WRC	A8 1
12.	A. AIGNER (A)	K. WICHA (D)	RED BULL - SKODA TEAM	Skoda Fabia WRC	A8 1
14.	T. GARDEMEISTER (FIN)	J. HONKANEN (FIN)	ASTRA RACING	Citroën Xsara WRC	A8 2
15.	X. PONS (E)	C. DEL BARRIO (E)	XAVIER PONS	Citroën Xsara WRC	A8 2
16.	C. ATKINSON (AUS)	G. MACNEALL (AUS)	SUBARU AUSTRALIA	Subaru Impreza WRC	A8 2
17.	J. KOPECKY (CZ)	F. SCHOVÁNEK (CZ)	CZECH RALLY TEAM SKODA- KOPECKY	Skoda Fabia WRC	A8 2
18.	F. DUVAL (B)	P. PIVATO (F)	FIRST MOTORSPORT	Skoda Fabia WRC	A8 2
20.	G. MAC HALE (IRL)	P. NAGLE (IRL)	GARETH MAC HALE	Ford Focus WRC	A8 2
21.	M. KAHLE (D)	P. GÖBEL (D)	SKODA AUTO DEUTSCHLAND GMBH	Skoda Fabia WRC	A8 2
22.	P. TSJOEN (B)	E. CHEVAILLIER (B)	PIETER TSJOEN	Ford Focus RS WRC	A8 2
23.	V. VOJTECH (CZ)	M. ERNST (CZ)	CZECH OMV RALLY TEAM	Peugeot 307 WRC	A8 2
24.	K. POULSEN (DEN)	O. R. FREDERIKSEN (DK)	KRISTIAN POULSEN	Toyota Corolla WRC	A8 2
25.	E. WEVERS (NL)	F. GODDE (B)	ERIK WEVERS	Toyota Corolla WRC	A8 2
32.	K. MEEKE (GB)	G. PATTERSON (GB)	KRIS MEEKE	Citroën C2 Super 1600	A6 3
36.	L. BETTI (E)	P. CAPOLONGO (I)	LUCA BETTI	Renault Clio Super 1600	A6 3
37.	P. VALOUSEK (CZ)	Z. HRUZA (CZ)	PAVEL VALOUSEK	Suzuki Swift Super 1600	A6 3
39.	C. RAUTENBACH (ZW)	D. SENIOR (GB)	CONRAD RAUTENBACH	Renault Clio Super 1600	A6 3
42.	J. PRESSAC (F)	J. BOYERE (F)	JULIEN PRESSAC	Citroën C2 Super 1600	A6 3
44.	M. KOSCIUSZKO (PL)	J. BARAN (PL)	MICHAL KOSCIUSZKO	Suzuki Ignis Super 1600	A6 3
49.	M. PROKOP (CZ)	J. TOMANEK (CZ)	JIPOCAR CZECH NATIONAL TEAM	Citroën C2 Super 1600	A6 3
50.	K. PINOMAKI (FIN)	M. MARKKULA (FIN)	KALLE PINOMAKI	Renault Clio Ragnotti	N3 3
51.	F. KARA (TR)	C. BAKANCOCUKLARI (TR)	FATIH KARA	Renault Clio Super 1600	A6 3
52.	B. CASIER (B)	F. MICLOTTE (B)	BERND CASIER	Renault Clio Super 1600	A6 3
53.	B. CLARK (GB)	S. MARTIN (GB)	STOBART, VK	Ford Fiesta ST	N3 3
54.	A. Nicolai BURKART (D)	T. GEILHAUSEN (D)	AARON NICOLAI BURKART	Citroën C2 Super 1600	A6 3
55.	B. TIRABASSI (F)	F. GORDON (F)	PH-SPORT	Citroën C2 Super 1600	A6 3
61.	M. VAN ELDIK (NL)	E. MOMBAERTS (B)	MARK VAN ELDIK	Subaru Impreza WRC	A8
62.	G. JONES (GB)	D. MOYNIHAN (IRL)	GARETH JONES	Subaru Impreza WRC	A8
64.	K. ROSENBERGER (A)	T. MONEGO (A)	KRIS ROSENBERGER	VW Golf IV Kitcar	A7
65.	N. SCHELLE (D)	M. WENZEL (D)	NIKI SCHELLE	Suzuki Swift Super 1600	A6
66.	T. VAN PARIJS (B)	K. HEYNDRICKX (B)	TIMOTHY VAN PARIJS	Ford Fiesta Super 1600	A6
68.	H. GASSNER (D)	K. THANNHÄUSER (D)	HERMANN GASSNER	Mitsubishi Lancer Evo IX	N4
70.	P. BIJVELDS (NL)	B. V.D.NIEUWENHUIJZEN (NL)	PETER BIJVELDS	Mitsubishi Lancer Evo VIII	N4
71.	F. AUER (D)	M. PETER (D)	GASSNER RALLISPORTS	Mitsubishi Lancer Evo VIII	N4
73.	S. SCHNEPPENHEIM (D)	J. LIMBACH (D)	STEFAN SCHNEPPENHEIM	Mitsubishi Lancer Evo VIII	N4
74.	P. HEINTZ (CH)	R. SCHERRER (CH)	PATRICK HEINTZ	Subaru Impreza WRX STi	N4
75.	H. VOSSEN (NL)	J. FINDHAMMER (NL)	HENK VOSSEN	Mitsubishi Lancer Evo VIII	N4
76.	J. VAN DEN HEUVEL (NL)	M. KOLMAN (NL)	JASPER VAN DEN HEUVEL	Mitsubishi Lancer Evo VIII	N4
77.	H. WEIJS JR. (NL)	J. RAVEN (NL)	HANS WEIJS JR.	Mitsubishi Lancer Evo VIII	N4
78.	E. MOREE (NL)	J. VAN WEEREN (NL)	ERIK MOREE	Mitsubishi Lancer Evo VIII	N4
79.	G. HENNEKY (NL)	R. SANDER (NL)	GERHARD HENNEKY	Mitsubishi Lancer Evo VIII	N4
80.	M. LISKA (CZ)	T. PLACHY (CZ)	MILAN LISKA	Mitsubishi Lancer Evo IX	N4
81.	T. LEGER (B)	F. DORTU (B)	AZUR	Subaru Impreza WRX STi	N4
82.	T. KUHLMANN (D)	A. SCHRODER (D)	THORSTEN KUHLMANN	Mitsubishi Lancer Evo VIII	N4
83.	Z. PENZES (H)	A. THURZO (H)	JO-ZI SE	Mitsubishi Lancer Evo VIII	N4
84.	M. ECKHAUS (NL)	E. EERTINK (NL)	MICHAEL ECKHAUS	Mitsubishi Lancer Evo VIII	N4
85.	A. BETTEGA (I)	S. SCATTOLIN (I)	TRT SRL	Ford Fiesta ST	N3
86.	M. BIASION (F)	C. BEYNET (F)	MATHIEU BIASION	Ford Fiesta ST	N3
87.	G. SCHAMMEL (LUX)	R. JAMOUL (B)	JPS JUNIOR TEAM LUXEMBOURG	Ford Fiesta ST	N3
88.	L. ATHANASSOULAS (GR)	N. MOUZAKIS (GR)	TEAM GREECE	Ford Fiesta ST	N3
89.	K. KESKINEN (FIN)	L. HIRVIJARVI (FIN)	PROGRESS MOTORSPORT FINLAND	Ford Fiesta ST	N3
90.	E. VERTUNOV (RUS)	G. TROSHKIN (RUS)	EVGENY VERTUNOV	Ford Fiesta ST	N3
91.	E. GILMOUR (NZ)	J. BENNIE (GB)	EMMA GILMOUR	Ford Fiesta ST	N3
92.	A. KJAER (N)	T. SVENDSEN (NOR)	ANDERS KJAER	Peugeot 206	A6
93.	D. HOLCZER (H)	G. MAGYAR (H)	HOLCZER RACING	Renault Clio Ragnotti	N3
94.	M. MOUFANG (D)	H. WALCH (D)	MARKUS MOUFANG	BMW 120 Diesel	N4
95.	T. STEBANI (D)	F. HEINDLMEIER (D)	SKODA AUTO DEUTSCHLAND GMBH	Skoda Fabia RS TDI	N4
96.	M. LUDWIG (D)	E. SCHMIDT (D)	MARC LUDWIG	OPEL Astra GTC Diesel	N4
97.	F. LAUER (D)	K. STOCKMAR (D)	FRANK LAUER	BMW 120 Diesel	N4
98.	D. JONES (GB)	S. SMALLBONE (GB)	DAVID JONES	Peugeot 206 XSI	A6
99.	T. YOSHII (J)	M. NABEKURA (J)	TAKAHIRO YOSHII	Honda Civic	N2
100.	M. WALLENWEIN (D)	S. KOPCZYK (D)	MARK WALLENWEIN	Suzuki Ignis Sport	N2
101.	N. KUNZE (D)	M. SCHWENDY (D)	PRIVATE RENNGEMEINSCHAFT SPANDAU	Citroën Saxo VTS	N2
102.	J. HOHLHEIMER (D)	W. KIPPE (D)	ADAC NORDBAYERN	Fiat Seicento Sporting	A5

Championship Classifications

FIA Driver (9/16)
1. Loeb — 6🏆 84
2. Grönholm — 3🏆 51
3. Sordo — 41
4. Stohl — 24
5. P. Solberg — 20
6. Hirvonen — 21
7. Gardemeister — 16
8. Galli — 11
9. Pons — 11
10. H. Solberg — 11
11. Bengué — 9
12. Atkinson — 9
13. Carlsson — 6
14. Kopecky — 6
15. Sarrazin — 6
16. Välimäki — 4
17. Rådström — 4
18. Duval — 4
19. Mac Hale — 3
20. Aigner — 3
21. Katajamäki — 3
22. Sohlberg — 3
23. Wilson — 1
24. Perez Companc, Arai... — 0

FIA Constructors (9/16)
1. Kronos Total Citroën WRT — 6🏆 114
2. BP-Ford World Rally Team — 3🏆 91
3. Subaru World Rally Team — 63
4. OMV-Peugeot Norway — 41
5. Stobart VK M-Sport Ford WRT — 20
6. Red Bull-Skoda Team — 22

FIA Production Car (4/8)
1. Al-Attiyah — 2🏆 34
2. Baldacci — 17
3. Arai — 1🏆 15
4. Kuzaj — 13
5. Nutahara — 1🏆 10
6. Pozzo — 8
7. Marrini — 8
8. Ligato — 8
9. Latvala — 7
10. Teiskonen — 6
11. Heath — 5
12. Uspenskiy — 4
13. Beltrán — 4
14. Vojtech — 2
15. Name — 1
16. Kamada — 0
17. Popov — 0
    Higgins Excluded 8

FIA Junior WRC (6/9)
1. Sandell — 1🏆 26
2. Andersson — 1🏆 21
3. Aava — 20
4. Rautenbach — 17
5. Meeke — 1🏆 16
6. Casier — 16
7. Prokop — 1🏆 14
8. Pressac — 12
9. Béres — 12
10. Tirabassi — 1🏆 11
11. Wilks — 1🏆 11
12. Valousek — 11
13. Burkart — 9
14. Kara — 7
15. Molder — 5
16. Kosciuszko — 5
17. Pinomäki — 4
18. Betti — 4
19. Zachrisson — 2
20. Bonato — 1
21. Clark, Bordignon — 0
    Cortinovis, Karlsson — 0

Special Stages Times

www.rallye-deutschland.de
www.wrc.com

SS1 Ruwertal/Fell 1 (20.04 km)
1.Loeb 11'44"6; 2.P.Solberg +8"8;
3.Sordo +15"9; 4.Stohl +19"5;
5.Grönholm +20"1; 6.Duval +24"4;
7.Pons +25"1; 8.Kopecky +25"2...
J-WRC > 16.Meeke/Rautenbach/Betti...
12'28"0

SS2 Dhrontal 1 (12.61 km)
1.Sordo 7'18"7; 2.Loeb +1"5;
3.Gardemeister +8"2; 4.P.Solberg +8"7;
5.Grönholm +9"7; 6.Duval +9"8;
7.Pons +10"5; 8.Aigner +10"6...
J-WRC > 23.Meeke/Wevers 8'03"1

SS3 Grafschaft Veldenz 1 (17.73 km)
1.Loeb 10'49"8; 2.Stohl +9"9;
3.Grönholm +10"9; 4.Sordo +11"6;
5.Hirvonen +13"9; 6.Aigner +14"3;
7.Gardemeister +14"5;
8.Atkinson +16"3...
J-WRC > 23.Meeke 12'07"5

SS4 Moselwein 1 (16.98 km)
1.Sordo 10'23"3; 2.Grönholm +2"5;
3.Loeb +5"9; 4.Hirvonen +6"9;
5.Gardemeister +10"7; 6.Aigner +12"4;
7.P.Solberg +12"6; 8.Stohl +13"6...
J-WRC > 21.Casier/Tirabassi 11'43"5

SS5 Ruwertal/Fell 2 (20.04 km)
1.Loeb 11'34"3; 2.Sordo +3"7;
3.Duval +11"7; 4.Grönholm +14"1;
5.Aigner +14"4; 6.P.Solberg +17"9;
7.Gardemeister +18"2; 8.Stohl +18"6...
J-WRC > 25.Burkart 12'54"1

SS6 Dhrontal 2 (12.61 km)
1.Sordo 7'18"2; 2.Loeb +0"4;
3.Atkinson/Gardemeister +6"1;
5.Pons +11"2; 6.Duval +11"4;
7.P.Solberg +12"0; 8.Sarrazin +17"7...
J-WRC > 18.Meeke 8'09"0

SS7 Grafschaft Veldenz 2 (17.73 km)
1.Loeb 10'57"9; 2.Sordo +16"7;
3.Gardemeister +41"8;
4.Grönholm +43"6; 5.Stohl +49"2;
6.Ekström +54"0; 7.Hirvonen +56"3;
8.P.Solberg +57"3...
J-WRC > 18.Casier 12'39"4

SS8 Moselwein 2 (16.98 km)
1.Loeb 10'20"4; 2.Hirvonen +0"7;
3.Sordo +2"6; 4.Grönholm +6"7;
5.Gardemeister +8"2; 6.Stohl +9"3;
7.Aigner +15"9; 8.P.Solberg +16"2...
J-WRC > 19.Meeke 11'23"6

Classification Leg 1
1.Loeb 1h20'35"0; 2.Sordo +42"7;
3.Gardemeister +2'06"0;
4.Grönholm +2'11"4;
5.P.Solberg +2'23"1; 6.Stohl +2'29"4;
7.Hirvonen +2'48"6; 8.Aigner +2'55"5...
J-WRC > 21.Casier 1h30'31"5

SS9 Bosenberg 1 (22.52 km)
1.Kopecky 13'02"7; 2.Sordo +0"9;
3.Loeb +9"4; 4.Sarrazin +10"3;
5.Gardemeister +10"8;
6.Hirvonen +11"5; 7.Stohl +18"4;
8.Aigner +23"0...
J-WRC > 23.Casier 15'01"8

SS10 Panzerplatte 1 (30.66 Km)
1.Sordo 18'09"5; 2.Loeb +6"8;
3.Hirvonen +14"0;
4.Gardemeister +17"4;
5.Grönholm +19"4; 6.Stohl +24"5;
7.Kopecky +28"0; 8.Sarrazin +28"4...
J-WRC > 16.Meeke 19'49"5

SS11 Erzweiler 1 (18.22 km)
1.Hirvonen 10'46"0;
2.Grönholm +0"6; 3.Sordo +4"6;
4.Loeb +6"9; 5.Gardemeister +12"3;
6.Stohl +14"8; 7.Kopecky +16"8;
8.Aigner +19"7...
J-WRC > 17.Meeke 11'50"3

SS12 Panzerplatte 2 (30.66 Km)
1.Grönholm 18'03"5; 2.Sordo +0"1;
3.Loeb +1"0; 4.Gardemeister +9"3;
5.Hirvonen +14"7; 6.Kopecky +16"5;
7.Stohl +18"0; 8.Latvala +18"9...
J-WRC > 16.Meeke 19'33"1

SS13 S. Erzweiler 2 (18,22 km)
1.Grönholm 10'42"4; 2.Hirvonen +2"6;
3.Kopecky +7"3; 4.Stohl +9"0;
5.Aigner +14"2; 6.Sarrazin +14"9;
7.Gardemeister +17"0; 8.Loeb +17"3...
J-WRC > 18.Meeke 12'03"9

SS14 Bosenberg 2 (22,52 km)
1.Kopecky 12'45"0; 2.Grönholm +2"9;
3.Loeb +3"0; 4.Hirvonen +4"9;
5.Sarrazin +6"9; 6.Atkinson +7"3;
7.Gardemeister +7"6;
8.Sordo/Stohl +8"3...
J-WRC > 16.Meeke 14'09"4

SS15 OMV SS St Wendel (5,84 Km)
1.Loeb 3'05"0; 2.Grönholm +0"6;
3.Sarrazin +0"9; 4.Stohl +2"0;
5.Sordo +2"8; 6.Gardemeister +3"8;
7.Kopecky +4"0; 8.Atkinson +4"1...
J-WRC > 17.Pressac 3'24"4

Classification Leg 2
1.Loeb 2h47'53"5; 2.Sordo +34"3;
3.Grönholm +2'14"1;
4.Gardemeister +2'39"8;
5.Hirvonen +2'56"4; 6.Stohl +3'20"0;
7.Aigner +4'42"1; 8.Sarrazin +4'54"7...
J-WRC > 15.Meeke 3h08'59"2

SS16 Freisen/Westrich 1 (19.07 Km)
1.Gardemeister 11'40"4; 2.Loeb +0"5;
3.Kopecky +1"4; 4.Sordo +2"3;
5.Atkinson +6"7; 6.Grönholm +7"4;
7.Aigner +10"8; 8.Ekström +11"6...
J-WRC > 18.Meeke 12'58"8

SS17 Birkenfelder Land (13.68 Km)
1.Sordo 7'52"3; 2.Loeb +1"0;
3.Gardemeister +2"5; 4.Grönholm +3"4;
5.Stohl +4"6; 6.Hirvonen +5"0;
7.Aigner +6"1; 8.Kopecky +6"6...
J-WRC > 18.Meeke 8'42"5

SS18 S. St Wendeler Land (16.37 Km)
1.Gardemeister 9'08"6;
2.Grönholm +1"7; 3.Sordo +3"1;
4.Loeb +3"7; 5.Latvala +11"0;
6.Kopecky +13"0; 7.Pons +13"6;
8.Aigner +14"4...
J-WRC > 19.Meeke 10'11"2

SS19 S. Freisen/Westrich 2 (19.07 Km)
1.Gardemeister 11'50"8;
2.Grönholm +1"1; 3.Sordo +2"6;
4.Loeb +3"3; 5.Pons +6"9;
6.Latvala +14"6; 7.Stohl +15"8;
8.Kopecky +21"6...
J-WRC > 17.Valousek 13'06"6

Results

	Driver - Co-driver	Car	Gr.	Time
1	Loeb - Elena	Citroën Xsara WRC	A8	3h28'34"1
2	Sordo - Marti	Citroën Xsara WRC	A8	+ 33"8
3	Grönholm - Rautiainen	Ford Focus RS WRC 06	A8	+ 2'19"2
4	Gardemeister - Honkanen	Citroën Xsara WRC	A8	+ 2'33"8
5	Stohl - Minor	Peugeot 307 WRC	A8	+ 4'25"9
6	Aigner - Wicha	Skodia Fabia WRC	A8	+ 5'42"6
7	Kopecky - Schovanek	Skodia Fabia WRC	A8	+ 5'45"8
8	Atkinson - Macneall	Subaru Impreza WRC	A8	+ 7'25"0
9	Hirvonen - Lehtinen	Ford Focus RS WRC 06	A8	+ 8'25"7
10	Mac Hale - Nagle	Ford Focus RS WRC 04	A8	+ 12'56"1
16	**Meeke - Patterson**	**Citroën C2 S1600**	A6/J	+ 25'26"6
17	Casier - Miclotte	Renault Clio S1600	A6/J	+ 26'05"2
19	Valousek - Hruza	Suzuki Swift S1600	A6/J	+ 26'55"3
21	**Gassner - Thannhäuser**	Mitsubishi Lancer Evo. IX	N4	+ 27'45"6

Leading Retirements (17)

SF16	Sarrazin - Prévot	Subaru Impreza WRC 2006	Gearbox
SF14	Kahle - Göbel	Skoda Fabia WRC	Engine
TC10C	Tsjoen - Chevaillier	Ford Focus RS WRC	Transmission
TC10	Vojtech - Ernst	Peugeot 307 WRC	Off
SF9	P. Solberg - Mills	Subaru Impreza WRC 2006	Engine
TC8D	Duval - Privato	Skoda Fabia WRC	Accident
TC8D	Tirabassi - Gordon	Citroën C2 Super 1600	Off

Mattias Ekström

Performers

	1	2	3	4	5	6	C6	NbSS
Loeb	6	5	4	3	-	-	18	19
Sordo	5	4	5	2	1	-	17	19
Gardemeister	3	-	4	2	4	1	14	19
Grönholm	2	6	1	4	3	1	17	19
Kopecky	2	-	2	-	-	2	6	19
Hirvonen	1	2	1	2	2	2	10	19
Stohl	-	1	-	3	2	3	9	19
P. Solberg	-	1	-	1	-	1	3	8
Sarrazin	-	-	1	1	1	1	4	15
Atkinson	-	-	1	-	1	1	3	19
Duval	-	-	1	-	?	3	4	6
Aigner	-	-	-	-	2	2	4	19
Pons	-	-	-	-	2	-	2	16
Latvala	-	-	-	-	1	1	2	11
Ekström	-	-	-	-	-	1	1	19

Leaders

SS1 > SS19   Loeb

Previous winners

2002	Loeb - Elena
	Citroën Xsara WRC
2003	Loeb - Elena
	Citroën Xsara WRC
2004	Loeb - Elena
	Citroën Xsara WRC
2005	Loeb - Elena
	Citroën Xsara WRC

Finland

10

Grönholm's revenge
Loeb was unbeatable on his favourite hunting ground in Germany and it was the same for Grönholm in Finland. Marcus won his national rally despite the attacks of a very motivated Frenchman who was after victory in one of the mythic events on the WRC calendar. After a nail-biting battle Loeb came home in second place splitting the two Fords, which closed the gap to Kronos in the manufacturers' Championship on the roads of Jyväskylä.

Finland

A very concentrated Sébastien Loeb was determined to win one of the mythic rallies on the calendar. But Marcus Grönholm had other ideas...

Marcus Grönholm is a hero to a whole nation, and he did not disappoint his fans who turned up en masse to cheer him on.

Manfred Stohl's hopes of a good result were dashed on the first day when a suspension arm broke on his car.

THE RALLY
Marcus dominates

The teams had not even a week's rest. After the long 2-month break August was the most hectic month for the entrants in the World Rally Championship. Hardly had the German event finished when the teams went straight to Jyväskylä, the nerve centre of the Finnish round, not only to take part in the rally but also to carry out reconnaissance early on in the week. It was a complete change of scenery between the Baumholder military camp in the Moselle valley and the Nordic forests of the 1000 Lakes. The only common feature was the weather. It was pouring rain when the start was given to the Finnish Rally on Friday after a super special on Thursday evening won by Loeb.
There wasn't much time for reflection on the Finnish roller coaster made all the trickier by the rain and mud, the pools and running water. It was a question of getting in behind the wheel, pressing the starter and then going for it. Just the type of challenge that Grönholm loves. Since 2000 he has lost only once on home territory - in 2003 when victory went to Markko Märtin in a Ford.

Marcus shot out of the starting blocks like a scalded cat and set the fastest times in the first three specials. He had no problems with the tricky surface. "The tracks were very wet in some places," he explained, "and dry in others. It was risky driving in such changeable conditions. Despite that we had constant grip. In fact, the rain was so heavy in the first special of the afternoon that the windscreen wipers were not quick enough! So visibility was pretty bad. You'd better believe me!"
It was no fun driving on such roads if one had not learned them beforehand as Loeb said: "To get into the Finnish rhythm so as not to let Marcus make the break is not obvious. It's even less so when the road is treacherous due to mud and puddles."

Loeb's cautious start to the rally dropped him to fourth place behind Grönholm, Hirvonen and Solberg where he stayed until the end of SS4. "Second time round," he said, "the road conditions were a bit better and our eyes began to get used to the incredible speed at which the trees flashed past us on either side of the car." To prove it he set the quickest time in Vellipohja (SS5) and then in Môkkiperä (SS6) after Grönholm stated that he was a teeny weeny bit tired!

"I decided to go for it right from the start," yawned the Finn. "I gave my all at the beginning of the rally and then when I saw my times I realised that I could lift off a little. I even drove a bit too carefully from time to time. But don't worry, it's not going to last."

Chris Atkinson was aiming at a place in the first six, until his gearbox broke.

Italian Gigi Galli was back for another race and finished in fifth place.

Dani Sordo made a good start to the rally only to be caught out at the end. It was a beginner's fault, and he was learning the hard way.

The leader underlined his words with the quickest time in SS7 but Loeb hit back and went faster in the following one taking completely crazy risks. "In the morning the passage of 100 cars had left deep ruts which filled with water in the afternoon due to the pouring rain. We emptied them for the others. In Mökkiperä 2 it was dry at the start and then suddenly the windscreen was awash with pouring rain. I didn't lift off, braked as late as possible in the dry, got bounced around in the ruts and started to aquaplane. There were a few very hairy moments but I'm delighted with the result."

The duel between the two drivers was awesome in the atrocious conditions and they returned to Jvyäskylä separated by only 12 seconds. "The game's still on,"

Loeb stated to which Gönholm shot back, "tomorrow there are a few specials where I'll knock the stuffing out of him!"

Behind, the other drivers tried to stay in contact as best they could. Mikko Hirvonen, who lives in Jyväsklayä, was out to shine in front of his local supporters and hung on to third place. Things in the Subaru camp were a little rosier thanks to an on-form Petter Solberg who set some good times and was in fourth place. He finished the first leg in front of his brother Henning and team-mate Chris Atkinson. The two Citroën-mounted Spaniards were completely at sea in the Finnish rally. Sordo was back in seventh place despite a minor off as it was his first time in a WRC on such roads. Pons's slow start cost him far too much

time to pose a threat to those ahead of him. He finished in twelfth place over 4 minutes behind the leader – a country mile!

The conditions were very different for the second leg. The sun shone down from a blue sky to the delight of the thousands of fans who had come to watch the event. And they got their money's worth. Seeing the two top rally drivers in the world going flat out on the most spectacular roads in the Championship was the answer to an enthusiast's prayer. Grönholm set the pace by winning the first special and Loeb hit back immediately coming first in the first section of the mythic Ouninpohja stage now divided into two parts. "I think I drove a perfect special," he gasped just afterwards delighted with his performance. "And I'm

Jan Kopecky kept up his scoring sequence. After his 2 points in Germany he bagged one in Finland.

Henning Solberg was the first non-works driver at the wheel of his 307 WRC, and also kept the family honour intact.

Finland

Sébastien Loeb has assimilated the special technique necessary to master the Finnish steeplechase and this helped him keep up constant pressure on Grönholm.

Grönholm and Rautiainen scored a telling victory but as Loeb and Elena finished second their gain was a meagre 2 points.

only 1.3s ahead of Marcus. Nothing." His average speed was a blinding 128 km/h. So much risk, such speed, such daring for such a tiny gain!

But he had to continue and drive even harder to hope to oust Grönholm from first place. Fate, though, had other ideas. In the second part of Ouninpojha Loeb hit a rock very hard as he explained: "I hit a rock on the inside of a left-hander which sent the car up into the air. The wheel was too badly damaged for the foam to work properly so we finished the stage on a flat tyre." It was a major setback and the result was a time that was 32.4s slower than the Finn's. Overall Marcus now led by 44.8s. The Frenchman knew the game was up given the difficulty of pulling back even a tenth of a second on such a surface.

Strangely enough, Grönholm had also hit the same piece of rock. "I was lucky as I hit it too and it wasn't in my notes; the corner has changed over the years and its apex has moved. So we took a different line and we dug up this stone. I heard a big "clunk" when I hit it. It was about the size of a football but the foam did its job perfectly and I was able to continue."

It was a strange turn-around. In Sardinia Grönholm destroyed his engine and with it his hopes of victory by hitting a big embedded stone which Loeb also thumped but without damage.

In Italy the Finn was in the lead and retired while in Finland Loeb was in second place and continued with the aim of holding on to his position and bagging the 8 points that went with it. "I had to concentrate on this to forget the disappointment," he said afterwards. "Obviously it was much less fun but that's part of the game."

Grönholm preferred to keep up the pace. "I didn't go absolutely flat out once Seb had his problem," admitted the Finn. "I tackled the jumps with a little less verve. I'll do the same thing tomorrow."

Behind, the ranks began to thin out. Petter Solberg was eliminated in a big shunt in the first part of Ouninpohja (SS11). It was the same thing for Xavier Pons who also crashed out in the eleventh stage. "In a right-hander just behind a hump," explained the Spaniard. "I slid towards the outside where I hit a stone that sent me cartwheeling off the road."

Later on in Ouninpohja second time round it was Dani Sordo's turn to get caught out. "I went straight on after a hump and landed a little bit sideways and when the car hit the ground it immediately pivoted to the outside where there was a rock wall." Loeb was able to give a little advice to his unfortunate stable companions due to his greater experience. "Dani got caught out by something rather special that I've gradually discovered. In a corner on a hump you think that you have to place the car but in fact, if you're all crossed up taking off when the car lands it blocks on the rear and pivots. I pay careful attention to tackle the jumps with the car as straight as possible." That was the voice of experience talking.

Petter Solberg's rally was yet another one to forget. This time it was his fault that he went off in the eleventh stage.

The Mitsubishi Lancer is still a quick motorcar. Jussi Välimäki finished in the points again adding a seventh place to his fifth in Sardinia.

Tuohino came home sixth in his Citroën Xsara making it four Finns in the first 8 places.

By Saturday evening it was all over bar the shouting. The first ten in the overall classification were exactly the same as the first ten on Saturday evening apart from the gaps that had changed. Grönholm let his young team-mate shine and Hirvonen set all the fastest times in the final leg. Once again the beanpole from Espoo was too strong for his rivals on home turf. "When I was a young driver back in the 90s I never realised that I was going to win this rally six times. I haven't had any problems this weekend. I had a good fight with Seb. My aim is to score victories in all the remaining rallies this season. With the Focus I've got just the right car to do it. Okay?" Taken as read Marcus! ∎

JUNIOR CHAMPIONSHIP
Wilks can thank Ouninpohja !

Ouninpohja whether it was part one or two will remain engraved in Citroën's memory as the 2006 special from hell. In WRC, Loeb, Pons, and Sordo all ran into trouble on it as already seen. In the Junior Championship it cost Chris Meeke the rally – a bit like the world champion. The Northern Irishman had been in the lead since the second special of the event but destroyed his engine on landing after one of the humps. This let Guy Wilks into first place, which he held until the end. The Suzuki driver scored a dominant victory fending off the attacks of P-G Andersson. It was his second win of the season and put him back in the title chase now led by the Swede. The 2004 champion

scored eight points and overtook his fellow-countryman Sandell who could do no better than seventh in Finland. The other unlucky driver in the rally was the Estonian Aava. He was in a strong position for victory when he was disqualified at the end of the first leg for a very strange reason; he was not wearing the fireproof underwear specified by the regulations! ∎

Mikko Hirvonen lives in Jÿvaskÿla and was out to fulfil his fans' dreams. But he had to thing of championship points before anything else and came home in third place.

You have to know how to do everything in rallying. You don't catch Michael Schumacher changing the wheels on his F1 Ferrari!

Finland results

56th RALLY OF FINLAND

Organiser Details
AKK Sports Ltd,
Box 54,
FIN-00551 Helsinki,
Finland
Tél.: +3589 72582239
Fax: +3589 72582240

Neste Oil Rally Finland

10th leg of FIA 2006 World Rally Championship for constructors and drivers.
7th leg of FIA WRC Junior Championship.

Date August 17 - 20, 2006

Route
1524.34 km divised in 3 legs.
21 special stages on dirt roads (351.61 km)

Starting Procedure
Thursday, August 17 (20:00),
Jyväskylä, 1 special stage (2.50 km)

Leg 1
Friday, August 18 (09:21/20:00),
Jyväskylä > Jyväskylä, 536.29 km;
8 special stages (146.49 km)

Leg 2
Saturday, August 19 (07:06/18:04),
Jyväskylä > Jyväskylä, 703.03 km;
8 special stages (144.90 km)

Leg 3
Sunday, August 20 (09:14/12:58),
Jyväskylä > Jyväskylä. 285.02 km;
4 special stages (60.22 km)

Entry List (107) - 101 starters

N°	Driver (Nat.)	Co-driver (Nat.)	Team	Car	Group & FIA Priority
1.	S. LOEB (F)	D. ELENA (MC)	KRONOS TOTAL CITROEN WRT	Citroen Xsara WRC	A8 1
2.	D. SORDO (E)	M. MARTI (E)	KRONOS TOTAL CITROEN WRT	Citroen Xsara WRC	A8 1
3.	M. GRÖNHOLM (FIN)	T. RAUTIAINEN (FIN)	BP FORD WORLD RALLY TEAM	Ford Focus RS WRC 06	A8 1
4.	M. HIRVONEN (FIN)	J. LEHTINEN (FIN)	BP FORD WORLD RALLY TEAM	Ford Focus RS WRC 06	A8 1
5.	P. SOLBERG (N)	P. MILLS (GB)	SUBARU WORLD RALLY TEAM	Subaru Impreza WRC 2006	A8 1
6.	C. ATKINSON (AUS)	G. MACNEALL (AUS)	SUBARU WORLD RALLY TEAM	Subaru Impreza WRC 2006	A8 1
7.	M. STOHL (A)	I. MINOR (A)	OMV - PEUGEOT NORWAY	Peugeot 307 WRC	A8 1
8.	H. SOLBERG (N)	C. MENKERUD (N)	OMV - PEUGEOT NORWAY	Peugeot 307 WRC	A8 1
9.	M. WILSON (GB)	M. ORR (GB)	STOBART - VK - M-SPORT FORD RALLY TEAM	Ford Focus RS WRC 04	A8 1
10.	K. KATAJAMÄKI (FIN)	T. ALANNE (FIN)	STOBART - VK - M-SPORT FORD RALLY TEAM	Ford Focus RS WRC 04	A8 1
14.	X. PONS (E)	C. DEL BARRIO (E)	XAVIER PONS	Citroen Xsara WRC	A8 2
15.	D. CARLSSON (S)	T. THORSZELIUS (SWE)	DANIEL CARLSSON	Mitsubishi WRC-05	A8 2
16.	J. KOPECKY (CZ)	F. SCHOVANEK (CZ)	CZECH RALLY TEAM SKODA- KOPECKY	Skoda Fabia WRC	A8 2
18.	J. VALIMAKI (FIN)	J. KALLIOLEPO (FIN)	JUSSI VALIMAKI	Mitsubishi Lancer WRC	A8 2
19.	K. SOHLBERG (FIN)	R. PIETILAINEN (FIN)	TEAM RED DEVIL ATOLYE KAZAZ	Subaru Impreza WRC 2005	A8 2
20.	J. TUOHINO (FIN)	M. MARKKULA (FIN)	JANNE TUOHINO	Citroen Xsara WRC	A8 2
21.	J. LATVALA (FIN)	M. SAIRANEN (FIN)	JARI-MATTI LATVALA	Toyota Corolla WRC	A8 2
22.	J. HANNINEN (FIN)	M. SALLINEN (FIN)	JUHO HANNINEN	Mitsubishi Lancer WRC	A8 2
24.	T. SCHIE (N)	G. BERGSTEN (S)	THOMAS SCHIE	Ford Focus RS WRC	A8 2
25.	G. GALLI (I)	G. BERNACCHINI (I)	GIANLUIGI GALLI	Peugeot 307 WRC	A8 2
26.	J. KETOMAKI (FIN)	K. RISBERG (FIN)	JUKKA KETOMAKI	Skoda Octavia WRC	A8 2
27.	M. OSTBERG (N)	O. KRISTIAN UNNERUD (N)	MADS OSTBERG	Subaru Impreza WRC	A8 2
32.	K. MEEKE (GB)	G. PATTERSON (GB)	KRIS MEEKE	Citroen C2	A6 3
33.	U. AAVA (EE)	K. SIKK (EE)	URMO AAVA	Suzuki Swift S1600	A6 3
35.	P. ANDERSSON (S)	J. ANDERSSON (S)	PER-GUNNAR ANDERSSON	Suzuki Swift Super 1600	A6 3
37.	P. VALOUSEK (CZ)	Z. HRUZA (CZ)	PAVEL VALOUSEK	Suzuki Swift 1600	A6 3
39.	C. RAUTENBACH (ZW)	D. SENIOR (GB)	CONRAD RAUTENBACH	Renault Clio	A6 3
41.	P. SANDELL (SWE)	E. AXELSSON (SWE)	PATRIK SANDELL	Renault Clio Super 1600	A6 3
42.	J. PRESSAC (F)	J. BOYERE (F)	JULIEN PRESSAC	Citroen C2	A6 3
43.	J. MOLDER (EE)	K. BECKER (EE)	JAAN MOLDER	Suzuki Ignis S1600	A6 3
44.	M. KOSCIUSZKO (PL)	K. BARAN (PL)	MICHAL KOSCIUSZKO	Suzuki Swift Super 1600	A6 3
45.	J. BÉRES (SK)	P. STARY (CZ)	JOZEF BERES	Suzuki Ignis	A6 3
46.	A. CORTINOVIS (I)	M. BOSSI (I)	ANDREA CORTINOVIS	Renault Clio	N3 3
47.	F. A BORDIGNON (I)	J. BARDINI (I)	FILIPPO BORDIGNON	Opel Astra OPC	N3 3
48.	G. WILKS (GB)	P. PUGH (GB)	GUY WILKS	Suzuki Swift Super 1600	A6 3
49.	M. PROKOP (CZ)	J. TOMANEK (CZ)	MARTIN PROKOP	Citroen C2	A6 3
50.	K. PINOMAKI (FIN)	J. LAAKSONEN (FIN)	KALLE PINOMAKI	Renault Clio Super 1600	A6 3
53.	B. CLARK (GB)	S. MARTIN (GB)	BARRY CLARK	Ford Fiesta	N3 3
55.	F. FIANDINO (F)	S. DE CASTELLI (F)	BRICE TIRABASSI	Citroen C2 R2	N3 3
59.	M. RANTANEN (FIN)	J. LONEGREN (FIN)	MATTI RANTANEN	Honda Civic Type R	N3 3
61.	P. FLODIN (S)	M. ANDERSSON (SWE)	PATRIK FLODIN	Subaru Impreza	N4
62.	O. SVEDLUND (S)	B. NILSSON (S)	OSCAR SVEDLUND	Subaru Impreza	N4
63.	A. ALÉN (FIN)	T. HANTUNEN (FIN)	TACK	Subaru Impreza	N4
64.	K. KUISTILA (FIN)	H. JOKINEN (FIN)	KAJ KUISTILA	Mitsubishi Lancer	N4
65.	R. TAHKO (FIN)	O. LAHTINEN (FIN)	RIKU TAHKO	Mitsubishi Lancer Evo VII	N4
66.	J. KANGAS (FIN)	J. KOLJONEN (FIN)	JARNO KANGAS	Mitsubishi Lancer Evo VII	N4
67.	J. HAKKINEN (FIN)	H. KAAPRO (FIN)	JUHA HAKKINEN	Mitsubishi Lancer Evo IX	N4
68.	J. YLIPAHKALA (FIN)	K. PYLVANAINEN (FIN)	JANI YLIPAHKALA	Mitsubishi Lancer Evo VIII	N4
69.	J. VUORELA (FIN)	A. KAPANEN (FIN)	JUHA VUORELA	Mitsubishi Lancer	N4
70.	R. GALLIGAN (IRL)	G. SHINNORS (IRL)	RORY GALLIGAN	Mitsubishi Lancer	N4
71.	J. METSALA (FIN)	S. OHRA-AHO (FIN)	JUKKA METSALA	Subaru Impreza WRX Sti	N4
72.	J. TIRI (FIN)	J. HAIPUS (FIN)	ARI HAIPUS	Subaru Impreza Sti	N4
73.	P. LEHTOVIRTA (FIN)	J. KANERVA (FIN)	PETRI LEHTOVIRTA	Subaru Impreza WRX Sti	N4
75.	R. TEODOSIO (P)	P. PRIMAZ (P)	RICARDO TEODOSIO	Mitsubishi Lancer	N4
76.	V. SVEDAS (LT)	Z. SAKALAUSKAS (LT)	VYTAUTAS SVEDAS	Mitsubishi Lancer Evo IX	N4
77.	F. FRISIERO (I)	A. BORDIN (I)	FABIO FRISIERO	Mitsubishi Lancer Evo IX	N4
78.	V. ROZUKAS (LT)	A. SHOSHAS (LT)	VILIUS ROZUKAS	Subaru Impreza WRX	N4
79.	F. DE SANCTIS (I)	I. ROSIGNOLI (I)	FABRIZIO DE SANCTIS	Mitsubishi Lancer	A8
80.	D. LEVYATOV (RUS)	A. SAPIRO (RUS)	SYRUS RALLY TEAM	Mitsubishi Lancer	N4
81.	N. BARRATT (GB)	C. PATTERSON (GB)	NATALIE BARRATT	Subaru Impreza Sti	N4
82.	I. SOKOLOV (RUS)	V. MIRKOTAN (RUS)	SYRUS RALLY TEAM	Mitsubishi Lancer	A8
83.	P. VIHMA (FIN)	K. NIEMELA (FIN)	PEKKA VIHMA	Mitsubishi Lancer Evo VIII	N4
84.	V. KUZMINYKH (RUS)	T. KAFAKOV (RUS)	VLADIM KUZMINYKH	Mitsubishi Lancer Evo VIII MR	N4
85.	O. GILLET (CH)	F. HELFER (CH)	OLIVIER GILLET	Subaru Impreza	N4
86.	M. JOKELA (FIN)	T. JARVINEN (FIN)	TAPIO JARVINEN	Mitsubishi Lancer Evo VII	A8
87.	P. SAVELA (FIN)	P. LAHTINEN (FIN)	PEKKA SAVELA	Mitsubishi Lancer	N4
88.	M. FRASSON (I)	C. VEZZARO (I)	MAURO FRASSON	Mitsubishi Lancer Evo VIII	N4
89.	M. OLEKSOWICZ (PL)	A. OBERBOWSKI (PL)	MACIEK OLEKSOWICZ	Subaru Impreza	N4
91.	A. VILLANUEVA (E)	A. TRAMONT (F)	ALEXANDER VILLANUEVA	Mitsubishi Lancer Evo VIII	N4
92.	A. BRUSCHETTA (I)	E. CIVIERO (I)	ALESSANDRO BRUSCHETTA	Mitsubishi Lancer Evo VIII	N4
93.	A. LLOVERA (AND)	L. CRUZ (E)	ALBERT LLOVERA	Mitsubishi Lancer Evo VIII	N4
94.	T. VUOKILA (FIN)	J. JAAKOLA (FIN)	TAPIO VUOKILA	Mitsubishi Lancer Evo IX	N4
96.	J. AROLAINEN (FIN)	T. SUOMINEN (FIN)	JOUNI AROLAINEN	Mitsubishi Lancer Evo IX	A8
97.	A. BETTEGA (I)	S. SCATEOLIN (I)	ALESSANDRO BETTEGA	Ford Fiesta	N3
98.	K. KESKINEN (FIN)	L. HIRVIJARVI (FIN)	PROGRESS MOTORSPORT FINLAND	Ford Fiesta	N3
99.	J. ARPIAINEN (FIN)	P. FLYTHSTROM (FIN)	MOTORSTAR OY LTD	Ford Fiesta ST	N3
100.	M. BIASION (F)	C. BEYNET (F)	MATHIEU BIASION	Ford Fiesta	N3
101.	G. CHAMMEL (F)	R. JAMOUL (B)	JPS JUNIOR TEAM LUXEMBOURG	Ford Fiesta	N3
102.	L. ATHANASSOULAS (GR)	N. MOUZAKIS (GR)	TEAM GREECE	Ford Fiesta	N3
103.	E. VERTUNOV (RUS)	G. TROSHKIN (RUS)	EVGENY VERTUNOV	Ford Fiesta	N3
104.	E. GILMOUR (NZ)	C. MOLE (GB)	EMMA GILMOUR	Ford Fiesta	N3
106.	V. SIMKUS (LV)	V. BARINOV (LV)	KASPARS SIMKUS	Honda Civic Type R	N3
107.	J. SALOMAA (FIN)	M. LAPPALAINEN (FIN)	JANI SALOMAA	Honda Civic Type R	N3
108.	T. HURSKAINEN (FIN)	K. MAKIRANTA (FIN)	TUOMAS HURSKAINEN	Ford Fiesta ST	N3
109.	J. LAAKSO (FIN)	I. RAJAMAKI (FIN)	JARI LAAKSO	Volkswagen Polo GTI	N2
110.	A. SAARI (FIN)	P. HAATAJA (FIN)	ANTERO SAARI	Nissan Micra 1.3 Super S	A5
111.	J. LAAKSO (FIN)	P. LEPPALA (FIN)	JORMA LAAKSO	Volkswagen Polo 1.4	A5
112.	R. KAISANLAHTI (FIN)	T. PULKKINEN (FIN)	RAIMO KAISANLAHTI	Volkswagen Polo	A5
113.	J. KOJO (FIN)	J. RAHIKAINEN (FIN)	JOOSE KOJO	Volkswagen Polo 1.4	A5
114.	J. NIEMINEN (FIN)	O. ALANKO (FIN)	JAAKKO NIEMINEN	Nissan Micra 1.3 Super S	A5
115.	T. LUKANDER (FIN)	P. HEDMAN (FIN)	PASI HEDMAN	Volkswagen Polo	A5
116.	V. RUOKANEN (FIN)	T. PALLARI (FIN)	VILLE RUOKANEN	Volkswagen Polo	A5
117.	S. LIIMATAINEN (FIN)	E. MIKKOLA (FIN)	SOINI LIIMATAINEN	Skoda Felicia	A5
118.	S. SALONEN (FIN)	J. HONKALATVA (FIN)	SEPPO SALONEN	Volkswagen Polo 16V 1.4	A5
119.	K. KOSKELAINEN (FIN)	F. VIRTANEN (FIN)	KARI KOSKELAINEN	Skoda Felicia	A5
120.	K. HYTONEN (FIN)	H. SALMEN (FIN)	KARI HYTONEN	Suzuki Ignis Sport	N2
121.	S. BIELTVEDT (NOR)	L. BRAENNA (N)	SVEINUNG BIELTVEDT	Ford Fiesta ST	N3
122.	F. SAVOLDELLI (I)	S. GRIGIS (I)	FLAVIO SAVOLDELLI	Seat Ibiza GT TDI	N4
123.	L. GRIOTTI (I)	G. GUZZI (I)	LUCA GRIOTTI	Renault Clio RS Light	N3
124.	A. NEIKSANS (LV)	E. UTANS (LV)	ANDIS NEIKSANS	Renault Clio	N3

Championship Classifications

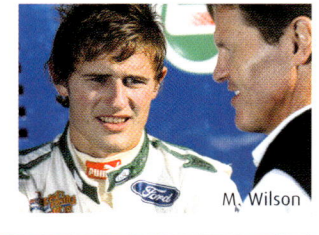

FIA Drivers (10/16)
1. Loeb — 6🏆 92
2. Grönholm — 4🏆 61
3. Sordo — 41
4. Hirvonen — 27
5. Stohl — 24
6. P. Solberg — 20
7. Gardemeister — 16
8. H. Solberg — 16
9. Galli — 15
10. Pons — 11
11. Bengué — 9
12. Atkinson — 9
13. Kopecky — 7
14. Carlsson — 6
15. Välimäki — 6
16. Sarrazin — 6
17. Rådström — 4
18. Duval — 4
19. Mac Hale — 3
20. Tuohino — 3
21. Aigner — 3
22. Katajamäki — 3
23. Sohlberg — 3
24. Wilson — 1
25. Perez Companc, Arai... — 0

FIA Constructors (10/16)
1. Kronos Total Citroën WRT — 6🏆 122
2. BP-Ford World Rally Team — 4🏆 107
3. Subaru World Rally Team — 65
4. OMV-Peugeot Norway — 50
5. Stobart VK M-Sport Ford WRT — 24
6. Red Bull-Skoda Team — 22

FIA Production Car (4/8)
1. Al-Attiyah — 2🏆 34
2. Baldacci — 17
3. Arai — 1🏆 15
4. Kuzaj — 13
5. Nutahara — 1🏆 10
6. Pozzo — 8
7. Marrini — 8
8. Ligato — 8
9. Latvala — 7
10. Teiskonen — 6
11. Heath — 5
12. Uspenskiy — 4
13. Beltrán — 4
14. Vojtech — 2
15. Name — 1
16. Kamada — 0
17. Popov — 0
Higgins Exclu 8

FIA Junior WRC (7/9)
1. Andersson — 1🏆 29
2. Sandell — 1🏆 28
3. Wilks — 2🏆 21
4. Aava — 20
5. Rautenbach — 17
6. Pressac — 17
7. Meeke — 1🏆 16
8. Casier — 16
9. Béres — 16
10. Prokop — 1🏆 15
11. Tirabassi — 1🏆 15
12. Valousek — 11
13. Burkart — 9
14. Molder — 8
15. Kara — 7
16. Rantanen — 6
17. Kosciuszko — 5
18. Pinomäki — 4
19. Betti — 3
20. Zachrisson — 2
21. Bonato — 1
22. Clark, Bordignon — 0
Cortinovis, Karlsson — 0

Special Stages Times

www.nesteoilrallyfinland.fi
www.wrc.com

SS1 Killeri 1 (2.50 km)
1.Loeb 1'21"4; 2.P.Solberg +0"2;
3.Hirvonen +0"5;
4.Carlsson/Grönholm +1"0;
6.Atkinson/Sordo/Katajamäki +1"3..
J-WRC > 33.Andersson 1'30"3

SS2 Lankamaa (24.97 km)
1.Grönholm 11'59"7; 2.Hirvonen +8"5;
3.P.Solberg +9"7; 4.Loeb +13"1;
5.Atkinson +15"7; 6.Sordo +36"4;
7.Galli +37"1; 8.Carlsson +37"3...
J-WRC > 23.Meeke 14'01"2

SS3 Laukaa (11.81 km)
1.Grönholm 5'40"8; 2.Hirvonen +0"1;
3.P.Solberg +3"2; 4.Loeb +3"6;
5.Atkinson +4"8; 6.H.Solberg +6"9;
7.Galli +8"9; 8.Carlsson +9"0...
J-WRC > 25.Meeke 6'28"2

SS4 Ruuhimaki (7.57 km)
1.Grönholm 3'57"2; 2.Loeb +0"9;
3.P.Solberg +1"9; 4.Hirvonen +3"6;
5.H.Solberg +5"0; 6.Atkinson +6"3;
7.Sohlberg +7"3; 8.Välimäki +7"8...
J-WRC > 27.Aava 4'32"1

SS5 Vellipohja 1 (36,38 km)
1.Loeb 17'51"9; 2.Grönholm +2"5;
3.Hirvonen +8"9; 4.P.Solberg +15"9;
5.H.Solberg +24"6; 6.Atkinson +29"6;
7.Sohlberg +38"8; 8.Hänninen +39"9...
J-WRC > 22.Meeke 20'04"1

SS6 Mokkipera 1 (12.60 km)
1.Loeb 6'11"2; 2.Grönholm +1"1;
3.H.Solberg +4"1; 4.Hirvonen +5"6;
5.P.Solberg +6"7; 6.Atkinson +11"6;
7.Välimäki +12"1;
8.Katajamäki +13"1...
J-WRC > 20.Meeke 7'05"9

SS7 Vellipohja 2 (36.38 km)
1.Grönholm 18'05"8; 2.Loeb +4"2;
3.Hirvonen +7"4; 4.P.Solberg +8"2;
5.Galli +20"5; 6.H.Solberg +21"1;
7.Sordo +27"5; 8.Stohl +33"5...
J-WRC > 18.Aava 20'14"8

SS8 Mokkipera 2 (12.60 km)
1.Loeb 6'20"1; 2.Grönholm +5"3;
3.H.Solberg +8"9; 4.Galli +10"1;
5.P.Solberg +15"4; 6.Välimäki +16"4;
7.Hirvonen +17"5; 8.Tuohino +17"6...
J-WRC > 19.Andersson 7'14"3

SS9 Killeri 2 (2.50 km)
1.Grönholm 1'21"6; 2.Loeb +0"1;
3.Sordo +0"6; 4.H.Solberg +0"8;
5.Pons +1"1; 6.Hirvonen +1"3;
7.Stohl +1"4; 8.Välimäki +1"5...
J-WRC > 29.Aava 1'31"1

Classification Leg 1
1.Grönholm 1h12'59"6; 2.Loeb +12"0;
3.Hirvonen +43"5; 4.P.Solberg +52"9;
5.H.Solberg +1'47"2;
6.Atkinson +2'17"1; 7.Sordo +2'45"0;
8.Galli +2'49"6...
J-WRC > 18.Meeke 1h22'53"2

SS10 Vaheri (19.90 Km)
1.Grönholm 9'47"6; 2.Loeb +1"7;
3.P.Solberg +5"5; 4.Hirvonen +8"3;
5.Katajamäki +18"9; 6.H.Solberg +20"3;
7.Sordo +21"1; 8.Galli +24"5...
J-WRC > 19.Wilks 11'02"7

SS11 Ouninpohja Lansi 1 (13.97 km)
1.Loeb 6'33"0; 2.Grönholm +1"3;
3.Hirvonen +4"0; 4.Katajamäki +11"8;
5.Sordo +12"7; 6.Galli +15"4;
7.Tuohino +15"8; 8.H.Solberg +16"2...
J-WRC > 18.Meeke 7'16"7

SS12 Ouninpohja Ita 1 (16.54 km)
1.Grönholm 7'51"7; 2.Galli +18"1;
3.H.Solberg +19"6; 4.Sordo +21"6;
5.Hirvonen +22"0; 6.Välimäki +23"7;
7.Tuohino +27"0; 8.Loeb +32"4...
J-WRC > 16.Wilks 8'52"5

SS13 S. Urria (10,00 km)
1.Grönholm 4'40"8; 2.Loeb +2"4;
3.Hirvonen +3"3; 4.H.Solberg +4"0;
5.Galli +5"4; 6.Atkinson +6"7;
7.Katajamäki +8"1; 8.Sordo +10"8...
J-WRC > 19.Wilks 5'16"0

SS14 Ouninpohja Lansi 2 (13.97 km)
1.Grönholm 6'30"7; 2.Loeb +0"7;
3.Hirvonen +2"3; 4.H.Solberg +4"9;
5.Atkinson +6"5; 6.Tuohino +8"5;
7.Katajamäki +8"8; 8.Galli +9"9...
J-WRC > 16.Wilks 7'08"5

SS15 Ouninpohja Ita 2 (16.54 km)
1.Grönholm 7'51"8; 2.Loeb +1"8;
3.Hirvonen +4"1; 4.H.Solberg +6"6;
5.Galli +9"4; 6.Atkinson +9"5;
7.Tuohino +13"6; 8.Katajamäki +14"0...
J-WRC > 16.Wilks 8'49"0

SS16 Moksi - Leustu (40.95 Km)
1.Grönholm 20'25"6; 2.Hirvonen +11"3;
3.Loeb +13"6; 4.Galli +29"0;
5.Katajamäki +32"8; 6.Tuohino +34"8;
7.H.Solberg +36"0; 8.Välimäki +43"8...
J-WRC > 17.Wilks 23'20"8

SS17 Himos (12.97 Km)
1.Grönholm 7'09"1; 2.H.Solberg +3"5;
3.Loeb +4"5; 4.Hirvonen +5"0;
5.Galli +5"9; 6.Katajamäki +7"4;
7.Atkinson +7"7; 8.Tuohino +12"5...
J-WRC > 17.Wilks 8'14"9

Classification Leg 2
1.Grönholm 2h23'51"2;
2.Loeb +1'07"8; 3.Hirvonen +1'42"5;
4.H.Solberg +3'37"0; 5.Galli +5'05"9;
6.Tuohino +5'38"1; 7.Välimäki +5'58"6;
8.Kopecky +8'50"5...
J-WRC > 14.Wilks 2h43'30"9

SS18 Kuohu 1 (7.80 Km)
1.Hirvonen 3'42"4; 2.Grönholm +1"2;
3.Loeb +1"5; 4.Atkinson +4"2;
5.Katajamäki +5"1; 6.H.Solberg +7"3;
7.Tuohino +7"9; 8.Galli +8"1...
J-WRC > 18.Wilks 4'11"4

SS19 Jukojarvi 1 (22.30 Km)
1.Hirvonen 10'46"6; 2.Loeb +1"6;
3.Grönholm +3"0; 4.H.Solberg +11"4;
5.Tuohino +13"4; 6.Atkinson +16"2;
7.Katajamäki +16"9; 8.Galli +18"6...
J-WRC > 18.Andersson 12'11"0

SS20 Kuohu 2 (7.80 Km)
1.Hirvonen 3'42"6; 2.Loeb +0"7;
3.H.Solberg +1"3; 4.Grönholm +1"7;
5.Atkinson/Katajamäki +1"8;
7.Tuohino +2"6; 8.Galli +3"0...
J-WRC > 17.Wilks 4'09"0

SS21 Jukojarvi 2 (22.30 Km)
1.Hirvonen 10'39"5; 2.Grönholm +2"1;
3.Loeb +3"1; 4.Atkinson +8"3;
5.H.Solberg +8"8; 6.Tuohino +11"0;
7.Galli/Katajamäki +12"3...
J-WRC > 17.Andersson 11'56"7

Results

	Driver - Co-driver	Car	Gr.	Time
1	Grönholm - Rautiainen	Ford Focus RS WRC 06	A8	2h52'50"3
2	Loeb - Elena	Citroën Xsara WRC	A8	+ 1'06"7
3	Hirvonen - Lehtinen	Ford Focus RS WRC 06	A8	+ 1'34"5
4	H. Solberg - Menkerud	Peugeot 307 WRC	A8	+ 3'57"8
5	Galli - Bernacchini	Peugeot 307 WRC	A8	+ 5'39"9
6	Tuohino - Markkula	Citroën Xsara WRC	A8	+ 6'05"0
7	Välimäki - Kalliolepo	Mitsubishi Lancer WRC 05	A8	+ 6'55"4
8	Kopecky - Schovanek	Skodia Fabia WRC	A8	+ 10'15"0
9	Stohl - Minor	Peugeot 307 WRC	A8	+ 13'28"0
10	Wilson - Orr	Ford Focus RS WRC 04	A8	+ 14'47"4
11	Alén - Hantunen	Subaru Impreza	N4	+ 17'10"3
15	Wilks - Pugh	Suzuki Swift S1600	A6/J	+ 23'15"4
18	Andersson - Andersson	Suzuki Swift S1600	A6/J	+ 25'52"9
21	Rantanen - Lönegren	Honda Civic Type R	A6/J	+ 32'01"3

Leading Retirements (33)

TC17C	Meeke - Patterson	Citroën C2 S1600	Engine
SF14	Sordo - Marti	Citroën Xsara WRC	Off
SF11	P. Solberg - Mills	Subaru Impreza WRC 2006	Off
SF11	Pons - Del Barrio	Citroën Xsara WRC	Off
TC9C	Aava - Sikk	Suzuki Swift S1600	Exclusion
TC9C	Carlsson - Thorszelius	Mitsubishi WRC-05	Off
TC6A	Sohlberg - Pietilainen	Subaru Impreza WRC 2005	Engine

Performers

	1	2	3	4	5	6	C6	Nb SS
Grönholm	12	6	1	2	-	-	21	21
Loeb	5	9	4	2	-	-	20	21
Hirvonen	4	3	7	4	1	1	20	21
H. Solberg	-	1	4	5	3	4	17	21
P. Solberg	-	1	4	2	2	-	9	10
Galli	-	1	-	2	4	1	8	21
Sordo	-	-	1	1	1	2	5	13
Atkinson	-	-	-	2	4	7	13	21
Katajamäki	-	-	-	1	4	2	7	18
Carlsson	-	-	-	1	-	-	1	7
Tuohino	-	-	-	-	1	3	4	21
Pons	-	-	-	-	1	-	1	10
Välimäki	-	-	-	-	-	2	2	21

Previous winners

1973	Mäkinen - Liddon Ford Escort RS 1600
1974	Mikkola - Davenport Ford Escort RS 1600
1975	Mikkola - Aho Toyota Corolla
1976	Alen - Kivimaki Fiat 131 Abarth
1977	Hamalaiinen - Tiukkanen Ford Escort RS
1978	Alen - Kivimaki Fiat 131 Abarth
1979	Alen - Kivimaki Fiat 131 Abarth
1980	Alen - Kivimaki Fiat 131 Abarth
1981	Vatanen - Richards Ford Escort RS
1982	Mikkola - Hertz Audi Quattro
1983	Mikkola - Hertz Audi Quattro
1984	Vatanen - Harryman Peugeot 205 T16
1985	Salonen - Harjanne Peugeot 205 T16
1986	Salonen - Harjanne Peugeot 205 T16
1987	Alen - Kivimaki Lancia Delta HF Turbo
1988	Alen - Kivimaki Lancia Delta Integrale
1989	Ericsson - Billstam Mitsubishi Galant VR4
1990	Sainz - Moya Toyota Celica GT-Four
1991	Kankkunen - Piironen Lancia Delta Integrale 16v
1992	Auriol - Occelli Lancia Delta Integrale
1993	Kankkunen - Giraudet Toyota Celica Turbo 4WD
1994	Mäkinen - Harjanne Ford Escort RS Cosworth
1995	Mäkinen - Harjanne Mitsubishi Lancer Evo 3
1996	Mäkinen - Harjanne Mitsubishi Lancer Evo 3
1997	Mäkinen - Harjanne Mitsubishi Lancer Evo 4
1998	Mäkinen - Mannisenmäki Mitsubishi Lancer Evo 5
1999	Kankkunen - Repo Subaru Impreza WRC
2000	Grönholm - Rautiainen Peugeot 206 WRC
2001	Grönholm - Rautiainen Peugeot 206 WRC
2002	Grönholm - Rautiainen Peugeot 206 WRC
2003	Märtin - Park Ford Focus RS WRC 03
2004	Grönholm - Rautiainen Peugeot 307 WRC
2005	Grönholm - Rautiainen Peugeot 307 WRC

Leaders

| SS1 | Loeb |
| SS2 > SS21 | Grönholm |

Japan

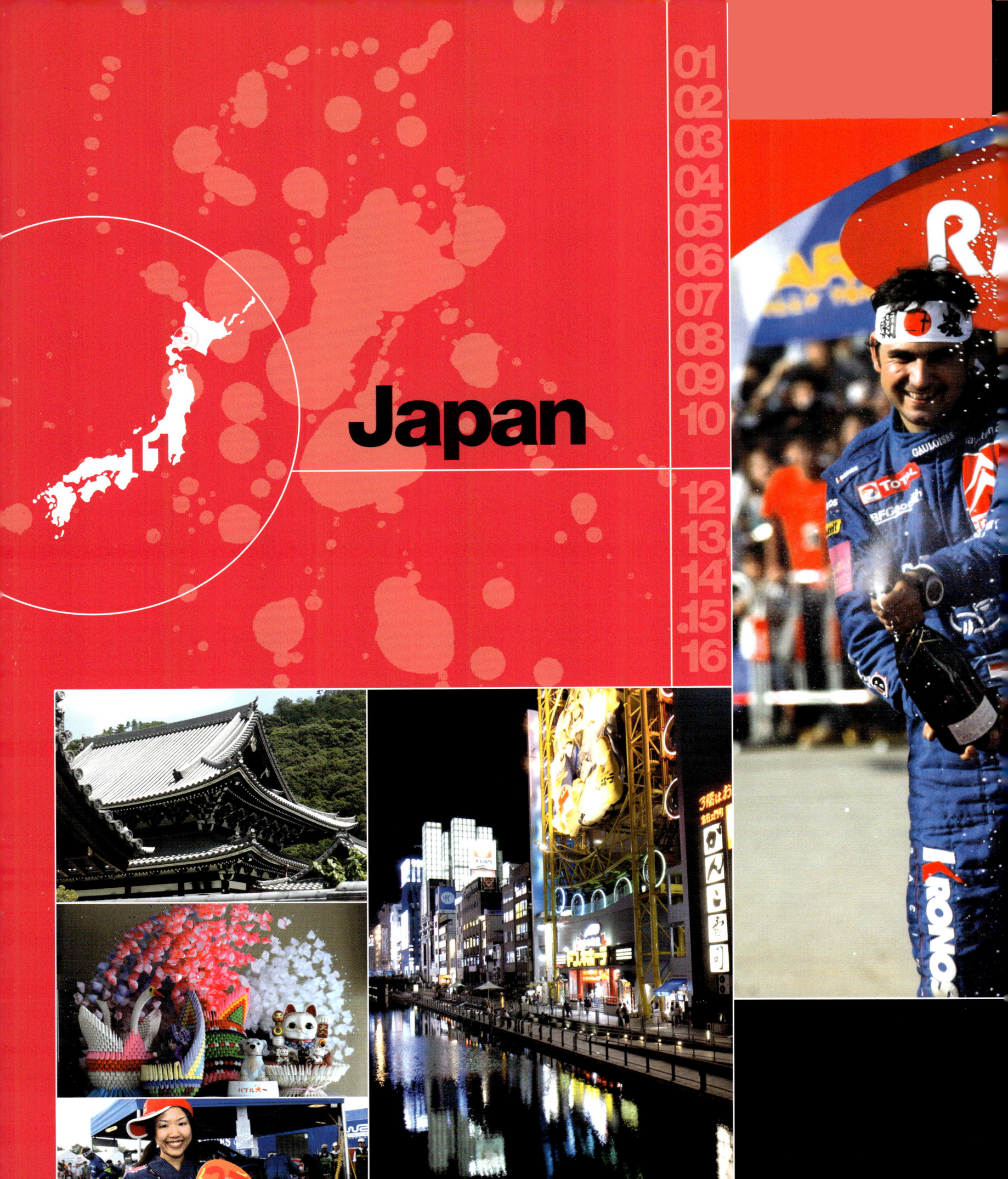

01
02
03
04
05
06
07
08
09
10

12
13
14
15
16

RALLY FINISH

King Seb!
After a rally that turned into a head-to-head battle by the two best drivers of the moment Sébastien Loeb became the world record holder of the number of victories in the WRC thanks to his 27th victory. The Frenchman was never able to let up, and occasionally went beyond the limit to win his seventh rally out of the eleven held so far this season.

11 Japan

Every year the Japanese give the competitors in their national rally a marvellous welcome. 2006 was no exception as Grönholm and Rautiainen found out!

Petter Solberg was hoping to shine in his manufacturer's home event. Once again it all went wrong for the Norwegian due to brake problems.

THE RALLY
Pushing the envelope

While the 2006 rally championship was a two-horse race between Marcus Grönholm and Sébastien Loeb, who completely overshadowed their rivals, their duels generated some thrilling moments of sporting intensity. When it went right down to the wire as in the 3rd Japanese rally it occasionally touched the sublime. The thousands of spectators who came to attend the opening ceremony and then rushed to the roadside got value for money as they saw a marvellous battle between the two men, which lasted the full 3 days as neither ran into mechanical problems or retired early on. Finally, no external elements that could have upset the balance like tyre choice for example intruded in the Homeric struggle waged between the Frenchman and his Finnish rival.

While it true that the cold facts often strip the sporting aspect of its heat and intensity those of the Japanese rally give an excellent overview of the closeness of the scrap: 27 special stages, 15 fastest times for Grönholm, 11 for Loeb (Hirvonen claimed the other one in the final super special). There were only 2 leaders, the Finn from SS1 to 13 and Loeb from SS14 to 27. At the finish the gap between the Citroën driver and his Ford-mounted adversary was 5.4s after it had been 25.6s at the start of the third leg.

If it were necessary to underline the performances of these two "Kings of the Road," Mikko Hirvonen's comment after the second leg sums it up: "I haven't had any problems so far but if I tried to match the pace of Marcus and Sébastien, I would have! They're incredibly quick and they're both able to keep up this infernal rhythm."

Right from the start the pace of the two men was far too hot for their opponents. Loeb has often been a bit slow getting into the swing of things while Grönholm's trademark has been his instant on-the-gas getaway. On the first day the Frenchman was slightly hindered, as he was first out on each stage on which the road was covered by gravel, but his rival's determination on the muddy, slippery surface was a pleasure to see. He won the first two stages pulling out a lead of 7.7s over Loeb in fourth place behind Hirvonen and Petter Solberg. But not for long. In Kanna the Citroën looked as if it was flying and the reigning world champion shot past the two cars in front of him thanks to a heavy right foot. "I'll have to revise my notes for this stage," grumbled Grönholm who was not very happy at having 3.8s sliced off his lead in only 14 kilometres. Second time

Mikko Hirvonen made a great start but then went off in the fourth special. He took things quietly after that to hold on to his third place.

Loeb, Stohl and the other drivers had to cover the same super special five times!

A very concentrated and determined Dani Sordo is about to enter into combat.

Seeing a car crossing a ford is always spectacular especially when it's an all-fired up Grönholm.

On Saturday morning the two were champing at the bit even more than the day before. "I'll have to be at 100% everywhere and perhaps a bit more," Loeb remarked as he got into his car.

Grönholm won the first two stages as the cars flew from one checkpoint to another. Taking huge risks he managed to pull out a lead of 13.1s in the general classification at speeds that sometimes exceeded 110 km/h. Loeb hit back in the third slashing his lead to 6.3s. It was pedal to metal all the way and no pussy footing.

The big Finn did not give up; he tripped up. In SS14, he dropped his Ford's wheel into a gully in a sharp right-hander in the opening kilometres of the Sipirkakim stage. The car was unbalanced and spun. "I found myself pointing in the wrong direction and on the narrow road I had to do a lot of manoeuvring to face the right way." His mistake cost him 18 seconds. He was unable to get back into the rhythm and lost another five.

"We didn't know if Marcus had run into problems or made a mistake so we continued flat out," grinned Loeb.

through he lost another 6.3 seconds, which did nothing to add to his good humour! However, he was the quickest through the remaining stages with the exception of the 2 super specials at the end. "My determination was reinforced by my victory in Finland and I arrived here full of confidence hence the very close battle with Seb. But I have to admit that I'd have liked to have had a bigger lead."

It was 10.5s, a mere trifle. For the others it was a nightmare. Hirvonen was back in third place 1m 02s down after hitting the coping of a cement bridge in SS4 and twisting a rim. Sordo was in fifth place 2m 54s in arrears in what was his apprenticeship on this type of terrain. In sixth, seventh and eighth came the Subaru trio of Atkinson, Araï and Solberg handicapped by recurrent brake, gearbox and differential problems.

Chris Atkinson was spared the problems that hit his team leader and came home in fourth place in Japan where he is always at home.

Manfred Stohl was racing in Japan for the first time in the only 307 WRC entered by the Bozian squad.

11 Japan

Marcus Grönholm threw caution to the wind in the third leg and took huge risks to try and pull back a few precious seconds. His efforts may have been in vain but the big Finn was not lacking in supporters!

Mikko Hirvonen's steadiness paid off again and he finished on the rostrum. But he was still not up to beating Loeb or Grönholm in a straight fight.

Sébastien Loeb once again displayed the full range of his immense talent. He pushed Grönholm into making a mistake and then controlled his comeback, not something everybody can do.

"It was the right decision as after his spin he went very quickly. We drove the nail home by winning Menan."

In addition, Grönholm was only a pale shadow of himself as he was upset by his mistake. In SS15, he went off, stalled and had to get the car pointing in the right direction once again. Loeb pulled out another 10.5s over his rival: "I don't understand why I make such mistakes," he moaned.
"Maybe he wanted to close the gap (27.9s) in one fell swoop," said his co-driver Timo Rautiainen, philosophically.

Once Marcus had got over his little upset he set off again at full speed but could only pull back 2.3s in the final stages of the second day. "I don't really know what to expect from the third leg but I'll do my best to catch Seb. I've got to get as close to him as possible and maybe he'll make a mistake. In any case I'm not giving up now," he concluded. When Marcus gets angry he flies. Only 6 specials remained, a total of 93.90 kms. The game was on again.

In SS22, he pulled back 4.5s, in SS23 he lost a tenth, in SS24, he sliced another 5.5s off his rival's lead and in SS25, 6.9s! At the start of the 24,8 km Penke 2 stage 8.8s separated the two men. Loeb wasn't having any. "At the start I reckoned that the eight points for second place would be a good bet in the championship chase. And then we decided to go for it. The battle was too good to err on the side of caution. It was a pretty emotional moment. Once Daniel and me set off we were only thinking of one thing: victory. We had no splits we had to go as fast as possible. Yes, we did take a few risks in the last special!"
"Victory was still possible, laughed Grönholm afterwards. There was no let-up in either camp."

"It was the wildest battle I've ever seen as a team manager," declared Malcolm Wilson. And the Ford man has been around long enough to know what he is talking about, as he looked after Colin McRae at the time of the Scot's great duels with Tommi Mäkinen. When the Franco-Monegasque pair arrived at the checkpoint they both grabbed the time sheets. Loeb thought he had lost as he reckoned that by pushing so hard he committed a plethora of mistakes.
"When I crossed the line, I didn't know where I was." Then he searched for his rival's time. 14m 21.5s and his was 14m 24.9s. He was home and dry!

"My mistakes on Saturday cost me victory," groaned the Finn.
"It took us fifteen to twenty seconds to understand that we'd won," warbled Daniel Elena after the rally. The final stage (a super special) had no bearing on the result.

The Citroën clan exploded with joy. "It was sheer madness," chortled Marc Van Dalen, the Kronos boss. "I don't really know what to feel: admiration for these exceptional guys Sébastien and Daniel or joy and pride in our team."

The crew was in seventh heaven, as its twenty-seventh victory that gave them the world record was also of one the best of their career. It began with an intense battle and ended on a bravura note. One doesn't become the world record holder for nothing. Courage, talent and a little bit of madness all play their part in such an achievement.

Fumio Nutahara's win in the Production championship was celebrated in typical Japanese style as he was at the wheel of a Japanese car (Mitsubishi) with Japanese tyres (Yokohama) and had Japanese sponsors.

The other aspects were of minor importance. Hirvonen finished third and Petter Solberg went home empty-handed yet again. Fumio Nutahara won the production category. Dani Sordo was disqualified after the event for not having put on his safety harness at the right moment. In the championship Loeb led the drivers' by 33 points while Citroën was 11 points in front in the manufacturers'. But these were mere footnotes to what had been an exceptionally thrilling event. ∎

THE RECORD
27 victories!

It took Carlos Sainz 15 years and 196 world championship rallies to set his record of 26 outright victories. Sébastien Loeb took 81 rallies since 2000 to rack up his 27 wins. In Japan, the Frenchman underlined the fact that no comparison was possible between the two achievements. It was a different era with very different types of events that were much longer and much trickier. The cars too were not the same; they were less reliable than those of today; the calendar was different with fewer rallies and of course the rivals were not the same (in 2006 Loeb's only real adversary was Grönholm). Loeb could have reached this figure earlier as in 2001 he lost the San Remo by the skin of his teeth to Gilles Panizzi, then the Monte Carlo in 2002 when he was disqualified, and Great Britain in 2005 because of a personal decision as he did not want to be crowned in the event that cost the life of Michael Parks.

This record will be a keystone in the career of the Frenchman. In Sardinia when he congratulated Daniel Elena on his becoming the record holder for the number of victories by a co-driver, he said that he could well imagine his right-hand man's joy as he was waiting for the very same thing. Concerning Michael Schumacher one remembers his record number of victories in addition to his world titles. Now it's done for the Alsatian with the panache that has always been part of his make-up.

Other challenges still await him: winning each rally on the calendar at least once (after Japan he was still missing Finland and Great Britain). The great Tommi Mäkinen also took it up and failed to achieve it. Then there is the record number of world titles held by Kankkunen and Mäkinen (4) to be beaten as well as becoming the first driver to win the world championship four times on the trot.
Only time will tell if he can accomplish these feats, but Sébastien Loeb has already left his mark on the history of rallying. ∎

"Toshi" Araï is a Subaru regular. He was at the wheel of a 2006 WRC and even if he had not driven one of the top-category cars for 4 years he still managed to finish sixth.

Sordo salutes the crowd. He was disqualified for not fastening his safety harness!

Number 27! This victory gave Sébastien Loeb the record in terms of WRC victories, and Daniel Elena took on the onerous job of uncorking the champagne!

11 Japan results

3rd RALLY OF JAPAN

Organiser Details
Event Competition Secretariat,
Homei Bldg Minami 4-9 Nangodori 19,
Shiroishi-ku, Sapporo,
Hokkaido, Japan 003-0022
Tel.: +8111 8642003
Fax: +8111 8641192

Rally Japan

11th leg of FIA 2006 World Rally Championship for constructors and drivers.
5th leg of FIA Production Car World Championship.

Date September 1st - 3, 2006

Route
1586.52 km divised in 3 legs.
27 special stages on dirt roads (345.72 km)

Starting Procedure
Thursday, August 31 (18:30),
Rally Show, central Obihiro

Leg 1
Friday, September 1st (08:03/18:55),
Kita Aikoku > Kita Aikoku, 610.14 km;
10 special stages (123.80 km)

Leg 2
Saturday, September 2 (07:26/18:55),
Kita Aikoku > Kita Aikoku, 600.82 km;
11 special stages (128.02 km)

Leg 3
Sunday, September 3 (07:19/14:09),
Kita Aikoku > Kita Aikoku, 375.56 km;
6 special stages (93.90 km)

Entry List (90) - 87 starters

N°	Driver (Nat.)	Co-driver (Nat.)	Team	Car	Group & FIA Priority
1.	S. LOEB (F)	D. ELENA (MC)	KRONOS TOTAL CITROEN WRT	Citroën Xsara WRC	A8 1
2.	D. SORDO (E)	M. MARTI (E)	KRONOS TOTAL CITROEN WRT	Citroën Xsara WRC	A8 1
3.	M. GRÖNHOLM (FIN)	T. RAUTIAINEN (FIN)	BP FORD WORLD RALLY TEAM	Ford Focus RS WRC 06	A8 1
4.	M. HIRVONEN (FIN)	J. LEHTINEN (FIN)	BP FORD WORLD RALLY TEAM	Ford Focus RS WRC 06	A8 1
5.	P. SOLBERG (N)	P. MILLS (GB)	SUBARU WORLD RALLY TEAM	Subaru Impreza WRC 2006	A8 1
6.	C. ATKINSON (AUS)	G. MACNEALL (AUS)	SUBARU WORLD RALLY TEAM	Subaru Impreza WRC 2006	A8 1
7.	M. STOHL (A)	I. MINOR (A)	OMV - PEUGEOT NORWAY	Peugeot 307 WRC	A8 2
9.	M. WILSON (GB)	M. ORR (GB)	STOBART - VK - M-SPORT FORD RALLY TEAM	Ford Focus RS WRC 06	A8 1
10.	L. PEREZ COMPANC (RA)	J. MARIA VOLTA (RA)	STOBART - VK - M-SPORT FORD RALLY TEAM	Ford Focus RS WRC 06	A8 1
12.	G. MACHALE (IRL)	P. NAGLE (IRL)	GARETH MACHALE	Ford Focus RS WRC 04	A8 2
14.	T. ARAI (J)	T. SIRCOMBE (NZ)	SUBARU WORLD RALLY TEAM	Subaru Impreza WRC 2006	A8 2
32.	M. LIGATO (RA)	R. GARCIA (RA)	MARCOS LIGATO	Mitsubishi Lancer Evo IX	N4 3
33.	F. NUTAHARA (J)	D. BARRITT (GB)	ADVAN-PIAA RALLY TEAM	Mitsubishi Lancer Evo IX	N4 3
34.	S. BELTRÁN (RA)	R. ROJAS (RCH)	SEBASTIÁN BELTRÁN	Mitsubishi Lancer Evo IX	N4 3
35.	G. POZZO (RA)	D. STILLO (RA)	GABRIEL POZZO	Mitsubishi Lancer Evo IX	N4 3
36.	M. BALDACCI (RSM)	G. AGNESE (I)	MIRCO BALDACCI	Mitsubishi Lancer Evo IX	N4 3
37.	J. LATVALA (FIN)	M. ANTTILA (FIN)	JARI-MATTI LATVALA	Subaru Impreza WRX Sti Spec	N4 3
38.	L. KUZAJ (PL)	M. SZCZEPANIAK (PL)	AUTOMOBILKUB RZEMIESLNIK WARSZAWA	Subaru Impreza WRX Sti Spec	N4 3
40.	S. MARRINI (I)	T. SANDRONI (I)	ERRANI TEAM GROUP	Mitsubishi Lancer Evo VII	N4 3
41.	T. KAMADA (J)	D. GIRAUDET (F)	SUBARU TEAM QUASYS	Subaru Impreza WRX Sti	N4 3
42.	L. BALDACCI (RSM)	D. D'ESPOSITO (I)	SUBARU RALLY TEAM RUSSIA	Subaru Impreza WRX Sti	N4 3
45.	M. TEISKONEN (FIN)	M. TEISKONEN (FIN)	SYMS RALLY TEAM	Subaru Impreza WRX Sti Spec	N4 3
61.	K. TAGUCHI (J)	M. STACEY (AUS)	TEAM PIAA RALLIART	Mitsubishi Lancer Evo IX	N4
62.	H. YANAGISAWA (J)	T. MISAIZU (J)	CUSCO RACING	Subaru Impreza WRX Sti 2004	N4
63.	D. HERRIDGE (AUS)	W. HAYES (AUS)	SUBARU RALLY TEAM JAPAN	Subaru Impreza WRX Sti	N4
64.	N. KATSUTA (J)	M. YAMAMOTO (J)	SUBARU RALLY TEAM JAPAN	Subaru Impreza WRX Sti	N4
65.	S. TAGUCHI (J)	S. HIROTA (J)	SEIICHIRO TAGUCHI	Mitsubishi Lancer Evo VII	N4
66.	E. IWASHITA (J)	A. TAKAHASHI (J)	TEAM OKUYAMA	Mitsubishi Lancer Evo VIII	N4
68.	A. MASUMURA (J)	K. WATANABE (J)	SUPER ALEX TROOP	Mitsubishi Lancer Evo IX	N4
69.	S. ARAI (J)	H. SAKAKI (J)	MITSUBISHI RALLY TEAM GUNMA ARAI SHINSUKE	Mitsubishi Lancer Evo VIII	N4
70.	D. YAMADA (J)	T. TAKAHASHI (J)	TEAM PACK R	Subaru Impreza WRX Sti	N4
71.	M. ISHIDA (J)	S. ANDOU (J)	TEAM C-ONE SPORT	Mitsubishi Lancer Evo IX	N4
72.	S. OHBA (J)	H. TAKAHASHI (J)	SEISUKE OHBA	Mitsubishi Lancer Evo VII	N4
73.	O. FUKUNAGA (J)	H. OKUMURA (J)	OSAMU FUKUNAGA	Mitsubishi Lancer Evo VII	N4
74.	H. MIYOSHI (J)	H. ICHINO (J)	HIDEAKI MIYOSHI	Mitsubishi Lancer Evo IX	N4
75.	G. NAGAYOSHI (J)	T. YOSHIMOCHI (J)	GENTO NAGAYOSHI	Mitsubishi Lancer Evo VII	N4
76.	H. NIWA (J)	T. YASUE (J)	HIROMICHI NIWA	Mitsubishi Lancer Evo VII	N4
77.	T. SAKAUE (J)	N. HARA (J)	TETSUJI SAKAUE	Mitsubishi Lancer Evo VII	N4
78.	K. KAMATA (J)	C. KAMATA (J)	KYOSUKE KAMATA	Mitsubishi Lancer EVO 7	N4
79.	K. TERAO (J)	K. SAKAI (J)	TOKACHI OFFICIAL NETWORK	Subaru Impreza WRX Sti	N4
80.	Y. TAGUCHI (J)	T. SATO (J)	BESTCAR-FENEK RALLY TEAM	Mitsubishi Lancer Evo IX	N4
81.	Y. KUDO (J)	S. OTSUKA (J)	YUKIHIRO KUDO	Mitsubishi Lancer Evo VII	N4
82.	H. OSHIMA (J)	T. IDEUE (J)	HAROU OSHIMA	Mitsubishi Lancer Evo IX	N4
83.	K. AMOU (J)	H. TAKEYABU (J)	KEISUKE AMOU	Mitsubishi Lancer Evo VII	N4
84.	K. OI (J)	Y. TOYAMA (J)	TAKAYAMA COLLEGE RALLY TEAM	Mitsubishi Lancer EVO 7	N4
85.	T. NISHI (J)	A. FUKUSHIRO (J)	TAKASHI NISHI	Subaru Impreza WRX Sti	N4
86.	R. HORIKAWA (J)	T. KAJIYAMA (J)	RYUJI HORIKAWA	Mitsubishi Lancer Evo VII	N4
87.	Y. WATANABE (J)	S. IKEDA (J)	YOZO WATANABE	Mitsubishi Lancer Evo VIII	N4
88.	H. YOSHITANI (J)	K. YAMAKITA (J)	HISATOSHI YOSHITANI	Mitsubishi Lancer Evo VIII	N4
89.	S. HOLMES (NZ)	G. COWAN (NZ)	TERAOKA AUTO DOOR	Subaru Impreza WRX Sti 2002	N4
90.	S. YAMAUCHI (J)	N. ODAGIRI (J)	BEST CAR FENEK RALLY TEAM	Mitsubishi Lancer Evo VIII	N4
91.	F. TAKAHASHI (J)	M. NAKAMURA (J)	AHRESTY RALLY TEAM	Subaru Impreza WRX Sti	N4
92.	Y. MITANI (J)	M. ARAI (J)	YOSHIZAKU MITANI	Mitsubishi Lancer Evo VIII	N4
93.	M. AOKI (J)	F. AOKI (J)	MITSUHIRO AOKI	Mitsubishi Lancer Evo IX	N4
94.	M. NAKAMURA (J)	Y. FUJISHIMA (J)	MITSUGU NAKAMURA	Mitsubishi Lancer Evo VII	N4
95.	A. MITSUKURI (J)	M. HASEGAWA (J)	ARITOSHI MITSUKURI	Mitsubishi Lancer Evo VII	N4
96.	M. NAKAJIMA (J)	N. KUROSAKI (J)	MASAHIRO NAKAJIMA	Subaru Impreza WRX Sti	N4
97.	T. SAITO (J)	A. ENDO (J)	TATSURU SAITO	Mitsubishi Lancer Evo IX	N4
98.	H. NAMBA (J)	T. SEKIGUCHI (J)	HIDEAKI NAMBA	Mitsubishi Lancer Evo VII	N4
99.	E. NAKAMURA (J)	H. MIYABE (J)	RS.TAKEDA WORLD RALLY TEAM	Mitsubishi Lancer Evo IX	N4
100.	Y. NAKATA (J)	M. KIKUCHI (J)	YUJI NAKATA	Mitsubishi Lancer Evo VI	N4
101.	Y. IKEMACHI (J)	A. NAKATA (J)	YOSHIO IKEMACHI	Subaru Impreza WRX Sti	N4
102.	D. MIZUNO (J)	M. KIHARA (J)	YASUHARU MIZUNO	Mitsubishi Lancer Evo VIII	N4
103.	K. BABA (J)	M. ONAYA (J)	KOJI BABA	Mitsubishi Lancer Evo IX	N4
104.	Y. HAGIWARA (J)	M. TAKAHASHI (J)	TEAM HAS RALLY	Subaru Impreza WRX Sti	N4
105.	T. MINAMINO (J)	P. SANTO (NZ)	TERAOKA AUTO DOOR	Mitsubishi Lancer Evo VIII	N4
106.	K. KITAMURA (J)	M. HIRUTA (J)	AHRESTY RALLY TEAM	Subaru Impreza WRX Sti	N4
107.	M. MURANO (J)	K. TAKEMORI (J)	TEAM KENICHI TAKEMURA	Subaru Impreza WRX Sti	N4
108.	M. FUKUMOTO (J)	H. UMENO (J)	HIDEKI UMENO	Subaru Impreza WRX Sti	N4
109.	M. SUGIYAMA (J)	M. ITOH (J)	MASAMI SUGIYAMA	Mitsubishi Lancer Evo VI	N4
110.	K. SHIMADA (J)	T. KAYAHARA (J)	TEAM YM WORKS	Toyota Celica ST202	A7
111.	Y. AWAZUHARA (J)	S. GOTOH (J)	YUTAKA AWAZUHARA	Peugeot 206RC	A7
112.	T. IRINATSU (J)	J. IIDA (J)	TEAM-ASE	Suzuki 2005 Swift (RS)	A6
113.	K. ONODERA (J)	M. KURODA (J)	TEAM DCCS	Honda Civic 3 Door SiR	A6
114.	C. OHMOMO (J)	A. TSUYUKI (J)	CHIAKI OHMOMO	Daihatsu Boon	A5
115.	T. HIRATSUKA (J)	H. SUZUKI (J)	TEAM DCCS	Honda Civic 3 Door SiR	N2
116.	T. AMANO (J)	Y. INOUE (J)	ECOLOGY I . A TECHNICA	Daihatsu Boon	A5
117.	Y. HARA (J)	S. HARA (J)	YASUSHI HARA	Toyota Yaris 3 Door	A5
118.	M. NAKANISHI (J)	N. KAYAHARA (J)	MASATO NAKANISHI	Daihatsu Boon	N1
119.	B. SEARCY (AUS)	C. MURPHY (AUS)	BEN SEARCY	Honda Integra Type-R	N3
120.	R. HIRAYAMA (J)	N. YAMAGISHI (J)	RISA HIRAYAMA	Toyota Yaris 3 Door	A5
121.	K. ISHIGAKI (J)	A. URUSHIDO (J)	KENJI ISHIGAKI	Honda Civic 3 Door SiR	A6
122.	M. ITO (J)	J. CHIGAMI (J)	MASUHIRO ITO	Honda Civic 3 Door SiR	N2
123.	M. OGURA (J)	M. HIRAYAMA (J)	MASATOSHI OGURA	Daihatsu Boon	N1
124.	T. NAKANO (J)	S. HAYASHI (J)	TAKAKO NAKANO	Daihatsu Boon	N1
125.	K. OHKURA (J)	Y. OTAKI (J)	TEAM FOX	Subaru Vivio Sedan 4WD	N1
126.	Y. FUKUZAWA (J)	T. AKABA (J)	YOKO FUKUZAWA	Suzuki Ignis Sport	N2
				Mitsubishi Lancer Evo VIII	N4

Championship Classifications

FIA Drivers (11/16)
1. Loeb 7♛ 102
2. Grönholm 4♛ 69
3. Sordo 41
4. Hirvonen 33
5. Stohl 28
6. P. Solberg 22
7. Gardemeister 16
8. H. Solberg 16
9. Galli 15
10. Atkinson 14
11. Pons 11
12. Bengué 9
13. Kopecky 7
14. Carlsson 6
15. Välimäki 6
16. Sarrazin 6
17. Rådström 4
18. Duval 4
19. Arai 3
20. MacHale 3
21. Katajamäki 3
22. Sohlberg 3
23. Aigner 3
24. Tuohino 3
25. Wilson 1
26. Nutahara 1
27. Perez Companc, Pozzo... 0

FIA Constructors (11/16)
1. Kronos Total Citroën WRT 7♛ 132
2. BP-Ford World Rally Team 4♛ 121
3. Subaru World Rally Team 74
4. OMV-Peugeot Norway 50
5. Stobart VK M-Sport Ford WRT 29
6. Red Bull-Skoda Team 22

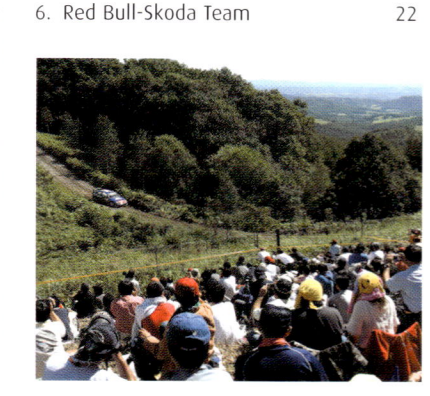

FIA Production Car WRC (5/8)
1. Al-Attiyah 2♛ 34
2. Nutahara 2♛ 20
3. Teiskonen 11
4. Baldacci 19
5. Arai 1♛ 15
6. Kuzaj 17
7. Pozzo 16
8. Ligato 14
9. Marrini 11
10. Latvala 7
11. Heath 5
12. Uspenskiy 4
13. Beltrán 4
14. Vojtech 2
15. Kamada 1
16. Name 1
Higgins Excluded 8

FIA Junior WRC (7/9)
1. Andersson 1♛ 29
2. Sandell 1♛ 28
3. Wilks 2♛ 21
4. Aava 20
5. Rautenbach 17
6. Pressac 17
7. Meeke 1♛ 16
8. Casier 16
9. Béres 16
10. Prokop 1♛ 15
11. Tirabassi 1♛ 11
12. Valousek 11
13. Burkart 9
14. Molder 8
15. Kara 7
16. Rantanen 6
17. Kosciuszko 5
18. Pinomäki 4
19. Betti 4
20. Zachrisson 2
21. Bonato 1
22. Clark, Bordignon 0
Cortinovis, Karlsson 0

Special Stages Times

www.rallyjapan.jp
www.wrc.com

SS1 Pawse Kamuy 1 (9.05 km)
1.Grönholm 4'38"2; 2.Hirvonen +0"2;
3.P.Solberg +1"0; 4.Loeb +4"1;
5.Stohl +5"6; 6.Atkinson +6"4;
7.Araï +8"9; 8.Wilson +12"2...
P-WRC > 11.Nutahara 5'01"8

SS2 Rikubetsu 1 (2.73 km)
1.Grönholm 2'12"1; 2.Hirvonen +2"3;
3.P.Solberg +2"4; 4.Araï +3"0;
5.Loeb +3"6; 6.Stohl +5"2;
7.Sordo +6"1; 8.Atkinson +6"3...
P-WRC > 10.Nutahara 2'21"0

SS3 Kanna 1 (13.86 km)
1.Loeb 8'06"3; 2.Grönholm +3"8;
3.Hirvonen +9"4; 4.Atkinson +11"0;
5.Sordo +22"2; 6.Stohl +23"8;
7.Araï +25"0; 8.P.Solberg +26"1...
P-WRC > 12.Nutahara 9'00"0

SS4 Puray 1 (34.96 km)
1.Grönholm 19'45"3; 2.Loeb +5"4;
3.Hirvonen +29"7; 4.Atkinson +30"2;
5.Stohl +38"1; 6.Araï +45"3;
7.Sordo +1'01"8; 8.Wilson +1'13"6...
P-WRC > 12.Latvala 21'53"4

SS5 Pawse Kamuy 2 (9.05 km)
1.Grönholm 4'32"9; 2.Hirvonen +1"3;
3.Atkinson/Loeb +4"3;
5.P.Solberg +4"9; 6.Stohl +7"6;
7.Araï +10"1; 8.Perez Companc +12"7...
P-WRC > 12.Baldacci 5'05"2

SS6 Rikubetsu 2 (2.73 km)
1.Grönholm 2'07"9; 2.Loeb +0"1;
3.Hirvonen +0"4; 4.P.Solberg +1"1;
5.Stohl +1"3; 6.Sordo +1"6;
7.Perez Companc +2"7; 8.Araï +3"3...
P-WRC > 13.Nutahara 2'16"8

SS7 Kanna 2 (13.86 km)
1.Loeb 7'52"2; 2.Grönholm +6"3;
3.Hirvonen +11"3; 4.Atkinson +16"6;
5.Stohl +20"5; 6.Sordo +20"6;
7.P.Solberg +22"1; 8.Wilson +28"0...
P-WRC > 12.Baldacci 8'51"7

SS8 Puray 2 (34.96 km)
1.Grönholm 19'06"7; 2.Loeb +4"1;
3.Hirvonen +15"4; 4.Stohl +43"7;
5.Sordo +44"0; 6.P.Solberg +48"2;
7.Atkinson +53"0; 8.Wilson +1'09"1...
P-WRC > 12.Pozzo 21'31"3

SS9 Obihiro 1 (1.30 km)
1.Loeb 1'14"2; 2.Grönholm +0"5;
3.Sordo +2"0; 4.Hirvonen +2"1;
5.P.Solberg +3"1; 6.Wilson +3"2;
7.Atkinson +3"3;
8.Perez Companc +3"4...
P-WRC > 12.Baldacci 1'18"9

SS10 Obihiro 2 (1.30 Km)
1.Loeb 1'15"0; 2.Grönholm +0"5;
3.Sordo +1"0; 4.Hirvonen +1"1;
5.P.Solberg +1"6; 6.Atkinson +1"9;
7.Stohl +2"2; 8.Wilson +2"8...
P-WRC > 9.Baldacci 1'18"3

Classification Leg 1
1.Grönholm 1h11'01"9; 2.Loeb +10"5;
3.Hirvonen +1'02"1; 4.Stohl +2'20"7;
5.Sordo +2'54"5; 6.Atkinson +2'56"1;
7.Araï +3'20"5; 8.P.Solberg +3'35"0...
P-WRC > 12.Latvala 1h19'12"6

SS11 Emina (8.18 km)
1.Grönholm 5'42"1; 2.Loeb +2"0;
3.Hirvonen +5"7; 4.Atkinson +11"3;
5.Stohl +14"1; 6.P.Solberg +15"5;
7.Sordo +21"0; 8.MacHale/Araï +26"2...
P-WRC > 11.Ligato 6'16"8

SS12 Rikubetsu 3 (2.73 km)
1.Grönholm 2'07"4; 2.Hirvonen +0"3;
3.Loeb +0"6; 4.P.Solberg +1"4;
5.Sordo +2"6; 6.Stohl +2"9;
7.Araï/Atkinson +3"3...
P-WRC > 11.Nutahara 2'15"9

SS13 Niueo 1 (20.75 km)
1.Loeb 12'10"6; 2.Grönholm +6"8;
3.Hirvonen +13"9; 4.Atkinson +16"7;
5.Sordo +25"0; 6.MacHale +29"1;
7.P.Solberg +30"6; 8.Araï +34"2...
P-WRC > 11.Ligato 13'23"2

SS14 Sipirkakim 1 (22.43 km)
1.Loeb 12'17"0; 2.Hirvonen +1"3;
3.Atkinson +15"4; 4.Stohl +22"1;
5.Grönholm +23"7; 6.P.Solberg +35"8;
7.Perez Companc +49"3; 8.Araï +38"5...
P-WRC > 11.Ligato 13'21"2

SS15 Menan (16.25 Km)
1.Loeb 10'17"3; 2.Hirvonen +5"4;
3.Atkinson +10"4; 4.Grönholm +10"5;
5.Sordo +16"8; 6.Stohl +17"3;
7.Araï +25"1; 8.Perez Companc +26"6...
P-WRC > 11.Ligato 10'55"1

SS16 Rikubetsu 4 (2.73 km)
1.Grönholm 2'04"2; 2.Hirvonen +1"6;
3.P.Solberg +1"7; 4.Loeb +1"9;
5.Sordo +3"3; 6.Stohl +3"6;
7.Perez Companc +4"5;
8.Atkinson +4"8...
P-WRC > 10.Latvala 2'16"1

SS17 Niueo 2 (20.75 km)
1.Loeb 11'35"9; 2.Grönholm +5"1;
3.P.Solberg +13"8; 4.Hirvonen +16"5;
5.Atkinson +18"0; 6.Sordo +20"6;
7.Sordo +23"4; 8.Perez Companc +25"8...
P-WRC > 11.Latvala 12'54"0

SS18 Sipirkakim 2 (22.43 km)
1.Grönholm 12'09"0; 2.P.Solberg +1"7;
3.Loeb +3"0; 4.Hirvonen +10"6;
5.Atkinson +11"7; 6.Stohl +25"1;
7.Perez Companc +28"7; 8.Araï +30"1...
P-WRC > 11.Nutahara 13'33"6

SS19 Menan Short (9.17 Km)
1.Grönholm 5'33"5; 2.P.Solberg +0"3;
3.Loeb +3"1; 4.Hirvonen +5"6;
5.Atkinson +7"4; 6.Sordo +8"2;
7.Araï +9"8; 8.Stohl +11"7...
P-WRC > 11.Pozzo 6'02"7

SS20 Obihiro 3 (1.30 Km)
1.Loeb 1'13"1; 2.Grönholm +0"3;
3.Hirvonen +0"7; 4.Sordo +1"0;
5.P.Solberg +1"1;
6.Perez Companc +1"3;
7.Stohl +1"4; 8.MacHale +2"4...
P-WRC > 10.Nutahara 1'16"5

SS21 Obihiro 4 (1.30 Km)
1.Loeb 1'12"6; 2.Grönholm +0"3;
3.Hirvonen +0"5; 4.Perez Companc +0"9;
5.Sordo +1"1; 6.P.Solberg/Stohl +1"5;
8.MacHale +2"3...
P-WRC > 11.Latvala 1'15"6

Classification Leg 2
1.Loeb 2h27'45"7; 2.Grönholm +25"6;
3.Hirvonen +1'43"1;
4.Atkinson +4'24"1; 5.Stohl +4'40"4;
6.Sordo +5'25"6; 7.P.Solberg +5'31"7;
8.Araï +6'39"7...
P-WRC > 11.Latvala 2h43'46"1

SS22 Rera Kamuy (8.76 Km)
1.Grönholm 5'07"2; 2.Loeb +4"5;
3.Hirvonen +9"3; 4.P.Solberg +11"6;
5.Stohl +11"9; 6.Atkinson +12"0;
7.Araï +12"9; 8.Sordo +19"2...
P-WRC > 10.Ligato 5'36"8

SS23 Panke Nikorpet 1 (17.04 Km)
1.Loeb 9'36"8; 2.Grönholm +0"1;
3.Hirvonen +6"8; 4.Atkinson +16"2;
5.Sordo +21"6; 6.Araï +26"7;
7.Stohl +27"3; 8.Wilson +40"4...
P-WRC > 10.Ligato 10'26"9

SS24 Penke 1 (24.88 Km)
1.Grönholm 14'44"3; 2.Loeb +5"5;
3.Hirvonen +23"3; 4.Atkinson +29"5;
5.Araï +42"1; 6.Wilson +46"4;
7.Sordo +46"9; 8.Stohl +51"9...
P-WRC > 11.Pozzo 16'13"1

SS25 Panke Nikorpet 2 (17.04 Km)
1.Grönholm 9'13"4; 2.Loeb +6"9;
3.Hirvonen +14"6; 4.Atkinson +26"2;
5.P.Solberg +26"9; 6.Stohl +32"4;
7.Araï +35"7; 8.Sordo +36"5...
P-WRC > 11.Ligato 10'16"6

SS26 Penke 2 (24.88 Km)
1.Grönholm 14'21"5; 2.Loeb +3"4;
3.Hirvonen +29"9; 4.Atkinson +38"9;
5.Wilson +43"3; 6.Stohl +45"3;
7.Araï +45"7; 8.P.Solberg +53"6...
P-WRC > 9.Ligato 15'48"8

SS27 Obihiro 5 (1.30 km)
1.Hirvonen 1'11"0; 2.Loeb +0"2;
3.Grönholm +0"4; 4.Sordo +0"6;
5.Atkinson +1"4; 6.P.Solberg +1"5;
7.Stohl/Wilson +2"0...
P-WRC > 9.Baldacci 1'13"2

Results

	Driver - Co-driver	Car	Gr.	Time
1	Loeb - Elena	Citroën Xsara WRC	A8	3h22'20"4
2	Grönholm - Rautiainen	Ford Focus RS WRC 06	A8	+ 5"6
3	Hirvonen - Lehtinen	Ford Focus RS WRC 06	A8	+ 2'46"5
4	Atkinson - Macneall	Subaru Impreza WRC 2006	A8	+ 6'07"8
5	Stohl - Minor	Peugeot 307 WRC	A8	+ 7'10"7
6	Araï - Sircombe	Subaru Impreza WRC 2006	A8	+ 9'05"1
7	P. Solberg - Mills	Subaru Impreza WRC 2006	A8	+ 11'43"7
8	**Nutahara - Barritt**	**Mitsubishi Lancer Evo IX**	**N4/P**	**+ 22'57"4**
9	Pozzo - Stillo	Mitsubishi Lancer Evo IX	N4/P	+ 23'24"8
10	Ligato - Garcia	Mitsubishi Lancer Evo IX	N4/P	+ 23'58"6

Leading Retirements (9)

TC27C	Sordo - Marti	Citroën Xsara WRC	Excluded
TC27C	MacHale - Nagle	Ford Focus RS WRC 04	Off
TC10C	Baldacci - D'Esposito	Subaru Impreza WRX Sti	Off

Fumio Nutahara

Performers

	1	2	3	4	5	6	C6	NbSS
Grönholm	15	9	1	1	1	-	27	27
Loeb	11	9	4	2	1	-	22	27
Hirvonen	1	7	14	4	-	-	26	27
P. Solberg	-	2	4	3	5	5	19	27
Atkinson	-	-	2	9	4	3	18	27
Sordo	-	-	2	2	9	3	16	27
Stohl	-	-	-	2	6	10	18	27
Araï	-	-	-	1	1	2	4	27
Perez Companc	-	-	-	1	-	1	2	25
Wilson	-	-	-	-	1	2	3	19
MacHale	-	-	-	-	-	1	1	24

Leaders

SS1 > SS13   Grönholm
SS14 > SS27   Loeb

Previous winners

2004   Solberg - Mills
       Subaru Impreza WRC 2004
2005   Grönholm - Rautiainen
       Peugeot 307 WRC

Cyprus

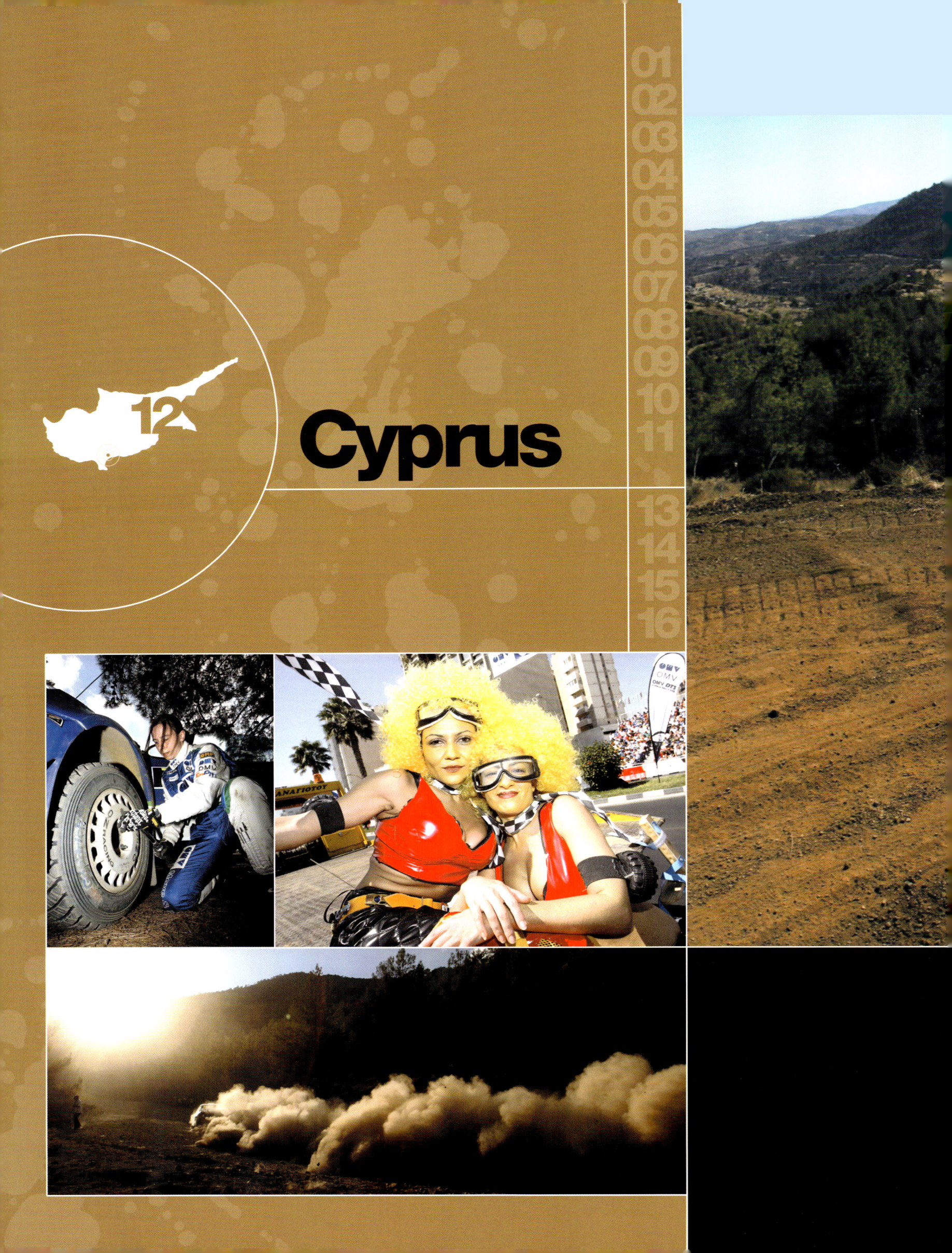

12

Loeb rubs it in
The world champion and his co-driver raised the world record to 28 victories after another battle with Marcus Grönholm. The Finn lost the event more because of a poor tyre choice than technical problems or bad driving. This success put Sébastien in an excellent position to win his third title on the trot.

12 Cyprus

THE RALLY
A two-horse race

The World Rally Championship and the 2006 season would be much less interesting were it not for the presence of Loeb and Grönholm. Backed up by their co-drivers Monegasque Daniel Elena and Timo Rautiainen from Finland, their exciting duel kept the spectators' enthusiasm at fever pitch in what was an exceptional year. The performance of the other WRC crews in the Cyprus Rally was sleep inducing to say the least!

This was possibly the last time that the WRCs would parade through the streets of Limasol in the context of a world championship rally, as the event is not on the 2007 calendar.

A very concentrated Marcus Grönholm is about to enter the fray.

The two Skodas started the first special but did not see the end as they both went out in the opening kilometres. The pundits saw this as a sign of a big hole in the semi-works team's budget whose main sponsor is Red Bull. Team manager Armin Schwartz immediately shot back saying that this was not true, and the cause of the double retirement of the Fabia WRCs was electrical problems. This was little consolation for Aigner and Rovanperä. The event was yet another disaster for Subaru. The team management was more forthcoming than usual and gave detailed technical explanations for the difficulties met by the Imprezas. They suffered from erratic behaviour under braking and lacked grip in the corners. This got Petter Solberg all worked up and his famous "Hollywood" grin was noticeably absent. "That's enough," he raged. "Absolutely nothing has been done on the car since the Japanese Rally." At the start of the event he managed to set competitive times including fastest in Kato Amiantos-Platres (SS4). But what happened afterwards was not in keeping with either his aspirations or those of such a prestigious and experienced team. He lost all chances of a good result in the late afternoon as he was forced to cope with a gearbox blocked in second. He managed to grab the point for eighth place thanks to his determination as his technical problems continued; it was small beer for a driver of his skills. Chris Atkinson in the second works Impreza did not make it into the points and finished in ninth place after being delayed more by an accident at the end of the second leg than by the behaviour of his racing car - if such it can still be called!

It is no insult to the two drivers entered by Bozian in their 307 WRCs to say that they are not in the same league as Loeb and Grönholm. Manfred Stohl and Henning Solberg drive some good rallies and add excitement to the mid-field battles but are rarely in a position to aim at rostrum finishes. It was the case in Cyprus. The Austrian at the wheel of a reliable car came home in fourth place while Solberg saw the flag in sixth. It was a rather flattering position for the Norwegian who finished the event in the super rally having gone off on Saturday after being blinded by the sun. Nonetheless their gaps to the winner were a kind of black hole: 6m 39.7s for Stohl and 14m 40s for Solberg. In the not very distant past the fact of coming home over ten minutes behind the victor would have meant that the driver in question might just have scraped into the first fifteen. And their team-mates?

Twenty-six-year-old Mikko Hirvonen had a great 2006 season at Ford. His year got off to a rather erratic start but from then on he displayed excellent consistency. He provided top-class back-up to Grönholm and was quick enough to score some rostrum finishes as in Cyprus. However, when he tried to match the pace of either the Finn or the Frenchman he made a

Mikko Hirvonen added another third place to his tally behind the two stars after the two in Japan and Finland.

No Petter Solberg is not passing in front of the new Subaru headquarters, but the ruined house was perhaps an apt metaphor for the state of his team!

< Manfred Stohl drove another intelligent rally and finished fourth.

Toni Gardemeister found the going on the car-breaking Cypriot terrain very tough. He was less competitive than in previous events due to a puncture on the first leg.

few mistakes. He spun at the start of the Cyprus rally and drove more cautiously after that. 2006 was a learning year for him and the 6 points he scored in Cyprus put him in the running to finish third overall in the drivers' Championship. The way he drove was exactly what his employers expected of him; he gained Ford's trust and the possibility of hanging on to one of the most sought-after works seats of the field.

At Citroën, the 2 Spaniards Dani Sordo and Xavier Pons were given alternate possibilities to score points with Sordo succeeding Pons in the last few rallies. In Cyprus, they did not quite meet the expectations of Marc Van Dalen's team. Pons was back after his accident in Finland, spun in SS3 and then went off in SS8, which gave him a bad start to the rally. He went better in the second loop and got as high as sixth before broken transmission caused his retirement the next day. Thanks to the super rally he was finally classified in seventh spot. But it was not enough to overshadow Loeb! It was the same thing for Sordo. The 2005 Junior Champion was racing in Cyprus for the first time. He started off cautiously and then came to a halt in SS7 as he felt his engine suddenly losing power and preferred to stop rather than damage it. Once it was repaired he set off in the super rally and climbed back up to tenth place before losing the point he could have brought home for Citroën. In the super special laid out in town he missed his braking and made mincemeat of his Xsara against a wall on a roundabout! It was a very stupid mistake as it happened in a timed section whose aim was to entertain the public, but whose result had no bearing on the overall classification. All he had to do was to reach the finish. It was a debutante's fault, but this did not prevent Marc Van Dalen from going ballistic! "Dani," he said through clenched teeth, "made a bloody stupid mistake, all the more so as we know how vital each point is in the manufacturers' Championship."

It was further proof that neither teammates nor rivals were capable of matching the two stars of the 2006 Championship.
In Cyprus there was no let-up in the battle that raged between them. Like in the 2 previous rallies Grönholm, as is his wont, set off in a burst of sound and fury going pedal to metal right from the start to open up a critical advantage over Loeb. The latter as always set off more carefully and in addition had the task of sweeping the roads. So at the end of the first loop of 4 specials the mighty Finn had a lead of 17.9s over the Frenchman's Xsara. Then as usual in the afternoon Sébastien closed the gap over the same 4 stages and in the evening it was down to 6.4s: advantage Grönholm. "It's business as usual," commented Loeb. "We clean the way, pay for it and then we try to pull back the time lost. Sometimes that works like today and it looks like we're going to have a good scrap for the rest of the rally."

12 Cyprus

The Cypriot mule tracks were narrow but this made no difference to Marcus who pushed as hard as ever.

Loeb gives his Xsara a little wash in one of the fords before the inevitable champagne ejaculation on the rostrum.

The Finn said much the same: "This morning there was a thick layer of little stones so starting second was a bit of an advantage, but the difference was not too big." In fact, after the leg the Finn reckoned that his tyres had been responsible for his average performance. In the morning he had fitted the same rubber as Loeb, the BF Goodrich G-Force Gravels, in the afternoon the Citroën driver preferred the wider H1 type compounds while the Ford was on H2s with a narrower tread. These were the tyres Grönholm used in Greece where he won the rally, but they were not right for the Cypriot roads. "I didn't have the same grip," he explained, "and so my confidence wasn't 100%. I was not able to keep up the same pace. The roads had not been as well swept first time through as I'd expected."

It was the same story the next day. Both men went for it from the start and Grönholm managed to fight off his deadly foe. So intense was their battle that they finished the long special between Foini and Koilina (SS11, 30,3 kms) separated by only 1/10s! Out of the 4 stages in the morning two went to Grönholm and two to Loeb and the gap between them was 8.5s.

Second time through in the afternoon the balance of power swung Loeb's way as he was fastest in all four. He took the lead after SS14 (Akrounta-Apsiou 2) and opened up a 21.8s gap over the Finn.

The BF Goodrich H1s that were wider and provided a bigger contact patch were better suited to the conditions. "Yesterday, we realised that we could play a cat and mouse game with Marcus," explained the Frenchman. "The morning confirmed it and I'm particularly happy with the afternoon result." That gave Grönholm a lot of head-scratching to do. Would he be able to repeat his Japanese performance and put pressure on the Frenchman up to the finish? "Difficult," the Ford leader growled. "But I'll do my best and I hope he's not going to sleep too well tonight!"

In fact, Marcus was never in a position to threaten Loeb in the 5 stages of the final leg (the super special in the town did not count in the results) and nothing changed. Sébastien scored his twenty-eighth victory (new record) with 21.2s in hand over Grönholm while into third came Hirvonen some 5 minutes (exactly 5m 16.41s) behind.

Paradoxically both Loeb and Ford left Cyprus in a happy state of mind; the former because he could be crowned in the next event (he was 35 points in front of Grönholm with 4 rallies still to run), and the latter was back to within 7 points of Kronos-Citroën thanks to the 14 scored by its two drivers in the Cypriot rally. ∎

Once again Chris Atkinson had to cope with indifferent road holding on his 2006 Impreza.

Henning was the better of the Solberg brothers in Cyprus. The elder was at the wheel of a Bozian-entered 307 WRC that may have excited the envy of his younger sibling!

Loeb and Grönholm not only fought each other on the roads; they also carried on the combat wheel changing, checking the stae of the car etc.

PRODUCTION
Al-Attiyah trips up

Nasser Al-Attiyah will curse the Cyprus Rally for a long time especially if he fails to win the title. He arrived on the island in the Championship lead, and immediately went into first place in the sixth round on the calendar. He opened up a comfortable cushion over his rivals once he had got past Fumio Nutahara in the fifth special. At the end of the first leg he was 27.5s ahead of his adversaries. But he went off in the longest stage of the rally, Foini-Koilina, and stuck his Subaru into a deep ditch. The Japanese in his Mitsubishi took advantage of this unexpected gift and sailed on to his third win in four starts (in Mexico he did not score any points after being excluded by the Stewards – see report) this season. Al-Attiyah salvaged what he could thanks to the super rally, finished fifth and scored four points. The man from Qatar was not going to race in Australia while Nutahara still had the last two event to do so Al –Attiyah had to win in New Zealand, the final round of the Production Championship, if he wanted to beat his Japanese rival. Toshihiro Araï (Subaru) lost any chance he might have had of claiming the title. He was the reigning champion and went off only 1.4 kms after the start of the first special! At the end of the rally he had set twelve fastest times (super rally) and he finished sixth overall. ■

Dani Sordo's big boo-boo: he missed his braking in the special in the town, hit a little wall and retired. Stupid really, as the times were not counted in the overall classification.

Cyprus results

34th CYPRUS RALLY

Organiser Details
The Cyprus Automobile Association (CAA),
12 Chr Mylona str,
CY-2014 Nicosia
Cyprus
Tel.: +3572 2590555
Fax: +3572 2358443

Cyprus Rally

12th leg of FIA 2006 World Rally Championship for constructors and drivers.
6th leg of FIA Production Car WRC Championship.

Date September 22 - 24, 2006

Route
1172.74 km divised in 3 legs.
23 special stages on dirt roads and 1 special stage on tarmac foreseen (331.34 km),
21 special stages raced (319.11 km)

Starting Procedure
Thursday, September 21 (20:30)
Limassol
Leg 1
Friday, September 22 (09:43/17:25),
Limassol > Limassol, 375.80 km;
8 special stages (111.48 km)
Leg 2
Saturday, September 23 (08:38/17:19),
Limassol > Limassol, 444.24 km;
8 special stages (122.28 km)
Leg 3
Sunday, September 24 (08:54/14:56),
Limassol > Limassol, 323.56 (352.70 km);
7 special stages foreseen (97.58 km),
5 special stages raced (85.35 km)

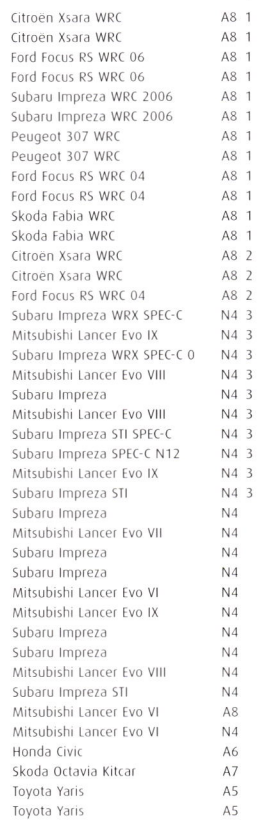

Entry List (41) - 40 starters

N°	Driver (Nat.)	Co-driver (Nat.)	Team	Car	Group & FIA Priority
1.	S. LOEB (F)	D. ELENA (MC)	KRONOS TOTAL CITROEN WRT	Citroën Xsara WRC	A8 1
2.	D. SORDO (E)	M. MARTI (E)	KRONOS TOTAL CITROEN WRT	Citroën Xsara WRC	A8 1
3.	M. GRÖNHOLM (FIN)	T. RAUTIAINEN (FIN)	BP FORD WORLD RALLY TEAM	Ford Focus RS WRC 06	A8 1
4.	M. HIRVONEN (FIN)	J. LEHTINEN (FIN)	BP FORD WORLD RALLY TEAM	Ford Focus RS WRC 06	A8 1
5.	P. SOLBERG (N)	P. MILLS (GB)	SUBARU WORLD RALLY TEAM	Subaru Impreza WRC 2006	A8 1
6.	C. ATKINSON (AUS)	G. MACNEALL (AUS)	SUBARU WORLD RALLY TEAM	Subaru Impreza WRC 2006	A8 1
7.	M. STOHL (A)	I. MINOR (A)	OMV - PEUGEOT NORWAY	Peugeot 307 WRC	A8 1
8.	H. SOLBERG (N)	C. MENKERUD (N)	OMV - PEUGEOT NORWAY	Peugeot 307 WRC	A8 1
9.	M. WILSON (GB)	M. ORR (GB)	STOBART - VK - M-SPORT FORD RALLY TEAM	Ford Focus RS WRC 04	A8 1
10.	L. PEREZ COMPANC (RA)	J. MARIA VOLTA (RA)	STOBART - VK - M-SPORT FORD RALLY TEAM	Ford Focus RS WRC 04	A8 1
11.	H. ROVANPERÄ (FIN)	R. PIETILAINEN (FIN)	RED BULL - SKODA TEAM	Skoda Fabia WRC	A8 1
12.	A. AIGNER (A)	K. WICHA (D)	RED BULL - SKODA TEAM	Skoda Fabia WRC	A8 1
14.	T. GARDEMEISTER (FIN)	J. HONKANEN (FIN)	ASTRA RACING	Citroën Xsara WRC	A8 2
15.	X. PONS (E)	C. DEL BARRIO (E)	PONS XAVIER	Citroën Xsara WRC	A8 2
17.	J. PABLO RAIES (RA)	J. PEREZ COMPANC (RA)	STOBART - VK - M-SPORT FORD RALLY TEAM	Ford Focus RS WRC 04	A8 2
31.	T. ARAI (J)	T. SIRCOMBE (NZ)	SUBARU TEAM ARAI	Subaru Impreza WRX SPEC-C	N4 3
33.	F. NUTAHARA (J)	D. BARRITT (GB)	ADVAN-PIAA RALLY TEAM	Mitsubishi Lancer Evo IX	N4 3
39.	N. AL-ATTIYAH (QAT)	C. PATTERSON (GB)	QMMF	Subaru Impreza WRX SPEC-C 0	N4 3
40.	S. CAMPEDELLI (I)	D. FAPPANI (I)	ERRANI TEAM GROUP	Mitsubishi Lancer Evo VIII	N4 3
41.	K. AL QASSIMI (UAE)	N. BEECH (GB)	SUBARU TEAM QUASYS	Subaru Impreza	N4 3
43.	A. NICOLAI BURKART (D)	T. GEILHAUSEN (D)	OMV CEE RALLY TEAM	Mitsubishi Lancer Evo VIII	N4 3
45.	A. TEISKONEN (FIN)	M. TEISKONEN (FIN)	SYMS RALLY TEAM	Subaru Impreza STI SPEC-C	N4 3
46.	N. HEATH (GB)	S. LANCASTER (GB)	NIGEL HEATH	Subaru Impreza SPEC-C N12	N4 3
59.	A. TSOULOFTAS (CY)	S. LAOS (CY)	ANDREAS TSOULOFTAS	Mitsubishi Lancer Evo IX	N4 3
60.	S. PAVLIDES (CY)	T. VASSILIADES (CY)	SPYROS PAVLIDES	Subaru Impreza STI	N4 3
62.	K. KOUTSAKOS (CY)	P. LAOS (CY)	KIKIS KOUTSAKOS	Subaru Impreza	N4
63.	C. TIMOTHEOU (CY)	P. SIALOS (CY)	CHARALAMBOS TIMOTHEOU	Mitsubishi Lancer Evo VII	N4
64.	G. ZAKOS (CY)	K. EVANGELOU (CY)	GEORGIOS ZAKOS	Subaru Impreza	N4
65.	A. PHILIPPOU (CY)	C. KOURTELLAS (CY)	ANDREAS PHILIPPOU	Subaru Impreza	N4
66.	Y. HARTOUPALOS (CY)	M. VASSILIADES (CY)	YIOTIS HARTOUPALOS	Mitsubishi Lancer Evo VI	N4
67.	L. LIMNIOTIS (CY)	G. PIKIS (CY)	LAMBROS LIMNIOTIS	Mitsubishi Lancer Evo IX	N4
69.	S. SAVVA (CY)	C. CONSTANTINOU (CY)	SAVVAS SAVVA	Subaru Impreza	N4
70.	C. KOMODROMOS (CY)	Y. EVRIPIDOU (CY)	CHARIS KOMODROMOS	Subaru Impreza	N4
71.	K. DOBSON (GB)	B. SPADEMAN (GB)	KEN DOBSON	Mitsubishi Lancer Evo VIII	N4
74.	P. PAMBOUKKA (CY)	L. CHRISTOFI (CY)	PANTELIS PAMBOUKKA	Subaru Impreza STI	N4
75.	M. KOULOUMAS (CY)	C. GEORGIOU (CY)	MANOLIS KOULOUMAS	Mitsubishi Lancer Evo VI	A8
77.	S. KLEOVOULOU (CY)	M. MICHAEL (CY)	STAVROS KLEOVOULOU	Mitsubishi Lancer Evo VI	N4
80.	S. ACHILLEOS (CY)	F. CHRISTOFI (CY)	STAVROS ACHILLEOS	Honda Civic	A6
81.	E. WEISS (D)	Z. SZECHENYI (HU)	EDITH WEISS	Skoda Octavia Kitcar	A7
82.	A. MAKARONIS (GR)	S. KAVVADIAS (GR)	AKIS MAKARONIS	Toyota Yaris	A5
83.	P. PANTELI (CY)	Y. ARISTODEMOU (HU)	PETROS PANTELI	Toyota Yaris	A5

Championship Classifications

FIA Drivers (12/16)
1. Loeb 8🏆 112
2. Grönholm 4🏆 77
3. Sordo 41
4. Hirvonen 39
5. Stohl 33
6. P. Solberg 23
7. Gardemeister 20
8. H. Solberg 19
9. Galli 15
10. Atkinson 14
11. Pons 13
12. Bengué 9
13. Kopecky 7
14. Carlsson 6
15. Välimäki 6
16. Sarrazin 6
17. Rådström 4
18. Duval 4
19. Arai 3
20. MacHale 3
21. Katajamäki 3
22. Sohlberg 3
23. Aigner 3
24. Tuohino 3
25. Wilson 1
26. Nutahara 1
27. Perez Companc, Pozzo... 0

FIA Constructors (12/16)
1. Kronos Total Citroën WRT 8🏆 142
2. BP-Ford World Rally Team 4🏆 135
3. Subaru World Rally Team 79
4. OMV-Peugeot Norway 59
5. Stobart VK M-Sport Ford WRT 30
6. Red Bull-Skoda Team 22

FIA Production Car (6/8)
1. Al-Attiyah 2🏆 38
2. Nutahara 3🏆 30
3. Teiskonen 19
4. Baldacci 19
5. Arai 1🏆 18
6. Kuzaj 17
7. Pozzo 16
8. Ligato 14
9. Marrini 11
10. Latvala 7
11. Al Qassimi 6
12. Heath 5
13. Campedelli 5
14. Uspenskiy 4
15. Beltrán 4
16. Vojtech 2
17. Kamada 1
18. Name 1
19. Jereb, Nassoulas, 0
    Popov, Baldacci, 0
    Burkart, Tsouloftas, 0
    Pavlides 0
    Higgins Excluded 8

FIA Junior WRC (7/9)
1. Andersson 1🏆 29
2. Sandell 1🏆 28
3. Wilks 2🏆 21
4. Aava 20
5. Rautenbach 17
6. Pressac 17
7. Meeke 1🏆 16
8. Casier 16
9. Béres 16
10. Prokop 1🏆 15
11. Tirabassi 1🏆 11
12. Valousek 11
13. Burkart 9
14. Molder 8
15. Kara 7
16. Rantanen 6
17. Kosciuszko 5
18. Pinomäki 4
19. Betti 4
20. Zachrisson 2
21. Bonato 1
22. Clark, Bordignon 0
    Cortinovis, Karlsson 0

Special Stages Times

www.cyprusrally.org.cy
www.wrc.com

SS1 Xyliatos-Kapouras 1 (8.09 km)
1.Grönholm 7'43"3; 2.Loeb +2"2;
3.Gardemeister +2"6; 4.Hirvonen +5"1;
5.Pons/Atkinson +5"2; 7.Sordo +7"0;
8.P.Solberg +7"2...
P-WRC > 15.Nutahara 8'15"0

SS2 Kapouras-Asinou 1 (10.17 km)
1.Grönholm 9'14"1; 2.Loeb +4"0;
3.P.Solberg +5"1;
4.Gardemeister +9"5; 5.Stohl +9"6;
6.Pons +10"5; 7.Hirvonen +11"5;
8.Atkinson +13"6...
P-WRC > 13.Al-Attiyah 9'56"8

SS3 Asinou-Nikitari 1 (25.61 km)
1.Grönholm 26'52"4; 2.Loeb +1"9;
3.Hirvonen +23"8; 4.Stohl +25"8;
5.Gardemeister +27"7;
6.Atkinson +32"5; 7.Sordo +38"0;
8.P.Solberg +45"9...
P-WRC > 13.Nutahara 28'53"3

SS4 Kato Amiantos-Platres 1 (11.87 km)
1.P.Solberg 9'33"4; 2.Grönholm +1"5;
3.Hirvonen +5"6; 4.H.Solberg +8"9;
5.Gardemeister +11"2; 6.Loeb +11"3;
7.Pons +14"2; 8.Sordo +14"5...
P-WRC > 13.Al-Attiyah 10'14"9

SS5 Xyliatos-Kapouras 2 (8.09 km)
1.Grönholm 7'26"5; 2.Loeb +0"6;
3.Hirvonen +5"7; 4.Sordo +8"1;
5.Stohl +8"7; 6.P.Solberg +9"4;
7.Pons +9"8; 8.H.Solberg +14"7...
P-WRC > 12.Al-Attiyah 8'07"3

SS6 Kapouras-Asinou 2 (10.17 km)
1.Loeb 8'56"4; 2.Grönholm +1"6;
3.Hirvonen +8"2; 4.P.Solberg +9"0;
5.Pons/Stohl +11"0;
7.Sordo +11"6; 8.H.Solberg +20"3...
P-WRC > 12.Al-Attiyah 9'46"2

SS7 Asinou-Nikitari 2 (25.61 km)
1.Loeb 26'07"1; 2.Grönholm +6"4;
3.Hirvonen +29"2; 4.Stohl +33"8;
5.Gardemeister +37"5; 6.Pons +39"9;
7.H.Solberg +49"9; 8.Wilson +59"4...
P-WRC > 11.Al-Attiyah 28'40"3

SS8 Kato Amiantos-Platres 2 (11.87 km)
1.Loeb 9'26"8; 2.Grönholm +4"1;
3.Hirvonen +9"6;
4.Gardemeister +10"8; 5.Stohl +12"7;
6.Atkinson +19"1;
7.Perez Companc +24"6...
P-WRC > 8.Nutahara 10'12"0

Classification Leg 1
1.Grönholm 1h45'33"6; 2.Loeb +6"4;
3.Hirvonen +1'25"1; 4.Stohl +1'50"7;
5.Atkinson +3'01"0; 6.Pons +4'05"2;
7.Gardemeister +4'05"3;
8.Perez Companc +5'22"9...
P-WRC > 12.Al-Attiyah 1h54'11"6

SS9 Kellaki-Foinikaria 1 (9.49 km)
1.Grönholm 8'01"2; 2.Loeb +2"9;
3.Hirvonen +12"7; 4.Stohl +14"2;
5.P.Solberg +15"8; 6.Atkinson +17"3;
7.Gardemeister +17"5; 8.Sordo +23"7...
P-WRC > 13.Araï 8'40"4

SS10 Akrounta-Apsiou 1 (7.99 Km)
1.Grönholm 7'44"9; 2.Loeb +0"9;
3.Hirvonen +8"3; 4.Stohl +10"5;
5.Atkinson +10"6; 6.P.Solberg +12"0;
7.Gardemeister +13"7; 8.Pons +16"0...
P-WRC > 11.Araï 8'16"4

SS11 Foini-Koilinia 1 (30.33 km)
1.Loeb 26'20"8; 2.Grönholm +0"1;
3.Gardemeister +45"0; 4.Stohl +45"7;
5.Hirvonen +47"5; 6.P.Solberg +51"1;
7.Pons +1'00"4; 8.Atkinson +1'04"6...
P-WRC > 12.Araï 28'37"9

SS12 Galatareia-Pentalia 1 (13.33 km)
1.Loeb 8'17"8; 2.Grönholm +1"6;
3.Hirvonen +10"1; 4.P.Solberg +16"0;
5.Stohl +20"6; 6.Atkinson +22"3;
7.Pons +25"6; 8.Gardemeister +28"4...
P-WRC > 11.Araï 9'10"2

SS13 Kellaki-Foinikaria 2 (9.49 km)
1.Loeb 8'01"7; 2.Grönholm +0"6;
3.P.Solberg +7"5; 4.Hirvonen +9"0;
5.Gardemeister +9"3;
6.Atkinson +10"9; 7.Stohl +12"3;
8.H.Solberg +14"3...
P-WRC > 12.Araï 8'51"8

SS14 Akrounta-Apsiou 2 (7.99 Km)
1.Loeb 7'35"4; 2.Grönholm +8"9;
3.Hirvonen +13"7; 4.P.Solberg +13"9;
5.Stohl +14"5; 6.Gardemeister +16"6;
7.Atkinson +17"5; 8.Pons +18"8...
P-WRC > 12.Araï 8'24"2

SS15 Foini-Koilinia 2 (30.33 km)
1.Loeb 25'56"1; 2.Grönholm +16"7;
3.Gardemeister +47"9; 4.Sordo +49"2;
5.Hirvonen +55"7; 6.P.Solberg +58"5;
7.Stohl +1'01"0; 8.Pons +1'02"3...
P-WRC > 10.Araï 28'41"5

SS16 Galatareia-Pentalia 2 (13.33 km)
1.Loeb 8'09"7; 2.Grönholm +4"1;
3.Hirvonen +14"4; 4.P.Solberg +15"4;
5.Sordo +19"3; 6.Gardemeister +21"4;
7.H.Solberg +23"2; 8.Stohl +23"6...
P-WRC > 10.Araï 9'04"6

Classification Leg 2
1.Loeb 3h25'51"6; 2.Grönholm +21"8;
3.Hirvonen +4'06"1; 4.Stohl +5'02"9;
5.Gardemeister +7'14"8;
6.Pons +8'06"2; 7.P.Solberg +11'35"7;
8.H.Solberg +12'46"2...
P-WRC > 12.Nutahara 3h48'39"5

SS17 Vavatsinia-Mandra Kambiou 1 (25.24 Km)
1.Loeb 22'24"1; 2.Grönholm +7"3;
3.P.Solberg +33"5; 4.Gardemeister +35"2;
5.Hirvonen +42"7; 6.Stohl +47"0;
7.Sordo +54"0; 8.Pons +56"1...
P-WRC > 13.Araï 24'34"1

SS18 Machairas-Agioi Vavatsinias 1 (12.94 Km)
1.Grönholm 10'56"6; 2.Loeb +2"0;
3.Hirvonen +15"6; 4.H.Solberg +20"2;
5.Gardemeister +21"6; 6.Pons +21"8;
7.Stohl +22"2; 8.Sordo +23"8...
P-WRC > 12.Araï 11'49"3

SS19 Lageia-Kalavasos 1 (8.99 Km)
1.Grönholm 7'21"6; 2.Loeb +1"5;
3.Hirvonen +7"4; 4.Stohl +12"0;
5.H.Solberg +13"7; 6.Pons +14"1;
7.Atkinson +15"5; 8.P.Solberg +16"0...
P-WRC > 13.Araï 7'53"3

SS20 Down Town Special (3.40 Km)
Cancelled

SS21 Vavatsinia-Mandra Kambiou 2 (25.24 Km)
1.Pons/Hirvonen/Grönholm/Atkinson/
P.Solberg/Loeb/H.Solberg/Stohl...
23'19"8...
P-WRC > 11.Araï/Teiskonen/Nutahara...
23'43"9...

SS22 Machairas-Agioi Vavatsinias 2 (12.94 Km)
1.Grönholm 10'48"8; 2.Loeb +4"2;
3.Hirvonen +12"2; 4.Gardemeister +16"4;
5.H.Solberg +16"9; 6.Stohl +23"5;
7.Atkinson +29"4; 8.Wilson +32"7...
P-WRC > 10.Araï 11'54"5

SS23 Lageia-Kalavasos 2 (8.99 Km)
Cancelled

Results

	Driver - Co-driver	Car	Gr.	Time
1	Loeb - Elena	Citroën Xsara WRC	A8	4h40'50"4
2	Grönholm - Rautiainen	Ford Focus RS WRC 06	A8	+ 21"2
3	Hirvonen - Lehtinen	Ford Focus RS WRC 06	A8	+ 5'16"1
4	Stohl - Minor	Peugeot 307 WRC	A8	+ 6'39"7
5	Gardemeister - Honkanen	Citroën Xsara WRC	A8	+ 8'40"4
6	H. Solberg - Menkerud	Peugeot 307 WRC	A8	+ 14'40"0
7	Pons - Del Barrio	Citroën Xsara WRC	A8	+ 14'46"7
8	P. Solberg - Mills	Subaru Impreza WRC 2006	A8	+ 15'21"5
9	Atkinson - Macneall	Subaru Impreza WRC 2006	A8	+ 17'15"0
10	Wilson - Orr	Ford Focus RS WRC 04	A8	+ 25'21"0
11	**Nutahara - Barritt**	**Mitsubishi Lancer Evo IX**	**N4/P**	**+ 29'52"9**
12	Teiskonen - Anttila	Subaru Impreza STI SPEC-C	N4/P	+ 34'10"4
13	Al Qassimi - Beech	Subaru Impreza	N4/P	+ 35'52"1

Leading Retirments (13)

TC22D	Sordo - Marti	Citroën Xsara WRC	Off
TC18	Raies - Perez Companc	Ford Focus RS WRC 04	Retirement, co-driver ill
TC15	Burkart - Geilhausen	Mitsubishi Lancer Evo VIII	Off
TC8C	Rovanperä - Pietilainen	Skoda Fabia WRC	Electronics
TC8C	Aigner - Wicha	Skoda Fabia WRC	Electronics

Performers

	1	2	3	4	5	6	C6	Nb SS
Loeb	10	9	-	-	-	1	20	20
Grönholm	9	11	-	-	-	-	20	20
P. Solberg	1	-	3	4	1	4	13	20
Hirvonen	-	-	14	2	3	-	19	20
Gardemeister	-	-	3	4	5	2	14	20
Stohl	-	-	-	6	6	2	14	20
H. Solberg	-	-	-	2	2	-	4	19
Sordo	-	-	-	2	1	-	3	17
Atkinson	-	-	-	-	2	5	7	18
Pons	-	-	-	-	2	4	6	20

Leaders

SS1 > SS13	Grönholm
SS14 > SS22	Loeb

Previous winners

2000	Sainz - Moya Ford Focus WRC	2002	Grönholm - Rautiainen Peugeot 206 WRC	2004	Loeb - Elena Citroën Xsara WRC
2001	C. McRae - Grist Ford Focus RS WRC 01	2003	Solberg - Mills Subaru Impreza WRC 2003	2005	Loeb - Elena Citroën Xsara WRC

Fumio Nutahara

13

Turkey

No Loeb!
Sebastian Lobe was missing after his fall from a bicycle and was replaced in the no.1 Sara by Colin McRae. The 1995 world champion, who was out of practice, joined the Kronos-Citroën team at very short notice. Victory, as expected, went to Marcus Grönholm after what was a pretty dull rally.

13 Turkey

Xevi Pons had one of his best rallies when he was not nominated to score points; He came home fourth as in Sardinia.

Petter Solberg tries to explain the erratic behaviour of his Subaru to ex-Peugeot engineer, François-Xavier Demaison.

Marcus Grönholm must have felt a bit lonely, as his sparring partner was absent.

The track conditions of this rally were dreadful as Mikko Hirvonen found out.

THE RALLY
Easy-peasy for Grönholm

The Turkish rally was hit by a violent storm that began on Wednesday evening when the teams were just finishing their pre-race preparations. A powerful gust of wind struck the service park carrying off the two Kronos tents. It was another blow to the Franco-Belgian team that was still coming to terms with the loss of its star driver, Sébastien Loeb (see below), replaced by Colin McRae. The bad weather continued and on Friday, the first day of the rally, the organisers were obliged to cancel three out of the nine special stages scheduled leaving the drivers with a meagre day's racing. Fog prevented the medical helicopter from over flying stages 1 and 2 (Perge and Myra) so it was out of the question to allow the 67 entries to start. SS4 (Perge 2) was also cancelled as torrential rain had transformed it into a completely impassable torrent of mud even for the 4-wheel drive WRC cars. For similar reasons SS5 (Myra 2) was shortened from 24.1 kms to 13 kms.

None of this made any difference to Marcus Grönholm who dominated the storm-shortened first day. He went into the lead in the first special (SS3, Kumluca 1) and set the first three fastest times with consumate ease after which he let his rivals led by Petter Solberg pick up the crumbs. The Finn had to win the event in order to maintain the very slim chance he had of a third world title in the absence of Sébastien Loeb. This he did without ever being under threat throughout the rally. He won the first leg by 26.1s from Solberg and the second by over 2 minutes from his own team-mate, Mikko Hirvonen. He went on to score his twenty-third World Championship success (one more than the mythic Juha Kankkunen) without problems. The big Finn was obviously happy with his first place, but regretted the way in which he had emerged victorious. Marcus likes nothing better than a good scrap and in Turkey nobody got even remotely near him.

"Winning in this way on these very difficult roads without the slightest technical problem is a magnificent achievement for the whole team" he enthused at the finish. "The conditions in the second leg were some of the worst I've ever experienced in the World Championship. It's true that I didn't drive as aggressively as I normally do when Seb is here. Petter put on a good show before his retirement but it wasn't the same. Obviously this victory closes the gap a little (25 at the finish instead of 35 at the start) but quite honestly I reckon that my title hopes are very slim. My priority is to help Ford win the manufacturers' championship."

Mikko Hirvonen continued in his role as the ideal team-mate and helped Ford to have both its drivers on the rostrum giving the Blue Oval its first double in 2006. He too had no problems and preferred to allow the flying Solberg to blast off into the distance early on until his retirement rather than taking big risks to try

The Belgians love motor sport as shown by François Duval at the wheel of his Skoda Fabia WRC.

Dani Sordo drove a much calmer rally after his Cypriot blunder. He finished seventh.

Henning Solberg got better and better as the season unfolded. In Turkey, he finished third, his best WRC performance.

and overhaul him. When the Norwegian retired Mikko took over second place. "It's great for Ford and for Finland," he laughed at the finish. "The car was so good that it would've been a real shame not to score a double."

The main news was the fact that Ford went into the manufacturers' championship lead with 3 events left till the end of the season. With no Sébastien Loeb to put a spanner in the works Malcolm Wilson and his men looked on course to give the American giant its first manufacturers' title since 1979 (in 1981 Ari Vatanen won the drivers' championship at the wheel of a Ford Escort). It would be a fitting reward for a company that has remained faithful to top-level rallying for so long.

"It's the best performance by the Ford Focus WRCs in their first season of rallying," underlined Jost Capito, the Ford RS team manager. "What's most impressive is to have done so in atrocious weather and road conditions, and the cars did not have a single problem. And now we're in the lead in the manufacturers' championship."

Ford's only rival up to then, the Kronos-Citroën squad that had led the championship since Mexico, slipped back as Loeb's absence was a huge blow to the team. McRae set promising times in the first leg including a third but was a bit out of breath by the end of the day. The team's 2 Spaniards, like the Scot, made the wrong tyre choice. Medium, hard, retreaded or not? It was not easy and the accumulation of these strategic errors cost Citroën heavily at the end.

They managed to pull back places by the end of the short third leg and finished in the points with Pons fourth and Sordo seventh. There was just one hitch, the former had not been nominated to score points so the two added to the team's total was pretty meagre especially when compared to Ford's 18! Kronos was not helped by Colin McRae's retirement (alternator) in the very last special when he was heading for seventh place. So it was a rally to forget for the Franco-Belgian outfit.

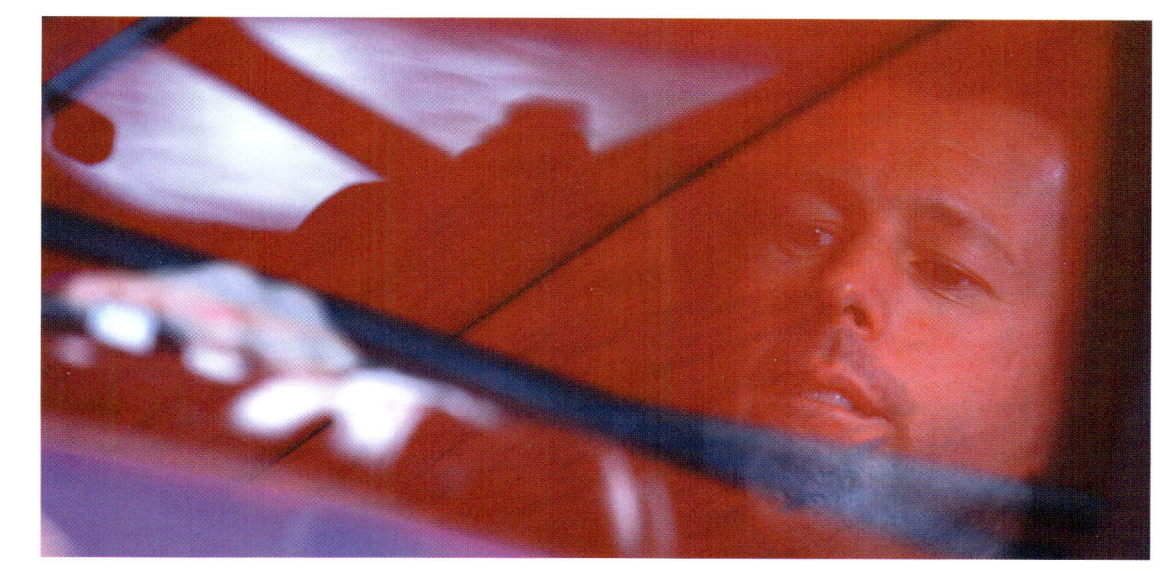

Colin McRae was called in at the last minute to replace Sébastien Loeb. The Scot made a good start to the rally but then fell back due to lack of practice and a poor tyre choice.

145

13 Turkey

The heavy rain before the start resulted in swollen rivers as Grönholm demonstrates.

Manfred Stohl was never really at home in Turkey and he also suffered engine problems.

For Subaru the Turkish rally brought a tiny glimmer of hope after what had been a disastrous season so far. Early on in the event the 2006 version of the Subaru at last showed some real pace and enabled Petter Solberg to display his talent. "Hollywood" took advantage of the fact that Grönholm was not really pushing and installed himself in second place finishing the first leg 26.1s behind the Flying Finn. In the second Petter's jinx struck again as he hit a stone and could not stop his car falling into a ditch. He continued in the super rally in which he saw the flag in thirteenth spot, a big disappointment as second overall was well within his grasp. However, he had the satisfaction of winning the highest number of stages in the event with 7 fastest times. But his performance in Mexico where he had hassled Loeb was but a distant memory. A cautious Chris Atkinson crept home in sixth place.

Petter's misfortune was his brother's opportunity and Henning got onto the rostrum during the second leg, and stayed there for the rest of the rally in his Bozian Team 307 WRC, his best-ever performance in a World Championship event.

The other WRC drivers like Aigner, Kopecky, Stohl, Duval etc. never shone. The only one to make a bit of a splash was Marcus Grönholm's protégé Katajamäki who was heading for a rostrum finish in his 2004 Ford Focus until hit by gear selection problems at the end of the rally when he was pipped by Xavier Pons.

While the adjective "exciting" could not be applied to the battle for honours in the WRC category, it was exactly the opposite in the Junior Championship. Guy Wilks was quickest out of the starting blocks and took advantage of the problems that hit his direct rivals, a puncture for Aava, an off and long repairs for Andersson and windscreen wiper failure for Meeke, to take the lead. But Wilks too ran into big trouble at around half distance. In SS12 his exhaust broke and he could no longer hear the pace notes of his co-driver Phil Pugh with the result that he cartwheeled off the road in the following stage, and lost a lot of time waiting for help to put his car back on its wheels. He finally finished fourth. This let Aava into the lead but not for long. In SS14, he also ran into a similar exhaust problem on his Swift, which, combined with another puncture, let Andersson into the lead. One very happy Swede saw the flag in first place as his win meant another title after that of 2004. His joy was short-lived, however. He was disqualified by the stewards for having carried out repairs in a zone where such an act was forbidden. And so Urmo Aava inherited victory, his first of the season and it gave him the lead in the championship 1 point ahead of Andersson, 2 ahead of Sandell (11th in Turkey), 4 ahead of Wilks, 5 in front of Rautenbach (2nd in Turkey), 8 in hand over Beres (3rd in the event) and 10 in front of Meeke (5th).

The result of the Turkish rally ensured that the last round in the British rally in December would a suspense-filled one, as apart from Rautenbach who was not taking part, the other six would go at it hammer and tongs for the title. ■

Kosti Katajamäki could have finished third were it not for a gear selection problem. He finally came fifth, his best WRC performance to date.

LOEB'S FALL!
A stupid accident (is there any other kind?!)

Two days after the Cyprus rally Sébastien Loeb went to do a bit of mountain biking a few kilometres from his home as part of his fitness-training programme. Suddenly when he was going down a wooded slope a big stone blocked his front wheel. The bike stopped but Loeb didn't! He fell heavily, all the more so as his feet were firmly wedged on the pedals, and he was unable to protect himself. "I fell on my shoulder and that broke my arm immediately," he explained once he had been operated on and was back in his Swiss home while the Turkish rally was unfolding. He tried to get back onto the saddle but realised that his arm was hanging by his side. "On the spot I was in pain without knowing exactly what the problem was. At the hospital they saw that I had smashed my arm (in fact, it was the head of the right-hand humerus that was broken). When something like that happens I immediately think of the rally and the championship. It's not an easy situation. I knew straight away that I wouldn't be able to drive in Turkey. These are difficult moments to bear. You have to have a lot of patience and allow nature to do its job, but it takes a long time."

Of course, he was haunted by the obsession of losing his title, as he did not yet know if he would be able to get back into a car before the end of the season. "Marcus has an open road in front of him now and he's going to exploit it to the full. But it won't be easy for him to win everything. I hope I'll be back before the end of the year to defend my title. It's a strange sensation. I'd prefer to be there in Turkey fighting for the championship and in addition all my friends were supposed to go there. But that's how it is and you have to accept it. My aim was to win the championship in Turkey; now it's to come back as soon as possible." ∎

In 2006, the little world of F1 said that the prettiest grid girls were Turkish, and in the rally Mikko Hirvonen could not but agree!

Chris Atkinson is always spectacular but he managed to control his fiery temperament probably helped by his team's briefing.

It is difficult to replace Sébastien Loeb. The omnipresent French photographers hounded Colin McRae even when he was out of the car.

The twilight of a god? Citroën gave McRae another chance. Will we see the Scot, one of the most spectacular drivers in the history of rallying, back in the world championship again?

Turkey results

Entry List (73) - 67 starters

N°	Driver (Nat.)	Co-driver (Nat.)	Team	Car	Group & FIA Priority
1.	C. MCRAE (GB)	N. GRIST (GB)	KRONOS TOTAL CITROEN WRT	Citroën Xsara WRC	A8 1
2.	D. SORDO (E)	M. MARTI (E)	KRONOS TOTAL CITROEN WRT	Citroën Xsara WRC	A8 1
3.	M. GRÖNHOLM (FIN)	T. RAUTIAINEN (FIN)	BP FORD WORLD RALLY TEAM	Ford Focus RS WRC 06	A8 1
4.	M. HIRVONEN (FIN)	J. LEHTINEN (FIN)	BP FORD WORLD RALLY TEAM	Ford Focus RS WRC 06	A8 1
5.	P. SOLBERG (N)	P. MILLS (GB)	SUBARU WORLD RALLY TEAM	Subaru Impreza WRC 2006	A8 1
6.	C. ATKINSON (AUS)	G. MACNEALL (AUS)	SUBARU WORLD RALLY TEAM	Subaru Impreza WRC 2006	A8 1
7.	M. STOHL (A)	I. MINOR (A)	OMV - PEUGEOT NORWAY	Peugeot 307 WRC	A8 1
8.	H. SOLBERG (N)	C. MENKERUD (N)	OMV - PEUGEOT NORWAY	Peugeot 307 WRC	A8 1
9.	M. WILSON (GB)	M. ORR (GB)	STOBART - VK - M-SPORT FORD RALLY TEAM	Ford Focus RS WRC 04	A8 1
10.	K. KATAJAMAKI (FIN)	T. ALANNE (FIN)	STOBART - VK - M-SPORT FORD RALLY TEAM	Ford Focus RS WRC 04	A8 1
11.	H. ROVANPERA (FIN)	R. PIETILAINEN (FIN)	RED BULL - SKODA TEAM	Skoda Fabia WRC	A8 1
12.	A. AIGNER (A)	K. WICHA (D)	RED BULL - SKODA TEAM	Skoda Fabia WRC	A8 1
14.	X. PONS (E)	C. DEL BARRIO (E)	XAVIER PONS	Citroën Xsara WRC	A8 2
15.	J. KOPECKY (CZ)	F. SCHOVANEK (CZ)	CZECH RALLY TEAM SKODA- KOPECKY	Skoda Fabia WRC	A8 2
16.	F. DUVAL (B)	P. PIVATO (F)	FIRST MOTORSPORT	Skoda Fabia WRC	A8 2
19.	M. BESLER (TR)	O. YILMAZ (TR)	FORD RALLYE SPORT TURKEY	Ford Focus WRC	A8 2
20.	E. KAZAZ (TR)	S. KURBANZADE (TR)	SUBARU RALLY TEAM JAPAN	Subaru Impreza WRC	A8 2
32.	K. MEEKE (GB)	G. PATTERSON (GB)	KRIS MEEKE	Citroën C2 S1600	A6 3
33.	U. AAVA (EE)	K. SIKK (EE)	URMO AAVA	Suzuki Swift S1600	A6 3
35.	P. ANDERSSON (S)	J. ANDERSSON (S)	PG ANDERSSON	Suzuki Swift S1600	A6 3
37.	P. VALOUSEK (CZ)	P. SCALVINI (CZ)	PAVEL VALOUSEK	Suzuki Swift S1600	A6 3
39.	C. RAUTENBACH (ZW)	D. SENIOR (GB)	CONRAD RAUTENBACH	Renault Clio S1600	A6 3
41.	P. SANDELL (SWE)	E. AXELSSON (SWE)	PATRIK SANDELL	Renault Clio S1600	A6 3
42.	J. PRESSAC (F)	J. BOYERE (F)	JULIEN PRESSAC	Citroën C2 S1600	A6 3
43.	J. MÖLDER (EE)	R. BECKER (EE)	JAAN MÖLDER	Suzuki Ignis S1600	A6 3
44.	M. KOSCIUSZKO (PL)	J. BARAN (PL)	MICHAL KOSCIUSZKO	Suzuki Ignis S1600	A6 3
45.	J. BERES (SK)	P. STARY (CZ)	JOZEF BERES	Suzuki Ignis S1600	A6 3
46.	A. CORTINOVIS (I)	F. ZANELLA (I)	ANDREA CORTINOVIS	Renault Clio	N3 3
48.	G. WILKS (GB)	P. PUGH (GB)	SUZUKI SPORT EUROPE UK	Suzuki Swift S1600	A6 3
49.	M. PROKOP (CZ)	J. TOMANEK (CZ)	JIPOCAR CZECH NATIONAL TEAM	Citroën C2 S1600	A6 3
51.	F. KARA (TR)	C. BAKANCOCUKLARI (TR)	FATIH KARA	Renault Clio S1600	A6 3
52.	B. CASIER (B)	B. MICLOTTE (B)	BERND CASIER	Renault Clio S1600	A6 3
54.	A. NICOLAI BURCANT (D)	T. GEILHAUSEN (D)	AARON NICOLAI BURCANT	Citroën C2 GT S1600	A6 3
55.	F. FIANDINO (F)	S. DE CASTELLI (F)	PH-SPORT	Citroën C2 R2 S1600	A6 3
61.	A. SARIHAN (TR)	B. GUCENMEZ (TR)	FORD RALLYE SPORT TURKEY	Ford Focus WRC	A8
62.	E. YURDAKUL (TR)	A. BAYDAR (TR)	FORD RALLYE SPORT TURKEY	Ford Focus WRC	A8
64.	G. BASSO (I)	M. DOTTA (I)	NEW BUSINESS 16 SPA	Fiat Punto Abarth Super 2	N4
65.	V. ISIK (TR)	G. KARAÇAR (TR)	FIAT MOTORSPORLARI	Fiat Grande Punto S2000	N4
67.	H. DINÇ (TR)	M. GUR (TR)	SUBARU TURKIYE RALLI TAKIMI	Subaru Impreza	N4
68.	H. UNAL (TR)	K. OZSENLER (TR)	FIAT MOTORSPORLARI	Fiat Punto S1600	N4
69.	B. CUKUROVA (TR)	A. ALAKOÇ (TR)	DELTA SPORT	Fiat Palio S1600	A6
70.	V. ROZUKAS (LT)	A. SHOSHAS (LT)	VILIUS ROZUKAS	Suzuki Ignis S1600	A6
72.	H. OZSEYHAN (TR)	F. INAN (TR)	SUBARU TURKIYE RALLI TAKIMI	Subaru Impreza	N4
73.	A. FARRAH (JO)	J. MATAR (RL)	TEAM JORDAN	Mitsubishi Lancer Evo IX	N4
74.	G. BOSTANCI (TR)	V. BOSTANCI (TR)	ST RACING	Mitsubishi Lancer Evo VIII	N4
75.	M. ERSONMEZ (TR)	B. ERDENER (TR)	TOKSPORT	Subaru Impreza N11	N4
76.	B. SINAN PULAT (TR)	G. SARAÇOGLU (TR)	TOKSPORT	Subaru Impreza GC-8	N4
77.	T. OKTEM (TR)	O. GÖKSEN (TR)	TOKSPORT	Mitsubishi Lancer Evo VIII	N4
79.	S. OZTEMIR (TR)	U. TEZEL (TR)	TOKSPORT	Mitsubishi Lancer Evo VI	A8
80.	V. RAZUMOVSKYY (UA)	I. SULTANOV (UA)	VALERIY RAZUMOVSKYY	Mitsubishi Lancer Evo IX	N4
82.	Y. SHAPOVALOV (UA)	L. SHUMAKOV (UA)	YURY SHAPOVALOV	Mitsubishi Lancer Evo IX	N4
83.	K. MURATOGLU (TR)	L. OZOKUTUCU (TR)	FORD RALLYE SPORT TURKEY	Ford Fiesta	N3
84.	D. UNLUDOGAN (TR)	A. SAMI CAN (TR)	FORD RALLYE SPORT TURKEY	Ford Fiesta	N3
85.	C. ÇELEBI (TR)	K. ALP (TR)	FORD RALLYE SPORT TURKEY	Ford Fiesta	N3
86.	A. KUÇUKSARI (TR)	B. AYAN (TR)	ST RACING	Renault Clio Ragnotti 2.0	N3
87.	B. ÇETINKAYA (TR)	N. YILMAZ (TR)	BURCU ÇETINKAYA	Ford Fiesta	N3
89.	A. ERDEN (TR)	A. EKMEKÇIOGLU (TR)	ALKAN ERDEN	Peugeot 106 GTI	A6
91.	Ö. ORHAN (TR)	S. TERZIOGLU (TR)	DELTA SPORT	Fiat Palio	N2
92.	H. OZAL (TR)	H. IPKIN (TR)	DELTA SPORT	Fiat Palio	N2
95.	O. ÖZDOGAN (TR)	B. KOÇOGLU (TR)	LASSA RALLY TEAM	Fiat Palio	N2
96.	B. TUGLU (USA)	A. YASAR (TR)	DELTA SPORT	Fiat Palio	N2
97.	H. OZAL (TR)	E. SEN (TR)	DELTA SPORT	Fiat Palio	N2
98.	M. DIKER (TR)	E. ORAL (TR)	DELTA SPORT	Fiat Palio	N2
99.	S. HONAMLI (TR)	B. UÇAK (TR)	DELTA SPORT	Fiat Palio	N2
101.	M. OKUR (TR)	B. SUEL (TR)	DELTA SPORT	Fiat Palio	N2
102.	D. ÇOKSAYAR (TR)	N. SAHIN (TR)	DELTA SPORT	Fiat Palio	N2
103.	S. DERICI (TR)	T. CANPOLAT (TR)	DELTA SPORT	Fiat Palio	N2

4th TURKISH RALLY

Organiser Details
Turkish Automobile and Motosports Federation (TOMSFED)
Göksuevleri, Kartopu caddesi No: B168/A
Anadoluhisari, Istanbul
TURKEY
Tel.: +90 (216) 465 11 55
Fax: +90 (216) 465 11 57

Rally of Turkey
13th leg of FIA 2006 World Rally Championship for constructors and drivers.
8th leg of WRC Junior Championship.

Date October 12 - 15, 2006

Route
1201.85 km divised in 3 legs.
19 special stages on dirt roads foreseen (351.01 km),
16 special stages raced (266.77 km)

Starting Procedure
Thursday, October 12th (19:45),
Cumhuriyet Square, Antalya

Leg 1
Friday, October 13 (07:58/19:22),
Kemer > Kemer, 587,13 km;
9 special stages (152.94 km)
6 special stages raced (70.71 km)

Leg 2
Saturday, October 14 (08:33/19:11),
Kemer > Kemer, 498.13 km;
7 special stages (147.11 km)

Leg 3
Sunday, October 15 (09:48/11:19),
Kemer > Kemer, 116.28 km;
3 special stages (50.96 km)

Championship Classifications

FIA Drivers (13/16)

1.	Loeb	8🏆 112
2.	Grönholm	5🏆 87
3.	Hirvonen	47
4.	Sordo	43
5.	Stohl	34
6.	H. Solberg	25
7.	P. Solberg	23
8.	Gardemeister	20
9.	Pons	18
10.	Atkinson	17
11.	Galli	15
12.	Bengué	9
13.	Katajamäki	7
14.	Kopecky	7
15.	Carlsson	6
16.	Välimäki	6
17.	Sarrazin	6
18.	Rådström	4
19.	Duval	4
20.	Arai	3
21.	Mac Hale	3
22.	Sohlberg	3
23.	Aigner	3
24.	Tuohino	3
25.	Wilson	1
26.	Nutahara	1
27.	Perez Compang, Pozzo...	0

FIA Constructors (13/16)

1.	BP-Ford World Rally Team	5🏆 153
2.	Kronos Total Citroën WRT	8🏆 145
3.	Subaru World Rally Team	83
4.	OMV-Peugeot Norway	67
5.	Stobart VK M-Sport Ford WRT	35
6.	Red Bull-Skoda Team	23

FIA Production Car (6/8)

1.	Al-Attiyah	2🏆 38
2.	Nutahara	3🏆 30
3.	Teiskonen	19
4.	Baldacci	19
5.	Arai	1🏆 18
6.	Kuzaj	17
7.	Pozzo	16
8.	Ligato	14
9.	Marrini	11
10.	Latvala	7
11.	Al Qassimi	6
12.	Heath	5
13.	Campedelli	5
14.	Uspenskiy	4
15.	Beltrán	4
16.	Vojtech	2
17.	Kamada	1
18.	Name	1
19.	Jereb, Nassoulas,	0
	Popov, Baldacci,	0
	Burkart, Tsouloftas,	0
	Pavlides	0
	Higgins Excluded	8

FIA Junior WRC (8/9)

1.	Aava	1🏆 30
2.	Andersson	1🏆 29
3.	Sandell	1🏆 28
4.	Wilks	2🏆 26
5.	Rautenbach	25
6.	Béres	22
7.	Meeke	1🏆 20
8.	Pressac	19
9.	Prokop	1🏆 18
10.	Casier	17
11.	Tirabassi	1🏆 11
12.	Valousek	11
13.	Burkart	9
14.	Molder	8
15.	Kara	7
16.	Rantanen	6
17.	Kosciuszko	5
18.	Pinomäki	4
19.	Betti	4
20.	Zachrisson	2
21.	Bonato	1
22.	Clark, Bordignon	0
	Cortinovis, Karlsson	0

Special Stages Times

www.rally-of-turkey.org
www.wrc.com

SS1 Perge 1 (22.43 km)
Cancelled

SS2 Myra 1 (24.15 km)
Cancelled

SS3 Kumluca 1 (9.90 km)
1.Grönholm 7'42"7; 2.P.Solberg +24"9;
3.Katajamäki +33"6; 4.H.Solberg +37"0;
5.McRae +37"9; 6.Hirvonen +38"7;
7.Aigner +43"7; 8.Pons +43"9...
J-WRC > 14.Wilks 9'02"5

SS4 Perge 2 (22.43 km)
Cancelled

SS5 Myra 2 (10.93 km / 24.15 km)
1.Grönholm 8'54"0; 2.Hirvonen +1"2;
3.Pons +4"8; 4.P.Solberg/McRae +5"9;
6.H.Solberg +8"8; 7.Sordo +11"1;
8.Katajamäki +12"1...
J-WRC > 18.Wilks 10'04"6

SS6 Kumluca 2 (9.90 km)
1.Grönholm 7'21"3; 2.Hirvonen +1"3;
3.McRae +3"3; 4.Atkinson +4"0;
5.P.Solberg/H.Solberg +6"2;
7.Pons +6"7; 8.Katajamäki +8"9...
J-WRC > 18.Meeke 8'08"6

SS7 Tekirova 1 (5.50 km)
1.P.Solberg 4'46"5; 2.Duval +2"0;
3.H.Solberg +5"0; 4.Katajamäki +6"0;
5.Grönholm +6"2; 6.Atkinson +7"4;
7.Hirvonen +9"8; 8.Stohl +10"2...
J-WRC > 18.Meeke 5'27"1

SS8 Phaselis 1 (29.28 km)
1.P.Solberg 24'17"1; 2.H.Solberg +2"1;
3.Grönholm +2"8; 4.Hirvonen +8"0;
5.Atkinson +19"9; 6.Katajamäki +20"3;
7.Rovanperä +30"9; 8.Pons +31"2...
J-WRC > 16.Aava 27'26"6

SS9 Akdeniz University 1 (5.20 km)
1.P.Solberg 4'12"6;
2.Hirvonen/McRae +0"7;
4.H.Solberg +1"3; 5.Grönholm +1"9;
6.Atkinson +2"1; 7.Katajamäki +2"2;
8.Stohl/Duval +3"2...
J-WRC > 19.Andersson 4'37"4

Classification Leg 1
1.Grönholm 57'25"1; 2.P.Solberg +26"1;
3.Hirvonen +48"8; 4.H.Solberg +49"5;
5.Katajamäki +1'12"2;
6.McRae +1'25"9; 7.Atkinson +1'26"5;
8.Pons +1'34"2...
J-WRC > 16.Wilks 1h05'01"7

SS10 Kemer 1 (20.50 Km)
1.P.Solberg 14'54"9; 2.Grönholm +2"2;
3.Hirvonen +9"0; 4.Sordo +12"2;
5.Pons +12"8; 6.H.Solberg +14"0;
7.McRae +16"2; 8.Duval +17"5...
J-WRC > 21.Andersson 17'22"7

SS11 Silyon 1 (27.36 km)
1.Grönholm 20'55"9; 2.Hirvonen +8"4;
3.P.Solberg +13"5; 4.Sordo +15"8;
5.H.Solberg +17"8; 6.Pons +25"9;
7.Duval +28"2; 8.Atkinson +29"6...
J-WRC > 18.Aava 22'59"0

SS12 Kemer 2 (20.50 Km)
1.Grönholm 14'26"7; 2.P.Solberg +2"6;
3.Hirvonen +5"8; 4.H.Solberg +8"8;
5.Pons +11"8; 6.Atkinson +16"9;
7.Duval +17"5; 8.McRae +17"9...
J-WRC > 19.Meeke 16'30"5

SS13 Silyon 2 (27.36 km)
1.Hirvonen 20'21"4; 2.Grönholm +0"5;
3.P.Solberg +3"9; 4.H.Solberg +8"7;
5.Atkinson +10"5; 6.Stohl +16"2;
7.Pons +22"1;
8.Katajamäki/Duval +23"1...
J-WRC > 18.Andersson 22'32"1

SS14 Chimera 1 (16.91 km)
1.P.Solberg 12'22"5; 2.Grönholm +9"2;
3.Atkinson +24"3; 4.Aigner +28"1;
5.McRae +28"6; 6.Katajamäki +30"1;
7.Hirvonen +32"2; 8.Duval +36"2...
J-WRC > 18.Meeke 14'14"9

SS15 Phaselis 2 (29.28 km)
1.Sordo 24'52"3; 2.Katajamäki +2"3;
3.Grönholm +6"3; 4.Atkinson +13"1;
5.Pons +17"5; 6.Rovanperä +22"5;
7.Stohl +22"9; 8.Aigner +30"3...
J-WRC > 15.Andersson 28'07"3

SS16 Akdeniz University 2 (5.20 km)
1.Hirvonen 4'06"5; 2.McRae +0"2;
3.Katajamäki +1"6; 4.Duval +1"8;
5.Stohl +2"1; 6.Pons/H.Solberg +3"0;
8.Atkinson +4"6...
J-WRC > 16.Aava/Andersson/Wilks 4'28"1

Classification Leg 2
1.Grönholm 2h49'50"4;
2.Hirvonen +2'05"2;
3.H.Solberg +2'45"6;
4.Atkinson +3'04"0;
5.Katajamäki +3'05"7; 6.Pons +3'29"5;
7.McRae +3'44"2; 8.Duval +4'12"2...
J-WRC > 17.Andersson 3h14'51"9

SS17 Tekirova 2 (5.50 km)
1.Duval 4'11"5; 2.Pons +0"4;
3.Stohl +0"9;
4.Grönholm/P.Solberg +1"4;
6.Atkinson +3"3; 7.Sordo +3"6;
8.Aigner +4"6...
J-WRC > 20.Wilks 4'48"9

SS18 Chimera 2 (16.91 km)
1.P.Solberg 12'06"9; 2.Grönholm +4"4;
3.Sordo +5"2; 4.Pons +8"6;
5.H.Solberg +9"4; 6.Stohl +9"9;
7.Hirvonen +11"2;
8.Katajamäki +16"9...
J-WRC > 19.Wilks 13'34"3

SS19 Olympos (28.55 Km)
1.P.Solberg 21'47"3; 2.Sordo +8"2;
3.Pons +9"1; 4.Grönholm +14"4;
5.Stohl +18"0; 6.Atkinson +19"3;
7.Hirvonen +20"8;
8.Katajamäki +21"4...
J-WRC > 18.Valousek 24'16"9

Results

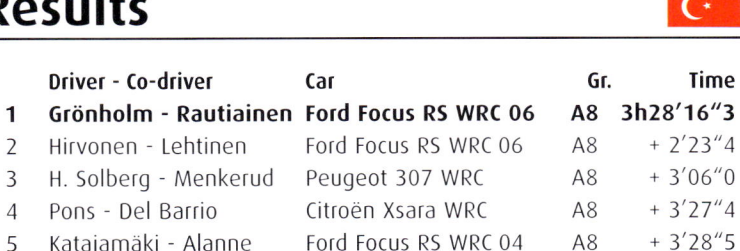

	Driver - Co-driver	Car	Gr.	Time
1	Grönholm - Rautiainen	Ford Focus RS WRC 06	A8	3h28'16"3
2	Hirvonen - Lehtinen	Ford Focus RS WRC 06	A8	+ 2'23"4
3	H. Solberg - Menkerud	Peugeot 307 WRC	A8	+ 3'06"0
4	Pons - Del Barrio	Citroën Xsara WRC	A8	+ 3'27"4
5	Katajamäki - Alanne	Ford Focus RS WRC 04	A8	+ 3'28"5
6	Atkinson - Macneall	Subaru Impreza WRC 2006	A8	+ 3'36"5
7	Sordo - Marti	Citroën Xsara WRC	A8	+ 4'24"8
8	Stohl - Minor	Peugeot 307 WRC	A8	+ 4'30"3
9	Duval - Privato	Skoda Fabia WRC	A8	+ 5'35"6
10	Aigner - Wicha	Skoda Fabia WRC	A8	+ 6'57"4
16	Aava - Sikk	Suzuki Swift S1600	A6/J	+ 33'50"2
17	Rautenbach - Senior	Renault Clio S1600	A6/J	+ 34'20"9
18	Béres - Stary	Suzuki Ignis S1600	A6/J	+ 34'29"7
23	Shapovalov - Shumakov	Mitsubishi Lancer Evo VIII	N4	+ 45'14"6

Leading Retirements (17)

SF18	Fiandino - De Castelli	Citroën C2 R2	Mechanical
TC19D	Andersson - Andersson	Suzuki Swift S1600	Excluded
SF19	McRae - Grist	Citroën Xsara WRC	Alternator
SF15	Kopecky - Schovanek	Skodia Fabia WRC	Off

Performers

	1	2	3	4	5	6	C6	NbSS
P. Solberg	7	2	2	2	1	-	13	14
Grönholm	5	4	2	2	2	-	15	16
Hirvonen	2	4	2	1	-	1	10	16
Sordo	1	1	1	2	-	-	5	16
Duval	1	1	-	1	-	-	3	16
McRae	-	2	1	1	2	-	6	15
Pons	-	1	2	1	3	2	9	16
Katajamäki	-	1	2	1	-	2	6	16
H. Solberg	-	1	1	4	3	3	12	16
Atkinson	-	-	1	2	2	5	10	16
Stohl	-	-	1	-	2	2	5	16
Aigner	-	-	-	1	-	-	1	16
Rovanperä	-	-	-	-	-	1	1	16

Leader

SS1 > SS19   Grönholm

Cato Menkerud / Henning Solberg

Urmo Aava

P.-G. Andersson, G. Wilks

Previous winners

2003	Sainz - Marti Citroën Xsara WRC
2004	Loeb - Elena Citroën Xsara WRC
2005	Loeb - Elena Citroën Xsara WRC

14 Australia

Marcus blows it!
Marcus Grönholm went off in the first leg and handed Sébastien Loeb his hat trick of world titles! Loeb, of course, was not there following his accident on his mountain bike and neither was Daniel Elena. Once again Marcus's impulsiveness killed his chances. Finally, victory went to his no.2 Mikko Hirvonen and Ford tightened its stranglehold on the manufacturers' title.

14 Australia

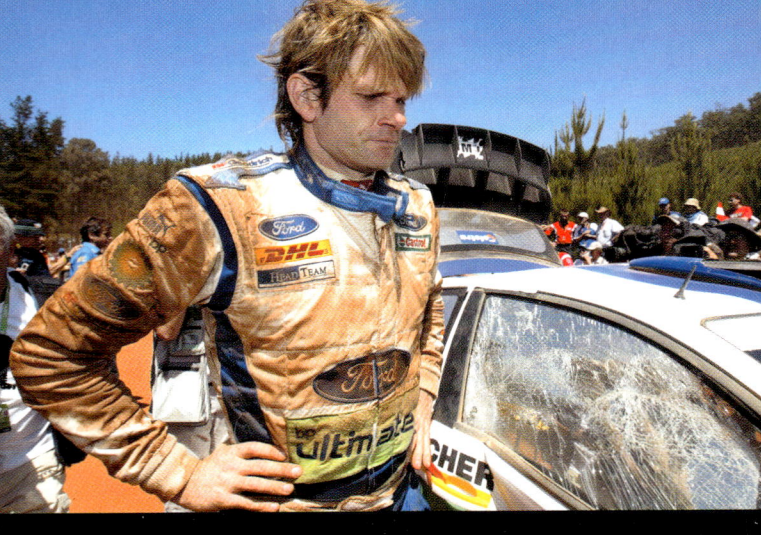

The Australian rally gave Subaru a slight hope of salvaging its disastrous season as Petter Solberg finished second.

Marcus Grönholm looks very downcast. His self-induced mistake has just cost him his chances of winning the drivers' championship.

THE RALLY
Thank you Marcus !

Sébastien sent his no.1 rival a little text message; it was a bit of a wind up but in fact both drivers have the highest respect for each other. When the Frenchman cannot take part in a rally Marcus misses him as his presence always drives him to surpass himself. And when the Finn is delayed for mechanical reasons or because he has gone off (as has happened to him on several occasions this year), Loeb's motivation goes down a notch or two.

So the words "Thank you!" appeared on the screen of Grönholm's mobile at the end of the rally. The message was, of course, from Sébastien Loeb, obliged to stay in Europe at the Capbreton re-education centre first of all after which he went back to his friends and family with whom he watched the 14th round of the world championship. Although he did not start he was crowned for the third time. Grönholm must have cursed himself as deep down he thought he could still win and become the first man to rack up three titles. Instead he handed it to Loeb on a plate. To remain in contention he had to finish at least third. It did not look too difficult, as down under the overall quality of the field was lower in relation to previous events; there were only ten WRCs at the start of the final Australian rally whose nerve centre was in Perth. In 2007, this event as dangerous as it is little known, will not be on the calendar. In 2008, perhaps, the Australian rally may be reinstated with the start in Brisbane. Five kilometres after Murray North the third stage on the programme, in fact the first after the 2 super specials the evening before won by Grönholm, the Ford driver was the victim of his own fieriness. "I hit a stone on the inside of a right-hand second-gear corner," he explained once he was back in the parc fermé. "The impact sent the car over to the other side of the track before it rolled. It turned over once and stopped on its roof. We got it back on its wheels with the help of a few spectators but it was stuck on a tree stump. We had to lift it to get it out. It cost us around ten minutes. I made a stupid mistake."

As always Marcus made no excuse and shouldered the blame for his driving error, which condemned him to play catch up. He was back in fifty-sixth and last place in the rally 10m 57.2s behind the leader, Chris Atkinson. So he had to pick off 53 cars to conserve even the slightest chance of winning the drivers' championship.
Once the Focus was back on its wheels his task looked even more difficult. It was working all right as damage was limited to the bodywork, but the windscreen was cracked and the side windows broken. There were still 4 stages (70 kms) to go before the service park and the cabin was filled with dust despite the repairs carried out by the two men. When they arrived in Perth after SS7 (Murray South) both men looked like they had spent the afternoon

rolling around on the Roland-Garros clay courts. "It was sheer hell inside," coughed Grönholm. "So much dust came in that I could hardly keep my eyes open. They're hurting me like hell, and I also twisted my back trying to get the car back on its wheels."

The Ford mechanics swarmed around the Focus to try and repair it changing the damaged bodywork and also the transmission. It took longer than the time allowed by the rules and Grönholm incurred an additional 20-second penalty. It was the straw that almost broke the camel's back.

He set off at full speed in fortieth place 12m 10.8s behind Petter Solberg and set three fastest times out of the four specials in the second loop. He finished the day in eighteenth place 12m 04.8s behind Mikko Hirvonen, the new leader since SS 9.

In fact, the two Subarus took advantage of Loeb's absence and Grönholm's boo-boo, and put on a performance that was more in keeping with their aspirations with Atkinson and then Solberg holding first place for a time. The Australian led until SS 6 (Murray North 2) after which he went off and his car caught fire. It was quickly extinguished with the help of the other competitors. The Norwegian replaced him in the lead before being badly handicapped by the hanging clouds of dust in Beraking 1 (SS 8) then Flynns 1 (SS 9), where he not only lost his way but also had to stop and wait for a semblance of visibility to return.

Unfortunately for Grönholm nothing much changed in the second and third legs. He really went for it setting five fastest times out of nine stages but it was difficult to climb back up the time sheets. On Saturday he was in seventh place and knew that his chances were very slim: "I did not go all out and now I'm not far off fifth place (under 50 seconds behind Ligato). That was the best we reckoned we could do after the accident. Anything else will be a bonus."
He finished fifth 8m 25.2s behind Manfred Stohl in third place as the order of the first four did not change. The 8 minutes lost near Murray proved crucial and with them the dreams of a third title went up in smoke - or rather dust.

And of course behind statements like, "delighted to have scored points for Ford after having lost so much time on Friday," or, "I'm very happy for Mikko; this win's going to give him more confidence in himself," or finally, "I'm sorry we won't be coming back to Perth. This is a fantastic rally," hid an immense disappointment.
"I knew that Seb was uncatchable after all his victories, in particular those in Japan and Cyprus. There was a tiny ray of hope but it was a kind of Mission Impossible. He's quick everywhere at the wheel of a very reliable car and he makes almost no mistakes. So it's not really surprising that he's won the title."

If Grönholm and Rautiainen were very disappointed Mikko Hirvonen and Jarmo Lehtinen were over the moon! The young 26-year-old Finn in his works Ford won his first world championship rally after his career had been relaunched thanks to his seat in the American works team. "It's fantastic. There was so much pressure on me not only to win but also to bring the car home in one piece, and score as many points as possible in the championship. Petter (Solberg) in second kept up the pressure on me but I tried not to allow him to get too close. It's one hell of a feeling winning from him."
"It's a very special day for us," added Jost Capito, the Ford RS team manager. "We bet on Mikko and Jarmo for this year and they scored their first victory. They're now up with drivers like Loeb and Grönholm as they're only the third pair to win this year."

Australian Chris Atkinson gets acquainted with one of his fellow-countrymen!

Manfred Stohl had a good rally down under in which he came home third.

Here Sordo fords a stream at the wheel of his Citroën Xsara that turned red in Australia (the colour that made it famous!).

Local driver Dean Herridge surprised some of the aces in the Production category by finishing on the rostrum.

¹⁴ Australia

Marcus Grönholm fell to the back of the field and then went pedal to metal to claw his way back into the top three, but in vain.

Petter Solberg enjoyed himself behind the wheel – for once!

The no.1 Xsara was entrusted to Spaniard Xavier Pons after McRae's disappointing performance in Turkey.

The other winner on Sunday 29th October was Jari-Matti Latvala who won the FIA Production round without his victory making much difference to the drivers' classification.

Al-Attiyah (Subaru, absent in Australia) was still in the lead from Nutahara (Mitsubishi, who finished in a disappointing eighth place down under).

Of course, the main event was Loeb's third title. The Alsatian with the cunning smile and modest bearing became the top rally driver of 2006, and also one of the greatest of all time in the history of the sport. ∎

THE CHAMPIONS
Meanwhile, back in France…

Sébastien Loeb and Daniel Elena were not in Australia to celebrate their third title. The Frenchman was unable to race in the event due to his mountain bike accident. Even if he owed his third title to Grönholm's error he fully deserved it having won eight out of 12 rallies up to the Cypriot event. After his brief stay in the Capbreton re-education centre the triple world champion had a funny kind of weekend in Toul with his family and friends.

A flying Mikko Hirvonen on his way to his first victory in the very quick Australian event.

Jari-Matti Latvala was a very happy bunny after scoring his first victory in the Production category in his Subaru.

Mirco Baldacci in his Mitsubishi had his best result of the year in Australia (2nd) but was never a threat to Latvala.

"It was a very special weekend living the rally in such a manner," commented Loeb once he knew the outcome. "It's a bit bizarre winning a championship when you're sitting on a sofa! But I have to tell you it's a big relief. When Marcus scored an easy victory in Turkey I began to doubt a little. The fact that he might win all the rallies till the end of the season could not be discounted. That's why I decided to go to the re-education centre to do everything in my power to race in New Zealand. Of course, I'm delighted to have won the title. It takes a lot of pressure off my having to come back. The conditions are different now. Marcus made a mistake; it was easier for me. The last night (Saturday/Sunday when the third leg was taking place due to the time difference) I didn't have a lot of sleep. Being in Marcus's shoes wasn't easy either. He had an open road ahead of him. He made a mistake; it happens; it's racing."

Loeb was not the only one to win the title in such a strange manner. Daniel Elena also racked up his third world championship. Marc Marti, Dani Sordo's co-driver, phoned him and woke him up to tell him about Grönholm's off. From then on the cheerful Monegasque followed the rally live.

"I sat down in front of my computer and I hardly left it throughout the rest of the stages. Then there were emails, text messages, web cams and what have you. Anything that would allow me to follow the rally as closely as possible. I watched the last special live with Kronos thanks to a web cam. It was really great!"

Meanwhile, the world champion was 20 000 kms away! Sébastien Loeb, the triple victor, was able to thank his best "enemy" Marcus Grönholm thanks to the wonders of modern communications technology.

That last night was a very hectic one for Elena who was also celebrating his birthday. He had a champagne breakfast and in the afternoon he went to see his favourite driver to continue the celebrations. The two men were already talking about the future. "One title's great, two are magnificent and three are fantastic!" said Elena with a roar of laughter after which he added: "four would be phenomenal and five historic! But we're not there yet. We're going to enjoy this one and for the rest we'll see what happens in the next few years." ■

14 Australia results

19th AUSTRALIAN RALLY

Organiser Details
Level 9, 2 Mill Street,
Perth WA 6000
Australia
Tel.: +61.89.262.17.00
Fax: +61.89.262.17.87

Telstra Rally Australia

14th leg of FIA 2006 World Rally Championship for constructors and drivers.
7th leg of FIA Production Car WRC Championship.

Date October 26 - 29, 2006

Route
1334.41 km divised in three legs.
26 special stages on dirt roads (348.51 km)

Starting Procedure
Thursday, October 26 (18:35),
Gloucester Park, East Perth
Prologue
Thursday, October 26 (19:12/19:21),
Gloucester Park;
2 special stages (4.00 km)
Leg 1
Friday, October 27 (09:23/19:34),
Perth > Murray > Perth, 540.47 km;
9 special stages incl. Prologue (124.83 km)
Leg 2
Saturday, October 28 (09:20/19:34),
Perth > Sotico > Perth, 496.94 km;
9 special stages (120.36 km)
Leg 3
Sunday, October 29 (07:03/12:14),
Perth > Mundaring > Perth, 297.00 km;
6 special stages (103.32 km)

Entry list (61) - 56 starters

N°	Driver (Nat.)	Co-driver (Nat.)	TEAM	Car	Group & FIA Priority
1.	X. PONS (E)	C. DEL BARRIO (E)	KRONOS TOTAL CITROEN WRT	Citroën Xsara WRC	A8 1
2.	D. SORDO (E)	M. MARTI (E)	KRONOS TOTAL CITROEN WRT	Citroën Xsara WRC	A8 1
3.	M. GRÖNHOLM (FIN)	T. RAUTIAINEN (FIN)	BP FORD WORLD RALLY TEAM	Ford Focus RS WRC 06	A8 1
4.	M. HIRVONEN (FIN)	J. LEHTINEN (FIN)	BP FORD WORLD RALLY TEAM	Ford Focus RS WRC 06	A8 1
5.	P. SOLBERG (N)	P. MILLS (GB)	SUBARU WORLD RALLY TEAM	Subaru Impreza WRC 2006	A8 1
6.	C. ATKINSON (AUS)	G. MACNEALL (AUS)	SUBARU WORLD RALLY TEAM	Subaru Impreza WRC 2006	A8 1
7.	M. STOHL (A)	I. MINOR (A)	OMV - PEUGEOT NORWAY	Peugeot 307 WRC	A8 1
8.	H. SOLBERG (N)	C. MENKERUD (N)	OMV - PEUGEOT NORWAY	Peugeot 307 WRC	A8 1
9.	M. WILSON (GB)	M. ORR (GB)	STOBART - VK - M-SPORT FORD RALLY TEAM	Ford Focus RS WRC 06	A8 1
10.	L. PEREZ COMPANC (RA)	J. MARIA VOLTA (RA)	STOBART - VK - M-SPORT FORD RALLY TEAM	Ford Focus RS WRC 06	A8 1
31.	T. ARAI (J)	T. SIRCOMBE (NZ)	SUBARU TEAM ARAI	Subaru Impreza WRX	N4 3
32.	M. LIGATO (RA)	R. GARCIA (RA)	MARCOS LIGATO	Mitsubishi Lancer Evo IX	N4 3
33.	F. NUTAHARA (J)	D. BARRITT (GB)	ADVAN-PIAA RALLY TEAM	Mitsubishi Lancer Evo IX	N4 3
34.	S. BELTRÁN (RA)	R. ROJAS (RCH)	SEBASTIAN BELTRAN	Mitsubishi Lancer Evo IX	N4 3
35.	G. POZZO (RA)	D. STILLO (RA)	GABRIEL POZZO	Mitsubishi Lancer Evo IX	N4 3
36.	M. BALDACCI (RSM)	G. AGNESE (I)	MIRCO BALDACCI	Mitsubishi Lancer Evo IX	N4 3
37.	J. LATVALA (FIN)	M. ANTTILA (FIN)	JARI-MATTI LATVALA	Subaru Impreza WRX	N4 3
40.	S. MARRINI (I)	T. SANDRONI (I)	ERRANI TEAM GROUP	Mitsubishi Lancer Evo IX	N4 3
41.	D. HERRIDGE (AUS)	B. HAYES (AUS)	SUBARU TEAM QUASYS	Subaru Impreza WRX	N4 3
42.	A. USPENSKIY (RUS)	D. EREMEEV (R)	SUBARU RALLY TEAM RUSSIA	Subaru Impreza WRX	N4 3
43.	J. POPOV (BG)	D. POPOV (BG)	OMV CEE RALLY TEAM	Mitsubishi Lancer Evo IX	N4 3
45.	A. TEISKONEN (FIN)	M. TEISKONEN (FIN)	SYMS RALLY TEAM	Subaru Impreza WRX	N4 3
61.	D. WINDUS (AUS)	J. MORTIMER (AUS)	DARREN WINDUS	Subaru Impreza WRX	N4
62.	W. ORDERS (AUS)	T. FEAVER (AUS)	WILL ORDERS	Subaru Impreza WRX	A8
63.	X. LANG (CHN)	D. MOSCATT (AUS)	XU LANG	Mitsubishi Lancer Evo VIII	N4
64.	T. CHALLIS (AUS)	A. CHUDLEIGH (AUS)	TOLLEY CHALLIS	Mitsubishi Lancer Evo VIII	A8
65.	S. LOWNDES (AUS)	C. RANDELL (AUS)	SPENCER LOWNDES	Mitsubishi Lancer Evo V	A8
66.	C. ANDERSON (AUS)	J. LITHGO (AUS)	MICHAEL ANDERSON	Subaru Impreza WRX	N4
67.	J. MURRAY (AUS)	G. MARTINOVICH (AUS)	JOHN MURRAY	Subaru Impreza WRX	N4
68.	T. HEYRING (AUS)	P. TURNER (AUS)	TOBY HEYRING	Subaru Impreza WRX	N4
69.	M. ANDERSON (AUS)	E. PLANE (AUS)	MICHAEL ANDERSON	Subaru Impreza WRX	N4
70.	M. STEWART (NZ)	M. FLETCHER (NZ)	MALCOLM STEWART	Mitsubishi Lancer Evo VI	A8
71.	J. MACARA (AUS)	G. MILES (AUS)	JOHN MACARA	Subaru Impreza WRX	A8
72.	J. ANDERSON (AUS)	B. SEARCY (AUS)	MICHAEL ANDERSON	Subaru Impreza WRX	N4
73.	S. EATHER (AUS)	A. KIRKHOUSE (AUS)	SHANE EATHER	Subaru Impreza WRX	A8
74.	L. BALDACCI (RSM)	D. D'ESPOSITO (I)	LORIS BALDACCI	Subaru Impreza WRX	N4
75.	G. FURNESS (AUS)	M. CIVIL (AUS)	GRAHAM FURNESS	Subaru Impreza WRX	N4
76.	D. MALLEY (NZ)	L. MALLEY (NZ)	NEIL ALLPORT MOTORSPORT	Mitsubishi Lancer Evo VIII	N4
77.	W. TUCKETT (AUS)	S. PERCIVAL (AUS)	WARREN TUCKETT	Mitsubishi Lancer Evo VIII	N4
78.	S. ITO (J)	F. BROOKHOUSE (AUS)	SATORU ITO	Mitsubishi Lancer Evo VII	N4
79.	R. MARKER (AUS)	K. HEIMSOHN (AUS)	RUSSELL MARKER	Subaru Impreza WRX	N4
80.	M. NAKAJIMA (J)	N. KUROSAKI (J)	MASAHIRO NAKAJIMA	Subaru Impreza WRX	N4
81.	S. MAITLAND (AUS)	B. D?ARCY (AUS)	STEVEN MAITLAND	Mitsubishi Lancer Evo V	A8
82.	R. FUNAKI (J)	H. SONODA (J)	RYO FUNAKI	Subaru Impreza WRX	N4
83.	R. WHYATT (AUS)	A. CHALLEN (AUS)	ROBERT WHYATT	Subaru Impreza WRX	N4
84.	J. BERNE (AUS)	S. BECKWITH (AUS)	JOHN BERNE	Subaru Impreza RS	N4
86.	R. ASH (AUS)	S. CARY (AUS)	ROBERT ASH	Subaru Impreza WRX	N4
88.	P. BENNISON (AUS)	T. ADAMS (AUS)	PETER BENNISON	Subaru Impreza WRX	N4
89.	K. SEITA (J)	K. NAKAMURA (J)	KEIJI SEITA	Honda Civic	N2
90.	S. ORKNEY (AUS)	T. BEST (AUS)	SHANE ORKNEY	Subaru Impreza WRX	N4
91.	T. ABBOTT (AUS)	M. STEELE (AUS)	TIMOTHY ABBOTT	Subaru Impreza WRX	N4
92.	P. STEEL (GB)	M. SFORCINA (AUS)	PHILIP STEEL	Subaru Impreza WRX	A8
93.	O. STICKELS (AUS)	A. KING (AUS)	OWEN STICKELS	Subaru Impreza WRX	N4
94.	K. KAMIYA (J)	S. TSUDA (J)	KAZUHIRO KAMIYA	Toyota Yaris	N1
95.	T. MATSUSHITA (J)	P. VAN DER MAY (AUS)	TOSHIYUKI MATSUSHITA	Toyota Yaris	N1
96.	P. WILLIAMS (AUS)	E. DELLA MADDALENA (AUS)	PAUL WILLIAMS	Subaru Impreza WRX	N4

Championship Classifications

FIA Drivers (14/16)
1. Loeb 8🏆 112
2. Grönholm 5🏆 91
3. Hirvonen 1🏆 57
4. Sordo 43
5. Stohl 40
6. P. Solberg 31
7. H. Solberg 25
8. Pons 23
9. Gardemeister 20
10. Atkinson 17
11. Galli 15
12. Bengué 9
13. Katajamäki 7
14. Kopecky 7
15. Carlsson 6
16. Välimäki 6
17. Sarrazin 6
18. Rådström 4
19. Duval 4
20. Arai 3
21. Mac Hale 3
22. Aigner 3
23. Tuohino 3
24. Latvala 3
25. Sohlberg 3
26. Baldacci 2
27. Wilson 1
28. Nutahara 1
29. Herridge 1
30. Perez Companc, Joge... 0

FIA Constructors (14/16)
1. BP-Ford World Rally Team 6🏆 167
2. Kronos Total Citroën WRT 8🏆 151
3. Subaru World Rally Team 94
4. OMV-Peugeot Norway 73
5. Stobart VK M-Sport Ford WRT 37
6. Red Bull-Skoda Team 23

FIA Production Car (7/8)
1. Al-Attiyah 2🏆 38
2. Nutahara 3🏆 32
3. Baldacci 27
4. Teiskonen 24
5. Arai 1🏆 18
6. Latvala 1🏆 17
7. Kuzaj 17
8. Marrini 14
9. Uspenskiy 8
10. Al Qassimi 6
11. Herridge 6
12. Heath 5
13. Campedelli 5
14. Vojtech 2
15. Kamada 1
16. Name 1
17. Jereb, Nassoulas, 0
    Popov, Baldacci, 0
    Burkart, Tsouloftas, 0
    Pavlides 0
Pozzo Excluded 16
Ligato Excluded 14
Higgins Excluded 8
Beltrán Excluded 4

FIA Junior WRC (8/9)
1. Aava 1🏆 30
2. Andersson 1🏆 29
3. Sandell 1🏆 28
4. Wilks 2🏆 26
5. Rautenbach 25
6. Béres 22
7. Meeke 1🏆 20
8. Pressac 19
9. Prokop 1🏆 18
10. Casier 17
11. Tirabassi 1🏆 11
12. Valousek 11
13. Burkart 9
14. Molder 8
15. Kara 7
16. Rantanen 6
17. Kosciuszko 5
18. Pinomäki 4
19. Betti 4
20. Zachrisson 2
21. Bonato 1
22. Clark, Bordignon 0
    Cortinovis, Karlsson 0
    Fiandino 0

Special Stages Times

SS1 Perth City Super I (2.00 km)
1.Grönholm 1'21"1; 2.P.Solberg +0"9; 3.Hirvonen +1"0; 4.Stohl +1"2; 5.Sordo +1"5; 6.H.Solberg +1"9; 7.Atkinson/Pons/Perez Companc +2"1...
P-WRC > 11.Araï 1'26"6

SS2 Perth City Super II (2.00 km)
1.Grönholm 1'20"7; 2.Hirvonen +0"9; 3.P.Solberg +1"2; 4.Stohl +1"3; 5.Sordo +1"8; 6.Perez Companc +2"0; 7.Pons +2"3; 8.Atkinson +2"5...
P-WRC > 11.Araï 1'25"9

SS3 Murray North I (15.92 km)
1.Atkinson 8'55"4; 2.P.Solberg +3"3; 3.Hirvonen +4"3; 4.Pons +14"4; 5.Stohl +14"6; 6.H.Solberg +21"6; 7.Perez Companc +33"7;
P-WRC > 8.Herridge 9'41"7...

SS4 Murray South I (20.12 km)
1.Atkinson 11'34"9; 2.Hirvonen +8"0; 3.P.Solberg +13"4; 4.Pons +13"8; 5.Stohl +18"8; 6.H.Solberg +38"4; 7.Grönholm +44"1;
P-WRC > 8.Baldacci 12'26"2...

SS5 Holyoake (3.13 km)
1.Atkinson 1'53"4; 2.P.Solberg +0"9; 3.Grönholm +3"3; 4.Hirvonen +4"0; 5.Pons/H.Solberg +6"7; 7.Stohl +8"8;
P-WRC > 8.Araï 2'05"2...

SS6 Murray North II (15.92 km)
1.P.Solberg 8'50"0; 2.Hirvonen +0"1; 3.Pons +10"1; 4.Stohl +15"1; 5.Grönholm +29"2;
P-WRC > 6.Herridge +37"3 (9'27"3); 7.Latvala +38"3; 8.Baldacci +43"5...

SS7 Murray South II (20.12 km)
1.P.Solberg 11'31"1; 2.Hirvonen +4"1; 3.Pons +6"5; 4.Stohl +13"1; 5.Grönholm +16"7;
P-WRC > 6.Herridge +44"8 (12'15"9); 7.Baldacci +45"5; 8.Teiskonen +46"3...

SS8 Beraking I (22.84 km)
1.Grönholm 13'05"7; 2.Hirvonen +6"7; 3.P.Solberg +8"1; 4.Pons +17"7; 5.Stohl +24"4;
P-WRC > 6.Teiskonen +57"5 (14'03"2); 7.Araï +58"0; 8.Ligato +1'02"4...

SS9 Flynns I (18.78 km)
1.Grönholm 11'07"2; 2.Hirvonen +15"4; 3.Stohl +40"4; 4.P.Solberg +42"5; 5.Pons +55"9;
P-WRC > 6.Teiskonen +1'26"5 (12'33"7); 7.Araï +1'32"3; 8.Herridge +1'32"8...

SS10 Perth City Super III (2.00 km)
1.Grönholm 1'22"6; 2.Pons +0"7; 3.Stohl +0"8; 4.Hirvonen +0"9; 5.P.Solberg +1"0;
P-WRC > 6.Nutahara +3"9 (1'26"5); 7.Araï +4"4; 8.Latvala/Ligato +4"6...

SS11 Perth City Super IV (2.00 km)
1.Pons 1'22"2; 2.Grönholm +0"1; 3.Hirvonen +0"4; 4.P.Solberg +0"7; 5.Stohl +0"9;
P-WRC > 6.Nutahara +3"9 (1'26"1); 7.Herridge +4"1; 8.Ligato +5"1...

Classification Leg 1
1.Hirvonen 1h13'10"1; 2.P.Solberg +26"2; 3.Pons +1'24"4; 4.Stohl +1'33"6; P-WRC > 5.Herridge +5'37"0 (1h18'47"1); 6.Araï +5'40"3; 7.Baldacci +5'53"8; 8.Teiskonen +5'55"0...

SS12 Bannister North I (17.71 km)
1.Hirvonen 8'34"7; 2.Grönholm +1"7; 3.P.Solberg +2"0; 4.Stohl +10"0; 5.Atkinson +10"5; 6.Pons +16"5; 7.Sordo +26"6;
P-WRC > 8.Araï 9'20"9...

SS13 Bannister Central I (17.85 km)
1.Hirvonen 9'20"8; 2.P.Solberg +0"2; 3.Grönholm +2"1; 4.Stohl +12"1; 5.Atkinson +13"6; 6.Pons +14"9; 7.Sordo +22"7
P-WRC > 8.Araï 10'08"6...

SS14 Bannister Loop (3.62 km)
1.Grönholm 1'57"5; 2.Hirvonen +1"1; 3.P.Solberg/Pons +1"2; 5.Stohl +1"3; 6.Atkinson +2"4; 7.Sordo +3"9; 8.Perez Companc +7"9;
P-WRC > 9.Nutahara 2'06"8

SS15 Bannister North II (17.71 km)
1.Grönholm 8'30"5; 2.P.Solberg +0"1; 3.Hirvonen +3"3; 4.Stohl +5"7; 5.Atkinson +11"1; 6.Pons +14"4; 7.Sordo +14"9; 8.Perez Companc +37"5...
P-WRC > 10.Araï 9'17"9

SS16 Bannister Central II (17.85 km)
1.Hirvonen 9'15"0; 2.Grönholm +0"2; 3.P.Solberg +1"1; 4.Stohl +9"9; 5.Atkinson +10"9; 6.Pons +12"6; 7.Sordo +14"4; 8.Perez Companc +47"3...
P-WRC > 10.Araï 10'04"3

SS17 Beraking II (22.84 km)
1.P.Solberg 12'34"5; 2.Hirvonen +1"5; 3.Grönholm +3"1; 4.Atkinson +17"3; 5.Stohl +18"4; 6.Pons +19"0; 7.Sordo +43"4; 8.Perez Companc +57"9...
P-WRC > 10.Latvala 13'41"1

SS18 Flynns II (18.78 km)
1.Grönholm 10'48"1; 2.Hirvonen +0"3; 3.P.Solberg +4"7; 4.Stohl +10"6; 5.Atkinson +12"7; 6.Pons +20"4; 7.Sordo +25"5; 8.Perez Companc +39"6...
P-WRC > 10.Latvala 11'46"9

SS19 Perth City Super V (2.00 km)
1.Grönholm 1'21"8; 2.Sordo/Pons +0"5; 4.Hirvonen +1"1; 5.Stohl +1"3; 6.Atkinson +1"8; 7.P.Solberg/Perez Companc +1"9...
P-WRC > 10.Marrini 1'26"8

SS20 Perth City Super VI (2.00 km)
1.Hirvonen/Grönholm 1'21"5; 3.Pons +0"5; 4.Sordo +0"6; 5.Stohl +1"3; 6.Perez Companc +1"6; 7.Atkinson +2"1; 8.P.Solberg +2"2...
P-WRC > 10.Latvala 1'26"8

Classification Leg 2
1.Hirvonen 2h17'01"8; 2.P.Solberg +32"3; 3.Stohl +2'36"9; 4.Pons +2'57"1; P-WRC > 5.Latvala +11'53"1 (2h28'54"9); 6.Grönholm +12'04"6; 7.Teiskonen +12'14"0; 8.Herridge +12'29"0...

SS21 Atkins I (4.42 km)
1.P.Solberg 3'06"1; 2.Grönholm +0"5; 3.Hirvonen +1"2; 4.Atkinson +3"5; 5.Stohl +4"6; 6.Pons +5"7; 7.Sordo +6"1; 8.Perez Companc +10"5:
P-WRC > 9.Herridge 3'17"5

SS22 Helena North I (29.93 Km)
1.Hirvonen 17'06"0; 2.P.Solberg +0"8; 3.Grönholm +9"9; 4.Stohl +21"5; 5.Sordo +40"6; 6.Pons +44"1; 7.Atkinson +44"2; 8.Perez Companc +1'07"9...
P-WRC > 10.Baldacci 18'30"6

SS23 Helena South I (17.31 Km)
1.Hirvonen 8'57"8; 2.Grönholm +5"0; 3.P.Solberg +5"2; 4.Stohl +14"4; 5.Pons +18"7; 6.Atkinson +20"3; 7.Sordo +21"7; 8.Perez Companc +26"9...
P-WRC > 10.Baldacci 9'46"4

SS24 Atkins II (4.42 km)
1.P.Solberg 3'01"3; 2.Grönholm +0"6; 3.Hirvonen +1"0; 4.Sordo +3"3; 5.Atkinson +3"4; 6.Pons +5"7; 7.Stohl +6"3; 8.Wilson +7"8...
P-WRC > 10.Baldacci 3'12"3

SS25 Helena North II (29.93 Km)
1.P.Solberg 16'59"1; 2.Hirvonen +1"6; 3.Grönholm +1"8; 4.Atkinson +15"1; 5.Stohl +23"2; 6.Pons +26"5; 7.Sordo +28"7; 8.Wilson +55"3...
P-WRC > 10.Latvala 18'16"4

SS26 Helena South II (17.31 Km)
1.Hirvonen 8'55"9; 2.P.Solberg +2"6; 3.Grönholm +5"2; 4.Atkinson +8"8; 5.Pons +11"4; 6.Stohl +15"5; 7.Sordo +17"6; 8.Perez Companc +22"1...
P-WRC > 10.Baldacci 9'42"5

Results

	Driver - Co-driver	Car	Gr.	Time
1	Hirvonen - Lehtinen	Ford Focus RS WRC 06	A8	3h15'11"8
2	P. Solberg - Mills	Subaru Impreza WRC 2006	A8	+ 37"1
3	Stohl - Minor	Peugeot 307 WRC	A8	+ 3'58"6
4	Pons - Del Barrio	Citroën Xsara WRC	A8	+ 4'45"4
5	Grönholm - Rautiainen	Ford Focus RS WRC 06	A8	+ 12'23"8
6	Latvala - Anttila	Subaru Impreza WRX Sti	N4/P	+ 17'09"2
7	Baldacci - Agnese	Mitsubishi Lancer Evo IX	N4/P	+ 17'42"9
8	Herridge - Hayes	Subaru Impreza WRX	N4/P	+ 18'22"0
9	Atkinson - Macneall	Subaru Impreza WRC 2006	A8	+ 27'05"5
10	Teiskonen - Teiskonen	Subaru Impreza WRX	N4/P	+ 27'19"3

Leading Retirements (11)

SF18	Arai - Sircombe	Subaru Impreza WRX	Engine
SF9	H. Solberg - Menkerud	Peugeot 307 WRC	Off
TC0	Ligato - Garcia	Mitsubishi Lancer Evo IX	Excluded
TC0	Pozzo - Stillo	Mitsubishi Lancer Evo IX	Excluded
TC0	Beltrán - Rojas	Mitsubishi Lancer Evo IX	Excluded

Performers

	1	2	3	4	5	6	C6	NbSS
Grönholm	10	6	6	-	2	-	24	26
Hirvonen	7	10	6	3	-	-	26	26
P. Solberg	6	7	8	2	1	-	24	26
Atkinson	3	-	-	4	6	3	26	20
Pons	1	2	4	3	3	11	24	26
Sordo	-	1	-	2	3	-	6	17
Stohl	-	-	2	11	10	1	24	26
H. Solberg	-	-	-	1	3	4	5	
Perez Companc	-	-	-	-	-	2	2	19
Teiskonen	-	-	-	-	-	2	2	24
Herridge	-	-	-	-	-	2	2	26
Nutahara	-	-	-	-	-	2	2	21

Leaders

SS1 > SS2	Grönholm
SS3 > SS5	Atkinson
SS6	Hirvonen
SS7 > SS8	P. Solberg
SS9 > SS26	Hirvonen

Previous winners

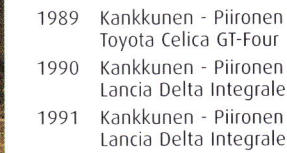

1989	Kankkunen - Piironen Toyota Celica GT-Four	1995	Eriksson - Parmander Mitsubishi Lancer Ev.2	2001	Grönholm - Rautiainen Peugeot 206 WRC
1990	Kankkunen - Piironen Lancia Delta Integrale	1996	Mäkinen - Harjanne Mitsubishi Lancer Ev.3	2002	Grönholm - Rautiainen Peugeot 206 WRC
1991	Kankkunen - Piironen Lancia Delta Integrale	1997	McRae - Grist Subaru Impreza WRC	2003	Solberg - Mills Subaru Impreza WRC 2003
1992	Auriol - Occelli Lancia Delta HF Integrale	1998	Mäkinen - Mannisenmäki Mitsubishi Lancer Ev.5	2004	Loeb - Elena Citroën Xsara WRC
1993	Kankkunen - Grist Toyota Celica Turbo 4WD	1999	Burns - Reid Subaru Impreza WRC	2005	Duval - Smeets Citroën Xsara WRC
1994	McRae - Ringer Subaru Impreza	2000	Grönholm - Rautiainen Peugeot 206 WRC		

Jari-Matti Latvala

New Zealand

01 02 03 04 05 06 07 08 09 10 11 12 13 14 16

27 years after...
As Sébastien Loeb was still convalescing the New Zealand rally was a cakewalk for the two works Fords with Marcus Grönholm winning easily from Mikko Hirvonen. This double gave the American giant the 2006 manufacturers' title, which it had been chasing since 1979! The other highlight of this rally was the presence of motorbike star Valentino Rossi at the wheel of a Subaru.

15 New Zealand

Marcus Grönholm was back on the winning path in the beautiful New Zealand settings.

THE RALLY
Ford dominates

Malcolm Wilson is a big worrier under his affable, dynamic exterior. He lived through hell in the final kilometres of the New Zealand rally that his drivers had dominated from the start. Everything went swimmingly for the two Ford aces. At the end of the first stage (Pirongia West, 20,38 kms) Marcus Grönholm-Timo Rautiainen and Mikko Hirvonen-Jarmo Lehtinen in their Ford Focuses filled the first two places. And that was how it stayed for the rest of the event as no one was able to match the pace of the two Finns. Grönholm set all the fastest times in the first leg and Hirvonen came second with one exception, the 3,14 km Mystery Creek super special (SS 5) won by Atkinson in his Subaru.

The rest of the rally followed the same pattern. The big Finn set thirteen scratch times out of a possible seventeen. Hirvonen set one (SS 10, Te Akau North) and finished second on 9 occasions.

Malcolm Wilson really had nothing to worry about. With just one round still to run the M-Sport boss, who looks after the development and entry of the Focus WRC RSs in the world championship, was able to present his employer with its first manufacturers' world title since 1979! The former driver who had become a team manager and spent all his career working for Ford was over the moon and made no bones about expressing his delight. "Winning this title gives me great personal satisfaction. Ford has been so close to it several times in the past. We've worked so hard and I'm very proud that my team has done it at last. It required a huge effort on the part of everybody, not only the people working for M-Sport but also those from BF Goodrich who provided us with tyres and all our other suppliers like Pipo Motors. This victory is the culmination of all those years in which we've patiently built up and developed a world-class team in terms of both infrastructure and resources that's capable of beating the best." In his torrent of praise Malcolm did not forget the drivers either: "Marcus Grönholm is one of the greatest drivers in the world and we were

Once again Chris Atkinson emerged pointless after another big shunt.

Dani Sordo did his job by scoring points in what was unexplored territory for him.

expecting him to be in the thick of battle, but not many people at the start of the year reckoned that Mikko Hiroven could reach such a high level so quickly. He's now one of the top rally drivers in the business."

"It's a very special feeling to have won the rally and at the same time brought the world title home to Ford," exulted the winner. "It wasn't really a difficult race but I have to say that the car was perfect from start to finish. When I joined this team I was expecting that the Ford would be on the pace, as it was a new car that was quick out of the box. But the fact that it's been so fast and reliable throughout the whole season is a big bonus."

"It's been a great year," said an enthusiastic Hirvonen. "What's more I've assured myself of third place in the drivers' championship. But the main thing at this stage of my career is to have helped Ford win the manufacturers' title."

The company's big cheeses saluted this historic performance with the same enthusiasm. "For a few years now I thought that our team was one of the best," warbled Jost Capito, the manager of the Ford Team RS. "This victory is a huge achievement for this outfit, and also a magnificent reward for all Ford's employees and enthusiasts throughout the world who give us their full unconditional support."

John Fleming, the Chairman of Ford Europe, was also a very happy man: "Henry Ford said that the only important history was the one that was built day by day. Today, we're proud to add another glorious page to the saga of Ford in motor sport."
The major focal point of interest of this event that took place mostly on new stages whose centre was not far from Hamilton some 150 kms from Auckland, the country's economic capital, was the attribution of the manufacturers' title after the drivers' one.
The other crews were reduced to walk-on roles.

Manfred Stohl put on another good performance after Australia and brought his 307 WRC home in third place despite a few wrong tyre choices due to the changing weather conditions on the first day. In the duel between the two Spanish drivers in their Citroëns Xavier Pons emerged victorious over Dani Sordo and he might even have been able to wrest third from Stohl had he not spun on 2 occasions: in SS 1 (Pirongia West and again in SS 14 (Whaanga Coast). They bagged 9 points for Kronos but once again Loeb's absence was sorely felt as the Spaniards were not nearly as quick as the Frenchman.

For the umpteenth time in 2006 the Subarus were completely off the pace. The Impreza was still not competitive and suffered from erratic behaviour, a strange tyre choice. Atkinson, who was trying too hard, crashed and retired in strange circumstances. While he was changing a wheel after an off the Subaru's jack collapsed and he watched helplessly as the car sank in

Valentino Rossi drove a black Subaru in his second WRC event.

Mikko Hirvonen attended the pre-race press conference made up like a Scotsman! It was the result of a bet with his mechanics after his first victory.

The New Zealand event is the favourite of the teams in the world championship. It is easy to understand why given the magnificent landscapes.

15 New Zealand

the mud! In fact, the damage caused by the contact with the rock that led to his accident was too serious because the rollbar was too badly damaged to allow him to continue.

Solberg came home in a lowly sixth place ahead of Argentinean, Perez-Companc, who scored his first 2 points of the season. In WRC the star attraction finished in eleventh place 20m 38.8s behind the winner. It was of course the 7-times motorcycle world champion Valentino Rossi who was back to try his hand on four wheels again. His first attempt was in 2002 in the British rally, and he did not make much of an impression going off in the first few kilometres. That year he was at the wheel of a 206 financed by Michelin. This time it was Pirelli which paid for his striking-looking black 2005 Impreza WRC. "I just came along for the pleasure and to try and finish the race," laughed

Petter Solberg's Impreza fell back into its bad old habits after its promising display in Australia.

Mikko Hirvonen kept up the good work. After his win down under he came home second in NZ giving Ford a double and the manufacturers' title to boot!

Manfred Stohl did manage to fasten his harness and drove on to third place in the rally.

the bike rider before the start. "Now I'm going to get to grips with the car and work on my note-taking with Carlo (Cassina, his co-driver) to see what I'm worth as a rally driver!"

Rossi talked about his experiences on 4 wheels, his tests with Ferrari and his recent outing in a DTM Mercedes-Benz, and admitted that rallying was "my real passion in motor sport but I'm less at home here than on a circuit. It may seem strange but it's easier for me to go quicker in F1 because of finding braking points and the right lines." The improvisation necessary for road racing is not always in the genes of circuit drivers.

He went very carefully in the first stage (36th time out of 42) and underlined the courage required to go flat out in certain tricky sections. Then he upped the pace little by little and ended the race of a high note by setting seventh time in a stage 2/10s in front of Petter Solberg! "I enjoyed myself very much," he smiled at the end of the event. " I finished without too many problems and without damaging the car which is very important. It was a real-life experience in a major rally. I tried to get to grips with the track and the car and to improve as the kilometres rolled by. It wasn't easy but I really liked it. And my times got better and better. Of course, if I want to continue I'll have to work harder. But it gives me pleasure and this time probably won't be the last!" David Richards the boss of Prodrive which develops and enters the Subarus in the world championship confirmed shortly afterwards that Rossi had talked to him about his reconversion to road racing. "One of his aims once he has finished his motorbike career is to do a few seasons in WRC. Subaru's going to study this very closely and we'll give him every opportunity to dial himself in." ■

Latvala doubled up in the Antipodes thanks to his victory in New Zealand after his success in Australia.

PRODUCTION
Al-Attiyah wins his bet

Nassar Al-Attiyah is an oddball. The Qatari, who is a crack shot and came fourth in the 2004 Athens Olympics, set himself another challenge over 3 years. This year's objective was to become the Production champion in the World Rally Championship. And he was at the end of the third and last season of his game plan. Of course you have to know how the ropes but his achievement is worthy of respect. All the more so as he won in a year that was full of surprises and upsets in which no fewer than 5 drivers emerged victorious in at least one of the eight rounds on the calendar. In any case, Al-Attiyah gave his country its first world title in motor sport obtained in a paradoxical manner as he did not see the end of the New Zealand rally, but scored 2 points in the super rally.

He was strolling home to the finish after basing his race on that of his direct rival for the crown, Fumio Nutahara, when his Subaru's engine gave up the ghost four stages from the end. "All I could do was to sit and wait. My aim was to finish scoring a lot of points. We didn't manage that but Nutahara had problems before us. And so..."

The Japanese in his Mitsubishi was not very happy on the New Zealand roads and punctured in SS 7 (Klondyke) before going off in the next one (Wairamaramara). He finished sixth overall thanks also to the super rally. His 3 points were not enough to close the gap of 5 that separated him from Al-Attiyah at the start.

In the rally itself victory went to Jari-Matti Latvala (Subaru) after an event full of upsets from Mirco Baldacci in his Mitsubishi.

Al Attiyah's next challenge was to defend the gold medal he won in the 2002 Asiatic Games as the 2006 competition was being held in his own country. In Doha in his role as world champion he was given the honour of carrying the torch at the opening ceremony. ∎

Henning Solberg somersaulted in SS 10 and lost 14 minutes. He was able to continue as his car was only superficially damaged.

Sébastien Loeb came to New Zealand as a tourist to do a bit of reconnaissance. The guys in this photo have 12 world titles between them: seven for Rossi, four for Loeb (three WRCs plus one Junior) and one for Petter Solberg.

The champions! Al-Attiyah gave Qatar its first world title in motor sport. Marcus Grönholm made an enormous contribution to Ford's manufacturers' title orchestrated by Malcolm Wilson, the M-Sport boss.

15 New Zealand results

36th RALLY NEW ZEALAND

Organiser Details
PO Box 62021, Mt Wellington,
Auckland,
New Zealand
Tel.: +6492 760882
Fax: +6492 760881

Rally of New Zealand

15th leg of FIA 2006 World Rally Championship for constructors and drivers.
8th and last leg of FIA Production Car WRC Championship.

Date November 16 - 19, 2006

Route
1354.26 km divised in three legs.
17 special stages on dirt roads (358.48 km).

Starting Procedure
Thursday, November 16 (19:30),
Hood Street, Hamilton

Leg 1
Friday, November 17 (09:33/18:00),
Mystery Creek > Pirongia > Mystery Creek,
427.21 km; 5 special stages (131.66 km)

Leg 2
Saturday, November 18 (09:23/18:15),
Mystery Creek > Te Akau > Mystery Creek,
542.49 km; 6 special stages (131.34 km)

Leg 3
Sunday, November 19 (07:38/12:59),
Mystery Creek > Te Akau > Mystery Creek,
384.56 km; 6 special stages (95.48 km)

Entry List (48) - 44 starters

N°	Driver (Nat.)	Co-driver (Nat.)	TEAM	Car	Group & FIA Priority
1	X. PONS (E)	C. DEL BARRIO (E)	KRONOS TOTAL CITROEN WRT	Citroën Xsara WRC	A8 1
2	D. SORDO (E)	M. MARTI (E)	KRONOS TOTAL CITROEN WRT	Citroën Xsara WRC	A8 1
3	M. GRÖNHOLM (FIN)	T. RAUTIAINEN (FIN)	BP FORD WORLD RALLY TEAM	Ford Focus RS WRC 06	A8 1
4	M. HIRVONEN (FIN)	J. LEHTINEN (FIN)	BP FORD WORLD RALLY TEAM	Ford Focus RS WRC 06	A8 1
5	P. SOLBERG (N)	P. MILLS (GB)	SUBARU WORLD RALLY TEAM	Subaru Impreza WRC 2006	A8 1
6	C. ATKINSON (AUS)	G. MACNEALL (AUS)	SUBARU WORLD RALLY TEAM	Subaru Impreza WRC 2006	A8 1
7	M. STOHL (A)	I. MINOR (A)	OMV - PEUGEOT NORWAY	Peugeot 307 WRC	A8 1
8	H. SOLBERG (N)	C. MENKERUD (N)	OMV - PEUGEOT NORWAY	Peugeot 307 WRC	A8 1
9	M. WILSON (GB)	M. ORR (GB)	STOBART - VK - M-SPORT FORD RALLY TEAM	Ford Focus RS WRC 06	A8 1
10	L. PEREZ COMPANC (RA)	J. MARIA VOLTA (RA)	STOBART - VK - M-SPORT FORD RALLY TEAM	Ford Focus RS WRC 06	A8 1
31	T. ARAI (J)	T. SIRCOMBE (NZ)	SUBARU TEAM ARAI	Subaru Impreza WRX Spec C	N4 3
33	F. NUTAHARA (J)	D. BARRITT (GB)	ADVAN-PIAA RALLY TEAM	Mitsubishi Lancer Evo IX	N4 3
36	M. BALDACCI (RSM)	G. AGNESE (I)	MIRCO BALDACCI	Mitsubishi Lancer Evo IX	N4 3
37	J. LATVALA (FIN)	M. ANTTILA (FIN)	JARI-MATTI LATVALA	Subaru Impreza WRX Spec C	N4 3
38	L. KUZAJ (PL)	M. SZCZEPANIAK (PL)	AUTOMOBILKUB RZEMIESLNIK WARSZAWA	Subaru Impreza WRX	N4 3
39	N. AL-ATTIYAH (QAT)	C. PATTERSON (GB)	QMMF	Subaru Impreza WRX Spec C 6	N4 3
41	T. KAMADA (J)	D. GIRAUDET (F)	SUBARU TEAM QUASYS	Subaru Impreza WRX	N4 3
42	A. DOROSINSKIY (R)	D. EREMEEV (R)	SUBARU RALLY TEAM RUSSIA	Subaru Impreza WRX Spec C	N4 3
43	N. BARRATT (GB)	D. MOSCATT (AUS)	OMV CEE RALLY TEAM	Mitsubishi Lancer Evo VIII	N4 3
44	N. HEATH (GB)	S. LANCASTER (GB)	NIGEL HEATH	Mitsubishi Lancer EVO	N4 3
45	A. TEISKONEN (FIN)	W. HAYES (AUS)	SYMS RALLY TEAM	Subaru Impreza WRX Spec C	N4 3
46	V. ROSSI (I)	C. CASSINA (I)	VALENTINO ROSSI	Subaru Impreza WRC 2005	A8 2
59	R. MASON (NZ)	S. RANDALL (NZ)	RICHARD MASON MOTORSPORT	Subaru Impreza WRX	N4 3
60	C. WEST (NZ)	G. COWAN (NZ)	WINGER SUBARU/SUBARU NZ	Subaru Impreza WRX	N4 3
61	J. HÄNNINEN (FIN)	M. SALLINEN (FIN)	JUHO HANNINEN	Mitsubishi Lancer Evo IX	N4
62	A. HAWKESWOOD (NZ)	J. CRESS (NZ)	FORCE MOTORSPORT	Mitsubishi Lancer Evo VII	A8
63	E. GILMOUR (NZ)	C. COBHAM (NZ)	EMMA GILMOUR	Subaru Impreza WRX	N4
64	D. SUMNER (NZ)	P. FALLON (NZ)	ITM RALLY TEAM	Mitsubishi Lancer Evo VIII	N4
65	G. INKSTER (NZ)	G. GOLDRING (NZ)	ETCO RALLY TEAM	Mitsubishi Lancer Evo VI	A8
66	S. TAYLOR (NZ)	W. SEARLE (NZ)	TAYLOR MOTORSPORT LTD	Mitsubishi Lancer Evo IX	N4
67	M. STEWART (NZ)	M. FLETCHER (NZ)	MALCOLM STEWART	Mitsubishi Lancer Evo VI	A8
68	D. AYLING (NZ)	G. KENNY (NZ)	AYLING RALLI SPORT	Subaru Impreza WRX	A8
69	B. TAYLOR (NZ)	C. RAMSAY (NZ)	RALLY DRIVE NZ	Mitsubishi Lancer Evo VI	N4
70	L. BALDACCI (RSM)	D. D'ESPOSITO (I)	LORIS BALDACCI	Subaru Impreza WRX	N4
71	P. MALLEY (NZ)	R. BENNETT (NZ)	M RALLY TEAM	Mitsubishi Lancer Evo VII	N4
72	M. KAHLFUSS (D)	R. BAUER (D)	MIKA TEAM	Mitsubishi Lancer Evo VI	N4
73	K. SHAW (IRL)	J. ALLEN (AUS)	NEIL ALLPORT MOTORSPORTS	Mitsubishi Lancer Evo VII	N4
74	K. NELSON (NZ)	M. BRUNT (NZ)	RICHARD MASON MOTORSPORT	Subaru Impreza WRX	N4
75	M. SHINNORS (IRL)	A. WILKEY (GB)	RALLY DRIVE NZ	Mitsubishi Lancer Evo VI	N4
76	D. MALLEY (NZ)	L. MALLEY (NZ)	M RALLY TEAM	Mitsubishi Lancer Evo VIII	N4
77	R. IVE (GB)	L. LOUGHLIN (NZ)	PROSPEED DEVELOPMENTS	Subaru Impreza WRX	N4
78	A. BAMBA (J)	J. KIBBLE (NZ)	AKIRA BAMBA	Mitsubishi Lancer Evo VIII	N4
79	G. STEVENSON (NZ)	M. PEDEN (NZ)	GREG STEVENSON	Mitsubishi Lancer Evo VII	N4
80	N. STEVENSON (NZ)	W. MARTIN (NZ)	GREG STEVENSON	Mitsubishi Lancer Evo VII	N4

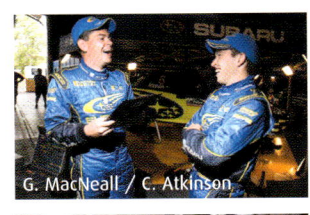

Championship Classifications

FIA Drivers (15/16)
1. Loeb ◊ 8♛ 112
2. Grönholm 6♛ 101
3. Hirvonen 1♛ 65
4. Sordo 47
5. Stohl 46
6. P. Solberg 34
7. Pons 28
8. H. Solberg 25
9. Gardemeister 20
10. Atkinson 17
11. Galli 15
12. Bengué 9
13. Katajamäki 7
14. Kopecky 7
15. Carlsson 6
16. Välimäki 6
17. Sarrazin 6
18. Rådström 4
19. Duval 4
20. Latvala 4
21. Arai 3
22. Mac Hale 3
23. Aigner 3
24. Tuohino 3
25. Sohlberg 3
26. Perez Companc 2
27. Baldacci 2
28. Wilson, 1
29. Nutahara 1
30. Herridge 1
31. Hänninen, Joge 0
    Panizzi, Teiskonen... 0

FIA Constructors (15/16)
1. BP-Ford World Rally Team ◊ 7♛ 185
2. Kronos Total Citroën WRT 8♛ 160
3. Subaru World Rally Team 97
4. OMV-Peugeot Norway 80
5. Stobart VK M-Sport Ford WRT 39
6. Red Bull-Skoda Team 23

FIA Production Car (8/8)
1. Al-Attiyah ◊ 2♛ 40
2. Nutahara 3♛ 35
3. M. Baldacci 31
4. Latvala 2♛ 27
5. Teiskonen 24
6. Arai 1♛ 18
7. Kuzaj 17
8. Marrini 14
9. Mason 8
10. Uspenskiy 8
11. Al Qassimi 6
12. Herridge 6
13. Dorosinskiy 6
14. Heath 6
15. Kamada 6
16. Campedelli 5
17. Vojtech 2
18. Name 1
19. Jereb, Nassoulas 0
    Popov, L. Baldacci 0
    Burkhart, Tsouloftas 0
    Pavlides, Barratt 0
    West 0
    Pozzo Excluded 16
    Ligato Excluded 14
    Higgins Excluded 8
    Beltrán Excluded 4

FIA Junior WRC (8/9)
1. Aava 1♛ 30
2. Andersson 1♛ 29
3. Sandell 1♛ 28
4. Wilks 2♛ 26
5. Rautenbach 25
6. Béres 22
7. Meeke 1♛ 20
8. Pressac 19
9. Prokop 1♛ 18
10. Casier 17
11. Tirabassi 1♛ 11
12. Valousek 11
13. Burkart 9
14. Molder 8
15. Kara 7
16. Rantanen 6
17. Kosciuszko 5
18. Pinomäki 4
19. Betti 4
20. Zachrisson 2
21. Bonato 1
22. Clark, Bordignon 0
    Cortinovis, Karlsson 0
    Fiandino 0

Special Stages Times

www.rallynz.org.nz
www.wrc.com

SS1 Pirongia West 1 (20.38 km)
1.Grönholm 15'09"7; 2.Hirvonen +5"9?;
3.Stohl +11"0; 4.Sordo +21"7;
5.P.Solberg +41"5; 6.Pons +46"2;
7.Perez Companc +46"8;
8.Wilson +50"7...
P-WRC > 10.Latvala 16'20"2

SS2 Te Koraha 1 (43.88 km)
1.Grönholm 29'44"7;
2.Hirvonen +11"8; 3.Stohl +19"9;
4.Sordo +27"2; 5.P.Solberg +38"4;
6.Pons +39"3; 7.H.Solberg +56"5;
8.Perez Companc +1'14"4...
P-WRC > 12.Baldacci 31'47"2

SS3 Pirongia West 2 (20.38 km)
1.Grönholm 14'53"6; 2.Hirvonen +4"8;
3.Stohl +5"2; 4.Pons +7"7;
5.Sordo +12"3; 6.H.Solberg +16"2;
7.P.Solberg +18"3;
8.Perez Companc +28"4...
P-WRC > 11.Latvala 15'43"6

SS4 Te Koraha 2 (43.88 km)
1.Grönholm 29'10"2; 2.Hirvonen +5"7;
3.Pons +6"7; 4.P.Solberg +9"2;
5.Sordo +13"4; 6.H.Solberg +32"1;
7.Stohl +37"1; 8.Atkinson +37"8...
P-WRC > 11.Latvala 30'39"6

SS5 Mystery Creek Super 1 (3.14 km)
1.Grönholm 2'59"8; 2.Atkinson +0"4;
3.P.Solberg +0"9; 4.Sordo +1"6;
5.Perez Companc +2"3; 6.Pons +2"6;
7.Hirvonen +3"0; 8.H.Solberg +3"4...
P-WRC > 10.Baldacci 3'06"7

Classification Leg 1
1.Grönholm 1h31'58"0;
2.Hirvonen +31"2; 3.Sordo +1'16"2;
4.Stohl +1'18"4; 5.Pons +1'42"5;
6.P.Solberg +1'48"3;
7.H.Solberg +2'43"5;
8.Perez Companc +3'23"8...
P-WRC > 10.Hänninen 1h37'33"5

SS6 Port Waikato (18.18 km)
1.Grönholm 10'25"3; 2.Pons +0"2;
3.Hirvonen +3"8; 4.P.Solberg +6"0;
5.Sordo +6"7; 6.Stohl +7"4;
7.Atkinson +8"2; 8.Wilson +16"7...
P-WRC > 11.Baldacci 11'06"2

SS7 Klondyke (13.88 km)
1.Atkinson 11'18"9; 2.Grönholm +5"7;
3.Sordo +9"9; 4.Hirvonen +11"7;
5.Pons +12"6; 6.Stohl +14"6;
7.H.Solberg +21"6; 8.Wilson +22"7...
P-WRC > 11.Latvala 11'55"2

SS8 Wairamarama (31.58 km)
1.Atkinson 22'23"7; 2.Pons +19"5;
3.Grönholm +20"6; 4.Hirvonen +21"4;
5.Sordo +22"4; 6.H.Solberg +24"2;
7.Stohl +27"0; 8.Wilson +48"1...
P-WRC > 11.Latvala 23'48"1

SS9 Te Akau South (31.92 km)
1.Grönholm 18'37"4;
2.Hirvonen +8"2; 3.Stohl +14"3;
4.H.Solberg +21"5; 5.P.Solberg +22"7;
6.Pons +26"0; 7.Sordo +32"2;
8.Wilson +36"3...
P-WRC > 11.Baldacci 20'03"2

SS10 Te Akau North (32.64 km)
1.Hirvonen 18'08"2; 2.Grönholm +0"3;
3.P.Solberg +6"6; 4.Stohl +8"1;
5.Sordo +18"9; 6.Pons +21"3;
7.Perez Companc +33"4;
8.Wilson +59"8...
P-WRC > 10.Baldacci 19'21"1

SS11 Mystery Creek Super 2 (3.14 km)
1.Grönholm 2'59"9; 2.Hirvonen +0"6;
3.H.Solberg +2"4; 4.Pons +2"9;
5.Stohl +3"0; 6.Sordo +3"4;
7.Rossi +3"6; 8.P.Solberg +3"8...
P-WRC > 10.Latvala 3'09"4

Classification Leg 2
1.Grönholm 2h56'17"2;
2.Hirvonen +50"3; 3.Stohl +2'06"2;
4.Sordo +2'23"1; 5.Pons +2'38"4;
6.P.Solberg +3'25"1;
7.Perez Companc +8'41"1;
P-WRC > 8.Baldacci 3h07'29"6

SS12 Maungatawhiri 1 (6.69 km)
1.Grönholm 3'40"6; 2.Hirvonen +0"3;
3.P.Solberg +2"3; 4.Sordo +3"0;
5.Pons +3"1; 6.Stohl +4"8;
7.Wilson +5"5; 8.H.Solberg +8"1...
P-WRC > 12.Latvala 3'57"9

SS13 Te Hutewai 1 (11.23 km)
1.Grönholm 7'56"2; 2.Pons +1"8;
3.Hirvonen +3"1; 4.P.Solberg+5"3;
5.Wilson +8"1; 6.Stohl +10"1;
7.H.Solberg +10"5; 8.Sordo +11"2...
P-WRC > 12.Araï 8'26"5

SS14 Whaanga Coast 1 (29.82 km)
1.Grönholm 21'38"1;
2.Hirvonen +1"8; 3.Stohl +7"8;
4.P.Solberg +14"6; 5.Sordo +21"4;
6.Pons +24"8; 7.Wilson +38"0;
8.Perez Companc +44"2...
P-WRC > 11.Araï 22'47"8

SS15 Maungatawhiri 2 (6.69 km)
1.Grönholm 3'37"5; 2.Hirvonen +0"1;
3.P.Solberg +0"8; 4.Pons +1"7;
5.Sordo +5"3; 6.Stohl +5"7;
7.Wilson +10"1;
8.Perez Companc +12"8...
P-WRC > 12.Araï 3'55"5

SS16 Te Hutewai 2 (11.23 km)
1.Grönholm/Pons 7'57"7;
3.Hirvonen +1"4; 4.P.Solberg +5"4;
5.Stohl +6"6; 6.Wilson +7"8;
7.Sordo +10"0;
8.H.Solberg +11"2...
P-WRC > 11.Araï 8'21"8

SS17 Whaanga Coast 2 (29.82 km)
1.Pons 21'09"7; 2.Stohl +11"8;
3.Hirvonen +12"7; 4.Grönholm +13"7;
5.P.Solberg +17"3; 6.Sordo +20"4;
7.H.Solberg +34"4;
8.Perez Companc +43"8...
P-WRC > 11.Latvala 22'40"0

Results

	Driver - Co-driver	Car	Gr.	Time
1	**Grönholm - Rautiainen**	**Ford Focus RS WRC 06**	**A8**	**4h02'30"7**
2	Hirvonen - Lehtinen	Ford Focus RS WRC 06	A8	+ 56"0
3	Stohl - Minor	Peugeot 307 WRC	A8	+ 2'39"3
4	Pons - Del Barrio	Citroën Xsara WRC	A8	+ 2'56"1
5	Sordo - Marti	Citroën Xsara WRC	A8	+ 3'20"7
6	P. Solberg - Mills	Subaru Impreza WRC 2006	A8	+ 4'57"1
7	Perez Companc - Maria Volta	Ford Focus RS WRC 06	A8	+ 10'51"6
8	**Latvala - Anttila**	**Subaru Impreza WRX Sti**	**N4/P**	**+ 16'22"4**
9	Hänninen - Sallinen	Mitsubishi Lancer Evo IX	N4	+ 17'30"2
10	Mason - Randall	Subaru Impreza WRX	N4/P	+ 20'20"0
11	Rossi - Cassina	Subaru Impreza WRC 2005	A8	+ 20'38"8
16	Dorosinskiy - Eremeev	Subaru Impreza WRX Spec C	N4/P	+ 32'09"2

Leading Retirements (7)

TC14C	Kuzaj - Szczepaniak	Subaru Impreza WRX	No more tyre
SF14	Barratt - Moscatt	Mitsubishi Lancer Evo VIII	Gearbox
SF8	West - Cowan	Subaru Impreza WRX	Off
SF9	Atkinson - Macneall	Subaru Impreza WRC 2006	Suspension
TC1	Teiskonen - Hayes	Subaru Impreza WRX Spec C	Electricals

Performers

	1	2	3	4	5	6	C6	Nb SS
Grönholm	13	2	1	1	-	-	17	17
Pons	2	3	1	3	2	6	17	17
Atkinson	2	1	-	-	-	-	3	8
Hirvonen	1	9	4	2	-	-	16	17
Stohl	-	1	5	1	2	5	14	17
P. Solberg	-	-	4	5	4	-	13	17
Sordo	-	-	1	4	7	2	14	17
H. Solberg	-	-	1	1	-	3	5	17
Wilson	-	-	-	-	1	1	2	14
Perez Companc	-	-	-	-	1	-	1	17

Leader

SS1 > SS17 Grönholm

Previous winners

1977	Bacchelli - Rosetti Fiat 131 Abarth
1978	Brookes - Porter Ford Escort RS
1979	Mikkola - Hertz Ford Escort RS
1980	Salonen - Harjanne Datsun 160J
1982	Waldegaard - Thorzelius Toyota Celica GT
1983	Rohrl - Geistdorfer Opel Ascona 400
1984	Blomqvist - Cederberg Audi Quattro A2
1985	Salonen - Harjanne Peugeot 205 T16
1986	Kankkunen - Piironen Peugeot 205 T16
1987	Wittmann - Patermann Lancia Delta HF 4WD
1988	Haider - Hinterleitner Opel Kadett GSI
1989	Carlsson - Carlsson Mazda 323 Turbo
1990	Sainz - Moya Toyota Celica GT-Four
1991	Sainz - Moya Toyota Celica GT-Four
1992	Sainz - Moya Toyota Celica Turbo 4WD
1993	McRae - Ringer Subaru Legacy RS
1994	McRae - Ringer Subaru Impreza
1995	McRae - Ringer Subaru Impreza
1996	Burns - Reid Mitsubishi Lancer Ev.3
1997	Eriksson - Parmander Subaru Impreza WRC
1998	Sainz - Moya Toyota Corolla WRC
1999	Mäkinen - Mannisenmäki Mitsubishi Lancer Evo 6
2000	Grönholm - Rautiainen Peugeot 206 WRC
2001	Grönholm - Rautiainen Peugeot 206 WRC
2002	Grönholm - Rautiainen Peugeot 206 WRC
2003	Grönholm - Rautiainen Peugeot 206 WRC
2004	Solberg - Mills Subaru Impreza WRC 2004
2005	Loeb - Elena Citroën Xsara WRC

Nasser Al-Attiyah

Great Britain

16

The mighty Finn racks up no.25
Once again nobody able to hold a candle to Marcus Grönholm, and he won the last round of the 2006 championship held in diabolical conditions in a canter. It was his 25th WRC victory making him the Finnish record holder as he beat Tommi Mäkinen's score of 24.

16 Great Britain

The Welsh tracks are wild and grandiose, as Dani Sordo would agree.

The most serious consequences of Hirvonen's off-course excursion were not visible. The team withdrew the car after only 3 specials because the roll bar had been damaged in the incident compromising the crew's safety.

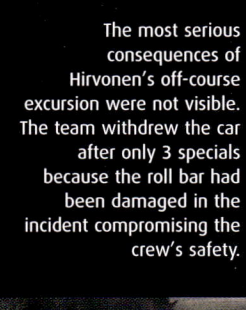

THE RALLY
Two points too far!

All that stood between Marcus Grönholm and his third world title was a measly 2 points. His victory in the final rally of the season was a doddle and he ended the year with 111 points, one fewer than Sébastien Loeb. Had they dead-heated the Frenchman would still have won thanks to his 8 victories compared with the Finn's 7. With 113 points Marcus would have won his third drivers' championship. He should have finished the Australian rally in third and not fifth place to achieve this aim. It all boiled down to a careless accident.

Of course, it could be argued that had Loeb not fallen off his bicycle after the Cyprus rally Grönholm would never have found himself in such a favourable position. Overall, the best driver won as the Frenchman had scored enough points before his accident to protect himself from a Grönholm comeback. But in terms of points Marcus nearly made it. Had the Alsatian started the final rally of the year he might have been beaten and things might have been different. Statistics don't lie (!) and the winner in 2006 scored 112 points, the runner-up 111 and Hirvonen in third 65, a measure of the way in which the first two dominated the season.

Loeb was unable to compete in the British rally, as his broken arm was not sufficiently healed. Right from the start in the first stage (Port Talbot 1) the Finn went into a lead he was never to lose. He won four of the six specials in the first leg (sharing one with Petter Solberg) while the other two went to Manfred Stohl and the Norwegian. The conditions in Wales were pretty diabolical, and the muddy roads were made all the more difficult by the heavy rain that had fallen the night before. They posed no problems for the Focus 06 driven by the two Finns, Grönholm and Rautiainen, on its BF Goodrich tyres. "The state of the roads was normal for this part of the world," explained Marcus, "with a lot of mud but no standing water. In the afternoon I lifted off a little, too much perhaps as Petter got quite close. But I am where I want to be on the evening of the first leg and I'll give it another go tomorrow!"

He was 25.8s ahead of a sparkling Solberg. "I really went for it today, I can tell you," laughed the Norwegian. "But it's the only way to drive if I want to have even the slightest chance of winning. Everything went well apart from the ten seconds I lost in the first special when I stalled in a hairpin. I pulled back quite a lot of time afterwards. In any case it's the first time for

Petter Solberg gave his all in this rally that he likes so much, and had several off-course excursions as the sate of his Subaru shows.

Xevi Pons has a difficult first day. He then buckled down to the task in hand and fought his way back to the front.

Jari-Matti Latvala was given a 2006 Focus for the last rally of the season and he did not waste this opportunity.

ages that we've been able to put up a fight and it's really motivating." Into third came an ebullient Manfred Stohl in his 307 WRC followed by Latvala, who was at the wheel of a 2006 Focus for the first time this year. The two Citroën drivers, Sordo and Pons were in fifth and sixth places.

There were two important retirements in the first leg. Andreas Aigner somersaulted off in his Skoda Fabia and Mikko Hirvonen also bit the dust. The young Finn was expecting a lot from this rally until he was withdrawn by his team at the first service halt. During the first special he hit a big stone very hard damaging his Focus's roll bar. It did nothing to diminish the car's performance – he set the second-quickest time in the first 3 specials - but as the crew's safety was at stake and the damage could not be repaired, the car was

withdrawn. "I just slid a bit wide," he mumbled, "and I hit stones on the verges. I made a stupid mistake because there was lots of room. I wanted to continue as the car was still very quick but it wouldn't have been very safe. It's really disappointing; we were behind Marcus and we could've scored another double to end the season on a high note for Ford."

Petter Solberg was in maximum attack mode in the second leg. The Norwegian reckoned that he could catch Grönholm and drove hell for leather right from the first special (Crychan 1 (SS 7). He overdid things in thick mud (after more rain) and poor visibility. "Honestly, I pushed too hard," he groaned. "I chose a new tyre and took a few too many risks and I went off. The car got stuck and it took us 30 seconds to get back on the road."

Manfred Stohl stole past Petter into second place but the Norwegian drove like crazy and repassed the Austrian after SS9. He then had another slight off in SS 11 damaging his steering so Manfred got back in front.

Xevi Pons moved up behind these two and finished the leg in fourth place after overtaking Latvala among others. "I had a good feeling throughout the day," smiled the Spaniard. "This afternoon it was raining very hard at the start of SS 10 but my tyres were good. I had no problems unlike yesterday." Things were not going so swimmingly for Dani Sordo who was plagued by transmission problems that condemned him to cover several stages at low speed.

Sunday 3rd December 2006: Marcus Grönholm duly strolled home to an uncontested victory increasing Ford's margin in the manufacturers' championship ahead of Kronos Citroën and Subaru. He also racked up his seventh victory of the season bringing his total to 25 one behind Carlos Sainz whose record had been beaten by Loeb earlier in the year. He also became the winningest driver in his home country by overtaking Tommi Mäkinen who had a total of 24. Given the love of rallying in Finland this really means something. The Big Finn grew even bigger!

Manfred Stohl proudly carried the Peugeot colours and scored a remarkable second place in Wales.

16 Great Britain

Marcus Grönholm was head and shoulders over his rivals in the last rally of the 2006 season and a rainbow greeted his seventh victory!

François Duval knows who to use the width of the road to the full, an essential part of driving on the very greasy terrain in the British rally.

Manfred Stohl's second place ahead of Petter Solberg slowed by a puncture and a spin was his best result of the season. It was probably the finest drive in the 34-year-old Austrian's career, and his third rostrum finish on the trot allowed him to snatch fourth place in the drivers' ratings from Dani Sordo. "This second place is worth much more than the one in Cyprus in 2005," he said delightedly. "There I was over 5 minutes behind the winner and today the gap is only 1m 35s. To be a privateer among the works teams is a real dream for me."

Petter Solberg finally came home in third place after a hard-charging drive ahead of the brilliant Latvala who deserves another outing in a really competitive car. He was followed by Pons who spun, Chris Atkinson, Dani Soro and the last to score a point was Belgian François Duval.

Thus, 2006 ended on a low note after a rally, which did not have much influence on the overall results. It was run in diabolical conditions, and the year came to a close as it had begun with a Ford victory, but in the meantime Sébasien Loeb had left his mark on the season. ■

Manfred Stohl and his co-driver, Ilka Minor, were delighted with this third rostrum finish on the trot; it was certainly their best performance of the year.

THE JUNIORS
The debutantes' ball

There were six drivers at the start of the British round of the Junior Championship who had a mathematical chance of winning the title. Aava, Andersson, Sandell, Wilks, Bères and Meeke at the wheel of 4 Suzukis, 1 Citroën and 1 Renault respectively were still in contention after 8 rounds, so a dream final in Wales looked on the cards. It kept its promises and the quickest out of the starting blocks was Guy Wilkes who was in the lead at the end of the first special. Kris Meeke set the quickest time in SS 2 and took over first place. The Citroën driver continued to show his rivals a clean pair of heels until the start of the second leg when he came a cropper in SS 7 (Crychan 1). He pushed a bit too hard and a few kilometres after the start off he went. "I came into a series of corners too quickly - right-left-right. The Citroën oversteered, then understeered and we clobbered a big stone on the exit with the right-hand front corner. The car was unable to continue. I'm really furious with myself and I'm very sorry for the team which gave me a winning car." Meeke could at least say that he was the driver who scored the highest number of stage victories during the year, but that is not the same thing as a title.

Chris Atkinson was outclassed by his team leader, Petter Solberg, in the final round of the 2006 championship.

Henning Solberg finished the year on a low note being largely dominated by Stohl in the same type of 307 WRC.

The other contenders had also run into different kinds of trouble while Meeke dominated. Urmo Aava, the overall leader in the category before Wales, broke a suspension wishbone in SS 2, which dropped him down to the bottom of the time sheets. In the next special Josef Bères was stopped by gearbox failure, and Andersson also had a suspension breakage on his Suzuki in the final stage of the first leg. All 3 rejoined on the morrow in the super rally but way behind Meeke and then Wilks who went into the lead after the Citroën driver's off. Just when it looked like the Brit, who had driven a cautious rally till then, was home and dry with the title in his pocket his Suzuki's gearbox blocked in SS 9 (Halfway 1). This let 19-year-old Estonian Jan Mölder into first place, which he held to the finish apart from a brief period at the end of Brechfa 1 (SS 14) when Patrik Sandell took up the running. Mölder was soon back in front and scored his first victory in this category without setting any scratch times. Behind him came Luca Betti and Aaron Burkart all of whom had their best result of the season in Wales. In addition, Mölder became the youngest driver ever to win a round since the creation of the Junior Championship. The title went to Patrik Sandell the only one of the favourites not to run into major problems. The young Swede succeeded Dani Sordo confirming the tradition that the title is always won by a driver in his first season. "My plan functioned perfectly," he chortled at the finish. "I drove at around 80% in the first leg so as not to make any mistakes. In the second I upped the pace a little to gain a few places, and in the final one I just hung in there to win the title. It was a rather strange rally but that's racing. My aim this year was to gather experience in view of 2007. This result is way beyond what I was expecting. All I want to do now is to be able to win the title for the second time next year." ■

Patrik Sandell and his co-driver Emil Axelsson scored an unexpected victory in the Production category in their very first year in the competition.

Was Andreas Aigner looking for a bit more aerodynamic grip? Whatever the case the Austrian finished his season in total anonymity retiring in SS 7 after rolling his car.

16 Great Britain results

62th RALLY OF GREAT BRITAIN

Organiser Details
International Motor Sports Ltd,
Motor Sports House, Riverside Park,
Colnbrook, Slough, SL3 0HG,
United Kingdom
Tel.: +44 1753 765 100
Fax: +44 1753 765 106

Wales Rally GB

16th and last leg of FIA 2006 World Rally Championship for constructors and drivers.
9th and last leg of FIA WRC Junior Championship.

Date December 1st - 3, 2006

Route
1206.67 km divised in 3 legs.
17 special stages on dirt roads (355.92 km)

Starting Procedure
Thursday, November 30 (19:30),
Cardiff, Millenium Stadium

Leg 1
Friday, December 1st (09:17/15:10),
Cardiff > Swansea, 313.74 km;
6 special stages (139.62 km)

Leg 2
Saturday, December 2 (08:50/17:06),
Swansea > Swansea, 479.17 km;
7 special stages (104.30 km)

Leg 3
Sunday, December 3 (07:47/12:43),
Swansea > Cardiff, 413.76 km;
4 special stages (112.00 km)

Entry List (118) - 115 starters

N°	Driver (Nat.)	Co-driver (Nat.)	Team	Car	Group& FIA Priority
1.	X. PONS (E)	C. DEL BARRIO (E)	KRONOS TOTAL CITROEN WRT	Citroën Xsara WRC	A8 1
2.	D. SORDO (E)	M. MARTI (E)	KRONOS TOTAL CITROEN WRT	Citroën Xsara WRC	A8 1
3.	M. GRÖNHOLM (FIN)	T. RAUTIAINEN (FIN)	BP FORD WORLD RALLY TEAM	Ford Focus RS WRC 06	A8 1
4.	M. HIRVONEN (FIN)	J. LEHTINEN (FIN)	BP FORD WORLD RALLY TEAM	Ford Focus RS WRC 06	A8 1
5.	P. SOLBERG (N)	P. MILLS (GB)	SUBARU WORLD RALLY TEAM	Subaru Impreza WRC 2006	A8 1
6.	C. ATKINSON (AUS)	G. MACNEALL (AUS)	SUBARU WORLD RALLY TEAM	Subaru Impreza WRC 2006	A8 1
7.	M. STOHL (A)	I. MINOR (A)	OMV - PEUGEOT NORWAY	Peugeot 307 WRC	A8 1
8.	H. SOLBERG (N)	C. MENKERUD (N)	OMV - PEUGEOT NORWAY	Peugeot 307 WRC	A8 1
9.	M. WILSON (GB)	M. ORR (GB)	STOBART - VK - M-SPORT FORD RALLY TEAM	Ford Focus RS WRC 06	A8 1
10.	J. LATVALA (FIN)	M. ANTTILA (FIN)	STOBART - VK - M-SPORT FORD RALLY TEAM	Ford Focus RS WRC 06	A8 1
11.	H. ROVANPERÄ (FIN)	R. PIETILÄINEN (FIN)	RED BULL - SKODA TEAM	Skoda Fabia WRC	A8 1
12.	A. AIGNER (A)	K. WICHA (D)	RED BULL - SKODA TEAM	Skoda Fabia WRC	A8 1
15.	F. DUVAL (B)	P. PIVATO (F)	FIRST MOTORSPORT SKODA	Skoda Fabia WRC 06	A8 2
16.	M. HIGGINS (GB)	R. KENNEDY (IRL)	MARK HIGGINS	Ford Focus	A8 2
17.	G. MACHALE (IRL)	P. NAGLE (IRL)	GARETH MACHALE	Ford Focus	A8 2
18.	J. KOPECKY (CZ)	F. SCHOVANEK (CZ)	CZECH RALLY TEAM SKODA - KOPECKY	Skoda Fabia WRC	A8 2
19.	A. MIKKELSEN (N)	O. FLOENE (N)	STOBART - VK - M-SPORT FORD RALLY TEAM	Ford Focus RS WRC 04	A8 2
20.	M. ØSTBERG (NOR)	O. KRISTIAN UNNERUD (N)	ADAPTA	Subaru Impreza WRC	A8 2
25.	G. COX (GB)	T. HOBBS (GB)	GAVIN COX	Mitsubishi Lancer Evo	N4
32.	K. MEEKE (GB)	G. PATTERSON (GB)	KRIS MEEKE	Citroën C2	A6 3
33.	U. AAVA (EE)	K. SIKK (EE)	URMO AAVA	Suzuki Swift	A6 3
35.	P. ANDERSSON (S)	J. ANDERSSON (S)	PER-GUNNAR ANDERSSON	Suzuki Swift	A6 3
36.	L. BETTI (E)	P. CAPOLONGO (I)	LUCA BETTI	Renault Clio	A6 3
41.	P. SANDELL (SWE)	E. AXELSSON (SWE)	PATRIK SANDELL	Renault Clio	A6 3
43.	J. MÖLDER (EE)	K. BECKER (D)	JAAN MÖLDER	Suzuki Swift	A6 3
45.	J. BÉRES (SK)	P. STARY (CZ)	JOZEF BÉRES	Suzuki Ignis	A6 3
46.	A. CORTINOVIS (I)	F. ZANELLA (I)	ANDREA CORTINOVIS	Renault Clio	N3 3
48.	G. WILKS (GB)	P. PUGH (GB)	SUZUKI SPORT EUROPE UK	Suzuki Swift	A6 3
50.	E. KAUR (EE)	A. KRISTOV (EE)	EGON KAUR	Renault Clio	N3 3
51.	F. KARA (TR)	C. BAKANCOCUKLARI (TR)	FATIH KARA	Renault Clio	A6 3
52.	B. CASIER (B)	F. MICLOTTE (B)	BERND CASIER	Renault Clio	A6 3
53.	B. CLARK (GB)	S. MARTIN (GB)	BARRY CLARK	Ford Fiesta	N3 3
54.	A. BURKART (D)	K. ZEMANIK (D)	AARON BURKART	Citroën C2 GT	A6 3
59.	J. WOZENCROFT (GB)	R. FAGG (GB)	JAMES WOZENCROFT	Suzuki Ignis	A6 3
60.	T. WALSTER (GB)	P. WILLIAMS (AUS)	TOM WALSTER	Ford Fiesta ST	N3 3
61.	N. MCSHEA (GB)	G. SHINNORS (IRL)	NIALL MCSHEA	Subaru Impreza	N4
62.	A. MCRAE (GB)	G. NOBLE (GB)	ALISTER MCRAE	Toyota Corolla Super 2000	N4
63.	P. FLODIN (SWE)	M. ANDERSSON (SWE)	PATRIK FLODIN	Subaru Impreza	N4
64.	R. CHAMPION (GB)	C. THORLEY (GB)	RYAN CHAMPION	Mitsubishi Lancer Evo XI	N4
65.	O. SVEDLUND (S)	B. NILLSON (S)	SUBARU SWEDISH DEALER TEAM	Subaru Impreza	N4
66.	G. EVANS (GB)	H. LEWIS (GB)	GWYNDAF EVANS	Mitsubishi Lancer Evo XI	N4
68.	D. HIGGINS (GB)	I. THOMAS (GB)	DAVID HIGGINS	Mitsubishi Lancer Evo XI	N4
69.	B. MUNSTER (B)	S. PREVOT (B)	BERNARD MUNSTER	Subaru Impreza	N4
70.	A. ALÉN (FIN)	T. ALANNE (FIN)	OOO TACK	Subaru Impreza	N4
71.	J. MILNER (GB)	N. BEECH (GB)	JONNY MILNER	Mitsubishi Lancer Evo XI	N4
72.	D. WESTON (GB)	A. DAVIES (GB)	DAVE WESTON	Ford Focus WRC01	A8
73.	P. VAN HOOF (NL)	N. LEERMAKERS (NL)	PIET VAN HOOF	Mitsubishi Lancer Evo	A8
74.	S. JONES (GB)	C. PARRY (GB)	STUART JONES	Mitsubishi Lancer Evo XI	N4
75.	P. MORROW (GB)	D. BARRITT (GB)	PHILLIP MORROW	Mitsubishi Lancer Evo XI	N4
76.	M. BALDACCI (RSM)	G. AGNESE (I)	MIRCO BALDACCI	Mitsubishi Lancer Evoution	N4
77.	J. REYNOLDS (GB)	A. COOK (GB)	JULIAN REYNOLDS	Subaru Impreza	N4
78.	C. RAUTENBACH (ZW)	D. SENIOR (GB)	CONRAD RAUTENBACH	Subaru Impreza	N4
79.	P. BIJVELDS (NL)	B. V D NIEUWENHUIJZEN (NL)	PETER BIJVELDS	Mitsubishi Lancer Evo VII	N4
80.	M. SOLOWOW (PL)	M. BARAN (PL)	CERSANIT RALLY TEAM	Mitsubishi Lancer Evo XI	N4
81.	M. VAN ELDIK (NL)	M. GROENEWOUD (NL)	MARK VAN ELDIK	Mitsubishi Lancer Evo VII	N4
82.	N. MCCANCE (GB)	F. REGAN (IRL)	NEIL MCCANCE	Mitsubishi Lancer Evo XI	N4
83.	A. DE KONING (NL)	H. VERSCHUUREN (NL)	ARJEN DE KONING	Mitsubishi Lancer Evo	A8
85.	K. STEVENS (GB)	T. STURLA (GB)	KEVIN STEVENS	Subaru Impreza	N4
86.	J. HANNINEN (FIN)	M. SALLINEN (FIN)	JUHO HANNINEN	Citroën C2	A6
87.	R. SWANN (GB)	D. GARROD (GB)	ROBERT SWANN	Subaru Impreza	N4
88.	C. MCCLOSKEY (GB)	D. CONNOLLY (IRL)	CONNOR MCCLOSKEY	Mitsubishi Lancer Evo XI	N4
89.	G. MANFRINATO (I)	C. PISANO (I)	GIOVANNI MANFRINATO	Mitsubishi Lancer Evo XI	N4
90.	B. GROUNDWATER (GB)	J. WYLIE (GB)	BARRY GROUNDWATER	Mitsubishi Lancer Evo VII	N4
92.	M. PROKOP (CZ)	J. TOMANEK (CZ)	MARTIN PROKOP	Citroën C2 S1600	A6
93.	J. V D HEUVEL (NL)	M. KOLMAN (NL)	JASPER V D HEUVEL	Mitsubishi Lancer Evo	N4
94.	E. BOLDERHEIJ (NL)	S. RÖLING (NL)	EVERT BOLDERHEIJ	Mitsubishi Lancer Evo	N4
95.	J. SINKE (NL)	P. MEIJS (NL)	JAAP SINKE	Mitsubishi Lancer Evo	N4
96.	M. OLEKSOWICZ (PL)	A. OBREBOWSKI (PL)	MACIEK OLEKSOWICZ	Subaru Impreza	N4
97.	L. BALDACCI (RSM)	D. D'ESPOSITO (I)	LORIS BALDACCI	Subaru Impreza	N4
98.	W. UTTING (GB)	M. UTTING (GB)	MAX UTTING	Subaru Impreza	N4
99.	S. SIMPSON (GB)	P. WALSH (GB)	STEPHEN SIMPSON	Hyundai Accent WRC	A8
100.	N. KENNY (GB)	N. PARRY (GB)	NICK KENNY	Subaru Impreza	N4
101.	B. KELLY (IRL)	D. BRANNIGAN (IRL)	BRENDAN KELLY	Mitsubishi Lancer Evo XI	N4
102.	J. DALE (GB)	A. BARGERY (GB)	JUSTIN DALE	Renault Clio	N3
103.	J. LLOYD (GB)	P. GULLICK (GB)	JOHN LLOYD	Subaru Impreza	N4
104.	R. BUTOR (I)	I. TOTH (H)	ROBERT BUTOR	Suzuki Ignis S1600	A6
105.	D. SHEPHERD (USA)	P. GLADYSZ (USA)	DOUG SHEPHERD	Subaru Impreza	N4
106.	P. JONES (GB)	D. ROBERTS (GB)	PAUL JONES	Mitsubishi Lancer Evo	N4
107.	V. ROZUKAS (LT)	A. SHOSHAS (LT)	VILIUS ROZUKAS	Suzuki Ignis S1600	A6
108.	T. NAUGHTON (GB)	C. THOMPSON (GB)	THOMAS NAUGHTON	Mitsubishi Lancer Evo XI	N4
109.	P. JAMES (GB)	D. DAVIES (GB)	PAUL JAMES	Mitsubishi Lancer Evo VII	N4
110.	A. BETTEGA (I)	S. SCATTOLIN (I)	ALESSANDRO BETTEGA	Ford Fiesta ST	N3
111.	C. MOORE (GB)	R. EDWARDS (GB)	CHRIS MOORE	Ford Fiesta ST	N3
112.	K. DAVIES (GB)	S. O'GORMAN (GB)	KEVIN DAVIES	Ford Fiesta ST	N3
113.	G. SCHAMMEL (LUX)	R. JAMOUL (B)	JPS JUNIOR TEAM	Ford Fiesta ST	N3
114.	L. ATHANASSOULAS (GR)	N. MOUZAKIS (GR)	TEAM GREECE	Ford Fiesta ST	N3
115.	E. GILMOUR (NZ)	C. MOLE (GB)	EMMA GILMOUR	Ford Fiesta ST	N3
116.	E. VERTUNOV (RUS)	G. TROSHKIN (RUS)	EVGENIY VERTUNOV	Ford Fiesta ST	N3
117.	W. RADFORD (GB)	C. DREW (GB)	WAYNE RADFORD	Mitsubishi Lancer Evo VII	N4
118.	H. JEFFREYS (GB)	A. CONNOR (GB)	HUW JEFFREYS	Subaru Impreza	N4
119.	A. BARNES (GB)	N. DASHFIELD (GB)	ANDREW BARNES	Subaru Impreza	N4
120.	R. GILL (GB)	A. HOWARD (GB)	ROB GILL	Subaru Impreza	N4
121.	S. PAVLIDES (CY)	T. VASILIADES (CY)	SPYROS PAVLIDES	Subaru Impreza	N4
122.	R. ROBERTS (GB)	W. ROBERTSON (GB)	RICHARD ROBERTS	Subaru Impreza	N4
123.	N. O'CONNOR (GB)	J. ROGAN (GB)	NATHAN O'CONNOR	Subaru Impreza	N4
124.	M. BEEBE (GB)	G. PRICE (GB)	MATT BEEBE	MG ZR 160	N3
125.	S. BIELTVEDT (NOR)	L. BRAENNA (N)	SVEINUNG BIELTVEDT	Ford Fiesta ST	N3
126.	H. WEIJS (NL)	H. VAN GOOR (NL)	HANS WEIJS	Ford Fiesta ST	N3
128.	D. FISCHER (H)	A. TABORSZKI (I)	RALLYE SPORT 2000SE	Ford Fiesta ST	N3
129.	T. JARDINE (GB)	J. MCEVOY (GB)	TONY JARDINE	Ford Fiesta ST	N3
130.	L. PINDER (GB)	K. BAKER (GB)	LUKE PINDER	Citroën C2	A6
131.	M. BOWMAN (GB)	K. BOWMAN (GB)	MANDY BOWMAN	Mitsubishi Lancer Evo	N4
132.	S. SMITH (NZ)	J. RICHARDSON (GB)	STEVE SMITH	Fiat Stilo	A7
134.	R. BENNETT (GB)	H. RICHARDSON (GB)	RODNEY BENNETT	Fiat Stilo	A7
135.	R. LLOYD (GB)	G. ROBERTS (GB)	RHYS LLOYD	MG ZR	N3
136.	A. LINTON (BDS)	J. LINTON (BDS)	JONATHAN LINTON	Opel Astra OPC	N3
138.	K. HEATH (GB)	P. HEATH (GB)	KATE HEATH	Subaru Impreza	N4
139.	D. JONES (GB)	P. BURLEY (GB)	DARREN JONES	Skoda Felicia	A5
140.	S. GRAHAM (GB)	T. GRAHAM (GB)	STEVE GRAHAM	MG ZR	N1
141.	F. MCCAUL (GB)	J. SMITH (GB)	FIN MCCAUL	Volkswagen Polo	N1
142.	F. FIANDINO (F)	S. DE CASTELLI (F)	FABIEN FIANDINO	Citroën C2	A6

U. Aava

P-G. Andersson

A. McRae

J. Mölder

A. Burkart

M. Østberg

Championship Classifications

FIA Drivers (16/16)

1.	Loeb	8🏆	112
2.	Grönholm	7🏆	111
3.	Hirvonen	1🏆	65
4.	Stohl		54
5.	Sordo		49
6.	P. Solberg		40
7.	Pons		32
8.	H. Solberg		25
9.	Gardemeister		20
10.	Atkinson		20
11.	Galli		15
12.	Bengué		9
13.	Latvala		9
14.	Katajamäki		7
15.	Kopecky		7
16.	Carlsson		6
17.	Välimäki		6
18.	Sarrazin		6
19.	Duval		5
20.	Rådström		4
21.	Araï		3
22.	MacHale		3
23.	Aigner		3
24.	Tuohino		3
25.	Sohlberg		3
26.	Perez Companc		2
27.	Baldacci		2
28.	Wilson		1
29.	Nutahara		1
30.	Herridge		1
31.	Rovanperä, Hänninen, Joge, Panizzi...		0 0

FIA Constructors (16/16)

1.	**BP-Ford World Rally Team**	8🏆	195
2.	Kronos Total Citroën WRT	8🏆	166
3.	Subaru World Rally Team		106
4.	OMV-Peugeot Norway		88
5.	Stobart VK M-Sport Ford WRT		44
6.	Red Bull-Skoda Team		24

FIA Production Car WRC (8/8)

1.	**Al-Attiyah**	2🏆	40
2.	Nutahara	3🏆	35
3.	M. Baldacci		31
4.	Latvala	2🏆	27
5.	Teiskonen		24
6.	Arai	1🏆	18
7.	Kuzaj		17
8.	Marrini		14
9.	Mason		8
10.	Uspenskiy		8
11.	Al Qassimi		6
12.	Herridge		6
13.	Dorosinskiy		6
14.	Heath		6
15.	Kamada		6
16.	Campedelli		5
17.	Vojtech		2
18.	Name		1
19.	Jereb, Nassoulas...		0

FIA Junior WRC (9/9)

1.	**Sandell**	1🏆	32
2.	Aava	1🏆	31
3.	Andersson	1🏆	29
4.	Wilks	2🏆	26
5.	Rautenbach		25
6.	Béres		22
7.	Meeke	1🏆	20
8.	Pressac		19
9.	Prokop	1🏆	18
10.	Mölder	1🏆	18
11.	Casier		17
12.	Burkart		15
13.	Betti		12
14.	Tirabassi	1🏆	11
15.	Valousek		11
16.	Kara		7
17.	Rantanen		6
18.	Clark, Kosciuszko		5
20.	Pinomäki		4
21.	Wazencroft		3
22.	Cortinovis, Zachrisson		2
24.	Bonato		1
	...		

Special Stages Times

www.walesrallygb.com
www.wrc.com

SS1 Port Talbot 1 (17.41 km)
1.Grönholm 9'08"7; 2.Hirvonen +3"7;
3.Stohl +9"2; 4.P.Solberg +9"7;
5.Pons +15"3; 6.Atkinson +17"8;
7.Latvala +18"4; 8.Higgins +24"4...
J-WRC > 27.Wilks 10'28"4

SS2 Resolfen 1 (24.49 km)
1.Grönholm 12'26"4;
2.Hirvonen +6"2; 3.Stohl +13"8;
4.P.Solberg +15"7; 5.Sordo +25"1;
6.Latvala +29"4; 7.Duval +35"9;
8.Higgins +36"6...
J-WRC > 21.Meeke 14'11"1

SS3 Rheola 1 (27.91 km)
1.Grönholm 15'34"5; 2.Hirvonen +9"2;
3.P.Solberg +9"3; 4.Stohl +17"6;
5.Latvala +21"8; 6.Pons +27"6;
7.Atkinson +29"4; 8.Duval +33"3...
J-WRC > 22.Meeke 17'37"5

SS4 Port Talbot 2 (17.41 km)
1.Stohl 9'10"9; 2.P.Solberg +1"4;
3.Grönholm +1"7; 4.H.Solberg +3"6;
5.Pons +6"3; 6.Sordo +9"3;
7.Atkinson +9"8; 8.Latvala +11"4...
J-WRC > 22.Meeke 10'23"4

SS5 Resolfen 2 (24.49 km)
1.Grönholm/P.Solberg 12'41"8;
3.Stohl +3"5; 4.Atkinson +10"5;
5.Sordo +10"8; 6.Latvala +13"8;
7.Duval/H.Solberg +14"9...
J-WRC > 16.Meeke 14'07"0

SS6 Rheola 2 (27.91 km)
1.P.Solberg 15'39"3; 2.Grönholm +8"6;
3.Stohl +14"3; 4.Pons +15"6;
5.Sordo +26"1; 6.H.Solberg +26"6;
7.Latvala +29"9; 8.Higgins +39"9...
J-WRC > 17.Meeke 17'37"6

Classification Leg 1
1.Grönholm 1h14'51"9;
2.P.Solberg +25"8; 3.Stohl +48"1;
4.Latvala +1'54"4; 5.Sordo +2'11"0;
6.Pons +2'11"9; 7.Atkinson +2'46"2;
8.Higgins +2'52"7...
J-WRC > 18.Meeke 1h25'21"8

SS7 Crychan 1 (19.47 km)
1.Pons 10'42"6; 2.Grönholm +1"6;
3.Stohl +3"8; 4.Sordo +7"8;
5.Latvala +9"5; 6.Atkinson +12"0;
7.H.Solberg +13"5; 8.Higgins +15"0...
J-WRC > 21.Meeke 11'51"9

SS8 Epynt 1 (13.76 km)
1.Grönholm 7'40"4; 2.Pons +0"9;
3.P.Solberg +1"8;
4.Duval/H.Solberg +4"4;
6.Atkinson/Stohl +5"5;
8.Latvala +6"2...
J-WRC > 29.Aava/Reynolds 8'43"7

SS9 Halfway 1 (18.37 km)
1.Grönholm 10'35"9; 2.P.Solberg +5"8;
3.Duval +6"0; 4.Latvala +6"5;
5.Pons +8"9; 6.H.Solberg +10"1;
7.Stohl 10"4; 8.Atkinson +12"9...
J-WRC > 25.Andersson 11'50"5

SS10 Crychan 2 (19.47 km)
1.Stohl 10'47"7; 2.P.Solberg +0"2;
3.Grönholm +0"3; 4.Pons +4"6;
5.Latvala +6"1; 6.Atkinson +6"3;
7.H.Solberg +6"9; 8.Duval +7"9...
J-WRC > 23.Andersson 11'59"8

SS11 Epynt 2 (13.76 km)
1.Grönholm 7'39"3; 2.Atkinson +0"8;
3.Pons +2"0; 4.Stohl +4"1;
5.Duval +4"4; 6.Latvala +5"8;
7.Sordo +6"2; 8.H.Solberg +7"2...
J-WRC > 24.Aava 8'43"5

SS12 Halfway 2 (18.37 km)
1.Grönholm 10'34"4; 2.Atkinson +0"5;
3.Pons +1"2; 4.Duval +2"4;
5.Sordo +4"6; 6.Latvala +7"4;
7.Stohl +7"6; 8.H.Solberg +11"1...
J-WRC > 23.Aava 11'45"7

SS13 Cardiff (1.10 km)
1.Grönholm 1'01"5; 2.Stohl +1"2;
3.Latvala +1"3; 4.Duval +1"4;
5.Sordo +1"6;
6.Mikkelsen/Wilson +1"9;
8.Kopecky/Rovanperä +2"7...
J-WRC > 15.Sandell 1'08"2

Classification Leg 2
1.Grönholm 2h13'55"6;
2.Stohl +1'18"8; 3.P.Solberg +2'08"7;
4.Pons +2'30"9; 5.Latvala +2'35"3;
6.Atkinson +3'25"9; 7.Duval +3'33"7;
8.Sordo +4'26"8...
J-WRC > 20.Mölder 2h35'54"7

SS14 Brechfa 1 (28.89 km)
1.P.Solberg 16'25"8;
2.Sordo +7"7; 3.Grönholm +15"5;
4.Atkinson +15"8;
5.Stohl/Latvala +16"1; 7.Pons +17"5;
8.Østberg +22"9...
J-WRC > 19.Andersson 18'24"0

SS15 Trawscoed 1 (27.11 km)
1.Sordo 16'19"3; 2.Latvala +8"1;
3.Atkinson +13"0; 4.Stohl +15"5;
5.Østberg +20"6; 6.Grönholm +22"8;
7.H.Solberg +25"7; 8.Duval +29"5...
J-WRC > 20.Wilks 18'11"9

SS16 Brechfa 2 (28.89 km)
1.P.Solberg 16'33"1; 2.Grönholm +6"5;
3.Latvala +8"7; 4.Sordo +9"1;
5.Atkinson +10"2; 6.Stohl +17"7;
7.Duval +18"3; 8.Pons +18"4...
J-WRC > 20.Wilks 18'39"1

SS17 Trawscoed 2 (27.11 km)
1.P.Solberg 16'22"2; 2.Grönholm +4"0;
3.H.Solberg +7"7; 4.Atkinson +11"4;
5.Sordo +13"5; 6.Stohl +16"2;
7.Latvala +17"7; 8.Pons +20"3...
J-WRC > 19.Aava 18'43"4

Results 🇬🇧

	Driver - Co-driver	Car	Gr.	Time
1	Grönholm - Rautiainen	Ford Focus RS WRC 06	A8	3h20'24"8
2	Stohl - Minor	Peugeot 307 WRC	A8	+ 1'35"5
3	P. Solberg - Mills	Subaru Impreza WRC 2006	A8	+ 1'55"2
4	Latvala - Anttila	Ford Focus RS WRC 06	A8	+ 2'37"1
5	Pons - Del Barrio	Citroën Xsara WRC	A8	+ 3'19"9
6	Atkinson - Macneall	Subaru Impreza WRC 2006	A8	+ 3'27"5
7	Sordo - Marti	Citroën Xsara WRC	A8	+ 4'08"3
8	Duval - Pivato	Skoda Fabia WRC 06	A8	+ 4'22"6
9	Rovanperä - Pietiläinen	Skoda Fabia WRC	A8	+ 8'00"3
10	Kopecky - Schovanek	Skoda Fabia WRC	A8	+ 8'27"8
13	Alén - Alanne	**Subaru Impreza**	N4	+ 21'34"2
20	Mölder - Becker	**Suzuki Swift**	A6/J	+ 34'39"9
22	Betti - Capolongo	Renault Clio	A6/J	+ 36'35"5
24	Burkart - Zemanik	Citroën C2 GT	A6/J	+ 40'25"4

Leading Retirements (29)
TC15A	Mikkelsen - Floene	Ford Focus RS WRC 04	Off
TC9A	Higgins - Kennedy	Ford Focus	Off
TC6D	Aigner - Wicha	Skoda Fabia WRC	Off
TC3C	Hirvonen - Lehtinen	Ford Focus RS WRC 06	Car endommaged

Performers

	1	2	3	4	5	6	C6	NbSS
Grönholm	9	4	3	-	-	1	17	17
P. Solberg	5	3	2	2	-	-	12	17
Stohl	2	1	5	3	1	3	15	17
Pons	1	1	2	2	3	1	10	17
Sordo	1	1	-	2	6	1	11	17
Hirvonen	-	3	-	-	-	-	3	3
Atkinson	-	2	1	3	1	4	11	17
Latvala	-	1	2	1	4	4	12	17
Duval	-	-	3	3	1	-	7	17
H. Solberg	-	-	1	2	-	2	5	17
Østberg	-	-	-	-	1	-	1	17
Mikkelsen	-	-	-	-	-	1	1	15
Wilson	-	-	-	-	-	1	1	17

Leaders

SS1 > SS17   Grönholm

Previous winners

1974	Mäkinen - Liddon / Ford Escort RS 1600
1975	Mäkinen - Liddon / Ford Escort RS
1976	Clark - Pegg / Ford Escort RS
1977	Waldegaard - Thorszelius / Ford Escort RS
1978	Mikkola - Hertz / Ford Escort RS
1979	Mikkola - Hertz / Ford Escort RS
1980	Toivonen - White / Talbot Sunbeam Lotus
1981	Mikkola - Hertz / Audi Quattro
1982	Mikkola - Hertz / Audi Quattro
1983	Blomqvist - Cederberg / Audi Quattro
1984	Vatanen - Harryman / Peugeot 205 T16
1985	Toivonen - Wilson / Lancia Delta S4
1986	Salonen - Harjanne / Peugeot 205 T16
1987	Kankkunen - Piironen / Lancia Delta HF
1988	Alen - Kivimaki / Lancia Delta Integrale
1989	Airikkala - McNamee / Mitsubishi Galant VR4
1990	Sainz - Moya / Toyota Celica GT-Four
1991	Kankkunen - Piironen / Lanica Delta Integrale
1992	Sainz - Moya / Toyota Celica Turbo 4WD
1993	Kankkunen - Piironen / Toyota Celica Turbo 4WD
1994	McRae - Ringer / Subaru Impreza
1995	McRae - Ringer / Subaru Impreza
1996	Schwarz - Giraudet / Toyota Celica GT-Four
1997	McRae - Grist / Subaru Impreza WRC
1998	Burns - Reid / Mitsubishi Carisma GT
1999	Burns - Reid / Subaru Impreza WRC
2000	Burns - Reid / Subaru Impreza WRC 2000
2001	Gronhölm - Rautiainen / Peugeot 206 WRC
2002	P. Solberg - Mills / Subaru Impreza WRC 2002
2003	P. Solberg - Mills / Subaru Impreza WRC 2003
2004	P. Solberg - Mils / Subaru Impreza WRC 2004
2005	P. Solberg - Mils / Subaru Impreza WRC 2005

Anton Alén

2006 FIA World Rally Championship / Drivers

	30 DRIVERS / 68	Nat.	1.Monte-Carlo	2.Sweden	3.Mexico	4.Spain	5.France	6.Argentina	7.Italy	8.Greece	9.Germany	10.Finland	11.Japan	12.Cyprus	13.Turkey	14.Australia	15.New Zealand	16.Great Britain	TOTAL
1.	Sébastien Loeb	(F)	8	8	10	10	10	10	10	8	10	8	10	10					112
2.	Marcus Grönholm	(FIN)	10	10	1	6	8	0	-	10	6	10	8	8	10	4	10	10	111
3.	Mikko Hirvonen	(FIN)	2	0	0	0	5	-	8	6	0	6	6	6	8	10	8	-	65
4.	Manfred Stohl	(A)	5	0	6	0	2	5	2	0	4	0	4	5	1	6	6	8	54
5.	Daniel Sordo	(E)	1	0	5	8	6	4	6	3	8	-	exc	-	2	0	4	2	49
6.	Petter Solberg	(N)	-	-	8	2	0	8	0	2	-	-	2	1	0	8	3	6	40
7.	Xavier Pons	(E)	0	2	-	-	3	0	5	1	0	-		2	5	5	5	4	32
8.	Henning Solberg	(N)	-	1	4			2	-	4		5		3	6	-	0	0	25
9.	Toni Gardemeister	(FIN)	6	-						5	5			4					20
10.	Chris Atkinson	(AUS)	3	0	2	0	0	3	0	0	1	0	5	0	3	0	-	3	20
11.	Gigi Galli	(I)	-	5			0	6	-			4							15
12.	Alexandre Bengué	(F)				5	4												9
13.	Jari-Matti Latvala	(FIN)	0		0					0		0		0		3	1	5	9
14.	Kosti Katajamäki	(FIN)		3					-		0				4				7
15.	Jan Kopecky	(CZ)	0	0		4	0		0	0	2	1						0	7
16.	Daniel Carlsson	(S)		6								-							6
17.	Jussi Välimäki	(FIN)							4	0		2							6
18.	Stéphane Sarrazin	(F)	4			1	1				-								6
19.	François Duval	(B)	-			3	-		1	0	-				0			1	5
20.	Thomas Rådström	(S)		4															4
21.	Toshihiro Arai	(J)		0			0		0				3	0		-	0		3
22.	Gareth MacHale	(IRL)	0		3	-		0	0		0		-					-	3
23.	Andreas Aigner	(A)	0	-		0	0		0	0	3			-	0			-	3
24.	Janne Tuohino	(FIN)		0								3							3
25.	Kristian Sohlberg	(FIN)							3			-							3
26.	Luis Perez Companc	(RA)			0			0	0	0			0	0		0	2		2
27.	Mirco Baldacci	(I)			0				0				0			2	0	-	2
28.	Matthew Wilson	(GB)	0	0	0	0	0	1	0	0	0	0	0	0	0	0	0	0	1
29.	Fumio Nutahara	(J)	0		exc								1	0		0	0		1
30.	Dean Herridge	(AUS)										0				1			1

31. Harri Rovanperä (FIN), Juho Hänninen (FIN), Jimmy Joge (S), Gilles Panizzi (F), Aki Teiskonen (FIN), Nasser Al-Attiyah (Q), Richard Mason (NZ), Anton Alén (N), Matias Ekström (S) 0
40. Valentino Rossi (I), D Windus (AUS), Patrick Flodin (S), Sergey Uspenskiy (RUS), Olivier Burri (CH), Federico Villagra (RA), Hiroshi Yanagisawa (J), Leszek Kuzaj (PL), 0
48. Erik Wevers (NL), Khalid Al Qassimi (UAE), Christopher Anderson (AUS), Eduardo Omar (RA), Stepan Vojtech (CZ), Brice Tirabassi (F), Pieter Tsjoen (B), Claudio Menzi (B), 0
56. Toby Heyring (AUS), Dean Sumner (NZ), Ercan Kazaz (TUR), Patrick Sandell (S), Guy Wilks (GB), Aris Vovos (GR), Simone Campedelli (I), James Anderson (AUS), 0
64. Stewart Taylor (NZ), Emre Yurdakul (TUR), Oscar Svedlund (S), Kristian Poulsen (DK), Seisuke Ohba (J) 0

2006 FIA World Rally Championship / Manufacturers

	MANUFACTURERS		1.Monte-Carlo	2.Sweden	3.Mexico	4.Spain	5.France	6.Argentina	7.Italy	8.Greece	9.Germany	10.Finland	11.Japan	12.Cyprus	13.Turkey	14.Australia	15.New Zealand	16.Great Britain	TOTAL
1.	BP-Ford World Rally Team	M1	14	12	4	12	14	1	8	16	10	16	14	14	18	14	18	10	195
2.	Kronos Total Citroën WRT	M1	11	13	10	10	15	10	16	11	18	8	10	10	3	6	9	6	166
3.	Subaru World Rally Team	M1	5	3	12	11	7	13	7	5	0	2	9	5	4	11	3	9	106
4.	OMV-Peugeot Norway	M2	6	4	11			10	5	5		9		9	8	6	7	8	88
5.	Stobart VK M-Sport Ford WRT	M2	0	7	2	1	0	5		2	3	4	5	1	5	2	2	5	44
6.	Red Bull-Skoda Team	M2	3	0		5	3		3	0	8		0	1			1		24

REGULATIONS: DRIVERS' CHAMPIONSHIP : All result count. 1st - 10 points, 2nd - 8 points, 3rd - 6 points, 4th - 5 points, 5th - 4 points, 6th - 3 points, 7th - 2 points, 8th - 1 point.
MANUFACTURERS' CHAMPIONSHIP: To be eligible, the constructors who have registered with FIA, must take part in all the events with a minimum of two cars. The first two cars score the points according to their finishing position. All results are taken into consideration. Points scale is the same as for the drivers.

World Championship for Manufacturers

1973	Alpine-Renault	1982	Audi	1991	Lancia	2000	Peugeot
1974	Lancia	1983	Lancia	1992	Lancia	2001	Peugeot
1975	Lancia	1984	Audi	1993	Toyota	2002	Peugeot
1976	Lancia	1985	Peugeot	1994	Toyota	2003	Citroën
1977	Fiat	1986	Peugeot	1995	Subaru	2004	Citroën
1978	Fiat	1987	Lancia	1996	Subaru	2005	Citroën
1979	Ford	1988	Lancia	1997	Subaru	2006	Ford
1980	Fiat	1989	Lancia	1998	Mitsubishi		
1981	Talbot	1990	Lancia	1999	Toyota		

World Championship for Drivers

1977	Sandro Munari (I)	1987	Juha Kankkunen (SF)	1997	Tommi Makinen (SF)
1978	Markku Alen (SF)	1988	Miki Biasion (I)	1998	Tommi Makinen (SF)
1979	Bjorn Waldegaard (S)	1989	Miki Biasion (I)	1999	Tommi Makinen (SF)
1980	Walter Rohrl (D)	1990	Carlos Sainz (E)	2000	Marcus Grönholm (SF)
1981	Ari Vatanen (SF)	1991	Juha Kankkunen (SF)	2001	Richard Burns (GB)
1982	Walter Rohrl (D)	1992	Carlos Sainz (E)	2002	Marcus Grönholm (SF)
1983	Hannu Mikkola (SF)	1993	Juha Kankkunen (SF)	2003	Petter Solberg (N)
1984	Stig Blomqvist (S)	1994	Didier Auriol (F)	2004	Sébastien Loeb (F)
1985	Timo Salonen (SF)	1995	Colin McRae (GB)	2005	Sébastien Loeb (F)
1986	Juha Kankkunen (SF)	1996	Tommi Makinen (SF)	2006	Sébastien Loeb (F)

1977-1978: FIA Cup for drivers

2006 FIA Production Car World Rally Championship (for drivers)

	DRIVERS	Nationalities	1.Monte-Carlo	2.Mexico	3.Argentina	4.Greece	5.Japan	6.Cyprus	7.Australia	8.New Zealand	TOTAL
1.	Nasser Al-Attiyah	(Q)	6	8	10	10		4		2	40
2.	Fumio Nutahara	(J)	10	exc			10	10	2	3	35
3.	Mirco Baldacci	(I)		6	6	5	2		8	4	31
4.	Jari-Matti Latvala	(FIN)	4	0		3	0		10	10	27
5.	Aki Teiskonen	(FIN)			-	6	5	8	5	-	24
6.	Toshihiro Arai	(J)		10	1	4		3	-	0	18
7.	Leszek Kuzaj	(PL)		5	8	-	4			-	17
8.	Stefano Marrini	(I)	5		2	1	3		3		14
9.	Richard Masson	(NZ)								8	8
10.	Sergey Uspenskiy	(RUS)		4	0	0			4		8
11.	Khalid Al Qassimi	(UAE)						6			6
12.	Dean Herridge	(AUS)							6		6
13.	Alexander Dorosinsky	(RUS)								6	6
14.	Nigel Heath	(GB)			5	0		-		1	6
15.	Takuma Kamada	(J)			-	0	1			5	6
16.	Simone Campedelli	(I)						5			5
17.	Stepan Vojtech	(CZ)		2							2
18.	Francisco Name	(MEX)		1							1
19.	Andrej Jereb	(SLO)				0					0
20.	Dimitris Nassoulas	(GR)				0					0
21.	Jasen Popov	(BG)	-								0
22.	Loris Baldacci	(I)					exc				0
23.	Aaron Nicolai Burkart	(D)							-		0
24.	Andreas Tsouloftas	(CY)						exc			0
25.	Spyros Pavlides	(CY)	-					-			0
26.	Natalie Barratt	(GB)	-							-	0
27.	Chris West	(NZ)	-							-	0

Production Car Championship (Gr. N)

- 1987 Alex Fiorio (I)
- 1988 Pascal Gaban (B)
- 1989 Alain Oreille (F)
- 1990 Alain Oreille (F)
- 1991 Grégoire de Mevius (B)
- 1992 Grégoire de Mevius (B)
- 1993 Alex Fassina (I)
- 1994 Jesus Puras (E)
- 1995 Rui Madeira (PT)
- 1996 Gustavo Trelles (RO)
- 1997 Gustavo Trelles (RO)
- 1998 Gustavo Trelles (RO)
- 1999 Gustavo Trelles (RO)
- 2000 Manfred Stohl (D)
- 2001 Gabriel Pozzo (RA)
- 2002 Karamjit Singh (MAL)
- 2003 Martin Rowe (GB)
- 2004 Niall McShea (GB)
- 2005 Toshihiro Arai (J)
- 2006 Nasser Al-Attiyah (Q)

2006 FIA Junior World Rally Championship (for drivers)

	DRIVERS	Nationalities	1.Sweden	2.Spain	3.France	4.Argentina	5.Italy	6.Germany	7.Finland	8.Turkey	9.Great Britain	TOTAL
1.	Patrick Sandell	(S)	8			8	10		2	0	4	32
2.	Urmo Aava	(EE)	6		8		6		exc	10	1	31
3.	Per-Gunnar Andersson	(S)	10			6	5		8	exc	-	29
4.	Guy Wilks	(GB)	0			10	1		10	5	0	26
5.	Conrad Rautenbach	(ZW)		3	6		8	0	0	8		25
6.	Josef Beres	(SK)	3	5	4				4	6	0	22
7.	Kris Meeke	(GB)		6	-			10	-	4	-	20
8.	Julien Pressac	(F)		-	5		2	5	5	2		19
9.	Martin Prokop	(CZ)	0	10			0	4	1	3		18
10.	Jaan Mölder	(EE)	0			5	0		3	-	10	18
11.	Bernd Casier	(B)		8	0	-		8		1	-	17
12.	Aaron Nicolai Burkart	(D)		-	2		4	3		0	6	15
13.	Luca Betti	(I)		-	-		3	1		-	8	12
14.	Brice Tirabassi	(F)		1	10		0	-		-		11
15.	Pavel Valousek	(CZ)	5		-		0	6	0	0		11
16.	Feith Kara	(TR)		2	3		-	2		0	-	7
17.	Matti Rantanen	(FIN)							6			6
18.	Barry Clark	(GB)		-	0		0	0	0		5	5
19.	Michal Kosciuszko	(PL)	1	4			0	0	-	0		5
20.	Kalle Pinomäki	(FIN)	4	0	0			-	0			4
21.	James Wazencroft	(GB)									3	3
22.	Andrea Cortinovis	(I)	0		0		0		0	0	2	2
23.	Peter Zachrisson	(S)	2									2
24.	Yoann Bonato	(F)			1							1
25.	Filippo Alessandro Bordignon	(I)	0	0			0		exc	-		0
26.	Johan Karlsson	(S)	0									0
27.	Tom Walster	(GB)								0		0
28.	Fabien Fiandino	(F)							-	-		0

World Junior Championship

- 2001 Sébastien Loeb (F)
- 2002 Daniel Solà (E)
- 2003 Brice Tirabassi (F)
- 2004 Per-Gunnar Andersson (S)
- 2005 Daniel Sordo (E)
- 2006 Patrick Sandel (S)l

DRIVERS WHO HAVE WON WORLD CHAMPIONSHIP RALLIES FROM 1973 TO 2006

DRIVERS	NATIONALITIES	Nbr. of VICTORIES	RALLIES
Andrea Aghini	(I)	1	**1992** I
Pentti Airikkala	(FIN)	1	**1989** GB
Markku Alen	(FIN)	20	**1975** PT · **1976** FIN · **1977** PT · **1978** PT, FIN, I · **1979** FIN · **1980** FIN · **1981** PT · **1983** F, I · **1984** F · **1986** I, USA · **1987** PT, GR, FIN · **1988** S, FIN, GB
Alain Ambrosino	(F)	1	**1988** CI
Ove Andersson	(S)	1	**1975** EAK
Jean-Claude Andruet	(F)	3	**1973** MC · **1974** F · **1977** I
Didier Auriol	(F)	20	**1988** F · **1989** F · **1990** MC, F, I · **1991** I · **1992** MC, F, GR, RA, FIN, AUS · **1993** MC · **1994** F, RA, I · **1995** F · **1998** E · **1999** C · **2001** E
Fulvio Bacchelli	(I)	1	**1977** NZ
Bernard Beguin	(F)	1	**1987** F
Miki Biasion	(I)	17	**1986** RA · **1987** MC, RA, I · **1988** PT, EAK, GR, USA, I · **1989** MC, PT, EAK, GR, I · **1990** PT, RA · **1993** GR
Stig Blomqvist	(S)	11	**1973** S · **1977** S · **1979** S · **1982** S, I · **1983** GB · **1984** S, GR, NZ, RA, CI
Walter Boyce	(CDN)	1	**1973** USA
Philippe Bugalski	(F)	2	**1999** E, F
Richard Burns	(GB)	9	**1998** EAK · **1999** GR, AUS, GB · **2000** EAK, PT, RA, GB · **2001** NZ
Ingvar Carlsson	(S)	2	**1989** S, NZ
Roger Clark	(GB)	1	**1976** GB
Gianfranco Cunico	(I)	1	**1993** I
Bernard Darniche	(F)	7	**1973** MA · **1975** F · **1977** F · **1978** F · **1979** MC, F · **1981** F
François Delecour	(F)	4	**1993** PT, F, E · **1994** MC
Ian Duncan	(EAK)	1	**1994** EAK
François Duval	(B)	1	**2005** AUS
Per Eklund	(S)	1	**1976** S
Mikael Ericsson	(S)	2	**1989** RA, FIN
Kenneth Eriksson	(S)	6	**1987** CI · **1991** S · **1995** S, AUS · **1997** S, NZ
Tony Fassina	(I)	1	**1979** I
Guy Frequelin	(F)	1	**1981** RA
Marcus Grönholm	(FIN)	18	**2000** S, NZ, F, AUS · **2001** FIN, AUS, GB · **2002** S, CY, FIN, NZ, AUS · **2003** S, NZ, RA · **2004** FIN · **2005** FIN, J · **2006** MC, S, GR, FIN, TR, NZ, GB
Sepp Haider	(A)	1	**1988** NZ
Kyosti Hamalainen	(FIN)	1	**1977** FIN
Mikko Hirvonen	(FIN)	1	**2006** AUS
Mats Jonsson	(S)	2	**1992** S · **1993** S
Harry Kallstom	(S)	1	**1976** GR
Juha Kankkunen	(FIN)	23	**1985** EAK, CI · **1986** S, GR, NZ · **1987** USA, GB · **1989** AUS · **1990** AUS · **1991** EAK, GR, FIN, AUS, GB · **1992** PT · **1993** EAK, RA, FIN, AUS, GB · **1994** PT · **1999** RA, FIN
Anders Kullang	(S)	1	**1980** S
Piero Liatti	(I)	1	**1997** MC
Sébastien Loeb	(F)	28	**2002** D · **2003** MC, D, I · **2004** MC, S, CY, TR, D, AUS · **2005** MC, NZ, I, CY, TR, GR, RA, D, F, E · **2006** MX, E, F, RA, I, D, J, CY
Colin McRae	(GB)	25	**1993** NZ · **1994** NZ, GB · **1995** NZ, GB · **1996** GR, I, E · **1997** EAK, F, I, AUS, GB · **1998** PT, F, GR · **1999** EAK, PT, GR · **2000** E, GR · **2001** ARG, CY, GR · **2002** GR, EAK
Timo Makinen	(FIN)	4	**1973** FIN, GB · **1974** GB · **1975** GB
Tommi Mäkinen	(FIN)	24	**1994** FIN · **1996** S, EAK, RA, FIN, AUS · **1997** PT, E, RA, FIN · **1998** S, RA, NZ, FIN, I, AUS · **1999** Mc, S, NZ, I · **2000** MC · **2001** MC, POR, EAK · **2002** MC
Markko Märtin	(EE)	5	**2003** GR, FIN · **2004** MX, F, E
Shekhar Mehta	(EAK)	5	**1973** EAK · **1979** EAK · **1980** EAK · **1981** EAK · **1982** EAK
Hannu Mikkola	(FIN)	18	**1974** FIN · **1975** MA, FIN · **1978** GB · **1979** PT, NZ, GB, CI · **1981** S, GB · **1982** FIN, GB · **1983** S, PT, RA, FIN · **1984** PT · **1987** EAK
Joaquim Moutinho	(PT)	1	**1986** PT
Michèle Mouton	(F)	4	**1981** I · **1982** PT, GR, BR
Sandro Munari	(I)	7	**1974** I, CDN · **1975** MC · **1976** MC, PT, F · **1977** MC
Jean-Pierre Nicolas	(F)	5	**1973** F · **1976** MA · **1978** MC, EAK, CI
Alain Oreille	(F)	1	**1989** CI
Jesus Puras	(E)	1	**2001** FR
Gilles Panizzi	(F)	6	**2000** F, I · **2001** IT · **2002** F, E, I · **2003** E
Rafaelle Pinto	(PT)	1	**1974** PT
Jean Ragnotti	(F)	3	**1981** MC · **1982** F · **1985** F
Jorge Recalde	(RA)	1	**1988** RA
Walter Röhrl	(D)	14	**1975** GR · **1978** GR, CDN · **1980** MC, PT, RA, I · **1982** MC, CI · **1983** MC, GR, NZ · **1984** MC · **1985** I
Harri Rovanperä	(FIN)	1	**2001** S
Bruno Saby	(F)	2	**1986** F · **1988** MC
Carlos Sainz	(E)	26	**1990** GR, NZ, FIN, GB · **1991** MC, PT, F, NZ, RA · **1992** EAK, NZ, E, GB · **1994** GR · **1995** MC, PT, E · **1996** RI · **1997** GR, RI · **1998** MC, NZ · **2000** CY · **2002** RA · **2003** TR · **2004** RA
Timo Salonen	(FIN)	11	**1977** CDN · **1980** NZ · **1981** CI · **1985** PT, GR, NZ, RA, FIN · **1986** FIN, GB · **1987** S
Armin Schwarz	(D)	1	**1991** E
Kenjiro Shinozuka	(J)	2	**1991** CI · **1992** CI
Joginder Singh	(EAK)	2	**1974** EAK · **1976** EAK
Petter Solberg	(N)	13	**2002** GB · **2003** CY, AUS, F, GB · **2004** NZ, GR, J, GB, I · **2005** S, MX, GB
Patrick Tauziac	(F)	1	**1990** CI
Jean-Luc Thèrier	(F)	5	**1973** PT, GR, I · **1974** USA · **1980** F
Henri Toivonen	(FIN)	3	**1980** GB · **1985** GB · **1986** MC
Ari Vatanen	(FIN)	10	**1980** GR · **1981** GR, BR, FIN · **1983** EAK · **1984** FIN, I, GB · **1985** MC, S
Bjorn Waldegaard	(S)	16	**1975** S, I · **1976** I · **1977** EAK, GR, GB · **1978** S · **1979** GR, CDN · **1980** CI · **1982** NZ · **1983** CI · **1984** EAK · **1986** EAK, CI · **1990** EAK
Achim Warmbold	(D)	2	**1973** PL, A
Franz Wittmann	(A)	1	**1987** NZ

A: Austria, AUS: Australia, B: Belgium, BG: Bulgaria, BR: Brazil, C: China, CDN: Canada, CI: Ivory Coast, CY: Cyprus, CZ: Czech Republic, D: Germany, E: Spain, EAK: Kenya, EST: Estonia, F: France, FIN: Finland, GB: Great Britain, GR: Greece, I: Italy, J: Japan, LT: Lithuania, MA: Marocco, MAL: Malaysia, MX: Mexico, MC: Monaco, N: Norway, NZ: New Zealand, PE: Peru, PL: Poland, PT: Portugal, PY: Paraguay, RA: Argentina, RI: Indonesia, RL: Leganon, ROK: Republic of Korea, ROU: Uruguay, RSM: San Marino, S: Sweden, TR: Turkey, USA : United States of America.